P9-DXT-118

$5

7/2022

THE LORD'S PRAYER
AND OTHER PRAYER TEXTS
FROM THE GRECO-ROMAN ERA

THE LORD'S PRAYER
AND OTHER PRAYER TEXTS
FROM THE GRECO-ROMAN ERA

———————— • ————————

Edited by James H. Charlesworth
with
Mark Harding and Mark Kiley

TRINITY PRESS INTERNATIONAL
Valley Forge, Pennsylvania

Copyright © 1994 Trinity Press International.

All rights reserved. No part of this book may be reproduced, stored in a retrieval system, or transmitted, in any form or by any means, electronic, mechanical, photocopying, recording, or otherwise, without the written permission of the publisher.

Trinity Press International, P.O. Box 851, Valley Forge, PA 19482–0851

Library of Congress Cataloging-in-Publication Data

The Lord's Prayer and other prayer texts from the Greco-Roman era /
  edited by James H. Charlesworth, with Mark Harding and Mark Kiley.
    p. cm.
  Includes bibliographical references and index.
  ISBN 1-56338-080-3
  1. Lord's prayer — Criticism, interpretation, etc. 2. Nunc
dimittis — Criticism, interpretation, etc. 3. Prayers — Comparative
studies. 4. Prayers, Early Christian. 5. Prayers. 6. Prayer —
Judaism — History 7. Judaism — Doctrines. 8. Prayer — Christianity —
History — Early church, ca. 30–600. 9. Rome — Religion. 10. Greece —
Religion. I. Charlesworth, James H. II. Harding, Mark.
III. Kiley, Mark Christopher.
BV230.L574 1994
291.4'3'09015–dc20   94-31
                                               CIP

Printed in the United States of America

94 95 96 97 98 99   10 9 8 7 6 5 4 3 2 1

CONTENTS

v

CONTRIBUTORS

Barbara E. Bowe is Associate Professor of Biblical Studies at Catholic Theological Union, Chicago. She received her Th.D. in New Testament and Christian Origins from Harvard University in 1986. Her thesis on *1 Clement* was published in the Harvard Dissertations in Religion series as *A Church in Crisis: Ecclesiology and Paraenesis in Clement of Rome* (Fortress Press, 1988). She is currently working on the Hermeneia commentary on *1 Clement.*

James H. Charlesworth, is the George L. Collord Professor of New Testament Language and Literature at Princeton Theological Seminary. He is also editor of the PTS Dead Sea Scrolls Project, which is preparing the first comprehensive edition of all the nonbiblical Dead Sea Scrolls (over four hundred).

Agneta Enermalm-Ogawa is Associate Professor at Union Theological Seminary, where she teaches New Testament and Hellenistic Greek. At present her research is devoted to the function of the hymns in Luke 1–2. She is also investigating apologetic features in Josephus's *Antiquities* in comparison with Luke-Acts and Hellenistic historiography at large.

Mark Harding received his Ph.D. from Princeton Theological Seminary in 1993. His published articles have appeared in *New Testament Studies* and in *Reformed Theological Review.* He is presently lecturer in Judaica and Biblical Studies at Macquarie University, North Ryde, N.S.W., Australia.

Mark Kiley received his Ph.D. in New Testament and Christian Origins from Harvard University in 1983 and is the author of *Colossians as Pseudepigraphy* (Sheffield, 1986). A member of the Philosophy/Theology Department of St. John's University, Staten Island, he chairs the Society of Biblical Literature's Group on Prayer in the Greco-Roman Period and is planning a critical anthology of prayer texts from that period. His monograph *The Lord's Prayer and Gospel Theologies* (Liturgical Press) is forthcoming.

Steven F. Plymale is Professor of Religious Studies and Campus Minister at Morningside College, Sioux City, Iowa. He is currently working on a book on Christian prayer for the laity.

Barbara E. Reid, O.P., is Associate Professor of New Testament Studies at Catholic Theological Union, Chicago. She holds a Ph.D. in Biblical Studies from the Catholic University of America and is author of *The Transfiguration: A Source- and Redaction-Critical Study of Luke 9:28–36* (Cahiers de la Revue Biblique 32; Paris: Gabalda, 1993) and *Choosing the Better Part: A Feminist-Critical Study of Women in the Gospel of Luke,* forthcoming from Liturgical Press.

PREFACE

The present volume contains the fruits of the Society of Biblical Literature's Working Group on "Prayer in the Greco-Roman Period." This group began as an SBL Consultation. It continued as such from 1989 to 1992 with the mandate to explore, from historical-critical methodologies, the prayers of the Hellenistic and Roman worlds from Alexander to Constantine. From the outset it was clear that a desideratum was an extensive bibliography of these prayers, which were isolated from one another due to the diverse disciplines within the academy and divergent departments within the university. This bibliography now is completed and published in the present volume. It was compiled by Mark Harding during his years as a doctoral candidate at Princeton Theological Seminary.

The appearance of *The Lord's Prayer and Other Prayer Texts from the Greco-Roman Era* coincides with the elevation of the aforementioned SBL Consultation to an SBL Working Group. The Steering Committee members are Mark Kiley (chair), David Aune, Pamela Mary Bright, James H. Charlesworth, Asher Finkel, Eileen Schuller, and Bonnie Bowman Thurston. The Steering Committee helped improve the bibliography and selected papers for inclusion in this volume. Other papers read at the annual meetings or studies developing out of our discussions have been polished in the following publications: S. Plymale, *The Prayer Texts of Luke-Acts* (New York: Peter Lang, 1992), M. Kiley, *The Lord's Prayer and Gospel Theologies* (forthcoming from Liturgical Press), E. Schuller, "The Psalm of 4Q372 within the Context of Second Temple Prayer," *CBQ* 54 (1992), 67–79, and B. Thurston, *Spiritual Life in the Early Church* (Minneapolis: Fortress, 1993).

I wish to express my appreciations to the Steering Committee, Mark Harding, and especially Mark Kiley for helping me edit these papers and complete this project. I have enjoyed working with the contributors to this volume and trust many will appreciate their thoughts and reflections. Dr. Hal Rast, as always, has been a delightful colleague, and I am grateful to Trinity Press International for publishing this volume in such a handsome fashion.

J. H. Charlesworth

· 1 ·

A CAVEAT ON TEXTUAL TRANSMISSION AND THE MEANING OF *ABBA*
A Study of the Lord's Prayer

James H. Charlesworth

Joachim Jeremias is widely and wisely heralded as one of the greatest New Testament scholars of this century.[1] Among his many influences on New Testament scholars are two that warrant reexamination. First, he contended that Luke's shorter version of the Lord's Prayer is earlier than Matthew's text because of the rule that liturgical texts are expanded through transmission. Second, he suggested (but never declared clearly) that Jesus' use of *Abba* is virtually synonymous with our familial "Daddy." This second suggestion by Jeremias has been misused to assert Jesus' uniqueness and even to imply that he was in a certain sense not Jewish.

The purpose of the present chapter is to discuss two reasons why both conclusions are invalid. First, I shall attempt to demonstrate that there is no law that liturgical texts tend to expand as they are transmitted by scribes. Second, I shall discuss whether it is appropriate to equate the Aramaic *abba* with the English "Daddy."[2] These caveats seem necessary in light of the vast amount of primary documents now available which date from the pre-Mishnaic period of Judaism, the period of Early Judaism or Second Temple Judaism.

A Caveat Regarding Transmission

Jeremias argued that Matthew's longer version of the Lord's Prayer is due to redactional expansion because "in the early period, before wordings were fixed, liturgical texts were elaborated, expanded, and enriched."[3] He continued by claiming that "we find elsewhere in the growth of liturgical texts" a "proclivity for sonorous expansions at the end."[4] Jeremias did not provide convincing proof for either of these claims. Yet they have generally been accepted as axiomatic among a generation of leading scholars. It is simply no longer sufficient to base an argument for expansion on the fact that *some* texts do seem to expand when transmitted. It is now necessary to examine the transmission of ancient sources to see if Jeremias was correct in claiming that "liturgical texts tend to be elaborated, and the shorter wording is usually the earlier."[5]

My study of the transmission of early Jewish writings dating from the four centuries before the compilation of the Mishnah in 200 C.E. reveals *no rule* that texts, including liturgical documents, are *expanded* through transmission. There is no "Gesetzmässigkeit der Überlieferung liturgischer Texte" (strict rule for the transmission of liturgical texts).[6]

A comparison of the Aramaic fragments of Enoch with the later Greek and Ethiopic texts shows that documents are frequently truncated by scribes. For example, the Astronomical Books of Enoch, that is, Ethiopic Enoch 72 to 82, were severely abbreviated when scribes transmitted them.[7] The abbreviation in this case was from a document that allegedly filled an entire scroll to a mere eleven chapters. A study of the transmission of the Enoch astronomical book raises the question of what scribes do when they copy a text, and — moreover — what distinguishes epitomes, literary abbreviations, excerpts, quotations, and allusions.

Many other examples could be brought forward from the study of the Jewish apocalypses. Another example is found in 2 *Enoch*.. Today we cannot simply follow the conclusion by N. Schmidt, A. Vaillant, and N. A. Meshchersky. They contended that the longer texts of 2 *Enoch* are later than the shorter texts; and they were able to reach that conclusion because of the assumption that there was a strict rule that in copying scribes expanded texts and heavily interpolated them. Now, as F. Andersen has demonstrated,[8] we are surely confronted with not only instances of expansion but also of contraction in the transmission of the so-called long text of 2 (Slavonic) Enoch.[9] The transmission of 2 *Enoch* is complex; sometimes the longer version may well preserve earlier and original material. Hence, a study of the transmission of 2 *Enoch,* according to the most recent research, indicates that texts were frequently expanded through transmission but also intermittently abbreviated.

The Qumran fragments of the Testaments of the Twelve Patriarchs are not yet fully published, but it is obvious that these Aramaic documents antedate the Greek text. Specialists who have studied the transmission of this complex document perceive the process of transmission as one of truncation as well as redactional expansion. Hence, the final document is longer; it was expanded by a second-century C.E. Christian; but the Christian scribe did not preserve all of the original text. It is obvious that in some places he abbreviated it.

This phenomenon of abbreviation along with expansion is not new to New Testament scholars who conclude that Mark is our earliest Gospel. They know that although Mark is the shortest canonical Gospel, in many pericopes it preserves the longest account. While the editor (or redactors) of the Gospel of John seem to have expanded an earlier edition of John (especially by adding chapters 1 and 21, and perhaps chapters 15–17 [later scribes added 7:53–8:11]), Matthew and Luke often transmit a pericope in Mark by resorting to abbreviation as well as expansion.

Sometimes we observe that two recensions of a document, one long and one short, existed in antiquity. This phenomenon confronts us especially with the transmission of Jeremiah, which is preserved in a long recension, represented in the *Biblia Hebraica,* and with a short recension preserved in the Septuagint and also in Hebrew fragments from Qumran Cave IV that antedate 150 B.C.E.[10] This textual evidence makes it clear that texts were not as a rule expanded by copying scribes.[11]

Obviously, we are at times faced with documents that are expanded through transmission. There are many well-known cases. The Septuagint was expanded with the addition of the Old Testament Apocrypha. The Greek New Testament grew as scribes desired to harmonize the Gospels and conflate readings. Expansion is also evident in the transmission of some major Qumran scrolls, especially the Rule of the Community,[12] the Damascus Document,[13] and the Temple Scroll.[14] These observations, however, should not be removed from the wide field of transmission and proclaimed as a pseudo-rule that texts were always expanded. There is no rule that texts were usually expanded through transmission. In fact — if we need a rule — it is surely this one: *scribes will do what they will do* in copying documents. Our task then is not to study texts in light of a preconceived rule; it is to observe what a scribe has accomplished in the process of copying.

At this point an objection should be raised. We have been looking primarily at literary documents: apocalypses, testaments, and Gospels. J. Jeremias had pointed to certain laws in the transmission of liturgical texts ("Gesetzmässigkeit der Überlieferung liturgischer Texte"). Today such a strict rule may be questioned in light of the excision of anti-Jewish and sexist passages in liturgies and hymns in most denominations over the past decade. In the ancient world, it is certainly exposed as an inaccurate assumption when we look at the transmission of the Five More Psalms of David, to take one example of the transmission of a liturgical text from pre-70 Judaism.

Psalm 151 is preserved in Hebrew, Greek, and Syriac. The Hebrew is the original language and antedates the second century B.C.E. The Syriac is much later and derived from the Septuagint. As the psalm was transmitted from Hebrew to Syriac, via Greek, it became truncated.[15] Note the first two verses:

Ps. 151:1–2, translating from the Hebrew:

I was the smallest among my brothers,
and the youngest among the sons of my father;
and he made me shepherd of his flocks,
and the ruler over his kids.

My hands made a flute,
and my fingers a lyre;
and I shall render glory to the Lord,
  I thought within myself.

Ps. 151:1–2, translating from the Syriac:

I was the smallest of my brothers,
and a child of my father's house.
I was tending my father's flocks;

My hands made instruments,
and my fingers fashioned lyres.

Through transmission the beautiful *parallelismus membrorum* of the Hebrew was lost; four stichoi are reduced to three and the poetic synonymity of "shepherd" with "ruler" and "flocks" with "kids" is turned into the prosaic "I was tending my father's flocks." The significance of this observation for the transmission of the Lord's Prayer will not be lost on those who have assumed that Matthew's *parallelismus membrorum,* which is lacking in Luke, is a later addition. In Psalm 151 we have at least one controlled case in liturgy in which the parallelism is truncated. Could not Luke have also abbreviated a parallelism?[16]

In conclusion, we can no longer assume that liturgical texts were expanded in transmission. There is *no strict rule.* Hence, it is conceivable that Matthew's longer version of the Lord's Prayer is older than Luke's. Matthew's *pater hēmōn ho en tois ouranois* is not necessarily an addition to Luke's *pater.*[17] Also, Matthew's *elthetō hē basileia sou, genēthētō to thelēma sou* is not *prima facie* an expansion of Luke's *elthetō hē basileia sou.* Matthew alone preserves the parallelism here, and we have seen that sometimes parallelisms are omitted in transmission; hence, the parallelism may well be older, and it is conceivably traceable to Jesus.[18]

The Jewishness of *pater hēmōn ho en tois ouranois* is obvious. This epithet for God was "well known among Jews and very usual with them";[19] and it is clearly linked with the familiar and ancient *'bynu šbšmym.* The Jewishness of this formula does not necessarily originate with Matthew's very Jewish community; it may well derive from Jesus, whose prayers are deeply indebted to Jewish liturgical forms. It is surprising to learn that Jeremias admits that Matthew's longer invocation, "Our Father who art in heaven," is not a Christian creation, but "shows that it was used as early as the first century AD."[20] The context indicates that Jeremias means this formula was used in "Jewish prayers" and he provides examples in a preceding line. Hence, if they exist in pre-70 Jewish circles, could they not have been used by Jesus?[21]

Scholars, notably Heinemann,[22] have also shown that early Jewish prayers were not concretized in a written form before 70 C.E. Spontaneous individual prayers, using traditional formulae, were customary in synagogue and Temple. The Mishnah contains the injunction not "to make any prayer a fixed form" (m. *Abot* 2:13). Hence, seeking for redactional expansion of such prayers is neither fruitful nor appropriate. We should not begin with the assumption that only one form is original; and we should allow for the fluidity of spontaneous oral expression.

The first point of this essay has been established. Jeremias contended that liturgical texts, like the Lord's Prayer, were expanded through transmission. We have seen that his contention does not accurately represent the varied phenomena in the transmission of texts. Sometimes liturgical texts were abbreviated.

A Caveat on the Meaning of *Abba*

Should we follow Jeremias and conclude that *Abba* means essentially "Daddy"? Such a conclusion should be drawn only after a thorough examination of pre-70 Jewish liturgies in light of Jesus' concept of God. As we shall see, the evidence does not support Jeremias's conclusion.

In the Jewish Sibylline Oracles, books 3 and 5, which clearly antedate the Mishnah, we read that it was God who begot all gods and people (3.228). God is "the one who has begotten all" (3.550; 5.285, 406, 488, 500). Surely it is not far from such affirmations to portray God as "Father." Liturgical intonations accompany the celebration of God. The reader is exhorted to praise through hymns "God the begetter" (3.726). God is addressed as the "begetter": "Be gracious, begetter of all..." (5.328). Surely Jesus would have concurred with the author who wrote, "It is necessary to love God, the wise eternal begetter" (5.360), although he would have been more distinctly Jewish than the author of Sibylline Oracles, books 3 and 5. Jesus affirmed his Jewishness and would have resisted the tendency to Hellenize the concept of God. For Jesus "wise eternal begetter" would have been simply "Father."

That observation clarifies a danger in some publications. Too often Christians seek to develop christologically some aspect of Jesus' life or thought by stressing his uniqueness. Many Christians around the world affirm that Jesus was Jewish; but they contend that he was a unique Jew, different from all other Jews. This bewitching oxymoron is proved to be false by further research into pre-70 Jewish liturgy. It also is seriously questioned by passages in the New Testament that with a high degree of probability derive ultimately from Jesus and reflect his own thought. He not only urged his disciples to go only to the house of Israel; but he also charged them not to go in the direction of the Gentiles. This ethnic-centered Jewish dimension of Jesus' teaching is preserved in Matthew 10. Also, according to the canonical Gospels, Jesus worshiped in the Jerusalem Temple and considered it his Father's house, the house for prayer.

The Testament of Levi and the Testament of Judah, both of which I am persuaded preserve in the excerpts below pre-Christian traditions, indicate that Jesus was not the only Jew who held that God is to be understood as "Father." Note these excerpts:

> And then the Lord will raise up a new priest...
> And his star shall rise in heaven like a king;...
> The heavens will be opened,
> and from the temple of glory sanctification will come upon him,
> with a *fatherly* voice, as from Abraham to Isaac.
>
> (TLevi 18:2–6; italics mine)

> And after this there shall arise for you a Star from Jacob in peace:
> And a man shall arise from my posterity like the Sun of righteous-
> ness,...
> And the heavens will be opened upon him to pour out the spirit as a
> blessing of the Holy *Father.*
>
> (TJudah 24:1–2; italics mine)

It seems likely that these passages were composed by a Jew and were later attractive to second-century Christians who read them in light of their interpretations of the traditions regarding Jesus' baptism.[23] The Jewish elements seem ancient and help us comprehend the concept of God as "Father" in Early Judaism. Jeremias incorrectly suggested that these passages "may be Christian" because of the messianic content of "my Father."[24] Rather than being messianology, they reveal the eschatological dimension of the epithet in some Jewish writings; and we must be cautious not to confuse messianology with eschatology, as have many scholars in the past.[25]

The Lucan "Father," the Matthean "our Father who art in heaven," and other forms, like "our Father" are found in Jewish texts antedating (clearly or probably) the Mishnah.[26] These were prayer formulae of Jesus' Jewish contemporaries. The formula "our Father who art in heaven" appears, for example, in the famous *'abynu šbšmym.*[27] The formula is traditionally linked to Rabbi Akiba, who allegedly stated that Israel is made clean solely by the merciful actions of "your Father in heaven" (m. Yoma 8.9). In the Mishnah (Sota 9.15) we find this form: "On whom can we depend? Only on our Father in heaven" (*al abinu šebbašshamayim*).[28]

The popular formula "our Father who art in heaven" appears in private prayers, especially those that are penitential and supplicatory and that employ the second person address to God and the imperative form of the verb.

These observations are apposite to the Lord's Prayer and caution against attributing the long invocation to Matthew's creativity because he and his community were fond of the noun "heaven." It is equally easy to argue that Luke, with his tendency to bring forth the universalistic and pro-Gentile nature of Jesus' teachings, could have omitted "who art in heaven" as too Jewish. It is no longer obvious that Matthew added these words to bring out the Jewishness of Jesus' message. Hence, it is conceivable that "our Father who art in heaven" may go back to Jesus.

"Our Father" is an epithet for God used long before 200 B.C.E.; for example, recall Trito-Isaiah: *attâ yhwh 'ābînû*, "thou, O Lord, art our Father" (63:16; cf. 64:7). The divine epithet "Our Father" is preserved in early Jewish prayers; it is found, for example, in the probably pre-Mishnaic Ahabah Rabbah:

> Our Father ['*abînû*], merciful Father,
> > you who are ever compassionate,
> > have pity on us
> > and inspire us to understand and discern,
> > to perceive, learn, and teach,
> > > to observe, do, and fulfill gladly
> > > all the teachings of your Torah.

"Our Father" appears also in the Amidah (18 Benedictions):

> 4. Graciously favor us, our Father ['*abînû]*, with understanding from you....
>
> 6. Forgive us, our Father ['*abînû*], for we have sinned against you.[29]

"Our Father" appears frequently also in the penitential prayers for public fast days, especially on Rosh Hashanah and Yom Kippur. The litany form of these prayers in the Selihot is like the form in the Lord's Prayer: the invocation "Our Father" is followed by a petition. Note the following example: "Our merciful Father, save us!"[30] In the Abinu Malkenu, which is said on fast days and between Rosh Hashanah and Yom Kippur, "Our Father" — Abinu — is voiced more than forty-four times by the congregation.

"Father" in the possessive form is found in the clearly pre-Christian and Jewish book titled the Wisdom of Solomon. The righteous man is one who "boasts that God is his father" (2:16; cf. 2:18, 5:5). The epithet then was used with regard to the individual; it was not only a collective concept.

The absolute form "Father" was used in prayers by Sirach, the great Jewish sage of the second century B.C.E., who invoked God with the following words: "O Lord, Father and Ruler of my life" (Sir. 23:1; cf. 23:4, 51:10). The absolute form "Father" appears in other early Jewish literature; it appears twice in 3 Maccabees 6:4–8 in Eleazar's prayer:

> Pharaoh, the former ruler of this Egypt . . . you destroyed in the depths of the sea with his proud host, *Father,* causing the light of your mercy to shine upon the people of Israel. . . . When Jonah was pining away unpitied in the belly of the monster of the deep, you, *Father,* restored him uninjured to all his household. (*OTP* 2:526, italics mine)

This passage should not be disregarded as only the literary license of a Jewish author; it may well reflect a title for God that was accepted by the author's contemporaries and used in their places of worship.

The author of Hodayot 9.35 employed the Jewish concept of "Father" when he portrayed God as the Father of the Qumran Community. Note his words: "You are Father to all your [sons] of truth."

The absolute form *pater* appears in other early Jewish prayers. One passage that has not been included in the scholarly discussion is preserved in a quotation from the lost Apocryphon of Ezekiel. Clement of Rome (1 Clem 8.3), Clement of Alexandria (*Paedagogus* 1.10), and the author of the Nag Hammadi Exegesis of the Soul (NHC II, 6:135, 31–136, 4)[31] preserve a quotation from this pseudepigraphon, which in *1 Clement,* the earliest source, reads as follows:

> If your sins reach from the earth to heaven, and if they are redder than scarlet or blacker than sackcloth, and you turn back to me with (your) whole heart and say, "Father," I will heed you as a holy people.[32]

The context of the quotation cannot be reconstructed, but the meaning is clear. The children of Israel are to repent and call upon God as "Father."

Most importantly, the absolute use of *Abba* is attributed to other Jews roughly contemporaneous with Jesus of Nazareth. For example, Honi the Circle-Drawer, who was stoned outside of Jerusalem during the civil war between Hyrcanus II and Aristobulus II, is reported to have called God *Abba.*[33] Moreover, he allegedly pleaded for a distinction between an earthly *Abba,* even a devout miracle worker like himself, and the heavenly *Abba.* Only the latter *Abba* has the power to give rain.[34]

The traditions about Honi are, of course, pre-Mishnaic, as proved by the account in Josephus (*Ant.* 14.22). As far as I know, no scholar has suggested we translate Honi's *Abba,* if he did use this term, as "Daddy." Since Josephus records that one of his invocations was "O God, king of the universe," it is unwise to conclude that he did not equate *Abba* with God, the King. Jesus' prayer certainly goes on to stress God as King and appeals for the dawning of God's kingdom. If our sources can be trusted to represent pre-70 phenomena, then G. Vermes was correct to argue that for Honi as well as for Jesus "God is *Abba*."[35]

Abba can mean "Daddy," and little children obviously addressed their fathers this way in ancient Israel as they do today in modern Israel. But there is no compelling evidence that Jesus used *Abba* in that sense, nor are we warranted in concluding that Jesus, in contrast to his contemporaries, thought of removing God from heaven and placing him on earth. The immanence of God was certainly stressed by many of Jesus' contemporaries and seems to be a feature of his own teachings. Not only the Qumranic *bēth qôdēš* but also the Jerusalem cult and many synagogues were conceived to be an antechamber of heaven in which God was experienced as present. Even in the apocalypses, which are misunderstood if they are seen to be only about the future or the heavens above, there is a continuous stress that the prayers of the faithful are before God's throne. In 3 Baruch the archangel Michael is described descending to accept human prayers and taking them to God (3 Bar. 11–14).[36] Humans, angels, and God are thereby depicted as united; that is, God is not out of touch with his people. In the Jewish Pseudepigrapha God is depicted as hearing the prayers of the righteous. He is present to hear and receive. Unfortunately, an abundance of recent research stresses far too much that the Jewish apocalyptists portrayed only the transcendent quality of God.

The essential point now is to recognize that we have found no warrant to conclude that *Abba* meant "Daddy" either in pre-70 Judaisms or in Jesus' teachings. This conclusion is also defended by other scholars. In 1985 J. Fitzmyer claimed that Jeremias's conclusion that *Abba* means "Daddy" was inappropriate.[37] In 1988 James Barr published two articles in the attempt to show that *Abba* does not mean "Daddy." He rightly showed that the words attributed to Honi — *abba abba hab lan mitra* — can be translated only by "Father, father, give us rain." He also showed that while there is no distinct word for "Daddy" in Hebrew or Aramaic, there are several in Greek, notably *papas* or *pappas*. Since neither is used in the New Testament, the rendering of *pater* as "Daddy" is incorrect.[38] Barr is correct to stress that *Abba* originates with adults and that children learn it from them. It is an adult's term; that is, children do not invent the word *Abba;* they are taught it by their parents.

Jeremias finally rejected his earlier idea that *Abba* in the sayings of Jesus indicated that "when Jesus spoke to his heavenly Father he took up the chatter of a small child."[39] Jeremias, however, continued to conclude that Jesus "spoke to God like a child to its father, simply, inwardly, confidently, Jesus' use of *abba* in addressing God reveals the heart of his relationship to God."[40]As attractive as this interpretation might seem to some Christians, it does not necessarily follow from the exegesis of the New Testament nor from a comparison of Jesus' prayers with early Jewish prayers. It has become impossible for me to agree with Jeremias's observation: "Nowhere in the literature of the prayers of ancient Judaism — an immense treasure all too little explored — is this invocation of God as *Abba* to be found, neither in the liturgical nor in the informal prayers."[41]

Conclusion

In conclusion, we cannot appeal to a "Gesetzmässigkeit der Überlieferung" and conclude either that Matthew's version of the Lord's Prayer (in the longer lines) cannot go back to Jesus or that Luke's shorter version of the Lord's Prayer derives from Jesus. It is conceivable that Matthew's longer invocation and parallel petitions derive from an earlier stage in the transmission of Jesus' sayings than Luke's, and that this stage (*mutatis mutandis*) may derive ultimately from Jesus. The only point that seems clear now is that by 85 c.e. there were two versions of the Lord's Prayer, and each was considered authentic. Each was used in at least one major Christian community.

What can be said about Jesus and the Lord's Prayer? Jesus customarily avoided the usual Jewish expressions for God (*elohim, adonai elohenu*) and called God *Abba,* as we know from Mark 14:36 (*abba, ho patēr*). Fitzmyer rightly underscores Jeremias's conclusion that *Abba* is an example of *ipsissima vox Jesu.*[42] The meaning, however, is not "Daddy." It is "Father."

Jesus also certainly did not reserve this address to God for himself as an indication of his unique sonship. It is found in Paul's letters (Gal. 4:6 and Rom. 8:15) which show that it was a part of the early Christian liturgy.

We cannot conclude with Jeremias, however, that Jesus' use of *Abba* "was something new, something unique and unheard of, that Jesus dared to take this step and to speak with God as a child speaks with his father, simply, intimately, securely. There is no doubt then that the *Abba* which Jesus uses to address God reveals the very basis of his communion with God."[43]

Abba and its equivalent in Jewish Greek texts, while not prevalent in early Jewish texts, was also used by Jews other than Jesus to address God.[44] We, therefore, should be cautious in concluding that, on the basis of a study of *Abba* in early Jewish texts, Jesus and God were locked in a unique communion. We simply are too ill informed of pre-70 Jewish prayer life in Palestine to conclude what is unique to Jesus.[45]

Rather than proving an unparalleled communion between himself and God, Jesus' use of *Abba* probably reminded the Jews who heard him of some familiar and ancient traditions. His *Abba* probably evoked in them an awareness of God the Father, who had been active on their behalf in history. According to Sacred Scriptures God had called his people "son" when he freed them from Egyptian slavery (Exod. 4:22–23) and he had adopted Israel's king as his special son during the enthronement ceremony (Ps. 2). While Jesus' message that God is *Abba* was not unexpectedly new, he does seem to have elevated it to prominence.

The Jewish nature of the Lord's Prayer is certain, whether it derives originally from Jesus (in some form) or from one of his Jewish followers. The frequent tendency in New Testament research to de-Semitize Jesus and the desire to prove his uniqueness should be observed and recognized to derive from modern concerns that falsify history.

Notes

1. See the heated debate between B. F. Meyer and E. P. Sanders in the *Journal of Biblical Literature:* Meyer, "A Caricature of Joachim Jeremias and His Work," *JBL* 110 (1991), 451–62; Sanders, "Defending the Indefensible," *JBL* 110 (1991), 463–77.

2. As James Barr observes, the notion of "Daddy" is clearly implied in Jeremias's consistent emphasis that *abba* is familial and childlike. This observation seems warranted in spite of the fact that Jeremias seems to have refrained from defending this translation explicitly. See Barr, "'Abba Isn't Daddy," *JThS* N.S. 39 (1988), 28. In a series of English lectures Jeremias preferred the translation "dear Father" for *abba* when found upon the lips of Jesus; but he employed the translations "Daddy" and "Dadda" when children are speaking. See Jeremias, *The Central Message of the New Testament* (New York: Scribner's, 1965), 19–20, 30.

3. Jeremias, *The Prayers of Jesus* (trans. C. Burchard and J. Reumann; London: SCM, 1967; repr. Philadelpha: Fortress, 1978), 90.

4. Jeremias, *Prayers,* 90.

5. Jeremias, *New Testament Theology* (New York: Scribner's, 1971), 195.

6. Jeremias, *Abba: Studien zur neutestamentlichen Theologie und Zeitgeschichte* (Göttingen: Vandenhoeck & Ruprecht, 1966), 158.

7. See the discussion by J. T. Milik in *The Books of Enoch: Aramaic Fragments of Qumrân Cave 4* (with M. Black; Oxford: Clarendon, 1976).

8. F. Andersen, "2 (Slavonic Apocalypse of) Enoch," in *The Old Testament Pseudepigrapha* (ed. J. H. Charlesworth; 2 vols.; Garden City, N.Y.: Doubleday, 1983–85), 1:92–94.

9. In fact, in some cases the "long" text is actually shorter in some expressions and sentences than the "short" text of 2 *Enoch.*

10. The Greek recension of Jeremiah is about one-eighth shorter than the Hebrew recension. It is no longer certain that Greek scribes abbreviated Jeremiah; a Hebrew version of Jeremiah, almost identical to the short text of the Septuagint, has been found in Qumran Cave IV. In antiquity two versions of Jeremiah existed; we are not confronted with a simple case of abbreviation or expansion of a document. See F. M. Cross, *Ancient Library of Qumran and Modern Biblical Studies* (Garden City, N.Y.: Doubleday, 1958), 186–87. Also see E. Tov, "Expanded Team of Editors at Work on Variety of Texts," *Biblical Archaeology Review* (July/August 1992), 69, 72–75.

11. Scribes could expand, abbreviate, or copy a text without significantly altering it. In fact, unfortunately, sometimes they did not copy a text and it disappeared from literary history.

12. See the interesting history of transmission represented by the 4Q fragments of the Rule of the Community; this transmission is appreciably different from what has been thought by looking only at the copy known as 1QS. The texts and translations of all these copies are presented in the first volume of the Princeton Theological Seminary Dead Sea Scrolls Project, *The Dead Sea Scrolls: Rules,* which is being published by J. C. B. Mohr (Paul Siebeck) in Tübingen.

13. See the critical edition of the fragments of the Damascus Document by J. Baumgarten in the second and third volumes of the Princeton Theological Seminary Dead Sea Scrolls Project (in press at Tübingen).

14. See the pioneering work by L. Schiffman and E. Qimron in the third volume of the Princeton Theological Seminary Dead Sea Scrolls Project (forthcoming).

15. The dropping of the *parallelismus membrorum* may well have occurred at the Greek stage, since the LXX sometimes does not preserve the Semitic poetic form.

16. This question is focused on methodology; it does not indicate that Matthew is more trustworthy in transmitting the Lord's Prayer than is Luke.

17. Methodologically this statement seems sound to me (although for other reasons I am convinced that it is more likely that Matthew added this phrase than it is that Luke omitted it; but then there are other possibilities, such as the possibility that two versions were known very early, perhaps before 50 C.E.).

18. I am convinced that some (perhaps many) of the parallelisms in the sayings of Jesus derive ultimately from him, and not from someone fond of him. Jesus does seem to be a Jew who was gifted in orality and influenced by the prophets who had mastered *parallelismus membrorum.* That technique is indicated by his prophetic consciousness and his desire to be understood (and remembered) by his original Jewish audience.

19. J. Lightfoot, *A Commentary on the New Testament from the Talmud and Hebraica: Matthew–1 Corinthians* (Oxford: Oxford University Press, 1859; repr. Baker, 1979, Hendrickson, 1989), 149. Also see the rabbinic texts cited by S. T. Lachs, *A Rabbinic Commentary on the New Testament* (Hoboken, N.J.: KTAV, 1987), 118, and by P. Billerbeck, *Kommentar zum Neuen Testament aus Talmud und Midrasch* (with H. L. Stack; 8th ed.; Munich: C. H. Beck, 1982), 1:410–11.

20. Jeremias, *Prayers,* 26.

21. As has been noted in many publications, the use of the criterion of dissimilarity has been discarded as a viable avenue for discerning Jesus' authentic traditions. What is obvious in the Judaism of Jesus' time may well be something he followed (but not created), since he was a devout Jew. See J. H. Charlesworth and W. Weaver, eds., *Jesus and Christology* (Valley Forge: Trinity Press International, forthcoming).

22. J. Heinemann, *Prayer in the Talmud: Forms and Patterns,* trans. R. S. Sarason (Berlin, New York: De Gruyter, 1977).

23. I do not think these passages were composed by a Christian. H. C. Kee judges these passages to be originally Jewish. The passage from the Testament of Levi appears to be a reference to an eschatological priest. Some specialists on the

Pseudepigrapha have interpreted the passage to refer to one of the Maccabean priests. The passage from the Testament of Judah is a pastiche of old biblical and Jewish traditions, including Numbers 24:17, Malachi 4:2, Psalm 45:4 (LXX), Isaiah 11:2, 53:9, 61:11, Joel 3:1, and CD 7.11–20. See Kee, *Old Testament Pseudepigrapha*, vol. 1, 794, 801.

24. Jeremias, *Prayers*, 16.

25. See especially the new perspectives and methodologies to be used in studying messianology in Early Judaism and Early Christianity; these are presented (in performing the task) by a team of international experts in J. H. Charlesworth (ed.), *The Messiah: Developments in Earliest Judaism and Christianity* (Minneapolis: Fortress, 1992).

26. The exact places are well known and readily traced through Strack-Billerbeck, Lightfoot's *Commentary*, and in most major commentaries on Luke and Matthew.

27. See Heinemann, *Prayer*, 190.

28. J. Fitzmyer, "Abba and Jesus' Relationship to God," in *À cause de l'Évangile: Mélanges offerts à Dom Jacques Dupont* (Paris: Cerf, 1985), 23. Surely we should not dismiss the mishnaic example cited above as too late, even though it is grammatically typical of the Late Aramaic that began to appear around 200 C.E.

29. Translating from the old Palestinian version according to the Genizah fragment. See S. Schechter, "Genizah Specimens," *JQR* O.S. 10 (1898), 654–59, esp. 657.

30. See Heinemann, *Prayer*, 150.

31. The Coptic is *maeiot*, "My Father"; Coptic frequently supplies the possessive pronoun in transmitting Greek texts.

32. Following J. Mueller, "The Apocryphon of Ezekiel," Ph.D. disser. Duke, 1986, 114. The Greek is on 113.

33. For a short, up-to-date discussion of Honi see J. H. Charlesworth, "Honi," *Anchor Bible Dictionary*, 3:282.

34. This tradition is preserved only in the fifth-century Babylonian Talmud; G. Shelbert and J. Neusner have concluded that it is too late to be informative of first-century use of *Abba*. See Fitzmyer, *À cause de l'Évangile*.

35. G. Vermes, *Jesus the Jew: A Historian's Reading of the Gospels* (London: Collins, 1973), 211.

36. See J. H. Charlesworth, "Jewish Prayers in the Time of Jesus," *Princeton Seminary Bulletin Supplementary Issue* 2 (1992), 36–55.

37. Fitzmyer, in *À cause de l'Évangile*.

38. Barr, *JThS* N.S. 39 (1988), 36–38. Also see Barr, " 'Abba, Father' and the Familiarity of Jesus' Speech," *Theology* 91 (1988), 173–79.

39. Jeremias, *Prayers*, 62.

40. Jeremias, *Prayers*, 62.

41. Jeremias, *Central Message*, 19.

42. Fitzmyer, *À cause de l'Évangile*. Contrast M. R. D'Angelo, who is persuaded that " 'abba' cannot be attributed to Jesus with any certainty" (D'Angelo, "*Abba* and "Father": Imperial Theology," *JBL* 111 [1992], 611–30; quotation is on 630). Contrast the conclusion of B. L. Cooke, who argues that "Jesus' awareness of his Abba as faithfully loving and supremely lovable, an awareness that

dominated his prayer and his teaching, was the most basic *word* communicated to him about the transcendent" (Cooke, *God's Beloved: Jesus' Experience of the Transcendent* [Philadelphia: Trinity Press International, 1992], 22). I would agree with R. G. Hammerton-Kelly, who perceived a consensus among the best scholars; they conclude that Jesus' *Abba* experience is the starting point of Christology. Hammerton-Kelly, "God the Father in the Bible," in *God as Father?* (Conc 143; Edinburgh: T. & T. Clark; New York: Seabury, 1981), 101.

43. Jeremias, *Central Message*, 21.

44. E. M. Schuller draws attention to a text found in Cave 4, the Prayer of Joseph, which begins as follows:

> My father and my God,
> do not abandon me into the hands of the nations;...

See Schuller, "The Psalm of 4Q372 1 within the Context of Second Temple Prayer," *CBQ* 54 (1992), 67–79, esp. 68. Also see her "4Q372 1: A Text about Joseph," *RdQ* 14 (1990), 349–76.

45. See the judicious comment by B. Gerhardsson, *The Origins of the Gospel Tradition* (Philadelphia: Fortress, 1979), 55.

· 2 ·

THE LORD'S PRAYER
AND MATTHEAN THEOLOGY

Mark Kiley

In this essay I propose to describe some of the linguistic and thematic affinities between the Matthean version of the Lord's Prayer (6:9–13) and the sayings that follow it in the Sermon on the Mount. In addition, I will attempt an overview of the prayer and its similarities to material outside the sermon, and I will focus primarily on material peculiar to Matthew.[1]

My purpose is not only to outline the similarities between the prayer and these various parts of the Matthean Gospel but to suggest that most of the sayings following the prayer in the Sermon on the Mount were placed there as a kind of commentary on the prayer, and further, to point out that the outline of the prayer bears a striking resemblance to much of the special Matthean, or M, material outside the sermon. I suggest that this special Matthean material outside the sermon sometimes acts in its own right as a commentary on the prayer, as in the thrice-repeated conjunction of Jesus' *coming* into a house with discussion of the *kingdom*. In other instances, the M material outside the sermon is the vehicle by which one may understand select sayings in the sermon as a commentary on the prayer, as in the case of the needle's eye of the kingdom and the sermon's narrow gate (19:24 and 7:13, 14).

In undertaking this task, I am preceded by two recent studies that examine the relationship between the prayer and other parts of Matthew. In a 1978 article in *New Testament Studies,* Günther Bornkamm suggested that much of the material in Matthew 6:19–7:12 is intended to serve as a kind of sayings commentary on the Lord's Prayer in 6:9–13.[2] And in 1981 in a collection of essays called *Standing before God,* Asher Finkel outlined a case that suggested that the prayer of Jesus served as ordering principle for the woes of chapter 23.[3] Because I am willing to look to special M material outside the sermon as commentary on the prayer and indeed to let special M material outside the sermon help define some sayings inside the sermon as commentary on the prayer, my thesis ends up being rather more extensive than Bornkamm's. Because Finkel's thesis is not really about Matthean material that comments on the prayer, I am not going to dwell at length on it here. However, I would say that a modified form of Finkel's suggestion is quite defensible, namely, that the material in 23:9–22 reflects the order of the theocentric petitions of the Lord's Prayer, but that the influence of the prayer leaves off at 23:22.[4]

Let us turn now to the Gospel at large. I propose to follow the order of the petitions of the prayer in the ensuing discussion. We will then be in a position to suggest a rendering of the prayer that is sensitive to its Matthean overtones.

Our Father in heaven:

There are about fifteen occurrences of this phrase in the special Matthean material. Of those, the vast majority have either "my" or "your" attached as an introductory modifier.[5] Jesus never speaks to the disciples about "our Father" except to give them permission to make that address in their prayer. This confirms the oft-noted thesis that the relationship presupposed by the prayer's address is one into which the disciples are invited by Jesus but one that is preeminently and in a unique way his own.[6]

Hallowed be your Name:

The otherness or sanctity of the Father title is underscored in 23:9: "call no man on earth Father."

In addition, another phenomenon of Matthew's text is relevant to this petition. The name "Jesus" is the Greek form of "Joshua," meaning "the Lord saves." That is, the name "Jesus" bears within it a component and reminder of the divine Name. And it is a startling fact of the Matthean Gospel that nobody ever addresses Jesus by the name "Jesus." Indeed, in both stories of double healings in chapters 8 and 20, Matthew drops the direct address "Jesus" present in his Markan source.[7] I find it hard to believe that both omissions of the direct address are gratuitous, and I would suggest that the prayer yields the rationale for the absence of any direct address to "Jesus." This omission, this reticence about addressing the divine Name in Jesus, is another way of sanctifying the divine Name.

Your kingdom come:[8]

We begin with sayings in the Sermon on the Mount that may be relevant to this petition of the prayer.

It is easy to see that 6:25–33 focuses on and ends with an admonition to seek first God's kingdom.[9] But what about the earlier discussion of treasure and the evil eye in 6:19–24? The sayings on treasure in heaven are probably best seen in relation to the description of the kingdom as a treasure (13:44). But is there a relation between the kingdom and the saying on the evil eye (6:23)? I would suggest that for that answer we look to the parable of the vineyard laborers in 20:1–16. That special Matthean parable in chapter 20 is presented as a depiction of the kingdom of heaven. The means of payment used by the householder, paying everyone a day's wage, is enough to send his longest-working employees into exercise of the evil eye, a reaction of jealousy about others' reception of the householder's belongings. The evil eye, Matthew intimates, must be eliminated from one's attitude toward the kingdom.[10] Seen collectively, then, the sayings in Matthew 6:19–24 are about the kingdom of heaven in which "treasure" is to be understood from God's point of view.[11]

Let us examine another example of potential kingdom material in the sermon: The main outline of Matthew 7:13, 14 concerning the narrow gate leading to life is the same as in Q (see Luke 13:23, 24). But it is interesting to note that this is not the only narrow opening pictured in the Gospel. In the story of the rich young man, Jesus challenges him to sell his possessions and give to the poor to acquire treasure in heaven (19:16–30) and likens the process to a camel going through the eye of a needle (19:24), i.e., through a very narrow opening. Is the kingdom's eye of a needle related to the narrow gate leading to life? I think so. Indeed, the evangelist at 7:14 has inserted another phrase into the Q account, "the way is *hard* that leads to life," mirroring the theme in the rich man's story about the difficulty a rich man has in entering the kingdom of heaven. This understanding of 7:13, 14 as a saying about entry to the kingdom qualifies it as a sayings commentary on the kingdom petition of the prayer.

The just among the nations, those who inherit the kingdom in 25:31–46, constitute another example of special M material and give us an insight into Matthew's understanding outside the sermon of precisely what kind of kingdom it is for which the community prays. The just inherit the kingdom because they unwittingly serve Jesus in their midst in the least of his brothers and sisters. There has been an ongoing debate about the identity of "the least." Some have said that the least are all the world's needy. I tend to agree with those who say that the least are the disciples on worldwide mission and that the nations are distinct from the disciples and to be judged on their treatment of the disciples. However, the primary focus of these verses on the reception of the kingdom by the just in virtue of their meeting the needs of the disciples need not preclude the derivative inference that the disciples too will inherit the kingdom when they meet each other's or the world's needs.[12]

Another example of kingdom commentary in M concerns sun imagery. Matthew 13:43 describes the fate of the just in this way: "Then the just shall shine like the sun in their Father's kingdom." In another piece of peculiarly Matthean material, at the transfiguration, we read that Jesus' face shone "like the sun" (17:2). Lest the reader miss the force of the sun imagery, Matthew alone has the ailing boy in the next pericope be "moonstruck" (17:15). We may reasonably infer that what the disciples see in Jesus' face is a proleptic glimpse of the fate of the just in the Father's kingdom.[13]

One final note about the kingdom theme in M material: there is a dynamic of the M material that posits a very close link between Jesus' coming into the house [at Capernaum] and the presence of the kingdom of heaven. In three places in the Matthean editing, 9:28, 13:36, and 17:25, Jesus [is in Capernaum and] "comes into the house." Following each of these three instances occurs a discussion of the kingdom: in chapter 10, the focus is on its healing; in chapter 13, on its mystery; in chapter 18, on its exaltation of the child/little ones.[14] This kind of tight association of Jesus' coming into the house and the advent of an aspect of the kingdom may presuppose a Matthean community functioning along the model of a house church and depicts one of the ways in which the community expects an answer to its petition "Your kingdom come."[15]

Your will be done on earth as in heaven:[16]

I want to discuss three places that illustrate how this petition is reflected in the Gospel.

The statement in 7:21 focuses on the central importance of doing the Father's will. That is another clear indication to me that the sayings material, at least up to this point in the sermon (and not only to 7:12), acts as a commentary on the prayer.[17]

My next example, or rather cluster of examples, concerns much of the special M material in chapter 18, which has a high degree of affinity with this petition of the prayer. Matthew 18:14 reads, "It is not the will of my Father in heaven that one of these little ones perish." Moreover, 18:18 reflects the language at the end of the prayer's petition, that concerning heaven and earth: whatever the disciples bind on earth will have been bound in heaven, and what they loose on earth will have been loosed in heaven. Even the immediately following verse reflects the language of this petition: when two of you agree on any matter, it will be done (*genēsetai*) by my Father in heaven; compare the prayer's language concerning the doing (*genēthētō*) of the Father's will. Much attention in recent years has been directed toward defining the precise nature of what is bound or loosed in this chapter;[18] and it is true that the promise of 18:19 extends to any matter on which they agree. But I think it fair to say that the material here enjoins the disciples to at least one way of effecting the Father's will, i.e., to bind and loose whatever is necessary to insure that the little ones not perish.

Finally, most commentators recognize that Jesus' prayer in 26:42, although not peculiar to Matthew, has been crafted to conform closely to this petition. He says "your will be done."[19]

Give us today our daily [*epiousios*] bread:

I agree with the majority of commentators who see 6:34, the prohibition against anxiety about "tomorrow," as partly intended to serve as a commentary on this petition of the prayer and its focus on "today."[20] Otherwise, material derived from Mark and from Q acts as such a commentary. For example, mention of the evil human fathers whose sons ask for bread becomes Jesus' platform for insisting that the heavenly Father will give good things to those who ask. This verse (7:7) is widely recognized as intended to be seen in tandem with the bread petition of the prayer. Similarly, I agree that the correspondence of bread and fish in the sayings in 7:7–11 and in the feeding stories in chapters 14 and 15 serve to make of all this material an amplified commentary on the bread petition of the prayer.[21]

Having come this far in the prayer, we are in a position to read with fresh eyes the story of the Canaanite woman's plea for her daughter in 15:21–28. In a phrase unique to Matthew, Jesus says to her, "May it happen to you according to your will." One cannot help but notice the way in which her will coincides with the express intention of the Father's will in 18:14, namely, that "not one of these little ones perish."[22] Furthermore the emphasis of M that the woman is in full agreement with Jesus (the phrase "for yes" in 15:27) illustrates the principle that the agreement of any two will cause the Father to effect that will (18:19). And the story's banter about bread serves as prelude to the healing, just as in 7:7–11 the discussion of the prayer's bread acts as backdrop to a portrait of all the "good things" that the Father gives.[23]

Forgive us our debts for we have forgiven our debtors:

I agree with those who see the parable of the unforgiving servant (18:21–35) as an illustration of this petition of the prayer. The fate of that servant, who got back what he gave out, is also mirrored in the sayings in 7:1–5 about judgment and the measure.[24]

Do not bring us to test(ing):

We begin our inspection of this petition by turning to material taken over with little change from Mark and from Q because this will provide the best backdrop for the special Matthean redaction centering on this theme.

I believe that the best place to start to answer the question of what Matthew thinks is involved in this petition is the Markan Gethsemane scene, one of the sources for Matthew 26:36–46.[25] In Mark 14:38, Jesus counsels the disciples to "stay awake and pray that you not come to testing." If we let our understanding of this command be guided by the immediate scene, then we can describe testing in this way: a request made during perceived danger, demanding of God (you *can;* take it away!) that God act for someone according to the person's will; Jesus does not counsel the disciples to pray to succeed in negotiating such a situation, but to pray to be spared it altogether. Having himself experienced the weakness of the flesh, Jesus worries that the disciples, similarly afflicted, will choose their own will to the frustration of God's good purposes for others and indeed for themselves.

The option of Jesus' testing God is presupposed and explicitly rejected in the statement of Jesus to the devil in Matthew 4:7 "You shall not test the Lord your God." This bit of dialogue is part of a three-step conversation in Matthew between the devil and Jesus, which is described as Jesus' "being tested" (Matt. 4:1–10). The fact that Jesus faces the option of testing God and can also be described as "being tested" is known as well in Matthew's source, Mark. In Mark, Jesus faces the option of testing God in Gethsemane and is said to "be tested" by Satan in Mark 1:13. One could well say that the dynamic of Jesus' being tested is the description of Jesus' side of the experience of Gethsemane's testing of wills. Matthew's portrait of Jesus' "being tested" is more elaborate than Mark's laconic notice and bears a resemblance to the experience both of Israel in the desert and of Jesus' being tested by people.[26]

Having noted those affinities, however, one should stress that the central dynamic of the Matthean temptation scene in 4:1–10 is the one confronted in Mark's Gethsemane: the tempter's offers focus on all that God (or the tempter) can do for Jesus, offers presumably calculated to appeal to a weakened human will. And there is a consistency to Jesus' manner of dealing with those offers: he chooses what the Markan Gethsemane scene calls God's will; what Matthew will portray in 4:1–10 as a choice to adhere to God's lifegiving word even in the midst of temporary human deprivation, to affirm God's independence from being manipulated into simply doing what God can do (or, from an anthropological point of view, to trust in God's presence without benefit of miraculous proof), to assert the Lord's exclusive right to worship and service over all other claimants. In these scenes, the Matthean Jesus is showing the Matthean community how to negotiate the testing when the prayer to avoid it is no longer answered positively, when indeed they come into testing.

Matthew has also incorporated several scenes in which people and not the devil test Jesus, scenes that may show us something about what the evangelist thought should be considered when the community prays "lead us not into testing." In three of the four Matthean scenes when people approach Jesus to "test" him (Matt. 16:1, 19:3, and 22:18), the scenes are largely similar to those in which the Markan Jesus is tested (Mark 8:11, 10:2, 12:15) in that Jesus refuses in each case to do or endorse without qualification what is proposed to him as merely possible.

But a special bit of Matthean pedagogy in one of these scenes is worth noting for the way in which it interacts with chapter 4 to produce a statement about surviving the test. In chapter 16, after the Pharisees and Sadducees test him with the challenge to perform a sign, the evangelist has added to his Markan base references in Matthew 16:10, 11, 12 to "loaves" in the plural, mirroring the uniquely Matthean portrayal in 4:3 of the devil challenging Jesus to produce "loaves" in the plural. In 16:12, the evangelist says that Jesus warned them not (in a literal sense) against the yeast of the loaves, but against the teaching of the Pharisees. By its allusion to the loaves of chapter 4, this comment warns the disciples to adopt the same stance as Jesus did there. Rather than cling to what comes out of the mouths of the Pharisees and Sadducees, they are to cling to whatever comes out of the mouth of God.[27]

Matthew has also created a fourth scene in which people test Jesus, based on a scene in which Mark had no such testing reference. In chapter 22, the evangelist has added a reference to people testing Jesus in the dialogue about the great commandment (cf. Matt. 22:35ff. and Mark 12:28–31). Jesus responds by citing the Shema concerning the primacy of loving the Lord, but immediately adjoins to it the commandment to love neighbor as self, asserting that on these (both) hang the Law and the prophets. The evangelist's choice to describe Jesus' articulation of neighbor love as a survival of a "test" brings this narrative as well within the ambit of the temptation scenes in chapter 4. Together the narratives assert that Jesus' choice in chapter 4 to worship the Lord instead of worshiping the tempter was not a choice to switch allegiance from the service of one despot to the service of another tyrant. Rather, when read in the light of 22:35ff., 4:10 asserts that Jesus' choice to worship the Lord is a choice to worship the true God, whose service is love of others.[28]

Moreover, this description of the command to neighbor love as a survival of a test also has relevance for our thesis that the sayings following the Lord's Prayer in the Sermon on the Mount comment on the prayer. For 7:12, the golden rule, enjoins treating others as one would want to be treated. In light of the fact that 22:35f. links testing and neighbor love, one can say that the golden rule of 7:12 is a sayings commentary on the prayer's petition "do not bring us to testing" (6:13).[29] Matthew's community is being told first to pray to be spared the test, but that when the test comes, one of the means of choosing well during the test is to choose love of neighbor.

But deliver us from evil:

I wish to cite only two relevant examples.[30] At Jesus' cross, in M material in 27:43, the crowd jeers by citing Psalm 22:8: "Let God deliver him, if he wants (to deliver) him" (27:43). Let me also suggest that the warning in 7:15–23 against the tolerance of evil fruit in the community's midst functions on one level as a comment on the prayer's petition to deliver us from evil.[31]

Let us step back and attempt some summary observations. If the affinities I have outlined above are intended by the evangelist, we are facing a covert inner-community dialogue between prayer and narrative in the Gospel of Matthew. That has long since seemed to me to be the case; indeed, I attribute the terse statement in 7:6 to "guard what is holy and the pearls from the dogs and pigs" to this covert correspondence known most fully in the catechesis of Matthew's church and available only after entry into the community.[32] Indeed, such a thesis fits well with the attitude expressed in adjoining centuries toward catechesis. For example, Hippolytus (d. 235) speaks of catechesis as a privilege of the elect:

> If anything needs to be explained, let the bishop speak in private to those who have received baptism. Those who are not Christians are not to be told unless they first receive baptism.[33]

That this catechesis (presuming baptism or preparation for baptism) included attention to the Lord's Prayer is seen as late as the fifth-century sermonic commentaries on the prayer by Peter Chrysologus addressed "to the catechumens."[34]

Furthermore, I think we can say that Bornkamm was basically correct in his assertion that sayings following the Lord's Prayer in the Sermon on the Mount offer an amplification of and pedagogical commentary on it. But he prematurely ended his investigation of the sayings that provide a commentary on the prayer, a commentary that we can now say extends at least to 7:23. To his credit, he has brought widespread attention to a long-neglected aspect of Matthean theology and furnished some of the exegetical wherewithal to pray the prayer in a way that is sensitive to its especially Matthean overtones:

Our Father in heaven, to whom Jesus has given us access, **Hallowed be your name** (we call no one on earth "Father" and we decline to address your name in your Son).

Your kingdom come. Help us seek it, and override our evil eye, that blinds us to the nature of this treasure; this kingdom which is measured in our identification with the poor and in care for the least of Jesus' brothers and sisters; your kingdom where the face of the just shall shine, as does Jesus', like the sun; your kingdom whose healing and mystery and fellow children we welcome when Jesus comes into our house.

Your will be done on earth as in heaven in our care for the little ones, in even the most excruciating reversal of our plans for your kingdom's coming.

Give us today our daily bread, lest anxiety overtake us about tomorrow.

Forgive us our debts, for we have forgiven our debtors. Shatter the miserly scales of our measure and replace them with larger, more generous ones.

Bring us not to testing, but if you will not spare us from testing, help us choose your word, revere your independence from manipulation, worship you only, and serve you in neighbor-love.

But deliver us from evil that is within ourselves, and also from the evil without, as at the cross of Jesus.

Notes

1. This essay is based on a presentation made to the Society of Biblical Literature's Consultation on New Testament Prayer in Historical Context, New Orleans, November 1991.

2. G. Bornkamm, "Der Aufbau der Bergpredigt," *NTS* 24 (1978), 419–32. Anticipated independently by G. Giavini, "Abramo forse in Mt 6, 19–7, 11 il primo commento al 'Pater Noster'?" *RivBib* 13 (1965), 171–77.

3. A. Finkel, "The Prayer of Jesus in Matthew," in A. Finkel and L. Frizzell, eds., *Standing before God: Studies on Prayer in Scriptures and in Tradition with Essays in Honor of John M. Oesterreicher* (New York: KTAV, 1981), 131–70.

4. Finkel draws attention to the fact that, like the petition "your kingdom come," the first woe in 23:13–14 mentions the kingdom.

The next petition of the prayer concerns the effecting of God's will. The next woe focuses on the Pharisees' proselytizing activity. And Finkel makes the intriguing suggestion that the evangelist may have placed the woe here because it reflects a similar collocation of motifs in Psalm 40:9, 10, where the psalmist celebrates doing God's will as well as sharing God's good news. Matthew's excoriation of Pharisaic proselytizing would then be a repudiation of the claim that such proselytizing reflects God's will and a claim that the divine will is now more fully revealed in the Matthean Jesus. The latter part of the petition about God's will runs "on earth as in heaven." Although Finkel does not approach it in quite this way, I would suggest that language about heaven in 23:22 is placed here to reflect this aspect of the prayer.

A careful reading of the remainder of the woes will show the high degree of correlation between their language and that in the Beatitudes, e.g., the next woe in 23:23–24 explicitly reflects the language of justice in the Beatitudes, while other woes focus on the issues discussed in the Beatitudes, such as purity and the murder of the prophets.

5. Matt. 5:16, 45, 48. 6:1, 4, 6, 8, 15, 18; 7:11, 21; 10:20, 29, 32, 33; 12:50; 13:43; 15:13; 16:17; 18:10, 14, 35; 20:23; 21:31; 23:9; 25:34; 26:53; 28:19.

These verses are special Matthean material that speak of the "Father." Underlining indicates phrases in which the expression "heavenly" or "in heaven" occurs.

6. See especially 11:25–27.

7. Matthew 8:29; cf. Mark 5:7. Also Matthew 20:30; cf. Mark 10:47. These stories of double healings have other traits in common, e.g., the use of "Lord" and "son of David" in the "cry" of the petitioners.

8. I count some eleven verses in special Matthean material focusing on the kingdom: 4:23 and 9:35, 13:19, 13:38, 13:41, 13:43, 20:21, 21:31, 21:43, 24:14, 25:34. Some twenty additional verses in M mention the kingdom of heaven: 3:2, 5:10, 5:19, 5:20, 7:21, 13:24, 13:44, 13:45, 13:47, 13:52, 16:19, 18:1, 18:3, 18:4, 18:23, 19:12, 20:1 (22:11–14), 23:13, 25:1, 25:14.

9. E. Schweizer, The Good News according to Matthew (Atlanta: John Knox, 1975), 164–67.

10. For a recent relevant study of the evil eye, see J. Elliott, "The Evil Eye in the First Testament: The Ecology and Culture of a Pervasive Belief," in D. Jobling, P. L. Day, and G. T. Sheppard (eds.), The Bible and the Politics of Exegesis (Cleveland: Pilgrim, 1991), 147–60.

11. J. C. Fenton, The Gospel of Saint Matthew (Harmondsworth, Middlesex, England: Penguin, 1963), 104, sees the reference to treasure in 6:19 as most helpfully illuminated by 19:21 and the reference to "treasure in heaven." For what I consider to be a complementary and illuminating way to handle 19:21, see my comments on 7:13, 14.

12. See J. Donahue, The Gospel in Parable (Philadelphia: Fortress, 1988), 109–25.

13. Moreover, the focus in 17:2 on Jesus' face as sun-like and the peculiarly Matthean detail of his "falling on his face" in Gethsemane (26:39) sets up the reader for a new appreciation of the predicted darkening of the sun (24:29), which precedes the Son of Man's coming in his kingdom (24:30). In Matthew, the Son of Man has begun to come in his kingdom: the mention of power in 28:18 and sun (glory) in 17:2 are a deliberate actualization of the promise to the disciples that some will not taste death before they see the Son of Man coming in his kingdom (16:28). In favor of this thesis is also the fact that only a select number of disciples ("some") witness these two events. On 28:18, see J. Meier Matthew (Wilmington, Del.: Michael Glazier, 1980), 369. Although such a reading would lend weight to an often-defended thesis that Matthew conceives of the kingdom of the Son of Man as already having come, one should not then proceed to say that he reserves the language of "kingdom of heaven" for a future reality. Both phrases are variously used to describe a reality both present and future. See W. Walker, Jr., "The Kingdom of the Son of Man and the Kingdom of the Father in Matthew: An Exercise in Redaktionsgeschichte," CBQ 30 (1968), 573–79.

14. In the first case, he comes into the house and heals two blind men (9:28) in anticipation of instructions in chapter 10 wherein he sends out the apostles to announce the advent of the kingdom of heaven (10:7) by healing the sick (10:8) when they also "come into the house" of their host in each city (10:12). In 13:36, Jesus "comes into the house" to explain to his disciples the parable of the weeds and wheat, one of the parables of the kingdom of the Father (13:43) and of the kingdom of heaven (13:44, 45). In 17:25, he "comes into the house" to query

about the kings' children and then gives his teaching about who is greatest in the kingdom of heaven.

Moreover, the specific language used in 17:25 links the incident tightly to the Gospel's language about the kingdom; I refer to the fact that Jesus "anticipates" (*proephthasen*) Peter. This language is a cognate of the word used in Matthew 12:28 to explain Jesus' exorcisms: "The kingdom of God has come upon [*ephthasen*] you." The verb used to describe the kingdom's coming, *ephthasen*, derives from Q but occurs only here in Matthew and has its closest linguistic cognate in the discussion at 17:24–27. For that reason, and not only because Jesus discusses the children of kings, I see the temple tax discussion in this pericope primarily as another parable of the kingdom. I say this without prejudice to the complementary observations of D. Garland, "Matthew's Understanding of the Temple Tax (Matt. 17:24–27)," *Society of Biblical Literature Seminar Papers* (Atlanta: Scholars Press, 1987), 190–209.

15. See M. Crosby, *House of Disciples* (Maryknoll, N.Y.: Orbis, 1988).

16. I count seven occurrences of special Matthean material bearing an affinity with this third petition of the prayer: 7:21, 9:13, 12:7, 18:14, 20:15, 21:31, and 26:42.

17. G. Luz, *Das Evangelium nach Matthäus (Matt 1–7)* (Neukirchener: Benziger, 1985), 406, also says that the verse relates back to the "Our Father." This thesis gains added strength when one recognizes that the version of the saying in Q, Luke 6:46, reads "why do you call me 'Lord, Lord' and not do what I say?" whereas Matthew replaces "do what I say" with "do the will of my Father." Matthew has gone out of his way to stress the notion of the Father's will here; since it comes so soon after the prayer containing this very phrase, I think it foolhardy to ignore the possibility that the saying is intended as an amplification of this petition of the prayer.

18. H. W. Basser, "Marcus's Gates: A Response," *CBQ* 52, 2 (April 1990), 307–8. J. Marcus, "The Gates of Hades and the Keys of the Kingdom," *CBQ* 50, 3 (July 1988), 443–55. H. W. Basser, "Derrett's Binding Reopened," *JBL* 104, 2 (June 1985), 297–300.

19. F. Matera, *Passion Narratives and Gospel Theologies* (New York: Paulist, 1986), 96.

20. E.g., R. Gundry, *Matthew: A Commentary on His Literary and Theological Art* (Grand Rapids: Eerdmans, 1982), 107, 108.

21. Fenton, *Matthew*, 111, links 7:11 to the feeding stories.

22. E. Lohmeyer, *Das Evangelium nach Matthäus* (Göttingen: Vandenhoeck & Ruprecht, 1967), 256, sees the use of *genēthētō* in 15:28 as an echo of the third petition of the Lord's Prayer.

23. This story seems to mark the beginning of a shift from the more restricted notion of the sheep for whom Jesus is sent (15:24 and 10:5, 6) to the more generalized notion of 18:12–13.

24. P. Bonnard, *L'Évangile selon Saint Matthieu* (Geneva: Labor et Fides, 1982), 97: "Matt. 18:23–35 is an exact illustration of 7:2." Similarly, Gundry, *Matthew*, 121.

Bornkamm joins many others in recognizing their similar dynamics, for which a recent study by Lambrecht criticizes him: J. Lambrecht, *The Sermon on the Mount:*

Proclamation and Exhortation (Wilmington, Del.: Michael Glazier, 1985), 164. I find this criticism puzzling, for this is one of Bornkamm's strongest points, which enjoys a wide consensus.

25. For a thorough recent study of the Markan Gethsemane's relation to questions of theodicy, see S. Dowd, *Prayer, Power and the Problem of Suffering: Mark 11:22–25 in the Context of Markan Theology,* SBLDS 105 (Atlanta: Scholars Press, 1988).

26. The concern for bread because of their hunger that overrides their attention to God's command (Exod. 16), the people's doubt concerning God's presence (Exod. 17), worship of a God other than the Lord (Exod. 32). The Matthean scene also shares elements with the Markan scenes in which persons "test" Jesus: the demand for an exercise of power (Mark 8:11), the discussion of two scriptures (Mark 10:2), and the discussion of political power (Mark 12:15).

27. See the similar comments of Gundry, *Matthew,* 55, 56.

28. Luz, *Evangelium,* 164, notes other connections between the Matthean temptation scenes and special Matthean material elsewhere: Jesus forswears angelic help and remains obedient to Scripture at 26:52–54. The taunt "If you are the Son of God" is repeated at the cross (27:40). The mountain as scene of the discussion of kingdoms is echoed in the mountain of Jesus' authority at 28:16.

29. P. Bonnard, *L'Évangile,* notes that the "Law and the prophets" occurs in both 7:12 and 22:40. L. Sabourin, *The Gospel according to Saint Matthew* (Bandra Bombay: St. Paul, 1982), 430, notes the common occurrence of the golden rule in 7:12, 22:39, and 19:19.

30. There are some ten occurrences of *ponēros,* evil, in M: 5:37, 5:39, 5:45, 7:18, 13:19, 13:38, 13:49, 18:32, 20:15, 22:10.

31. My conclusion about the overtone of the "evil fruit" motif is in a more diffuse way anticipated by Fenton, *Matthew,* 112, when he says that the (latter part of the) Lord's Prayer may have set the tone of destruction for this section (7:13–27).

The provenance of the special M petition "deliver us from evil" is a tantalizing question. I have already mentioned the evangelist's knowledge of Psalm 22:8 about deliverance at Matthew 27:43. But there is another possibility. Matthew quotes Psalm 91:11, 12, in the second temptation and that psalm's third verse discusses deliverance ("he will deliver you from the fowler's snare"). Since Jesus, whom the Spirit-dove had filled, was delivered from death, did the evangelist feel it appropriate to supply to Jesus' prayer "deliver us from evil"? Also see Psalm 55:6, 7; 54:9; 124:7, and P. Bonnard, *L'Évangile,* 87.

32. Though, of course, this is one of many possible options for understanding the verse; e.g., Didache 9:5 relates it to the Eucharist, perhaps on the basis of texts like Exodus 29:33, 34, and Leviticus 22:10–16. After the interpretation that I have proffered above, the one I find most attractive is that of R. Gundry, *Matthew,* 122, who feels that the "no pearls to the swine" saying is a necessary counterbalance to the prohibition against judgment of one's fellow disciples in 7:1–5. The latter "might well lead to a church dominated by the false, unless care is taken not to allow into fellowship those who are recognizably undiscipled."

33. Apostolic Tradition 23:14; cited by E. J. Yarnold, *The Awe-Inspiring Rites*

of Initiation: Baptismal Homilies of the Fourth Century (Slough, England: Society of St. Paul, 1971), 51.

34. Baptismal catechesis on the prayer and the Creed is also reflected in the work of Theodore of Mopsuestia (d. 428): "It is fitting that we should speak today of the necessary things concerning the prayer which was taught by Our Lord, and which they [the Fathers] made to follow the words of the Creed, so that it should be learned and kept in memory by those who approach the faith of baptism" (A. Mingana, *Theodore of Mopsuestia: Commentary on the Lord's Prayer and on the Sacraments of Baptism and Eucharist* [Woodbrooke Studies 6; Cambridge: Heffer & Sons, 1933], 1).

· 3 ·

THE PRAYER OF SIMEON
(Luke 2:29–32)

Steven F. Plymale

With good reason the Nunc Dimittis is generally classified with the other nine hymns in the first two chapters of the third Gospel. Yet there is one formal, distinguishing characteristic of Simeon's canticle. Unlike the others, the words of Simeon are addressed directly to God in the form of a prayer. Luke employs this text to introduce his readers to the concept of universal salvation, which invites both Gentile and Jew into the kingdom of God, and to explain the place the Christ event holds on the continuum of God's salvation history.

Simeon's prayer is part of a larger section (2:22–38), which includes the occasion for Mary and Joseph's trip to the Temple, the introduction of Simeon, the Nunc Dimittis itself, the response of Joseph and Mary to Simeon's prayer, Simeon's words to Mary, and the role of the prophet Anna. This larger section is located in the midst of a series of accounts dealing with the birth announcements of Jesus and John, and Jesus' birth, infancy, and boyhood.

Luke's concern is not with the specifics of the Mosaic Law, though he wants the reader to understand that in general the Law is being fulfilled and that the *dramatis personae* are concerned for and motivated by the Law. Joseph and Mary bring the child to Jerusalem because of the Law (vv. 22 and 27) and to fulfill the Law (v. 24). Simeon (v. 25) and Anna (v. 37) are clearly to be understood as exemplars of proper, faithful Judaism, including right regard for the Law. Luke brings this section to a close with his own affirmation regarding adherence to the Law: "And when they had performed everything according to the Law of the Lord, they returned into Galilee, to their own city, Nazareth" (v. 39).

Furthermore, Luke wants the reader to remember the presentation of Samuel at the sanctuary at Shiloh (1 Sam. 1:21ff.). Hannah brought Samuel and an offering to "the house of the Lord at Shiloh" (v. 24) as Mary and Joseph brought Jesus to the Temple and offered sacrifice (Luke 2:22–24). Luke's phrase "to present him to the Lord" (v. 22) echoes 1 Sam. 1:22:

28

"that he [the child] may appear in the presence of the Lord." Luke's conclusion to the second chapter of the Gospel — "And Jesus increased in wisdom and in stature, and in favor with God and men" (2:52) — reminds the reader of another statement made about Samuel: "Now the boy Samuel continued to grow in stature and in favor with God and with men" (1 Sam. 2:26).

Following his introduction (2:22–23), Luke brings Simeon into the scene. Though the name "Simeon" was a common Jewish name and seems to carry no particular significance, the person of Simeon is consequential for Luke. The "righteous and devout" Simeon (v. 25) is fully subject to the Holy Spirit, which was upon him (v. 25) and had revealed to him that he would not experience death until he had seen the promised, expected Messiah (v. 26). The Holy Spirit prompts Simeon to be present in the Temple at just the right time and place to encounter Mary and Joseph with the child (v. 27).

There is no mistaking the significance of the emphasis on the Holy Spirit in the story of Simeon. Preceding the story of Jesus' presentation at the Temple, Luke eagerly showed the Holy Spirit as orchestrating the activities connected with the coming of the Messiah. All significant persons in these opening chapters of the third Gospel are filled with the Holy Spirit, e.g., Elizabeth (1:14) and Zechariah (1:67). Luke continues to emphasize the role of the Holy Spirit in leading Jesus (e.g., 3:22; 4:1, 14) and the early church (e.g., Acts 1:8; 2:1ff.).

The reader is aware that all Simeon does, experiences, and says is under the direct control of God. The doublet of Luke 1:35b equates the "Holy Spirit" and "the power of the Most High" in words addressed to Mary by the angel Gabriel: "The Holy Spirit will come upon you, and the power of the Most High will overshadow you." "The Holy Spirit" as an expression occurs in the Hebrew Scriptures only at Psalm 51:11 (LXX 50:13) and Isaiah 63:10–11. In the Psalm the Holy Spirit and the presence of God are equated. The passage from Isaiah speaks of the Holy Spirit (63:11) in terms of God's redeeming activity (63:12–14). Since there are so many Isaianic references in this section of the Gospel, we can reasonably suggest that Luke had the passage from Isaiah in mind as he mentioned the Holy Spirit's role in Simeon's life. He seems to be alerting the reader to the significance of the Simeon episode in God's plan of salvation.

Luke also describes Simeon as one "waiting for" ("expecting" [RSV: "looking for"]) the consolation (*paraklēsin*) of Israel. Isaiah 66:12–13 (LXX) uses the same basic words to describe God's consolation of Jerusalem. Interestingly, the Isaianic passage also mentions the "glory of the Gentiles" (cf. Luke 2:32), but in a less conciliatory light. Isaiah 40:1, too, speaks of the consolation of Israel: "Comfort, comfort my people, says your God." Undoubtedly Luke was mindful of the prophecy of Isaiah as he finalized this story of Simeon. Furthermore, the Jews addressed by Anna just moments after Simeon spoke to the holy family are described as "all who were looking for the redemption of Jerusalem" (2:38). Within the context of this pericope, the "redemption of Jerusalem" and the "consolation of Israel" (2:25) are different expressions of the same expectation. Simeon is an exemplar of a type: pious and devout Jews awaiting the fulfillment of the promises of God.

Simeon's patient waiting is rewarded when he encounters the Christ child. He took the child into his arms and "blessed God" (*eulogēsen ton theon*). The significance of Simeon's blessing is to be found not in the secular Greek use of *eulogeō* but in Hebrew tradition.[1] Simeon blesses God, for he immediately recognizes this child as the Messiah and Simeon's whole life had been lived in expectation of this very moment. "The Israelite who knows that his whole life is in the hands of the Creator cannot find any better expression for his faith and gratitude and hope than by giving God the glory."[2] The "blessing of YHWH is a cry of thanksgiving to him arising from manifestations past and present of his faithfulness toward his people."[3] God has been faithful on two counts: he has sent the promised Messiah and Simeon lived to see the advent.

Many scholars have noted that "universalism," particularly in the sense that the work of Christ is for all people, Jew and Gentile alike, is one of Luke's primary themes. It is significant that the first indication of the universal scope of the Messiah's mission is presented in Simeon's prayer. Richard J. Dillon states: "Luke 24:47 is the first explicit provision for the Gentile mission, in contrast to the prophetic hints in earlier passages (e.g., Luke 2:30–32; 4:25–27; 10:1f.; 14:16–24; etc.)."[4] But there is clearly more in Simeon's prayer than a "hint." Simeon celebrates that God has sent his Christ into the world and his prayer explicitly states that the benefit is for Gentiles as well as for Jews (vv. 31–32).

To understand more fully the intent of Simeon's prayer and its significance in the Lucan scheme of things, let us examine the text in detail. *Nyn* (Now), placed first in the sentence, an emphatic position in both Greek and English, stresses the current reality of fulfilled promise, indicating that whatever follows is a reality at the time the words are uttered.

Proving these words to be a prayer, Simeon addresses God directly with the vocative *despota*. Luke employs this term as an address of God both here and in Acts 4:24. In the Gospel the term serves three functions. It is a fitting and properly Jewish invocation of God in prayer, quite appropriate for such a devout and pious Jew as Simeon; it intends simply to identify and glorify God as God; it also serves in cooperation with Simeon's use of the self-designation *doulon sou* to establish his concept of his relationship with and responsibility toward God.

Since Luke alludes so frequently to Isaiah in these opening chapters of the Gospel, it should be noted that the LXX Isaiah also employs *despotēs* for God. Isaiah 1:24 is the beginning of a passage in which God declares that he will unleash his wrath upon the rebellious of Israel. Isaiah 3:1 and 10:33 make similar use of the term, using *o despotēs kyrios sabaōth*. All three passages speak of the judgment of God upon rebellious Israel and each conveys the warrior-god image. Luke's use of the term carries the same connotations, for he envisions a divine judgment upon the rebellious of Israel, not within the prayer text itself, but in the words immediately following the prayer and addressed to Mary: "Behold the child is set for the fall and rising of many in Israel" (Luke 2:34–35). The use of *despota* in Simeon's prayer conveys hope for some and judgment for others.

Doulos, Simeon's self-designation in this prayer, is intended to complement the use of *despota,* with each word strengthening and clarifying the other. Luke uses the term in the general sense of servant/slave throughout his writings, meaning one having complete faith in God (e.g., Mary in Luke 1:38); or in a more technical sense as an echo of the LXX *doulos tou theou,* meaning a prophet. "It is difficult to decide whether there is here a conscious adoption of the designation of the prophets as *doulai tou theou,* and therefore the appropriation of an official or honorary title, or a personal confession of absolute commitment to God."[5] At the very least "the term expresses his [Simeon's] life of righteousness (Ps. 27:9; 2 Ch. 6:23; Dan. 3:33, 44; Acts 4:29)."[6] Yet in view of Luke's stress on the connection between the Holy Spirit and Simeon — Luke mentions it three times and "for Luke, as for later Judaism in general, there is a close connection between the Holy Spirit and the spirit of prophecy"[7] — and in view of Simeon's prophetic utterance to Mary (vv. 34–35), perhaps it would be most accurate to conclude that Luke presents Simeon with the honorary, implied title "Prophet."

This prophetic figure addresses God: *Nyn apolyeis ton doulon sou, despota.* The verses immediately preceding this statement make it clear. Luke had taken care to identify Simeon as one to whom "it had been revealed that he should not see death before he had seen the Lord's Christ." Simeon's initial words in this prayer should be translated: "Now you are dismissing your servant, Lord." Simeon's God-given task had been to wait (watch) for the coming of the Messiah and, upon seeing the Christ child, he considers his life to be ending. He is able to rejoice for he is being allowed to die in peace, a recipient of a true promise of God. The phrase *kata to rēma sou* refers to the promise revealed to Simeon by the Holy Spirit (v. 26). The present indicative *apolyeis* is no petition; it is, for Simeon, a present reality. One purpose of the prayer is to give Simeon the opportunity to thank God for fulfilling his promise; Luke thereby sanctions the concept of the faithfulness of God.[8] The parallel construction found in v. 26 and vv. 29–30 add to the likelihood that these words of Simeon are his statement of his imminent death. Simeon will not see (*mē idein,* v. 26; *eidon,* v. 30) death (*thanaton,* v. 26; *apolyeis* v. 29) until (*prin,* v. 26; *Nyn,* v. 29) he sees God's salvation (*Christon kyriou,* v. 26; *sōtērion sou,* v. 30).[9]

When one reads of "God's salvation," "the biblical precedent which springs to mind is, of course, Ps. xcvii (xcviii).3, which has been strongly in the mind of the author of the *Magnificat* and *Benedictus*."[10] Psalm 97:2–3 (LXX) mentions *sōtērion* twice and speaks of the salvation being seen in the sight of all the earth. It is entirely appropriate to "see" salvation in this sense, for the word refers to the person who brings/offers salvation. "The term *sōtērion*, which we can only translate by *salvation*, is equivalent neither to *sōtēr*, Savior, nor to *sōtēria*, salvation. This word, the neuter of the adjective *sōtērios*, saving, denotes an apparatus fitted to save. Simeon sees in this little child the means of deliverance which God is giving to the world."[11] The "seeing" of salvation is implied by Luke in 10:23 and is included in a Lucan quote of Isaianic material: Luke 3:6 quoting Isaiah 40:5. Isaiah implies the same thing in 62:11 and states it in 52:10. For Luke as for his Hebrew ancestors, to "see" salvation is to witness God's active involvement in the world on behalf of his salvific purposes.[12]

This salvation has been made ready, prepared (*hetoimazō*) by God. Luke uses the same verb with the same basic meaning in 1:17d, for example. "When used of God the verb almost always = 'ordain.'"[13] "But the idea of the preparation of salvation is unique, and in the light of what follows, this must mean the providential preparation of *salvation* through Israel's history, according to prophecy and promise, until the time of fulfillment which is now recognized."[14] When Simeon holds the Christ child, he accepts the immediate presence of that salvation promised and made ready by God — the child is the present reality of salvation. Luke is concerned to demonstrate that the Christ event is a fulfillment of rather than a break from faithful, historical Judaism.

The salvation has been planned and brought to fruition by God *kata prosōpon pantōn tōn laōn*, v. 31. *Kata prosōpon* with a genitive, as it occurs in Luke, is an example of a LXX style found only in Luke (cf. Acts 3:13). The phrase can mean "over against" (e.g., Gen. 16:12; 33:18) or "before" (i.e., "in front of" as in Lev. 16:14, 15). Both examples from the Lucan material, Acts 3:13 and here in Simeon's prayer, are to be translated "before" or "in the presence of." The meaning is that God's salvation is in the open view of and accessible to *pantōn tōn laōn*.

The phrase "all the people" can only be understood literally. "This is not an event like other events; it is the event with universal implications."[15] The concept is inspired by Isaiah 52:10:

> The Lord has bared his holy arm
> before the eyes of all the nations;
> And all the ends of the earth shall see
> the salvation of our God;

though it also seems to be related to Isaiah 42:6 and 49:6. "Simeon sieht in diesem kindlein das Heil nicht für Israel, sondern auch für alle Völker"

("Simeon sees in this child the salvation not for Israel only, but for all people").[16]

The attempt by G. D. Kilpatrick to argue that *laōn* refers here to Israel only and that the next line may mean only that there is a light for the Gentiles to see but no salvation available[17] is rejected soundly by most scholars. Luke's use of *pantōn* and the listing of the two groups — Jews and Gentiles — in v. 32 as a definition of the *laōn*, can only mean that Simeon is announcing a universal salvation, i.e., one available to *all people*. "The salvation — which is the coming of the Messiah — is light to the Gentiles and the glory of Israel. In the light of the new thing that has happened, the Christian psalmist can stand back and see God's mighty work in relation to both Gentile and Jew."[18]

Regarding "light," *phōs* can be used by Luke as a symbol of judgment (Luke 8:16–17; 12:2–3) and as a symbol of salvation (Luke 16:8; Acts 9:3; 22:6, 9; 26:18). In this instance, due to the context, due to the Lucan use of Isaiah (cf. Isa. 42:6; 49:6; and 51:4), and in view of Acts 13:47 and 26:22–23, both of which equate light with a salvation that includes Gentiles, the *phōs* of Luke 2:32 must be seen as a symbol of salvation. It stands in apposition to "your salvation" of v. 30.

Simeon's prayer is the first statement in the Lucan writings of what proves to be an important, distinctive, and definitive theological concept: the Messiah, promised in the Hebrew Scriptures, arrives to offer salvation for Jew and Gentile alike. The theme is repeated throughout Luke's two-volume work. For example, consider the case of Jesus' speaking to the congregation in the synagogue at Nazareth (Luke 4:16–30; cf. Matt. 13:54–58; Mark 6:1–6a). All three Gospels report that Jesus taught in the synagogue in his own country. The Lucan account, however, contains material found in neither Matthew nor Mark: that Jesus read from Isaiah and that the reading stressed the work of the Spirit, etc. In 4:25ff. Luke adds the story of Elijah to the account, telling of the power of God being used for the benefit of non-Jews. In light of Simeon's initial proclamation of the universality of salvation, and in light of Luke's continued use of the theme of universal salvation, this account of Jesus' teaching should also be considered as another Lucan statement of the inclusion of Gentiles into God's plan of salvation. Prayer, with its sanctioning power, is Luke's chosen vehicle for the initial proclamation of this definitive Lucan theme.[19]

The response of Joseph and Mary to the prayer of Simeon casts additional light on its interpretation. They "marveled at what was said about" the child (v. 33). Simeon's response was first to bless these parents and then speak directly to Mary words concerning an Israel divided in response to the Christ and the pain Mary would one day be compelled to endure. Of course, the wonder and amazement on the part of Joseph and Mary is a typical motif in stories of miracles and revelations; but what was said of the Christ child to cause such a reaction? The only new element is the inclusion of the Gentiles. Up to this point, all statements about the Christ had been cast in terms that could easily be understood exclusively in the context of Israel, e.g., Mary's conversation with Gabriel (1:26–38), the proclamation to the shepherds (2:8–20, particularly v. 11), and the message to Mary (2:16–18). "The Nunc Dimittis makes an advance over the Song of the Angels at the birth of Jesus (2:14) in that the birth is now related not only to the welfare of Israel (2:32b) but salvation is now announced in the sight of all peoples, the Gentiles as well as Israel (2:32a)."[20] Due to the messianic expectations in the Jewish community and past proclamations to Mary, the new element of Simeon's prayer caused both Mary and her husband to marvel — even Gentiles will be included in God's plan of salvation!

Simeon says that not only are the Gentiles to be included; even the house of Israel will be divided over this matter. Those who fall and then rise will be the Jews who, after the initial rejection of Jesus, accept him as Messiah; those who speak against the sign are those who completely reject the Messiah. "Luke has hitherto been concentrating on obedient Jews, like Zechariah, Elizabeth, the shepherds and Simeon. Now, having mentioned the inclusion of the Gentiles, he turns in the words of Simeon's second oracle to the many in Israel who will be disobedient."[21] Luke may have Isaiah 8:14 in mind: "And [the Lord] will become a sanctuary, and a stone of offense, and a rock of stumbling to both houses of Israel, a trap and a snare to the inhabitants of Jerusalem." Certainly the division of Jews over the person of Christ is a major theme of Luke-Acts.

The inclusion of the pericope concerning the prophetess Anna serves to augment the "authority" of what has been disclosed by the prayer of Simeon and to affirm that the Christ event is part of God's plan for Israel. Bultmann sees Anna as a doublet for Simeon, with 2:38 paralleling vv. 29–32.[22] It is interesting to note that Luke seems to be fond of male/female pairs as representatives of Judaism: Zechariah and Elizabeth, Mary and Joseph, Simeon and Anna. This pairing of righteous and devout Jews seems to add another dimension to Luke's universality — all people are included, male and female, Gentile and Jew. The old dividing lines disappear with the advent of the Messiah.

The story of Anna emphasizes that everything done in the Temple had been accomplished "according to the Law," as the story of Simeon had already mentioned (2:22, 23, 24, 27, and 29), but Anna also underscores the prophetic dimension of Luke's account:

Luke identifies Anna as a prophetess (2:36), and he has Simeon moved by the Spirit to utter a prophecy about Jesus' future (2:34–35). Thus, added to the Law is the element of prophecy; "the Law and the prophets," as Luke describes the heritage of Israel (Luke 16:16; 24:27; Acts 13:15; 24:14; 26:22; 28:24), come together to establish the context for the beginning of Jesus' career.[23]

The proclamation presented in the prayer of Simeon is clear: the Gentiles are to be included in the salvation made possible by Christ. There can be no doubt about the theological centrality of this concept in Luke's two-volume work nor regarding the fact that it is in the words of Simeon that Luke chooses to introduce the theme to his readers. The question remains, though: why is the initial announcement of this definitive Lucan theological insight first offered the reader in the form of a prayer? There are two possible answers to the question. First, Luke could be preserving a form of traditional material as it came to him. Second, Luke could be using a prayer form to sanction a concept he considers to be of crucial significance. Let us examine each possibility.

Bultmann argued that Luke 2:22–40 "must have been current before the version used by Luke."[24] Perhaps Bultmann had in mind an earlier observation concerning the prayer of Simeon offered by Hermann Gunkel, whose thoughts were initiated by observing that the prayer is reminiscent of Hebrew poetic form.[25] Gunkel suggested a Hebrew or Aramaic original. That Luke is placing a traditional piece into his account seems strengthened by the observation that the Simeon prayer can be removed from the text without destroying the flow of the narrative. It is possible to read v. 27 followed by vv. 34ff. as an unbroken account. The prayer and the response to it by Joseph and Mary could be understood as material added to an existing narrative by Luke.

Minear allows for the possibility of a Lucan source at this point while arguing that the Nunc Dimittis still reveals something of Lucan theology. "We may be convinced, as I am, that the stories are thoroughly Lucan and are fully congenial in mood and motivation to his [Luke's] perspective as a whole. But this does not entitle us to treat them as an ad hoc composition, first produced by Luke to introduce the two volumes."[26] Though it is true that just because the stories are so fully Lucan in character one cannot assume that they are not sources taken over by Luke, we must also affirm the other side of that coin: even if this pericope is from a source, it nevertheless is employed by Luke for his own purposes and, therefore, is a full expression of Lucan theology.

After carefully examining this text, R. A. Aytoun discovered that "the Nunc Dimittis, when translated into Hebrew . . . is found to be in regular Hebrew metre."[27] He found that the piece fell neatly into three trimeter couplets. Paul Winter reached a similar conclusion some years later.[28] D. R. Jones concluded that the evidence "points to a Hebrew original, while justice is done to the evidence of a relationship to the LXX by supposing that the translation into Greek was made by someone intimately acquainted with the LXX."[29]

The evidence suggests that the words of Simeon are to be taken as an early Christian, pre-Lucan, prayer-hymn, composed originally in Hebrew. It undoubtedly issues from a Hebrew-Christian community steeped in the language and style of the Hebrew Scriptures. The very words of the prayer suggest that the community that composed it was concerned to affirm both the old and the new: the Christ event is God's new action in his efforts to offer salvation, but the Christ event cannot be properly or fully understood unless it stands in the context of the continuing dealings of God with his people — Israel.

Though originally composed in Hebrew, the Nunc Dimittis is thoroughly Christian and thoroughly Lucan (even though there is no evidence of Lucan redaction within the prayer itself). While reminiscent of Hebrew psalms, it is not exactly like any specific psalm-type, though it suggests the epiphany psalm style.[30] Since the theology is completely Christian, though the language and style are Hebrew, the purpose of the Nunc Dimittis "is revealed principally, not in an amplification of the older psalm structure, but *in the use* that is made of the older material. It is the fulfillment of the old which is new, and art is forgotten in preoccupation with the mighty acts of God."[31]

Luke is preserving an original form (and thereby affirming the connection between Judaism and Christianity), but there is another and equally important reason to express the concepts presented in the Nunc Dimittis in prayer form. Prayer texts afford an aura possible with no other form of expression. To be sanctioned in a prayer is to be identified by the reader — Hebrew or Greco-Roman — as something of particular importance, an invitation into the deepest chambers of the author's mind.

One additional question remains: since Luke is writing in approximately 85 C.E., years after the definitive split between Judaism and Christianity occasioned by the destruction of the Temple, why would Luke wish to stress the continuity between Judaism and Christianity, as he seems to do with Simeon's prayer? Let me suggest several possible answers to the question:

First, Luke could be simply reproducing earlier sources. Perhaps the early Hebrew-Christian community that first penned the Simeon prayer believed it personally necessary to stress Jewish-Christian continuity. Luke's concern may be to be true to his sources, allowing them to express the concerns they had in their day without assuming that their concerns remain particularly relevant for his own day. Luke might be reproducing Simeon's prayer as a piece of Christian history — informative, but not necessarily definitive for Luke's own community, particularly in light of the Temple's destruction.

Second, Luke may be including Simeon's prayer for the sake of his own Roman audience. The Romans of Luke's day held a basic distrust for "new" religions. Luke might be saying that Christianity is a continuation of Judaism and, therefore, is not a new religion. While stressing the continuity to counter Roman fears, Luke is also saying that Christianity offers a new element to the historically established faith of Judaism. Luke might be saying that Christianity shares Jewish history, but that it is clearly not the same faith. In Luke's mind, the fact that Simeon and Anna, the representatives of the Law and Prophets, are old individuals, close to death, may be a way of saying that Judaism is passing away, but its long standing history and tradition lives on in Christianity.

Third, the continuity between Christianity and Judaism could be a statement of Luke's faith in and theological understanding of what we might call a "Judeo-Christian heritage." Our terms "Judaism" and "Christianity" may be imposing on Luke a religious differentiation alien to Luke's own understanding. From among the people in covenantal relationship with God, there have always been those who refuse to accept God's continuing activity of revelation. Simeon's prayer includes both Israel and Gentiles in God's salvation; but following his prayer, Simeon speaks to Mary about the opposition to this new act of revelation within Israel itself (Luke 2:34–35), without denying the place of Israel in covenantal relationship with God. Luke repeats this understanding in Stephen's speech (Acts 7:2–53; e.g., in 7:51: "You stiff-necked people, uncircumcised in heart and ears, you are forever opposing the Holy Spirit, just as your ancestors used to do"). Even later in Acts, Paul's self defense after his arrest begins with the words, "I am a Jew" (Acts 21:39 and 22:3). This evidence may suggest that Luke does not present a rejection of Judaism by God. In fact, given the sanctioning power of prayer texts so evident in Luke-Acts, the prayer of Simeon, which speaks of Gentile inclusion into the people of God rather than rejection of Judaism, may be the clearest statement of Luke's own thought.

Notes

1. Beyer, *TDNT*, 2:754: "Of few words in the NT is it so plain as of *eulogeō* and *eulogia* that they do not take their meaning from secular Greek but from the fact that they are renderings of Hebrew words which acquired their religious significance in the OT and other Jewish writings."

2. Beyer, *TDNT*, 2:758.

3. W. S. Towner, "Shorter Communications 'Blessed Be YHWH' and 'Blessed Art Thou, YHWH' ": The Modulations of a Biblical Formula, *CBQ* 30, 3 (1968), 390.

4. R. J. Dillon, *From Eye Witnesses to Ministers of the Word* (Rome: Biblical Institute Press, 1978), 168, n. 35.

5. K. H. Rengstorf, *TDNT*, 2:273–74.

6. I. H. Marshall, *Commentary on Luke* (New International Greek Testament Commentary; Grand Rapids: Eerdmans, 1978), 120.

7. A. R. C. Leaney, *The Gospel according to St. Luke* (2d ed.; London: A. & C. Black, 1958), 38.

8. A search of the Hebrew Scriptures (LXX) reveals a relationship between *apoluō* and death in the Hebrew tradition available to Luke. See D. R. Jones, "The Background and Character of the Lukan Psalms," *JThS* 19 (1968), 40.

9. See Alfred Plummer, *A Critical and Exegetical Commentary on the Gospel according to St. Luke* (ICC; 5th ed.; Edinburgh: T. & T. Clark, 1977), 68.

10. Jones, 41.

11. F. Godet, *Commentary on the Gospel of St. Luke* (New York: Funk, 1881), 86.

12. J. A. Fitzmyer, *The Gospel according to Luke I–IX*, (Anchor Bible; Garden City, N.Y.: Doubleday, 1981), 428.

13. Plummer, *Critical and Exegetical Commentary*, 68.

14. Jones, "Background and Character," 42.

15. Jones, "Background and Character," 42.

16. Fritz Rienecker, *Das Evangelium des Lukas* (Wuppertal: R. Brockhaus, 1959), 68.

17. G. D. Kilpatrick, "Laoi at Luke II:31 and Acts IV:25, 27," *JThS* 16.1 (1965), 127. See also Jerome Kodell, "Luke's Use of LAOS, 'People,' Especially in the Jerusalem Narrative (Lk 19, 28–24, 53)," *CBQ* 31 (1969), 327–43. Kodell argues that Luke does not "follow a consistent pattern in employing the term" (327).

18. Jones, "Background and Character," 43.

19. Other examples of the Lucan expression of universalism are found in the mission of the Seventy (Luke 10:1ff.), the parable of the great supper (14:15–24); Jesus' commissioning of his disciples in 24:36–53; the message of Paul and Barnabas at Antioch (Acts 13:44ff.), with its Isaianic quotation (v. 47) and response of the Gentiles (v. 48); and Paul's self-defense at 26:19ff.

20. Fitzmyer, *Luke*, 422. See also N. Q. King, "Universalism in the Third Gospel," *Texte und Untersuchungen zur Geschichte der altchristlicher Literatur* 73 (1959), 199–200. King agrees with this interpretation.

21. R. E. Brown, "The Presentation of Jesus (Luke 2:22–40)," *Worship* 51 (1977), 8.

22. Rudolf Bultmann, *The History of the Synoptic Tradition* (trans. John Marsh; rev. ed.; New York: Harper & Row, 1963), 301–2.

23. Brown, "The Presentation of Jesus (Luke 2:22–40)," 4.

24. Bultmann, *History of the Synoptic Tradition*, 299–300, 302–3.

25. H. Gunkel, "Die Lieder in der Kindheitsgeschichte Jesu bei Lukas," *Festgabe von Fachgenossen und Freunden A. von Harnack* (ed. Karl Holl; Tübingen: Mohr, 1921), 52.

26. P. Minear, "Luke's Use of the Birth Stories," *Studies in Luke-Acts* (ed. L. Keck and J. Louis Martyn; Philadelphia: Fortress, 1980), 112.

27. "The Ten Lucan Hymns of the Nativity in Their Original Language," *JThS* 18 (1916–1917), 275. See F. Zimmermann, *The Aramaic Origin of the Four Gospels* (New York: KTAV, 1979), 97–98.

28. Paul Winter, "Some Observations on the Language in the Birth and Infancy Stories of the Third Gospel," *NTS* 1 (1954), 111–21, see 113.

29. Jones, "Background and Character," 47.

30. Jones, "Background and Character," 73–74.

31. Jones, "Background and Character," 47. Jones, on p. 48: "It may not be far from the mark to hazard the guess that the Nunc Dimittis reflects an early Christian response to the problem of the death of a believer at a time when the coming of the Lord was regarded as imminent (Acts 1:11)."

· 4 ·

PRAYER AND THE FACE
OF THE TRANSFIGURED JESUS

Barbara E. Reid

What really happened at the transfiguration? This title of a recent article by Jerome Murphy-O'Connor poses a question for which a universally accepted solution has never been reached.[1] The existing studies of the transfiguration are as varied as the synoptic accounts themselves. Past approaches range from regarding the transfiguration as a real, historical event[2] to viewing it as a mythic creation of the early church.[3] As G. B. Caird has remarked, "Almost every item in the narrative can be made the starting point of a theory."[4] A current judgment on the situation is given by J. A. Fitzmyer in his commentary on the Gospel of Luke. After giving a brief sketch of the various theories, he writes, "Given the diversity of the way in which the incident is reported, no real historical judgment can be made about it; to write it all off as mythical is likewise to go beyond the evidence. Just what sort of an incident in the ministry of Jesus — to which it is clearly related — it was is impossible to say."[5]

I believe that it is possible to overcome this impasse by taking a different approach to the tradition history of the three accounts of the transfiguration. Almost all scholars begin with the basic assumption that Mark's account was the primary source of the story and that the versions of Matthew and Luke are subsequent redactions of it. This presupposition has been questioned by M.-E. Boismard, who discerns a source in Luke that is independent of Mark.[6] Jerome Murphy-O'Connor agrees with Boismard and has argued that, when refined, this source contains a historical element that can easily be integrated into the ministry of Jesus.[7] Several other scholars have suggested Luke's dependence on a special source for the transfiguration narrative.[8] In my source- and redaction-critical study of Luke 9:28–36, I concluded that the best explanation for the Lucan account is that the third evangelist did, indeed, use a unique tradition.[9] This L material underlies the bulk of the first half of the story, vv. 28–33a and also v. 36b. An approximation of what was contained in the non-Marcan piece of tradition follows:

[28] *egeneto de meta tous logous toutous hōsei hēmerai oktō [kai] par-alabōn Petron kai Iōannēn kai Iakōbon anebē eis to oros proseuxas-thai.* [29] *Kai egeneto en tǭ proseuchesthai auton to eidos tou prosōpou autou heteron kai ho himatismos autou leukos exastraptōn.* [30] *Kai idou andres duo synelaloun autǭ,* [31] *hoi ophthentes en doxę̄ elegon tēn exodon autou hēn ēmellen plēroun en Ierousalēm.* [32] *Ho de Pet-ros kai hoi syn autǭ eidon tēn doxan autou kai tous duo andras tous synestōtas autǭ.* [33] *Kai egeneto en tǭ diachōrizesthai autous 'ap autou heurethē Iēsous monos.*[10]

Luke later combined this tradition with the Marcan tradition reflected in vv. 33b–35 to shape the account as we now have it. One can detect the special source from internal inconsistencies in the narrative, atypical vocab-ulary and usage, and details that are not adequately explained as redactions of the Marcan account. The peculiarly Lucan tradition told a somewhat different story than the final form of the transfiguration account. Of par-ticular interest is the fact that Luke alone sets the occurrence in a context of prayer. And, in contrast to Mark and Matthew, the third evangelist does not use the language of *metamorphōsis*. Rather, he says that the appear-ance of Jesus' face changed. This study will explore the significance of this one peculiarly Lucan detail: the change in Jesus' face during this prayer experience.

Luke 9:29: Semantic Possibilities

Luke 9:29 tells that while Jesus was praying on the mountain, the appear-ance of his face changed: *to eidos tou prosōpou autou heteron.* We will first explore Luke's use of each of the words of this phrase and their semantic range. We will then examine other expressions from the Hebrew Scriptures and early Jewish literature describing a change in countenance to see if they may shed light on the meaning of Luke's phrase. Finally, we will look to the wider literary context of Luke's Gospel and his ninth chapter in particular for interpretive clues.

The noun *eidos* occurs one other time in Luke's Gospel, in 3:22, at Jesus' baptism, where the Holy Spirit descends upon him in bodily form, *sōmatikǭ eidei*. In that example as well as in 9:19, *eidos* denotes "form, outward appearance," "the total visible appearance; what may be perceived and known by others."[11] In the LXX, *eidos* most frequently translated *mar'eh* ("appearance") or *tō'ar* ("form, appearance"). It is used of God in Genesis 32:31; Exodus 24:17; Numbers 12:8. It is used to de-scribe people of beautiful appearance in such expressions as *kalos tǭ eidei* (e.g., Gen. 29:17; 39:6; Deut. 21:11; 2 Sam. 11:2; 13:1), or *agathos tǭ ei-dei* (e.g., 1 Sam. 16:18; 25:3). Other descriptions are given with *eidos* + a genitive, such as *hōs eidos lepras* (Lev. 13:43); *hōs eidos pyros* (Num. 9:15, 16); and *eidos krystallou* (Num. 11:7).[12] In Exodus 26:30 and Numbers 8:4 *eidos* has the connotation "plan, pattern." The expression *to eidos tou prosōpou* is not found anywhere in the LXX, but a similar expression, *homoiōsis tōn prosōpōn autōn* is found twice in Ezekiel (1:10; 10:22). The references are to the faces of the living creatures that Ezekiel saw in visions. Similarly, in Daniel 3:19 (LXX) is found *hē morphē tou prosōpou autou* (in Theodotion's version, *hē opsis tou prosōpou autou*), referring to Nebuchadnezzar's countenance.

Regarding the noun *prosōpon*, its usage in the NT follows closely that of the LXX, which corresponds to the Hebrew usage of *pānîm* and *'ap*. In Lucan writings, *prosōpon* appears twelve other times in the Gospel, and eleven times in Acts. In some instances, *prosōpon* literally denotes "face, countenance," as in Acts 6:15. In most instances *prosōpon* is part of an idiomatic expression, such as *kata prosōpon* (Luke 2:31; Acts 3:13; 25:16), *pro prosōpou* (Luke 7:27; 9:52; 10:1; Acts 13:24), *apo prosōpou* (Acts 3:19; 5:41; 7:45), *lambanein prosōpon* (Luke 20:21), *prosōpon stērizein* (Luke 9:51), *prosōpon poreuesthai* (Luke 9:53), *to prosōpon tēs gēs* (Luke 12:56; 21:35; Acts 17:26), *piptein epi prosōpon* (Luke 5:12; 17:16), *klinein to prosōpon eis tēn gēn* (Luke 24:5). In these last two expressions, *prosōpon* also retains its literal connotation, as the gestures of reverence they describe involve an actual inclination of the face. The noun *prosōpon* can also connote the whole person, or personal presence, as in the expressions *meta tou prosōpou sou* in Acts 2:28 (=Ps. 16:11), *horan to prosōpon* in Acts 20:25, and *theōrein to prosōpon* in Acts 20:38. Luke 9:29 is one of the few examples in Luke-Acts where *prosōpon* carries a literal connotation of "face, countenance."[13]

The adjective *heteros* appears frequently in Luke-Acts. It is a dual adjective used to denote the "other" of two, to contrast a definite person or thing with another,[14] or to designate "another" of more than two.[15] It also occurs in the plural, *heteroi*, as "others."[16] It is also used in lists.[17] In the expression *tē heterą*, it is used to designate "the next day."[18] In Acts 13:35, *en heterǭ* denotes "in another place" (in Scripture). As a substantive, *heteros* appears in the expression *ouden heteron* in Acts 17:21. In Luke 9:29, the connotation of *heteron* is "another, different from what precedes,"[19] the only instance of such a nuance in Luke-Acts.[20]

The whole phrase *to eidos tou prosōpou autou heteron* in Luke 9:29 says simply that the visible appearance of Jesus' face changed. For clues to the significance of this expression, a search for other expressions describing a change in countenance yields some enlightening data. These will be examined with a view to identifying what it was that caused the change in facial expression in each case and what that change signifies.

Changes of Face in Jewish Literature

There are no examples in the LXX of *heteros* used with *prosōpon* to describe a change in facial expression. But there are several instances in which such a change is expressed with the verb *alloioō* + *prosōpon*.[21] One such example is found in Judith 10, where the process of how Judith beautified herself for her mission is described. When the ancients of the city saw her (v. 7), they noted that her face was changed, *ēn ēlloiōmenon to prosōpon autēs*, as well as her garments, *kai tēn stolēn metabeblēkuian autēs*. The transformation of Judith is one that is deliberately effected by her own devices, as described in 10:3–4 and recalled in 16:8–9, in preparation for her encounter with the Assyrian commander Holofernes. In Sirach 12:18, *alloiōsei to prosōpon autou* is said of an enemy whose true face will be revealed in time of adversity. The expression is found in a section containing advice not to trust in appearances. It admonished that their faces change and their true character is revealed. In the following chapter of the same book, in Sirach 13:25, is another saying about a change in countenance. There it is said that the heart of a person is what changes one's countenance, whether it be for good or evil, *kardia anthrōpou alloioi to prosōpon autou, ean te eis agatha ean te eis kaka*. A similar example is found in Sirach 25:17, in a section of sayings on wicked and virtuous women. It states that wickedness changes one's appearance, *ponēria gynaikos alloioi tēn horasin autēs kai skotoi to prosōpon autēs hōs arkos*.

One example in Isaiah 29:22 uses the verb *metaballō*, a synonym of *alloioō*, with *prosōpon*. Here it is said that Jacob shall no more be ashamed, neither shall he now change countenance, *ou nyn aischynthēsetai Iakōb oude nyn to prosōpon metaballei*. This expression occurs in the context of an oracle of redemption and signifies that the house of Jacob will no longer be afflicted or in fear.

There are several instances in Daniel in which a change of countenance is expressed with *alloioō* + *morphē* rather than *prosōpon*. In Daniel 3:19 (LXX), *morphē* translates the Aramaic *ṣᵊlēm 'anpôhî*, connoting "face." In this instance, the expression *hē morphē tou prosōpou autou ēlliōthē* refers to King Nebuchadnezzar, whose wrath toward Shadrach, Meshach, and Abednego caused his change of face. Nebuchadnezzar's previously favorable attitude toward them changed to fury when they refused to worship his golden statue. In Dan. 5:6, 9, 10; 7:28 (Θ), *morphē* translates the Aramaic *zîw*, which means "brightness of countenance." The change of countenance described in 5:6, 9, 10 reflects the great fear of King Belshazzar at the appearance of the fingers of a hand that wrote on the wall. In 7:28, it is Daniel's facial expression that is said to be altered, because of his being troubled over his night visions. A similar example is found in *Herm. Man.* 12.4.1, where a change in the appearance of the shepherd, expressed as *hē morphē autou ēlliōthē*, is due to his anger. Earlier in the work (*Herm. Vis.* 5.4), a change in the form of the shepherd, *ēlliōthē hē idea autou*, enables Hermas to recognize the angel of penance to whom he had been entrusted.

Although neither *alloioō* nor *metaballō* is used in Genesis 31:2, 5, another formulation with *prosōpon* is found there, expressing a change of face: *kai eiden Iakōb to prosōpon tou Laban, kai idou ouk ēn pros auton hōs echthes kai tritēn hēmeran*. Jacob perceives that Laban's attitude, or face, is not the same as before. Laban's previously favorable attitude changes when he sees that Jacob has outwitted him with regard to the livestock.

In 2 Maccabees 3:16 a change of face is expressed with the verb *parallassō* in conjunction with the nouns *opsis* ("face") and *chroa* ("color" of the skin; complexion). The phrase *hē gar opsis kai to tēs chroas parēllagmenon enephainen tēn kata psychēn agōnian* describes the change in the high priest: "His countenance and the changing of his color declared the inward agony of his mind." Similar vocabulary is used in Exodus 34:29–30 to describe the change in Moses' face following his encounter with God on Mount Sinai, *dedoxastai hē opsis tou chrōmatos tou prosōpou autou*, "the skin of his face had become radiant."

In 1 Samuel 1:9–18 a change in Hannah's face occurs after her prayer of lament over her childlessness. In the course of her prayer, she is given assurance that her petition will be answered. In response, she goes on her way and her countenance is no longer sad, *to prosōpon autēs ou synepesen eti* (1 Sam. 1:18, LXX).

In 1QapGen 2:16–17 is found another example that speaks of a change in countenance. The text deals with the birth of Noah and Lamech's anxiety about whether Lamech is, indeed, the real father of the child. Bitenosh, Lamech's wife, attempts to reassure him and queries, *lm' ṣlm 'npyk kdn' 'lyk šn' wšḥt wrwḥk kdn 'lyb'* "[Why is the expression] of your face so changed and deformed? Why is your spirit so depressed?"[22]

Two examples in 2 *Enoch* tell of a change of countenance in the visionary.[23] In 2 *En.* 1:7 Enoch's reaction to the two huge men sent by God is described, "...I was terrified; and the appearance of my face was changed because of fear."[24] In 2 *Enoch* 22:1–6, Enoch is permitted to see and stand in front of the face of God forever. That this encounter leaves an effect on the face of Enoch himself is evident from chapter 37, where an angel of God chills Enoch's face before he is returned to the earth, since otherwise, as God explains, "no human being would be able to look at your face."[25]

There is one instance, in Job 14:20, in which it is said that God changes a person's countenance, *šānâ pānîm*.[26] This expression occurs in the context of a poem on the misery and brevity of life, in which the phrase is interpreted as a graphic description of death, or even *rigor mortis*,[27] i.e., the ultimate change of countenance.

In these examples of phrases that express a change of countenance, there are several reasons given for the alteration of facial expression. In the case of Judith, the change was brought about by her own devices for the purpose of her mission. Many of the examples tell of a change of face that reflects a change in one's emotions. In Daniel 3:19 the alteration is caused by wrath; in *Herm. Man.* 12.4.1 by anger; in Isaiah 29:22; Daniel 5:6, 9, 10; 2 *Enoch* 1:7 by fear; in Daniel 7:28; IQApGen 2:16–17 by anxiety; in 2 Maccabees 3:16 by anguish of soul; in Genesis 31:2, 5, by disfavor. The maxims in Sirach speak of adversity changing the face to reveal one's true character (12:18), the heart changing one's countenance (13:25), and wickedness changing one's appearance (25:17). And in Job 14:20 it is death that effects the change. Several of the examples describe a change in countenance as a result of prayer or encounter with God: Exodus 34:29–30; 1 Samuel 1:18; Judith 10; 16; Psalm 34:5–6; 2 *Enoch* 22:1–6.

These various expressions describing a change of face may shed light on the understanding of the phrase *to eidos tou prosōpou autou heteron* in Luke 9:29. There is no indication in the Lucan text that the change was brought about by Jesus' own devices, as in the example of Judith. Nor would the sayings about wickedness changing the face, or about adversity altering the countenance to reveal one's true character be applicable to the change of Jesus' face in Luke's version of the transfiguration. However, the expressions that describe a change of face caused by an emotional or interior change and those that follow an encounter with God may provide a clue to the interpretation of Luke 9:29.

Inner Change and Alteration of Countenance

An indication that the expression *to eidos tou prosōpou autou heteron* may have to do with an inner change in Jesus, reflected on his face, is that numerous idiomatic expressions with *prosōpon* reflect the understanding that the face mirrors one's inner state. A face that falls is one that expresses anger or sadness (e.g., Gen. 4:5, *synepesen tō prosōpō;* 1 Sam. 1:18, *to prosōpon autēs ou synepesen eti*). But to fall on one's face, *piptein epi prosōpon* (e.g., 2 Sam. 9:6; 14:4, 22, 33; Matt. 17:6; 26:39; Luke 5:12; 17:16) is an act of obeisance. To set one's face, *prosōpon stērizein* (Luke 9:51) or *tassein prosōpon* (2 Kings 12:17), is to show determination.[28] Adding the preposition *epi* to *stērizein prosōpon* means to set oneself against someone, connoting disfavor or even enmity (e.g., Jer. 3:12; 21:10; Ezek. 6:2; 13:17), as does *ephistanai prosōpon* (Lev. 17:10; 20:3, 5, 6; 26:17). To turn one's face away, *apostrephein prosōpon* (Deut. 31:17, 18; Ps. 69:17), is another expression of displeasure. It can also mean "to overlook" (Ps. 51:9). Expressions for fear are *hypostellein prosōpon* (Deut. 1:17) and *ekklinein apo prosōpou* (Deut. 20:3). That the face reflects one's inner state or attitude is obvious from these expressions with *prosōpon*.

Even more explicit on this point are statements such as: "When the heart rejoices, the countenance is cheerful, but when it is in sorrow, (the countenance) is sad" (Prov. 15:13); "The mark of a happy heart is a cheerful face" (Sir. 13:26); and "A sensible person is known by the look on his face" (Sir. 19:29).

Against this background, Luke's expression *to eidos tou prosōpou autou heteron* can be understood as saying that a physical alteration of Jesus' facial expression took place that reflected a change in Jesus' inner being. This change was said to be visible to, and observable by, the three disciples who accompanied him to the hill country. The clues to the cause of this change in Jesus and its significance may be detected in the references to prayer in vv. 28, 29 and in the content of the conversation between Jesus, Moses, and Elijah in v. 31.

Prayer and a Change of Face

The change in Jesus occurs in the context of prayer, a time when Jesus explicitly seeks communion with God. Often one's relationship with God is expressed in terms of God's face and the face of the one praying. God's face connotes God's presence (e.g., Ps. 21:7, *t³haddēhû b³śimhâ 'et-pānêkā / euphraneis auton en charą̄ meta tou prosōpou sou*). Prayer itself is referred to as seeking the face of God: *biqqēš pānîm / zētein to prosōpon* (Ps. 27:8; 105:4), and also as turning one's face to God: *nātān pānîm 'el / didonai to prosōpon pros* (Dan. 9:3). Entreating God's favor in prayer is expressed as *deesthai to prosōpon* or even more colorfully in Hebrew, "softening God's face," *hillâ pānîm* (e.g., 1 Sam. 13:12; 2 Kings 13:4; Zech. 8:21), i.e., flattering or putting God in a gentler mood. God's response of showing favor is formulated as "lifting up of the face," *lambanein prosōpon* (Gal. 2:6) or *epairein prosōpon* (Num. 6:26), or looking upon the face, *epiblepein epi to prosōpon* (Ps. 84:9), or making God's face shine upon one, *epiphainein to prosōpon epi* (Num. 6:25; Ps. 67:1; 80:3, 7). God's face being hidden (Gen. 4:14; Deut. 31:17, 18) or turned away (Ps. 21:25; 101:3) connotes divine displeasure and the absence of the divine protective presence. Worship of God is expressed as "falling on the face," *piptein epi prosōpon* (Num. 20:6; Josh. 5:14). Seeing God face to face is an expression that is used to describe intense encounters with the divine, such as those of Jacob at Peniel (Gen. 32:31) and Moses on Mount Sinai (Deut. 5:4; 34:10). The psalmist expresses longing for God's presence as a desire to see God's face (Ps. 41:3; 94:2). However, seeing God's face also involves great peril, as in Exodus 33:20–23, where God's face cannot be seen though the divine presence is manifest. According to Revelation 22:4 (also 2 Esd. 7:98), seeing God's face is a favor that will be reserved to the final consummation.

In sum, expressions involving God's face or the face of the one praying are often used to describe one's relationship with God.

Of the OT examples of changes in countenance as a result of prayer or encounter with God, the most famous is Moses (Exod. 34:29–30). After his meeting with God on Mount Sinai, the skin of his face shone, so that others were afraid to approach him. The change in Moses' countenance is the result of his having talked with God (v. 29). The radiance of his face is a reflection of the divine glory and signifies Moses' privileged relationship with God. Just as Moses was afraid to look at God (Exod. 3:6), so the Israelites were fearful to behold Moses' countenance that radiated with God's glory.

In 1 Samuel 1:9–18 it is implied that the change in Hannah's facial expression is effected by what transpired during her communion with God. Deeply distressed about her childlessness, she prayed to God. After receiving assurance that her petition would be answered, she went on her way with her countenance no longer sad.

In the case of Judith, although her change of face is accomplished by her own efforts,[29] the description of the alteration of her countenance also follows immediately upon her prayer to God for power and protection. The psalmist also recognizes that when one prays, i.e., seeks God and looks to God, the resultant freedom from fear is reflected by the joyful radiance of the face (Ps. 34:5–6).

2 Enoch 37 reflects the same understanding that the countenance is altered when it beholds God. In 2 Enoch 22:1–6, Enoch is permitted to see and stand in front of the face of God forever. That this encounter leaves an effect on the face of Enoch himself is evident from chapter 37, where an angel of God chills Enoch's face before he is returned to the earth, since otherwise, as God explains, "no human being would be able to look at your face."[30]

The Lucan Context

These examples from the OT and early Jewish literature that juxtapose a change of face with prayer give an interpretive clue for understanding the phrase *to eidos tou prosōpou autou heteron* in Luke 9:29, which is set in the context of Jesus' prayer. As in the examples of Moses (Exod. 34:29–30), Hannah (1 Sam. 1:18), Enoch (2 En. 22:1–6; 37), and in the description of the psalmist (34:5–6), Luke also indicates that the alteration in Jesus' countenance reflected something that transpired between himself and God during his prayer. The subject of the exchange between Jesus and God in Luke's transfiguration story is not made explicit,[31] although the context of 9:28–36 and the content of the conversation between Jesus, Moses, and Elijah in v. 31 provide clues as to what Luke supposed it to be. The location of the episode, as the hinge between Jesus' Galilean and Jerusalem ministries, is an indication that Luke considered Jesus' mission to be the subject of his prayer at the transfiguration. As suggested by Murphy-O'Connor, the uniquely Lucan story of the transfiguration related how Jesus, conscious of his mission from God, yet also quite aware that "setting his face to go to Jerusalem" (9:51) would mean his death, took to the mountain to pray.[32] It was during this prayer that he understood that it was precisely through his death that his mission would be accomplished. It was this moment of revelation that caused Jesus' face to light up. Like the accounts of Jesus' baptism and agony in the garden, Luke depicts this time of prayer as a critical moment of transition in Jesus' mission.

The story does not elaborate on precisely what was the change in Jesus' face. But in the final form of the story, with its Mosaic and apocalyptic overtones, the references to *doxa,* and the description of Jesus' clothing becoming flashing white, the phrase *to eidos tou prosōpou autou heteron* evokes an image of a radiant change in Jesus' countenance. The notion that the perfected righteous will have radiant faces (the ultimate change of countenance) occurs frequently in apocalyptic literature. 2 Esdras 7:97 says of those who have kept the ways of the Most High, "Their face is to shine like the sun." Daniel 10:6 speaks of a man clothed in linen whose face is like lightning, *to prosōpon autou hōsei horasis astrapēs.* In a vision similar to that of Daniel, the seer in Revelation 1:16 beholds one whose face is described as shining like the sun, *hē opsis autou hōs ho hēlios phainei.* That this radiance on the faces of the righteous is a reflection of the divine glory is made explicit in 1 *Enoch* 18:4, "They shall not be able to look on the faces of the righteous because the Lord of spirits shall cause his light to shine on the faces of the saints and the elect righteous." Similarly, the Lucan description of the changed face of Jesus at the transfiguration, in the final form of the story, elicits the image of Jesus as God's righteous one.

It is not only the face of the righteous one that shines with the radiance of God, but the whole being, as in Daniel 12:3, "And those who are wise shall shine like the brightness of the firmament, and those who turn many to righteousness, like the stars for ever and ever." Similarly, 2 *Baruch* 51:10 says: "They shall be changed... from beauty to splendor, from light to the radiance of glory." In 1 *Enoch* 104:2, the righteous are assured, "You shall shine like the lights of heaven." And in the NT, Matthew 13:43 says, "the righteous shall shine like the sun," *hoi dikaioi eklampsousin hōs ho hēlios.*

The extension of the radiance goes even further to include the clothing. 1 *Enoch* 62:15 asserts, "The righteous and elect ones... shall wear the garments of glory." And in 2 *En.* 22:8, where Enoch is taken up to the tenth heaven, God directs that his earthly garments be taken from him and that he be clothed in "the clothes of my glory." The connection between the glory of the righteous and the divine glory is made explicit here. It is possible that Luke had these apocalyptic notions in mind when he connected the phrase *kai ho himatismos autou leukos exastraptōn* to *to eidos tou prosōpou autou heteron.* Part of Luke's intent, then, would be to portray Jesus as God's righteous one, with a changed face and garments of glory. In the final form of the story, the joining of these two phrases creates an aura of an event that is not merely natural. In this respect, Luke's final form of the narrative is like that of Mark.

The wider literary context of Luke's chapter 9 also gives a clue as to the significance of the transfiguration. The transfiguration episode comprises one of several responses to Herod's question, "Who is this?" (Luke 9:9).[33] The question of Jesus' identity had been recurring since 5:21, where it was first posed by Pharisees and teachers of the Law. In 7:19–20 it is reiterated by John the Baptist's disciples; in 7:49 by those who were at table in the home of Simon the Pharisee; and in 8:25 by Jesus' disciples after the calming of the storm. The answers to this question are given, some explicitly and some implicitly, in the nine episodes in Luke 9 that follow Herod's question.

In the first episode, the feeding of the five thousand (vv. 10–17), an implicit answer is given by way of the miracle. The feeding demonstrates what is stated in Acts 2:22: that Jesus is "a man attested by God with mighty works and wonders and signs." In the second episode, Peter's confession (vv. 18–21), an explicit answer is given: Jesus is the anointed one of God, *ho Christos tou theou.* In the third segment, the first announcement of the passion and the sayings about discipleship (vv. 23–27), the further answer provided to Herod's question is that Jesus is the suffering Son of Man. Closely linked with the previous episode, this identification serves as a corrective to the notions that the disciples had of Jesus' messiahship. The transfiguration, the fourth episode (vv. 28–36), gives both an implicit and an explicit answer to Herod's question. The voice from the cloud in v. 35 gives the explicit identification of Jesus as "my chosen Son." The implicit identification is found in the juxtaposition of Jesus with Moses and Elijah: Jesus stands in continuity with these OT figures, yet now supersedes them as the one in whom God's saving action is manifest. In the fifth episode, the cure of the possessed boy (vv. 37–43a), the same implicit answer is given in this miracle as in the first episode: Jesus is the one in whom the majesty of God is made manifest. The sixth scene, the second announcement of the passion (vv. 43b–45), reiterates the answer given in episode three: Jesus is the Son of Man who is to be handed over. The seventh vignette, the argument among the disciples over greatness (vv. 46–48), supplies an implicit identification of Jesus as one who is sent and who nevertheless identifies himself with the lowliness of a child. In the eighth episode, concerning the strange exorcist (vv. 49–50), Jesus is called *epistata,* a title that implies his mastery and authority. The final segment, the introduction to the travel account that relates the disciples' reaction to the inhospitable Samaritans

(vv. 51–56), provides a concluding answer to Herod's question with the title *Kyrie.*

Thus the nine episodes in Luke 9:10–56 produce a series of christological statements in answer to Herod's question, "Who is this?" Some of the answers are implicit and others are explicit; some are exclusively Lucan, and some reflect Luke's reworking of Marcan motifs. The transfiguration account, like the episode of Peter's confession, stands out as containing some of the most important christological affirmations in this string of episodes. Just as the annunciation of Jesus' passion in 9:22 serves as a corrective to Peter's declaration of Jesus' messiahship in 9:20, so too the transfiguration scene confirms Jesus' identity as *ho Christos tou theou* but also corrects the disciples' understanding of what Jesus' messiahship entails. They are to comprehend that Jesus' sonship is played out as the servanthood of God's chosen one, whose way through suffering and death leads to glory. The two heavenly figures confirm Jesus' identity as God's unique chosen one and herald a turning point in Jesus' ministry. Jesus is now to embark on the path to Jerusalem, where his "exodus" will fulfill God's saving plan.

In the final form of the Gospel, the answers to the question, "Who is this?" are directed to the reader (on the narrative level they are directed to the disciples). However, the original piece of Lucan tradition, vv. 28–33a, 36b, has Jesus as the focus. The event is initiated by and directed toward him. It is only when Luke combines this with the Markan tradition, detectable behind vv. 33b–35, that the disciples come to the fore. It is probable that in the original Lucan tradition *to eidos tou prosōpou autou heteron* described Jesus' own reaction to the answer he perceived in prayer to the question of his own identity and mission.

Early Christian Martyrs

Luke's depiction of Jesus' radiant visage in the face of death is echoed in the descriptions of other early Christian martyrs. In Acts 6:15, as Stephen faces the charges that will lead to his death, Luke says that the Sanhedrin "saw that his face was like the face of an angel" (*eidon to prosōpon autou hōsei prosōpon angelou*). Saints Perpetua and Felicity likewise went to their "day of victory...cheerful and bright of countenance."[34] As Polycarp faced martyrdom in Smyrna, "he was animated with courage and joy, and his countenance was suffused with beauty" (*to prosōpon autou charitos eplērouto*).[35] The martyrs of Lyons and Vienne also came forth gladly, with glory and grace mixed together on their faces, *hoi men gar hilaroi proēesan doxēs kai charitos pollēs tais opsesin autōn sygkekramenēs* (Eusebius, *Hist. Eccl.* 5.1.35).[36]

Conclusion

In attempting to come closer to an answer for the question with which we began, "What really happened at the transfiguration?" this study proposes that a unique piece of Lucan tradition provides some clues. The expression *to eidos tou prosōpou autou heteron* describes a change in Jesus' countenance that resulted from something that transpired between Jesus and God during his time of prayer. In the context of Luke's ninth chapter, the transfiguration provides one more answer to the question, "Who is this?" In the wider context of Luke's Gospel, the occurrence of the transfiguration at the transition point between Jesus' ministry in Galilee and that in Jerusalem provides a clue that the subject of Jesus' prayer was his mission. This insight is confirmed by the two heavenly figures who speak of Jesus' *exodus* that is to be accomplished in Jerusalem (9:31). The new understanding that his death will, indeed, be the fulfillment of his mission is what causes a change in Jesus' facial expression.

Of course any study that attempts to isolate a preresurrection event in the life of Jesus can provide only tentative conclusions. Keeping in mind the fragmentary nature of the evidence, the stages of the transmission of the tradition, and the purpose for which the Gospel stories were written, one can at best hypothesize as to what really happened. If the results of this study are true, there are important implications for understanding Lucan Christology. The portrait given of Jesus is that of one who knows God and knows his mission, yet needs to continue to go to God in prayer to discern his role in God's saving acts. In a very human way, Luke portrays on Jesus' face the radiant joy that comes from intimate relationship with God, a relationship that discloses his true identity and mission. The message for disciples is an invitation to follow in the footsteps of this Jesus, even when the paradoxes of his *exodus* of death and life, suffering and joy, are not clearly understood.

Notes

1. J. Murphy-O'Connor, "What Really Happened at the Transfiguration?" *Bible Review* 3 (1987), 8–21.

2. E.g., H. Baltensweiler, *Die Verklärung Jesu: Historisches Ereignis und synoptische Berichte* (AThANT 33; Zurich: Zwingli, 1959); J. Blinzler, *Die neutestamentlichen Berichte über die Verklärung Jesu* (NTAbh 17/4; Münster: Aschendorff, 1937); E. Dabrowski, *La transfiguration de Jésus* (Scripta Pontificii Instituti Biblici 85; Rome: Biblical Institute, 1939).

3. M. Dibelius, *From Tradition to Gospel* (New York: Scribner, 1934), 271; I. H. Marshall, *Commentary on Luke* (New International Greek Testament Commentary 3; Grand Rapids: Eerdmans, 1978), 380–89; D. F. Strauss, *The Life of Jesus Critically Examined* (Philadelphia: Fortress, 1972), 86–87.

4. G. B. Caird, "The Transfiguration," *ET* 67 (1955–56), 291.

5. J. A. Fitzmyer, *The Gospel according to Luke I–IX,* (Anchor Bible 28; Garden City, N.Y.: Doubleday, 1981), 796.

6. M.-E. Boismard, *Synopse des quatre évangiles en français* (Paris: Cerf, 1972), 2:50–55.

7. Murphy-O'Connor, "Transfiguration," 9–10.

8. J. V. Bartlet, "The Sources of St. Luke's Gospel," *Studies in the Synoptic Problem by Members of the University of Oxford* (ed. W. Sanday; Oxford: Clarendon, 1911), 322; W. Dietrich, *Das Petrusbild der lukanischen Schriften* (BWANT 5; Stuttgart: Kohlhammer, 1972), 104–9; B. S. Easton, *The Gospel according to St. Luke* (Edinburgh: T. & T. Clark, 1926), 142–46; E. E. Ellis, "La Composition de Luc 9 et les sources de sa christologie," *Jésus aux Origines de la Christologie* (ed. J. Dupont; BEThL 11; Gembloux: Leuven University, 1975), 193–200; R. H. Fuller, *The Foundations of New Testament Christology* (New York: Scribner, 1965), 172; W. Grundmann, *Das Evangelium nach Lukas* (THKNT 3; Berlin: Evangelische Verlagsanstalt, 1974), 191–92; K. H. Rengstorf, *Das Evangelium nach Lukas* (NTD 3; Göttingen: Vandenhoeck & Ruprecht, 1958), 123; T. Schramm, *Der Markus-Stoff bei Lukas: Eine literarkritische und redaktionsgeschichtliche Untersuchung* (SNTSMS 14; Cambridge: Cambridge University, 1971), 2.

9. *The Transfiguration: A Source- and Redaction-Critical Study of Luke 9:28–36* (Cahiers de la Revue Biblique 32; Paris: Gabalda, 1993). For a briefer version, see "Voices and Angels: What Were They Talking about at the Transfiguration? A Redaction-Critical Study of Luke 9:28–36," *BR* 34 (1989), 19–31.

10. Murphy-O'Connor ("Transfiguration," 16) and Boismard (*Synopse,* 2:250–55) arrive at a similar reconstructions.

11. BAGD, 221; J. Behm, *"morphē,"* TDNT (1967), 4:743. This same connotation is found in John 5:37, where *eidos autou* is used of God. There are two other instances in which *eidos* is found in the NT, but with slightly different connotations. In 2 Corinthians 5:7, where *eidos* appears in the expression *dia pisteōs...ou dia eidous* it is rendered "sight" (NRSV, NAB, NJB). In 1 Thessalonians 5:22 *eidos* carries the connotation "kind" (BAGD, 221), as reflected in the NAB (revised NT, 1986) translation of the phrase *apo pantos eidous ponērou,* "from every kind of evil." However, the nuance of "form," or "appearance" is also operative in this example, thus the NRSV and NJB render *eidos* as "form"; the NAB (1970 edition) as "semblance."

12. Other similar expressions are found in Exodus 24:10; Numbers 11:7; Judges 8:18; 13:6; Sirach 43:1; 45:11; Ezekiel 1:16, 26.

13. So defined in BAGD, 720.

14. Luke 5:7; 7:41; 14:31; 16:13; 17:34, 35; 18:10; Acts 23:6. This and the subsequent definitions of *heteros* are from BAGD, 315.

15. Luke 6:6; 9:56, 59, 61; 16:18; Acts 1:20 (= Ps. 108:8); 7:18 (= Exod. 1:8); 8:34.

16. Luke 3:18; 4:43; 8:3; 10:1; 11:26; 22:65; 23:32; Acts 2:13; 27:1.

17. Luke 8:6, 7, 8; 11:16; 14:19, 20; 16:7; 19:20; 20:11; 22:58.

18. Acts 20:15; 27:3.

19. As also in Mark 16:12; Romans 7:23; 1 Corinthians 15:40; Galatians 1:6; James 2:25.

20. See further J. K. Elliott, "The Use of *heteros* in the New Testament," *ZNW* 60 (1969), 140–41.

21. In several MSS of Luke 9:29 (D e sy[s.c.p] co) *ēlloiōthē* is found in place of *heteron*.

22. See further J. A. Fitzmyer, *The Genesis Apocryphon of Qumran Cave I* (2d ed.; BibOr 18A; Rome: Biblical Institute, 1971), 53, 90–91.

23. The designation of *2 Enoch* as an early Jewish work is not shared by all scholars. There are widely divergent views on the date and provenience of *2 Enoch*. Dates assigned to the work range from pre-Christian times to the late Middle Ages; the provenance from Hellenized Jewish first-century Alexandria to ninth-century Byzantium. See further F. I. Andersen, "2 (Slavonic Apocalypse of) Enoch," *The Old Testament Pseudepigrapha* (ed. J. H. Charlesworth; 2 vols.; Garden City, N.Y.: Doubleday, 1983), 1:94–97.

24. So the J recension. The A recension says, "the appearance of my face was glittering because of fear" (Andersen, "2 Enoch," 106–7).

25. This reference is from the longer (J) recension. The shorter (A) recension also tells of God allowing Enoch to stand in front of God's face forever in chapter 22, but is more sparse in the description of the "chilling" of Enoch's face in chapter 37. This account simply says that one of God's senior angels "refreshed my face, because I could not endure the terror of the burning of the fire." For discussion on the two recensions of *2 Enoch*, see Andersen, "2 Enoch," 92–94.

26. The LXX understood this verse differently and reads: *epestēsas autō to prosōpon*, "you set your face against him." Elsewhere in the OT, the expression *ephistēmi to prosōpon* translates *nātān pānîm* or *sîm pānîm*.

27. S. Driver and G. B. Gray, *A Critical and Exegetical Commentary on the Book of Job* (ICC; Edinburgh: T. & T. Clark, 1950), 131.

28. See C. A. Evans, "'He Set His Face,' Luke 9, 51 Once Again," *Bib* 68 (1987), 80–84, on the connotation of judgment in the expression *prosōpon stērizein*.

29. This is implicit in chapter 10, but made explicit in chapter 16. The description of Judith's activity of beautification in 10:3–4 focuses on her manner of clothing herself and applying exterior ornaments. But what draws attention repeatedly is the beauty of her face (Jdt. 10:14, 23; 11:21, 23; 16:7). It is not until the recounting of Judith's deeds in the song of chapter 16 that it is said explicitly that she anointed her face with ointment (v. 8).

30. This reference is from the longer (J) recension. The shorter (A) recension also tells of God allowing Enoch to stand in front of God's face forever in chapter 22, but is more sparse in the description of the "chilling" of Enoch's face in chapter 37. This account simply says that one of God's senior angels "refreshed my face, because I could not endure the terror of the burning of the fire." For discussion on the two recensions of *2 Enoch*, see Andersen, "2 Enoch," 92–94.

31. Of all the times that Jesus is said to be at prayer in Luke (3:21; 5:16; 9:18, 28–29; 11:1; 22:32, 41–42) only in 10:21–22; 22:32, 41–42 and 23:46 is the content of Jesus' prayer given.

32. "Transfiguration," 18.

33. See further J. A. Fitzmyer, "The Composition of Luke, Chapter 9," in C. H. Talbot, ed., *Perspectives on Luke-Acts* (Edinburgh: T. & T. Clark, 1978), 139–52; Ellis, "Composition," 193–200.

34. *The Passion of SS. Perpetua and Felicity* (trans. W. H. Shewring; London: Sheed & Ward, 1931), 37, par. 18. I am indebted to Boniface Ramsey, O.P., for these references to the early Christian martyrs.

35. *The Martyrdom of Saint Polycarp,* 12.1, in J. Quasten, ed., *Ancient Christian Writers* (trans. J. A. Kleist; Westminster, Md.: Newman, 1948), 95.

36. G. Bardy, text and translation. *Eusèbe de Césarée: Histoire Ecclésiastique* (Sources Chrétiennes 41; Paris: Cerf, 1955), 15.

· 5 ·

MAKING OLD THINGS NEW
Prayer Texts in
Josephus's *Antiquities* 1–11:
A Study in the Transmission
of Tradition[1]

Mark Harding

Josephus wrote his *Jewish Antiquities* to inform his Greek-speaking readership of the origin of the Jews, their historical experiences, the wars they fought up to the great war with Rome—a war in which he says they were "involuntarily engaged" (*hakontes pros Rōmaiōus katestēsan*, 1.6)—and their great law-giver (*nomothetēs*), Moses, the founder of their constitution (*politeia*).[2]

Josephus claims that Romans curious about the history of the Jews urged him to write the history. An apologetic tone is easy to discern in the work.[3] Although imperial patronage was constant under Vespasian and Titus and actually increased under Domitian, Josephus complains of constant attacks from his enemies.[4]

Moreover, Josephus wanted to be his generation's Eleazar. Eleazar was the mid-third-century B.C.E. high priest who authorized the translation of the Jewish Scriptures into Greek in the time of Ptolemy Philadelphus, thus making the Jewish law accessible to the Greek world. Josephus set out to follow Eleazar's precedent and make available for his contemporaries the treasure of the venerable Hebrew traditions (cf. *Against Apion* 2.293). But whereas Eleazar only imparted the Law (*Ant.* 1.12), Josephus intends to publish the whole deposit in order that the readers of his history might learn that those who orient themselves to the will of God and keep his laws prosper in all things (*Ant.* 1.14). Let readers judge for themselves, Josephus appeals (*Ant.* 1.15), whether Moses has indeed bestowed a worthy conception of God and his nature, a conception free from the unworthy speculations of mythology.

The *Antiquities*, therefore, may be viewed as a large-scale exercise in the transmission and actualization of tradition. The purpose of this essay is to investigate this thesis with respect to the prayers and benedictions of the *Antiquities* books 1–11. These books constitute Josephus's presentation of the biblical story up to the end of the immediate postexilic era (including the careers of Daniel and Esther). I will offer an analysis of the theology and apologetics of six prayers. These are:

1.272–73 (Isaac's benediction over Jacob),

2.335–37 (Moses' prayer on the shore of the sea),

4.40–50 (Moses' appeal to God on the occasion of the revolt of Korah and the Reubenites),

5.38–41 (Joshua's supplication to God after the defeat at Ai), and

8.107–8 with 8.111–17 (the two prayers offered by Solomon on the occasion of the consecration of the Temple).

What is Josephus's theology of prayer? He informs his readers in his *Life* that he is of priestly stock (1). His father, Matthias, was esteemed for his "uprightness" (*dikaiosynē*, 7). While Josephus boasts of his own learning (9), his religious convictions, however, are only stated in generalities. The account of his three-year discipleship (*zēlōtēs egenomēn autou*, 11) with the hermit Bannus lamentably is not narrated. Having satisfied his religious quest, "he began to function politically with deference to the Pharisees" (*ērxamēn politeuesthai tē Pharisaiōn hairesei katakolouthōn*, 12) when he was nineteen years old.[5] In danger of his life at Jotapata he entrusts his cause to divine providence (*pronoia*), an important concept for Josephus.[6] On one occasion (*Life*, 295) we do find him praying in a synagogue. However, he does not inform the reader about the content of his prayers.[7]

However, his views on the place of prayer in Judaism recorded in *Against Apion* 2.193–8 deserve some comment. Prayers for the community, he writes, take precedence over those for ourselves (*Against Apion* 2.196). We beseech God not to give us blessings, but for the capacity to receive and keep them, for he gives them spontaneously (*Against Apion* 2.197). Here he appears to be in conflict with a widespread popular attitude to prayer in both the ancient and modern eras in which the one who prays approaches the divinity contractually with requests for blessings on the basis of favors rendered in the past or vowed in the future.[8] I suspect that Josephus's attitude to prayer would have been affirmed by his cultivated, philosophically aware audience.

In other respects too Josephus aligns his presentation of biblical history with contemporary sensibilities. In these first eleven books of the *Antiquities* Josephus, writing for a sophisticated Greco-Roman (and non-Jewish)

audience, clearly portrays the great Hebrew heroes in terms readily understood by his historiographically and rhetorically informed readership. Thus Abraham and Moses are portrayed as resourceful and inventive. Abraham is a religious reformer.[9] Moses, the great bestower of the Hebrew constitution, is more ancient and venerable than Romulus, Homer, Lycurgus, and Solon.[10] Samuel declares his preference for an aristocratic over a (potentially tyrannic) monarchical constitution (see *Ant.* 6.36). The best and highest theological conceptions of the Greeks and Romans show that their philosophers and constitutional founders were, after all, pupils of Moses. The Hebrew patriarchs are the founding fathers of all that is recognized as reasonable and noble in Greco-Roman culture.[11]

What might we learn from the prayers of these books? To what extent does the content of their prayers and benedictions reflect Josephus's apologetic intent? Is it even possible that these prayers might derive from the first-century synagogue, from prayers that Josephus himself might have prayed in that context? Comparison of these with extant early Jewish prayers, as well as Greek prayers, is in order.

The Prayers and Benedictions in *Antiquities* 1–11

Much of the reference to prayer is in reported speech. Josephus informs the reader that "so and so prayed." This is to some extent a reflection of the Bible in which the formula "so and so called on the Lord" is frequently attested. The effect of this is to render *Antiquities* 1–11 full of references to occasions when prayer was offered without Josephus providing much more than an indication that prayer took place. Summaries of what was prayed are sometimes provided, but for Josephus to provide the direct speech of the prayers uttered on those occasions is, as already noted, a comparatively rare phenomenon. Josephus does not often feel constrained to provide the direct speech of prayers in those places even where the Bible explicitly does. He is, after all, writing a history, not a theology.[12] Consequently, he focuses on the human characters in the unfolding of the narrative.

The following note provides a list of the places in books 1–11 in which Josephus mentions a prayer being offered but where he provides no direct speech in contradistinction to the Bible in which the direct speech of the prayers offered on these occasions is given.[13]

In my analysis of books 1–11, then, there are six substantial prayers Josephus actually reports in direct speech.[14] These six prayers, as indicated above, are the main focus of attention in this essay. There are another four passages in which brief quotations of prayers are included.[15] As these are all one sentence in length I have not chosen to discuss these in any depth.

Among my six examples are prayers that are somewhat substantial literary creations on Josephus's part. In *Ant.* 1.272–73 we encounter Isaac's exquisite benediction of Jacob; Josephus does not include the benediction that was already at hand in Genesis 27:27–29. In 2.211 Amram's reported prayer finds no parallel in Exodus, as does God's reply. Moses' prayer by the sea in 2.335–37 likewise has no biblical parallel. Interestingly, the reader is told that as a consequence of the divine rescue at the sea, Moses composed a hymn of thanksgiving to God in hexameters, the content unfortunately unrecorded.[16] In 3.25 Josephus reports that Moses thanks God for the quail, a prayer for which there is no biblical precedent. In 4.40–50 Moses' appeal to God in the face of the rebellion (*stasis*) of Korah has no parallel in the Bible either.

Prayer #1, 1.272–73: Isaac Blesses Jacob

This is the first substantial prayer or benediction in the *Antiquities*. It is independent of Genesis 27:27–29. This prayer begins, as do most of Josephus's prayers, with an invocation to God as "master" (*despotēs*), adding the qualification "of every age" (*pantos aiōnos*). While I am focusing on the invocation of this prayer, it might be noted that Josephus never uses the common Jewish *berakah* formula, i.e., his prayers never begin with "blessed..." (*eulogētos*).

Josephus denotes God "master" ten times in books 1–11.[17] The use of the term can also be paralleled extensively in early Jewish literature,[18] as well as in Philo, the NT, and other early Christian literature.[19] It is found only rarely, however, in those books of the LXX that are translations of the Hebrew Scriptures. Genesis 15:2, 8 and Joshua 5:14, all Godward references, are the only passages in which it occurs.

Despotēs used of a god is also found in non-Jewish Greek invocations. Xenophon explains that Greeks do not pay homage to any master but to the gods alone.[20] The feminine *despotis* is also found.[21] The frequency of the formula *despot' anax* in Greek prayers testifies, observed Friedrich Heiler, to a universal expression of dependence, though he observed the Greeks did not approach the deities as their servants or slaves.[22] This accords with the contention that *despotēs* expresses the Greeks' perception of the gods as powerful and free in relation to humankind.[23] The Jews, on the other hand, stress a master-servant, even a master-slave relationship to the heavenly *despotēs*.[24] The *d. pantos aiōnos* of Josephus's invocation also finds its Jewish parallel in the common rabbinic phrase *ribbônô šel 'ôlām*.[25]

Josephus also invokes God in this prayer as *dēmiourge tēs holēs ousias*. Generally, he prefers to use *ktizō*, rather than *dēmiourgeō*, of God's creating activity. *Ktizō* is the verb he chooses when describing the creation in 1.27.[26] Nevertheless, the use of *dēmiourgeō* can be paralleled in other early Jewish literature. The Jewish prayers preserved in the *Apostolic Constitu-*

tions are particularly enamored of the concept of God as "maker of the universe."²⁷ Philo also denotes God *dēmiourgos*.²⁸

Abraham, writes Josephus in *Ant.* 1.155, was actually the first to call God *dēmiourgos*. The term is found in non-Jewish Greek literature, e.g., in Plato's *Timaeus* and *Republic*. Here the fashioning of the world is ascribed to a "demiurge" whose task it is to make the *kosmos* out of pre-existing chaos.²⁹ Interestingly the LXX avoids this nomenclature for God since, one may surmise, the term restricted the role of God to maker of the ordered world.³⁰ Josephus continually predicates the creation of the world (of matter) to the God of the Jews, and terms him on occasion *dēmiourgos*.³¹ If this prejudiced his apologia in circles sympathetic to Platonism, then his ascription of the first use of the epithet to the venerable sage Abraham might bear special significance.³²

The content of Isaac's benediction fits the context of the divine promises to Abraham. Isaac knows that God had promised good things to his father and his descendants and has provided all that Isaac possesses. As he prays that his son will be blessed in turn, one notes the absence of any contract in Isaac's approach, in contrast with many non-Jewish Greek prayers. The good things have already been promised and, therefore, do not need to be requested in the context of appealing to favors and benefits performed by the prayer toward the god in the past.³³ This magnanimity and graciousness of God, as I have anticipated above, is both a biblical distinctive and a Stoic tenet.³⁴

The benediction concludes with the petition "make him fearful to his enemies, but a treasure and a delight to his friends" (*poiēsas d'auton phoberon men echthrois philois de timion kai kecharismenon*). I find no parallel to this petition in biblical literature. The Mishnah records that R. Akiba "used to say that a father endows his son with [the blessings] of beauty, riches, wisdom and length of years."³⁵ However this potential parallel does not really come close.

Intriguingly the much closer parallel is to be found in the sentiment of the sixth-century B.C.E. Athenian law-giver Solon, who prays for himself that he might be sweet to his friends but bitter to his enemies (*einai de glykyn hōde philois', echthroisi de pikron*).³⁶ How likely is it that Josephus and his readers might have known this prayer or the conventional wisdom expressed in its sentiment? It would certainly have been a nice touch for Josephus to allude to this venerable Greek prayer. Though the parallelism of the phrases is reversed and there are differences in the choice of words, it is tempting to see an allusion here to the Solon tradition in Isaac's benediction.

Given Josephus's knowledge of Plato's *Republic* (see *Against Apion* 2.256; cf. 224–25), it is also possible that Josephus is recalling the discussion in book 1 of that work of a maxim of the poet Simonides on the subject of what constitutes just dealings with one's friends and enemies.[37] Socrates insists against the consensus that the good person harms no one, not even his enemies. Returning to Isaac's benediction, it is difficult to avoid the conclusion that Isaac prays that his son, protected and blessed by God, might in fact be "fearful" (*phoberos*) to his enemies, a sentiment that, like that expressed in the Solon tradition, would seem to sanction doing them harm.[38] Perhaps, though this is speculation on my part, the synagogue used a prayer that expressed the general sentiment of Isaac's petition on the occasion of the birth of a child or a coming of age.[39]

Prayer #2, 2.335–37: Moses' Prayer at the Sea

This prayer begins without an invocation of God.[40] According to Rengstorf's *Concordance*, the "inferior" mss. group SPL does in fact interpolate the invocation *ō despota* after the initial *oud' autos men agnoeis*.[41] The absence of invocation and an epithet in the Greco-Roman context would have struck the reader as unusual in the extreme. Greek prayers followed a standard pattern.[42] Finding the right epithets for the god one was invoking was of utmost importance.[43] To any reader familiar with the prayers of the synagogue the absence of epithet might also have seemed unusual. The Amidah, e.g., certainly lays stress on invoking God by means of theologically laden epithets, as can be seen in Benediction 1, and the conclusion of each Benediction. The Bible, however, does afford examples of characters praying without invocation (see, e.g., Moses' prayers in Exod. 17:3–4 and Num. 16:15).

As in the previous prayer, there is no contract in this prayer either, i.e., no claim on divine help on the basis of services rendered or vowed. There are, furthermore, echoes of that dependence on God encountered in the Bible in laments. Israel is without hope and without resource (*elpis kai mēchanēs*).[44] She looks (*aphoraō*) to God for salvation.[45] Moses prays that God might manifest his power.[46] Israel is despondent.[47] All the elements are in God's possession.[48] They are pliable at his command.[49] This celebration of God's power over creation is the natural corollary of the terminology encountered in our first prayer in which God is invoked as "Master of the Universe." All things are God's, Moses declares (337), a view with which Philo, the Stoics, and the Mishnah concur.[50]

Moses also makes mention here of God's providence (*pronoia*, 336). Couched in the Stoic terminology of divine providence, Josephus expresses the great hope of Israel that God will act on her behalf in his good ordering of events. I have already drawn attention to the importance of this concept for Josephus (see n. 6 above). In *Ant.* 10.278 he takes the Epicureans to task for their denial of the idea of God's ordering of the affairs of the world.

Prayer #3, 4.40–50: Moses' Prayer in the Rebellion
of Korah and the Reubenites

This passage records a lengthy prayer, or really a declaratory speech on Moses' part, in response to the *stasis* perpetrated by Korah and the Reubenites. Josephus begins by mentioning Moses' stance. Standing he raises his hands to heaven (*tas cheiras eis ton ouranon anaschōn*). Standing was the usual Greek stance for prayer. Greeks praying to the Olympian gods stretched out their hands toward the sky. One stretched out one's hands toward the sea if one were praying to a sea-god, or stretched them out toward the image of a god. Kneeling is unusual.[51] That the Greek should normally pray standing accords well with the alleged Greek sensitivity toward approaching the gods as their servants or slaves.[52] By contrast, the Persian adopted the posture of obeisance (*proskynēsis*).[53] In the Bible, and in Josephus as well, characters do frequently "fall on their faces" before God, in prayer or in distress. Indeed in Numbers 16:4, 5, 22 this is exactly what Moses does when confronted by the enormity of the rebellion. However, the Josephan Moses offers his prayer standing in the usual manner of the ancient Greek.

Nevertheless, Josephus does not shy away from portraying his characters praying silently to God in the gesture of obeisance, and aloud, in the case of Joshua in the next prayer to be discussed (5.38–41, see 42).[54] That God is invoked by Moses as "Master of heaven and earth and sea" reminds us of the similar invocation in Isaac's benediction in *Ant.* 1.272 with its array of Jewish parallels.

The prayer of Moses also alludes to Israel's experience of divine rescue when God took pity on the nation in its extremity. Since God has acted thus in Israel's past experience, Moses prays for a fresh act of divine mercy in this present emergency. "Come, hearer of my words" (*elthe moi toutōn akroatēs tōn logōn*, 4.40), he prays. The English translation offered in Loeb at this point introduces the unwarranted anthropomorphism "lend thine *ear* to my words." Adolf Schlatter rightly emphasized Josephus's playing down the anthropomorphisms of his biblical sources. With a few exceptions, he wrote, "die Vergleichung Gottes mit dem menschlichen Leib und seinen Gliedern hat J. gemieden" ("Josephus avoided making comparison between God and the human body and its members").[55] Apart from considering Josephus's own religious convictions on this question, one must take into account the possibility of Josephus's sensitivity to the sophisticated philosophical conceptions of his readers.[56]

God is called not only *dēmiourgos* in this prayer but also the *genesis* of all that is. We find the same combination in the reported prayer of David in *Ant.* 7.380, the only other place in which God is called *genesis*. Incidentally, God is also termed "Father" (*patēr*) in the David passage.[57]

The rebellion allows Moses the opportunity to rehearse before God and the people his faithful service to God in the face of the people's ingratitude. The Bible's mention of Moses' extreme anger (Num. 16:15) on this occasion is omitted from Josephus's account in favor of a rhetorically competent and measured display by the statesman-lawgiver. The manifest self-vindication of this Josephan prayer might be compared to the protestation of the innocence and righteousness of Job (Job 9:15, 20–21; 12:4) or of the psalmist in Psalm 26.

However the histories of the Hellenic and Hellenistic eras, and the experiences of Pericles and Lycurgus in particular, offer more instructive parallels.[58] Moses, we must remember, is the founder of the Hebrew *politeia*. His integrity is under threat by the ungrateful who are in the process of fomenting a *stasis* against both him and the constitution he has bestowed. Moses protests his innocence of wrongdoing. He has always upheld the common good of the people. He has not taken any "present" for himself.[59] By contrast, the rebels are rebels against "the ordered beauty of their constitution" (*ho kosmos tēs katastaseōs*, 4.37). Moses' speech is a spirited defense of the "ordered constitution" he has delivered to the people from God, and of himself as the constitutional "father." Like their wilderness forebears, the fomenters of the *stasis* that overwhelmed Jerusalem in the events of 66–70 C.E. were guilty of sedition against Moses and the Law.[60]

Prayer #4, 5.38–41: Joshua's Prayer after the Defeat at Ai

Joshua, we learn in section 42, offers this prayer in the attitude of proskynesis (*epi stoma pesōn ērōta ton theon*), as he does in the biblical parallel (see Josh. 7:6). The prayer does not begin with an invocation, though the vocative *despota* does occur toward the end in section 41. The occasion of the prayer is the unexpected defeat Israel has suffered at the hands of the inhabitants of Ai. The true cause is not failure of God's promises or of his will, but the theft by Achan of objects consecrated to God (see 42). Though Joshua does appeal to God to restore Israel's fortunes, Josephus omits Joshua's question (see Josh. 7:9) as to what God might do for his great name if the Canaanites were to defeat Israel.[61] The *Antiquities* is not the arena for matters of theodicy.

Perhaps the most prominent of Josephus's contributions to this prayer is the role of Moses. Israel, Joshua pleads to God, is only doing what Moses commanded. In the wake of the defeat at Ai, Joshua fears that the Mosaic legacy (his "predictions") has foundered (*ou bebaiōn tōn para sou kai ōn proeipe Mōusēs*, 40). This reinforces the Josephan idea of Moses as the great law-giver. He is the custodian of Israel's political well-being, and the one whose legislation and vision continue to be operative in the continuing life of the people of Israel — the Israel to which Josephus yet belongs. In the Bible, on the other hand, the threat to God's fulfillment of the promises made to the patriarchs assume greater prominence than in Josephus.

It is tempting to see both in the situation of Joshua, in the prayer, and in God's response, an analogy with the defeat suffered by the Jews in the Jewish War. It is well known that Josephus lays the blame for that defeat squarely in the hands of Jewish hotheads whose offenses perpetrated in Jerusalem amounted to sacrilege against Moses and the Law. Consequently, the horrific outcome of the Jewish War was indeed superintended and willed by God. There were Jews in Palestine — Josephus's own contemporaries — who, acting in a sacrilegious manner like Achan, had given cause for divine action against the whole nation.

Finally, I turn to book 8 and the two prayers recorded by Josephus that are based on the narrative in 1 Kings 8. In the biblical account of the consecration of the Temple, Solomon offers three prayers to God. The first (8:15–21) and third (8:54–61) are benedictions pronounced over the assembled people of God, framing the lengthy prayer addressed directly to God (8:23–53). Josephus follows the basic biblical order: Solomon's prostrate response to the filling of the Temple with the glory of God (1 Kings 8:12–13) followed by his blessing of the people (8:14–21), the lengthy prayer prayed with hands outstretched to heaven (8:22–53), and the final benediction (8:54–61). Some of the leading ideas of the biblical text's central prayer are reworked by Josephus into the two prayers he has Solomon pray standing. In Josephus, both prayers become vehicles for affirming Stoic theology. Once again, the reader should note the historian's avoidance of the *eulogētos* formula to be encountered in the biblical sources.

Prayer #5, 8.107–8: Solomon's First Prayer at the Consecration of the Temple

The first of Josephus's prayers corresponds in terms of its placement in the narrative with the response of the king in the biblical account to the infilling of the Temple with the cloud of the glory of God. God is addressed by Solomon as a philosopher "in words which he [Solomon] considered suitable to the divine nature and fitting for him to speak (107)."

Josephus has Solomon express a panentheistic view of God. God, he declares, has an eternal dwelling "in those things which Thou didst create for Thyself...in the heaven and air and earth and sea, through all of which Thou movest and yet art not contained by them" (107–8).[62] Those who saw the cloud fill the Temple were but subject to the "impression and appearance" (*phantasia kai doxa*, 106) that God had descended into the Temple and taken up residence. The prayer concludes with the observation that though God might be thought of as present in the Temple he is just as accessible as before to all who ask for "good omens" (108).[63] From the Temple prayers ascend to God, whose dwelling is in the air. God, therefore, is neither captive to Israel's national agenda nor the God of Israel exclusively.

For Israel, Josephus declares, as well as the nations God is "present and not remote" (*parei kai makran aphestēkas*). Eduard Norden noted the Stoic coloring of this phrase in his discussion of Paul's Areopagus address, in particular the phrase "he is not far from each one of us" in Acts 17:27.[64]

Prayer #6, 8.111–17: Solomon's Second Prayer at the Consecration of the Temple

The second prayer of Solomon is in part an announcement of a rational theology of prayer — suitable on the occasion of the consecration since the Temple has been built for offering prayer, as well as for making sacrifices and seeking good omens (108). The deity is in need of nothing, Solomon begins. Here Josephus uses the term *aprosdeēs,* a term used by the Stoics to denote divine independence from the created order.[65] This has significant consequences for the concept of the cult paid to a divinity. The term denies the propriety of the ubiquitous concept of contract in prayer (*do ut des*), for God needs nothing. Moreover, God is above recompense, the kind of recompense one might pay in the cultic arena in terms of material offering. Praise, therefore, as Solomon now asserts, is the only proper response not only with respect to the goodness and being of God, but also to a God who is on occasion and with good reason wrathful. This idea of praise as sacrifice is common enough in Greek philosophy.[66] It is also found in the Hebrew Bible, the NT, the Qumran corpus, and the rabbinic literature. Prayer and praise become the substitutes for Temple worship.[67]

The second element of the prayer is its stress on the universal accessibility of God and on his nearness to all who seek him. All who take refuge in the Temple are guaranteed his protection. God is the bestower of kindness upon all — Jews and Gentiles — who fall into error and plead to be delivered from their misfortunes (116). "May God," prays Solomon, "hearken to all who pray thus in God's Temple as though he were within." For this is why God provided for the Temple to be built in Israel. It was built so that those near and those far-off might draw near to God in his Temple, both to praise him and to seek restoration of divine benefits. Correspondingly, the Jews are not unfriendly to non-Jews. On the contrary, Jews are humane and welcoming to all honest and sincere seekers after the truth. The charge of misanthropy directed frequently against the Jews in antiquity is here countered by Josephus. The charge of exclusivism is soundly refuted.[68]

Conclusion

I have four observations.

1. Josephus, while not compromising distinctive biblical theology and the essentials of the salvation-historical perspective (he is no assimilationist), is in a position as a literate Jew in the Hellenistic milieu to represent the history and ideas of Israel to his non-Jewish readers in a way that commends its traditions to them and makes for understanding and mutual respect. To this extent, as Schlatter rightly concluded, Josephus has not closed the door on Hellenism.[69] Moreover, he stands within a Jewish apologetic tradition in which the best of Greek culture is claimed as originating in the Hebrew genius.

2. In common with the Greco-Roman philosophical tradition, Josephus rejects the notion of contract with respect to relating to the divine. He generally avoids the anthropomorphisms of the Bible. He can use terms at home in the Greek philosophical and religious heritage, such as *aprosdeēs* and *dēmiourgos,* as we have seen. In fact, Stoic terminology and theology pervade Josephus's presentation of the six prayers I have examined.

3. He is not bound to keep his account rigidly "Semitic." He does not portray anything that would underscore Greek or Roman prejudice against "Semitic superstition" without at the same time implicitly or explicitly stressing the surpassing venerability of Jewish custom. Moses the great law-giver does not fall on his face before God to pray the prayer Josephus has him pray in book 4. Moses, and other biblical characters, can pray standing with hands uplifted in the manner of the ancient Greek when the Bible has them praying prostrate. Nevertheless, it must be acknowledged that Josephus can also portray his characters praying to God prostrate, as this did not necessarily offend in Greco-Roman worship contexts. However, and this is an important point, he maintains the reserve of Greeks toward rendering proskynesis to persons, avoiding reproducing this where his Jewish sources indicate it (see n. 53 above). God can be invoked in terms that bridge the gulf between the Greek culture and the Jewish, yet, I would venture to claim, we find nothing here that the Mishnah and Talmud did not enshrine and to which it did not give its imprimatur.

4. It is certainly unusual, as I have been hinting, that Josephus does not use the ubiquitous *eulogētos* formula. Its presence in Jewish literature — Pseudepigrapha, Qumran scrolls, NT, the rabbinic literature, as well as the biblical prayers which served as Josephus's models — certainly testifies to its wide use.[70]

Does Josephus avoid the term precisely because it was *uniquely* Jewish? This certainly seems a most reasonable possibility.

Notes

1. I wish to thank Professor L. H. Feldman for his helpful criticism and teachers and friends at Princeton Theological Seminary for their support.

2. The twenty books of the *Antiquities* are modelled both in title and scope on the late first century B.C.E. Dionysius of Halicarnassus's *Roman Antiquities*. Josephus is setting out to show that his people have a "history comparable, nay in antiquity superior, to that of the proud Romans" (H. St. J. Thackeray, *Josephus, the Man and the Historian* [New York: KTAV Publishing House, 1967 repr.], 56).

3. See Thackeray's introduction to the *Antiquities* in vol. 4 of the Loeb edition of Josephus's Works. He writes that in design the *Antiquities* "was to magnify the Jewish race in the eyes of the Greco-Roman world by a record of its ancient and glorious history" (vii). See *Ant.* 1.15–17, in which Josephus urges his readers to judge for themselves whether Moses has imparted a "worthy conception of his [God's] nature," a conception devoid of "that unseemly mythology current among others" (15). Moses antedates ("born 2,000 years ago," 16) the Greek poets responsible for the Greek myths, Homer, Hesiod, and Theognis, "at which ancient date the poets never ventured to refer even to the birth of their gods, much less the actions and laws of mortals" (16). Josephus ventures a scathing attack on "unseemly mythology" and Greek religion in general in *Against Apion* 2.236–86. All this is in accord with the Greek philosophic tradition. Plato was prepared to banish poetry, even that of Homer, from his ideal state (see *Republic,* 398A), a fact of which Josephus is aware (*Against Apion* 2.256). Josephus, like Philo, is not the only Jewish writer of the era to write apologetically. See the fragments of the Jewish philosopher Aristobulus and of the Jewish historians in J. H. Charlesworth (ed.), *Old Testament Pseudepigrapha* (Garden City, N.Y.: Doubleday, 1985), 2:831–42, 855–903. Moses was the first wise man (fragment 1 of Eupolemus citing Alexander Polyhistor in *OTP* 2:865), the inventor of philosophy, and the bestower of all kinds of benefits on humankind (fragment 3 of Artapanus in *OTP* 2:898–99). Moreover, the Greeks were dependent on his laws (fragment 4 of Aristobulus in *OTP* 2:840–41; see also *Against Apion* 2.281).

4. See *Life,* 429. Domitian punished Josephus's Jewish enemies. See also T. Rajak, *Josephus* (Philadelphia: Fortress, 1984), 146. Thackeray, however, contends that during Domitian's rule, Josephus lost much of his royal patronage (*Josephus,* 52–53). He seems to base this conclusion on Domitian's anti-literary tendencies. Suetonius writes that the emperor's only reading was Tiberius's official reports (*Domitian,* 20).

5. I am following S. Mason, *Flavius Josephus on the Pharisees* (Leiden: Brill, 1991), 330–41, 342–56. Mason argues (against the consensus) that in his religious quest Josephus, far from becoming a Pharisee and owing Pharisaic allegiance, found none of the three "schools' satisfactory (see *Life,* 11). That is why he attached himself to Bannus as his *zēlōtēs.* This was his only "conversion." At the age of nineteen, he began political life ("entered politics," *ērchamēn politeuesthai*) "following the Pharisaic school" (*tē pharisaiōn airesei katakolouthōn, Life,* 12), i.e., with a "certain acknowledgment of, or deference to, the Pharisaic school" (Mason, 354–55).

6. *War* 3.387: *pisteuōn tō kēdemoni theō tēn sōtērian paraballetai.* Cf. the role

of providence (*pronoia*), God's benevolent and purposeful supervision of the natural order, in *Life,* 15, when shipwrecked. The term is a frequently encountered in Josephus (see, e.g., *Ant.* 4.47, *Against Apion* 2.180. For further discussion, see M. Pohlenz, *Die Stoa: Geschichte einer geistigen Bewegung* (Göttingen: Vandenhoeck & Ruprecht, 1948), 1:98–101; H. W. Attridge, *The Interpretation of Biblical History in the Antiquitates Judaicae of Flavius Josephus* (Missoula, Mont.: Scholars Press, 1976), ch. 3 (71–107); and J. A. Montgomery, "The Religion of Flavius Josephus," *JQR* 11 (1920–21), 277–305 (286–87).

7. *Life,* 295. We were, he writes, "proceeding with the ordinary service and engaged in prayer" (*ēde d' ēmōn ta nomima poiountōn kai pros euchas trapomenōn*).

8. See the discussion of this point in L. H. Feldman, *Josephus and Modern Research 1937–80* (New York/Berlin: Walter de Gruyter, 1984), 435 #1819. Josephus's views on prayer are, according to S. Hahn, "Josephus on Prayer in c. Ap. II. 197," in O. Komlos (ed.), *Études orientales à la mémoire de Paul Hirschler* [Budapest, 1950], 111–15, supposedly close to Horace, *Odes* 1.31, in which the poet prays to Apollo not for rich harvests or for other extravagantly good things, but professes his satisfaction with the simple fare of the olive, endive, and mallow, concluding his prayer with "Grant me, O Latoma's son, to be content with what I have, and, sound of body and of mind, to pass an old age lacking neither honor nor the lyre" (Loeb trans.). However, Feldman (*Josephus and Modern Research,* 435) is right to doubt the merits of Hahn's case for comparing the Ode with Josephus on the evidence of the sentiment expressed in *Against Apion* 2.197.

9. See *Ant.* 1.154–68. Abraham, a man of ready intelligence, subsequent to the divine call, "began to have more lofty conceptions of virtue than the rest of mankind, and determined to reform and change the ideas universally current concerning God" (155). He was the first to declare that God is "one." He was a physicist and astronomer (156). However, his enlightened ideas are not appreciated by the Mesopotamians, who are provoked to rise against him. At this point, Abraham decides that it is expedient to emigrate. In due course, he teaches arithmetic and astronomy to the Egyptians (167). Moses invents the clarion, which rouses the tribes (*Ant.* 3.291). His laws are characterized as "excellent beyond the standard of human wisdom" (3.223). See also the fragment of Ps-Eupolemus in *OTP* 2:880–81. Cf. the inventiveness of Abraham in Jub 11:23–24 and his wisdom in 12:25–27. See further L. H. Feldman, "Abraham the Greek Philosopher in Josephus," *TAPA* 99 (1968), 143–56.

10. See *Against Apion* 2.154. Cf. Philo, *Life of Moses* 2.12–20.

11. Cf. the striking praise of the Jewish Law and the excellence of the piety it instills in the concluding sections of *Against Apion* (2.291–95). See discussion in Montgomery, "The Religion of Flavius Josephus," 294, and the discussion in note 3 above on Moses and the superiority of Jewish laws.

12. The writing of a theological work (entitled *Customs and Causes*) is anticipated in *Ant.* 1.25, 192; 3.143; 4.198; and 20.268. Feldman observes that although Josephus "proclaims his theologizing and moralizing purpose in the preface," he actually plays down the theological, and especially the miraculous, element of the biblical narratives. See his discussion in "Mikra in the Writings of Josephus," in J. Mulder and H. Sysling (eds.), *Mikra: Text, Translation, Reading*

and Interpretation of the Hebrew Bible in Ancient Judaism and Early Christianity (Compendia Rerum Iudaicarum ad Novum Testamentum II, vol. 1; Assen/ Philadelphia: van Gorcum/Fortress, 1988), 503–7, esp. 504.

13.   1.218   Hagar's lament (Gen. 21:16)

     1.245   Abraham's servant with respect to finding the right wife for Isaac (Gen. 24:12–14)

     1.275   The diminished blessing of Esau (Gen. 27:39–40)

     2.194   Jacob's benedictions over his sons (Gen. 49)

     3.34   Moses offers prayer at the Rock (Exod. 17:4)

     4.124–25   Balaam's blessings over Israel are replaced by summary (Num. 23–24)

     5.159   Phinehas's petition (Judg. 20:38)

     5.263   Jephthah's rash vow (Judg. 11:30–31)

     5.280   Manoah's wife's prayer for a further vision of the Angel (Judg. 13:8, in which Manoah is the one who prays)

     5.344–45   Hannah's supplication in the house of God at Shiloh (1 Sam. 2)

     6.22   The people's confession on the eve of the battle with the Philistines (1 Sam. 7:5)

     7.328   David's confession after the census (2 Sam. 24:10, 17 = 2 Chron. 21:8, 17)

     7.357   Benaiah's benediction of Solomon (1 Kings 1:36–37)

     7.380–81   David's prayer for Solomon with a report of the people's response (1 Chron. 29:11–19, 20)

     8.119–21   Solomon entreats God and blesses the people (1 Kings 8:54–61)

     8.342   Elijah prays on Mt. Carmel (1 Kings 18:36–37)

     8.348   Elijah prays in the wilderness (1 Kings 19:4)

     9.8–9   Jehoshaphat's response to the impending crisis (2 Chron. 20:5–12)

     9.15   Jehoshaphat's victory (2 Chron. 20:26)

     9.55, 57   Elisha's prayers during the Syrian emergency (2 Kings 6:17, 20)

     10.16   The prayer of Hezekiah (2 Kings 19:15–19)

     10.26   Hezekiah supplicates God in his illness (2 Kings 20:3)

     11.143–44 Ezra's confession on behalf of the people (Ezra 9:6–15)

     11.229–30 Mordecai supplicates God not to turn away from his people (AddEsth 13:8–17 [Addition C]). Josephus cites part of the prayer in 230.

     11.231–33 Esther supplicates God (AddEsth 14:3–19 [Addition C])

14. 1.272–73; 2.335–37; 4.40–50; 5.38–41; 8.107–8 and 111–17. There are few other prayers of this length in the remainder of Josephus's output.

15. 8.23 (Solomon's request for wisdom, paraphrasing 1 Kings 3:9); 11.65 (Zerubbabel's thanksgiving, reworking of 1 Esdras 4:59–60), 162 (Nehemiah, summary of Neh 1:5–11), 230 (Mordecai, reworking of AddEsth 13:12 [C]).

16. See *Ant.* 2.346, cf. *Ant.* 4.303. Thackeray suggests that Josephus was possibly familiar with collections of chants based on the Bible sung by the Temple

choir, Loeb 4, 622 note d, and his *Josephus*, 90–91. In support of this contention he refers to the fact that Josephus does say that Jeremiah composed a funeral elegy on Josiah that "survives to this day" (10.78). The Greek hexameter was the meter of Homer's epics and the Homeric hymns, and for songs both sacred and secular. See C. M. Bowra, *Landmarks in Greek Literature* (Pelican Books, 1968), 10–11, 18, 316. The famous "Hymn to Zeus" of Cleanthes is a third-century B.C.E. example of a hexameter hymn. Oracles were also delivered in hexameters as in Herodotus, *Histories*, 1.47 and 7.220.

17. 1.272; 4.40, 46; 5.41; 8.23, 107, 111; 11.65, 162, 230. The vocative is read in 2.335 by inferior mss.

18. Some examples are as follows. 2 Maccabees 15:22: *su, despota, apesteilas ton aggelon sou;* 3 Maccabees 2:2: *despotēs pasēs ktiseōs;* Sirach 23:1, *kyrie, pater kai despota; AposCon* 8.9.8: *despota tōn holōn* (cf. 8.5.1: *despota... ho theos*). For further references, see R. A. Marcus, "Divine Names and Attributes in Hellenistic Jewish Literature," *AAJR* (1931–32), 43–120 (61–62).

19. See Philo, *Who Is the Heir?* 22; Luke 2:29; Acts 4:24; 2 Peter 2:1; Revelation 6:10; *1 Clem.* 8:2. *despotēs* corresponds to the ubiquitous *ribbônî*, and can be found, for instance, in the prayer of Onias in *m.Taʿan* 3:8.

20. *Anabasis*, 3.2.13: *oudena gar anthrōpon despotēn alla tous theous proskyneite.*

21. See the Isis aretalogy P. Oxy. 1380. 231: *su kai pantōn despotis.*

22. F. Heiler, *Das Gebet* (Munich: Ernst Reinhardt, 1921), 200.

23. *TDNT,* 2:45.

24. Thus Heinemann cites the aphorism that the "Eighteen Benedictions" is the "prayer of a servant before his master" (*Prayer in the Talmud* [trans. R. S. Sarason; Berlin/New York: de Gruyter, 1977], 243–44). Josephus himself stresses the master-servant relationship in Israel's approach to God. The Jews, he writes, are the *douloi tou theou*" (*Ant.* 11.90, 101).

25. *b.Taʿan* 23a. Cf. *b.Yoma* 87b: *ribbôn haʿôlāmîm.*

26. *en archē ektisen o theos....* The LXX has *poieō.* See A. Schlatter, *Wie sprach Josephus von Gott* in *Beiträge zur Förderung christlicher Theologie* 14 (Gütersloh: Bertelsmann, 1910), 43. L. H. Feldman, "Josephus' Commentary on Genesis," *JQR* 72 (1981–82), 121, points out that Josephus's use of *ktizō* "implies more clearly *creatio ex nihilo*" whereas *poieō* "implies *creatio ex aliquo.*"

27. See 8.40.2: *dēmiourge tōn holōn;* 8.37.2: *ho tōn holōn poiētēs;* 7.33.2: *ho theos pantōn holōn.*

28. *Creation of the World*, 16. The term *dēmiourgos* occurs in the NT only in Hebrews 11:10, in which God is described as the *technitēs kai dēmiourgos* of the heavenly city.

29. See Plato, *Tim* 28A, C; 31A; 40C; *Republic* 530A. Cf. Epictetus, *Discourses* 2.8.21.

30. See *TDNT,* 3:1025.

31. Josephus uses *dēmiourgos* of God in *Ant.* 1.155, 272, and 7.380 only. The verb is used of God only in Josephus's speech in *War* 3.372 (in which it denotes the fashioning of the human bodies out of perishable matter, while the rational soul is a "portion of the Deity housed in our bodies") and *Ant.* 1.32. This is clearly consonant with the Stoic concept of the human person as a microcosm of

the universe whose soul is God. See E. V. Arnold, *Roman Stoicism* (Cambridge: Cambridge University Press, 1911), 238–41; M. Pohlenz, *Die Stoa*, 1.81–93. See also Acts 17:28.

32. Cf. note 9 above.

33. R. MacMullen, *Paganism in the Roman Empire* (New Haven: Yale University Press, 1981), 52, notes the pervasive spirit of self-interest to be found in Greek prayers. Cf. W. Burkert, *Greek Religion* (Cambridge, Mass.: Harvard University Press, 1985), 75; E. Ferguson, *Backgrounds of Early Christianity* (Grand Rapids, Mich.: Eerdmans 1987), 149; K. von Fritz, "Greek Prayers," *RR* 10 (1945), 5–39 (21–22). The Greek, writes von Fritz, "flatters the god with the suggestion that he [the god] is already under an obligation to him." Von Fritz's discussion of the subtlety of Sappho's prayer to Aphrodite is illuminating.

34. See, e.g., Cicero, *On Divination*, 1.38 (92–93) in which the author cites Chrysippus: "But it is not true that the gods do not love us, for they are the friends and benefactors of the human race" (Loeb tr.). Divination is evidence of this care and concern on the part of the gods.

35. *m.'Eduyyot*, 2:9 in Danby, *The Mishnah* (Oxford: Oxford University Press, 1933), 426.

36. Elegy 1.5, in E. Diehl, *Anthologia Lyrica Graeca* (Leipzig: Teubner, 1925), 1.17.

37. L. H. Feldman suggested the Simonides parallel to me (*per litt.*). The discussion of Simonides' definition of justice occurs in 331E–335E. Simonides believed that justice consists in giving each person what is due (331E: *to ta opheilomena hekastō apodidonai dikaion esti*). Polemarchus interprets this to mean that the poet believes that friends ought to render some good to their friends and not evil (332A: *tois philois opheilein tous philous agathon men ti drąn, kakon de mēden*), but one ought to render something evil (*kakon ti*) to one's enemy since that is his due (332B). Socrates, however, demonstrates the inadequacy of this piece of conventional wisdom since the good and, therefore, just person ought not to harm anyone (see 335D).

38. Loeb translates, "make him a terror to his foes." Cf. MM, s.v. *phoberos* where the editors cite the text of a Christian amulet (P. Oxy. 1151.55, fifth century[?] c.e.) that bears some parallel with the sentiment of Psalm 110:9 (LXX): *hoti to onoma sou k(yri)e ho th(eo)s, epikalesa(m)ēn to thaumaston kai hyperendoxon kai phoberon tois hypenantiois.*

39. That Isaac should pray that Jacob should be *timios* (= *yāqār*) suggests a comparison with *Gen. Rabbah* 67.ii.3 in which the phrase *wĕhôn 'ādām yāqār ḥārûṣ* from Proverbs 12:27 is applied to Jacob. See J. Neusner, *Genesis Rabbah* (Atlanta: Scholars Press, 1985), 2:411: "But the substance of the man of glory is determined," i.e., it was so that Jacob would came [sic] and take the blessings, which in principle from the beginning of the world had been assigned to him."

40. Cf. the beginning of Joshua's prayer in 5.38–41. The invocation in that prayer occurs in 41.

41. According to Thackeray in the Introduction (xvii) to the Loeb edition of the *Antiquities*, SPL are generally inferior to the mss. followed by Niese, i.e., ROM. In this case ROM do not have the usual epithet.

42. See W. Burkert, *Greek Religion*, 74–75. Burkert claims that no ancient litur-

gical prayer formulae have been transmitted. There was, however, a basic prayer form. Prayers were spontaneous. E. Ferguson, *Backgrounds*, 149–50, notes two stages in Greek prayers: the early, marked by invocation, praise, and petition; and the later Hellenistic pattern of invocation "by names, nature, cult sites, genealogy, and relationship to other gods," general powers and accomplishments of the deity, specific works and miracles and inventions, personal requests.

43. See von Fritz, "Greek Prayers," 16–17.

44. Cf. Psalm 124; Job 19:10.

45. Cf. Micah 7:7; Psalm 84:9; 119:153.

46. Cf. Psalm 77:14; 90:16.

47. Cf. Isaiah 40:27.

48. Cf. Exodus 19:5; Psalm 104; 50:12; 60:6–8; 74:12–17.

49. Cf. Psalm 97:5; 104:32; 144:5–7.

50. *m.Aboth*, 4:22, *hakkōl šellô* See also *Ant.* 1.72, 272; 4.46. Cf. Romans 11:36; 1 Corinthians 8:6; Colossians 1:16–17; Hebrews 1:3; Revelation 4:11. See J. D. G. Dunn, *Romans 9–16* (Waco, Tex.: Word, 1988), 701, for six parallels from the philosophical tradition to the sentiment expressed in Romans 11:36, 1 Corinthians 8:6, and Colossians 1:16–17.

51. See Burkert, *Greek Religion*, 75, and n.19 on 376. Theophrastus, *Characters*, 16.5, regards the man as "superstitious" who kneels and worships (*epi gonata pesōn kai proskynēsas*) the smooth stones set up at crossroads. For hands outstretched to heaven, see *Iliad*, 15.371.

52. Heiler, *Das Gebet*, 200. The term *proskunein* is ubiquitous in the LXX as a translation for *hištaḥăweh,* indeed it appears in 167 out of 171 places in which the Hebrew verb appears. Josephus, on the other hand, prefers the terms *thrēskeia, eusebein, sebein,* and *timan* in describing the religious rectitude of the Israelites. The first term denotes cultic ritual. The second and third are among the Greeks' preferred terms for expression of religious obligation. Jews also stood for prayer. See, e.g., Luke 22:41.

53. Obeisance was used among the ancient Greeks when approaching the chthonian deities. See *Od* 4.522, in which Agamemnon, on landing *kynei haptomenos hēn patrida*. However, for the offensiveness to Greeks of offering proskynesis to persons, see M. M. Austin, *The Hellenistic World from Alexander to the Roman Conquest* (Cambridge: Cambridge University Press, 1981), 22–23. Austin cites Arrian's objections to obeisance rendered to Alexander, observing that obeisance is only appropriate in worshiping the gods (*History of Alexander,* 4.10.5–12.5). Josephus preserves the distinction as in Haman's demand for obeisance and Mordecai's resistance (see *Ant.* 11.209, 210, 230, 277). Interestingly Josephus in *Ant.* 2.194–95 does not have Joseph and his sons rendering proskynesis to Jacob, though the LXX has them doing so (see Gen. 48:12). See discussion of ancient Greek reservation with respect to obeisance in J. Horst, *Proskynein* (Gütersloh: Bertelsmann, 1932), 14–26, and especially 25 for the influence of oriental religious practice on earlier Greek reserve in the Hellenistic era and beyond.

54. Josephus does use *proskyneō* rather frequently (*Ant.* 7.381; 8.119; 9.11; 10.29). Joshua prays in this attitude in 5.38–41 (see 42), the only occasion where prayer is offered thus in direct speech in books 1–11. Usually the characters stand for prayer where the content is reported or direct speech, after bowing down to the

ground/bending the knee as a first response to a manifestation of God's blessing or to some emergency. Cf. 11.143, e.g., where Josephus has Ezra get up from his prostrate position to pray erect. The content of this prayer is given in reported speech.

55. A. Schlatter, *Wie sprach Josephus*, 22. Moses does, however, hear the voice of God at the Burning Bush (2.283) and on Mt. Sinai (3.90), as do Abraham, and Elijah (1.185 and 8.352). Josephus even terms himself a servant of the "voice of God" in *War* 4.626. One also encounters God's "eye" (*War* 1.84, 378) and God's "hand" (*Ant.* 7.323). Josephus does not refer to God's "ear," "mouth" or "face." Cf. the fragment of Aristobulus explaining anthropomorphisms in *OTP* 2:837–39.

56. Further evidence of this is found in Solomon's prayer in 8.111–13 (to be discussed below). "The Deity," he prays, "stands in need of nothing and is above recompense" (*aprosdeēs gar to theion hapantōn kai kreitton toiautēs amoibēs*). The term *aprosdeos* is a Stoic attribute of God (see W. C. van Unnik, "Eine merkwürdige liturgische Aussage bei Josephus" in O. Betz, K. Haacker, and M. Hengel (eds.), *Josephus — Studien* [Göttingen: Vandenhoeck & Ruprecht, 1974], 362–69 [366 n. 13]); Loeb vol. 5, 631, note d). The doctrine that God needs nothing was a commonplace in Greek philosophy. It implied a rejection of the contractual mentality of Greek prayers. See also Acts 17:25. *AposCon* 8.38.4 speaks of God as *ho asygkritos kai aprosdeēs*. See further L. H. Feldman, "Josephus as Biblical Interpreter: The "Aqedah," *JQR* 75 (1985), 212–52 (223–24, cf. 229–30).

57. This is the only occasion in Josephus that God is addressed in prayer as "Father." See Schlatter, *Wie sprach Josephus*, 14–15. Cf. *Ant.* 1.230, in which Abraham speaks to Isaac of God as the "Father of all."

58. In Thucydides, Pericles is frequently the target of the ungrateful. Though the people know that he is above bribery, they fine him on the pretext that he embezzled funds (*War* 2.65). Plutarch's *Life* of Lycurgus chronicles the reaction to his constitutional reforms. Pursued by the wealthy, Lycurgus is struck by a youth, Alcander. Lycurgus takes him home where the lad sees ample evidence that Lycurgus is gentle, simple in his habits, and industrious. Not surprisingly, Alcander becomes a devotee of the new *politeia*.

59. There is an interesting textual matter here. The MT reads "ass" (*ḥĕmôr*). The LXX reads *epithymēma* (*ḥāmûd*). Either Josephus knows only the textual tradition behind the LXX translation, or he wanted to downplay the culturally specific "ass."

60. See Josephus's speech in *War*, 5.401. See also *Ant.* 20.166. Cf. *Ant.* 8.120–21, in which Josephus reports an exhortation of Solomon to the people to remember the commandments as the means by which they might maintain their present blessings. For Josephus's view of the failure of first century C.E. Jews in this regard, see the discussion of relevant passages in P. Bilde, "The Causes of the Jewish War according to Josephus," *JSJ* 10 (1979), 179–202, esp. 191–94. Cf. S. J. D. Cohen, "Josephus, Jeremiah, and Polybius," *History and Theory* 21 (1982), 366–81.

61. See L. H. Feldman, "Josephus' Portrait of Joshua," *HTR* 82 (1989), 351–76 (367). Feldman demonstrates the de-theologizing tendency of Josephus's biblical narrative in general, and of his presentation of Joshua in particular (366–72).

62. Cf. the Stoic doctrine of the divine soul immanent in the universe, yet not totally identifiable with it. See discussion in E. V. Arnold, *Roman Stoicism,* 185.

63. Cf. Cicero, *On Divination,* 1.38 (92–93).

64. See his *Agnostos Theos* (Leipzig/Berlin: Teubner, 1913), 19 n.2. Cf. L. H. Feldman, "Josephus as an Apologist to the Greco-Roman World: His Portrait of Solomon," in E. Schüssler Fiorenza (ed.), *Aspects of Religious Propaganda in Judaism and Early Christianity* (Notre Dame, Ind.: University of Notre Dame Press, 1976), 69–98, esp. 90–92. See also the more general discussion of Stoic terminology in Josephus in L. H. Feldman, "Mikra in the Writings of Josephus," 498–500. See also note 6 above on *pronoia.*

65. See, e.g., Plato, *Tim* 33D; Seneca, *Ep* 41.1; 120.14; Plutarch, *Aristeides and Cato* 4. Among Jewish writers, see LetAris 211; 2 Maccabees 14:35; 3 Maccabees 2:9; Philo, *On the Unchangeableness of God,* 56. Josephus uses the term only twice, here (*Ant.* 8.111) and of the self-sufficiency of the Israelite army with God as their ally (*Ant.* 3.45).

66. See, e.g., the last three lines especially of Cleanthes' "Hymn to Zeus"; E. Vernon Arnold, *Roman Stoicism,* 234–5; E. Ferguson, "Spiritual Sacrifice in Early Christianity and in its Environment," *ANRW* II 23.2 (1980), 1151–89, esp. 1153–56.

67. See, e.g., Psalm 69:30–31; Hebrews 13:15; 1QS 9.3–6; and the rabbinic texts and discussion in G. F. Moore, *Judaism* (Cambridge, Mass.: Harvard University Press, 1927), 2:218–19; and E. Ferguson, "Spiritual Sacrifice," 1161. See further discussion in F.-E. Wilms, "Blutige Opfer oder Opfer der Lippen," *ALW* 25 (1983), 121–36.

68. See Tacitus, *Histories* 5.5, where the historian writes that the Jews "regard the rest of mankind with all the hatred of enemies." Josephus takes great pains in *Against Apion* 2.89–111, to rebut the slander of the Jews' supposed annual human sacrifice of a Greek in the Temple. While sacrificing him, the Jews are supposed to swear hatred to all Greeks (2.95). Josephus points out that not only is the story without foundation, but that the Temple was not a place for the celebration of Mysteries, and that Gentiles were admitted, at least to the outer courts. For further discussion see L. H. Feldman, "Anti-Semitism in the Ancient World," in D. Berger (ed.), *History and Hate: The Dimensions of Anti-Semitism* (Philadelphia: Jewish Publication Society, 1986), 30–32, and "Pro-Jewish Intimations in Anti-Jewish Remarks Cited by Josephus' *Against Apion,*" *JQR* 78 (1987–88), 211–18.

69. See Schlatter, *Wie sprach Josephus,* 7; he remarks that Josephus "ist nicht gegen das Griechentum verschlossen."

70. See, e.g., 1 Maccabees 4:24, 30, and 55; 2 Maccabees 1:17; 10:38, etc.; 1QS 11.15; 1QM 13.2; 1QH 5.19; 10.14; 11.27, 29, 32; 16.8; Ephesians 1:3; 1 Peter 1:3; 2 Corinthians 1:3; Romans 1:25; 9:5; Luke 1:68; and AposCon 8.38.4. *Eulogētos* does not appear in the hymns of the NT Apocalypse.

• 6 •

JOSEPHUS'S PARAPHRASE OF 1 MACCABEES IN *ANTIQUITIES* 12–13
Prayer in a Narrative Context

Agneta Enermalm-Ogawa

A reader who compares 1 Maccabees with the paraphrase in *Antiquities* 12–13 discovers interesting discrepancies. While the events as reported by Josephus normally correspond to those in 1 Maccabees,[1] the speeches are elaborated and embellished by him.[2] The prayers, on the other hand, are reduced to short passages almost negligible in the flow of narrative. A few times Josephus mentions the singing of hymns, but he does not indicate their content. In terms of prayers, he offers only five instances. The first one is uttered by Mattathias in close connection with his farewell speech. This prayer is not part of 1 Maccabees; the source simply reports that Mattathias blessed his sons (2:69). As I will attempt to show, this particular prayer is thematically the most important of all the prayers that are included in the paraphrase. That this prayer is introduced as an enhancement of the story has to do with its placement in close proximity to a speech. Instead of the prayer text 1 Maccabees 3:50–53, Josephus presents only an exhortation to supplication. The priestly prayer of 1 Maccabees 7:37–38, rich in content and in dramatic tension with its context, occurs in Josephus in a simpler form in order to harmonize with the plain style of his narrative: "They supplicated God to deliver them from their enemies." The two other passages, phrased in a similar vein, correspond to prayers in chapters 4 and 9 of 1 Maccabees, uttered by Judah and Jonathan respectively. Instead of the three prayers attributed to Judah in 1 Maccabees (4:10–11, 30–33, 7:41–42), Josephus has him utter only one, thus putting him on par with Jonathan, the lesser hero both in 1 Maccabees and in Josephus's version of the story. This discrepancy already suggests a literary devaluation of prayer in the Josephan narrative. Another example of this is Josephus's omission in 13.161 of the detail of Jonathan's rending his garments and praying (cf. 1 Macc. 11:71–72). Josephus prefers to use the literary form "speech" more than the form "prayer" as a vehicle of religious thought. In 1 Maccabees, the prayers carry more weight than the speeches as far as theological content is concerned. The purpose of this essay, then, is to study more closely how the Josephan speeches and prayers diverge from 1 Maccabees and also to determine what functions the prayers, reduced as they are, actually have in the Josephan narrative.

Before entering on a systematic study of the prayers, I will give attention to how Josephus lays out the story up to and including Mattathias's speech in *Ant.* 12.279–84. 1 Maccabees does not contain prayers technically speaking in this section. It does, however, employ prayer language.[3] The author introduces the story of the revolt by inserting a number of poetic texts,[4] to which prayers, cited later in the story, allude.[5] The observation of whether Josephus imitates the literary form of 1 Maccabees here, including its direct discourse, has a bearing on the form of prayers as they appear in the paraphrase.

The report on the Maccabean uprising in the *Antiquities* starts in 12.237. The beginning section, up to 240, focuses on the rivalry of the high priests. Here Josephus diverges from 1 Maccabees and seems to be informed by Jason of Cyrene or 2 Maccabees, or, even more likely, a source that used these works.[6] To start with Alexander the Great as does the report in 1 Maccabees is not an option for Josephus at this point.[7] in contrast to 1 Maccabees. At 240b, reflecting 1 Maccabees 1:11, Josephus makes full use of the book, although he does not indicate this. A formal introduction comes in 245, signaling that what follows is a detailed narrative differing from the summarized one (*kephalaiōdōs*) of the *Wars,* basically 1.31–40. This text does not concern us here, since prayers are not part of it.

A comparative study of the style of the two narratives up to Mattathias's appearance on the scene entails the following observations.[8] While Josephus avoids the poetic language of 1 Maccabees with its allusions to Psalms and Lamentations, he uses other means to depict the calamitous state of the people. The descriptive lament of 1 Maccabees 1:25–28 begins *kai egeneto penthos mega;* it is appropriately called *Themazeile* by Günther O. Neuhaus in his study of the poetic passages of 1 Maccabees.[9] Josephus gives respectful attention to this passage by saying *eis mega tous Ioudaious epi toutois penthos enebalen* (12.250). The dramatic importance is conveyed by the use of *hyperbaton,* a displacement of words forming a syntactical unit.[10] The Josephan expression, keeping the fairly vapid qualifier "great," illustrates Shaye Cohen's statement that Josephus retains some of the original's manner,[11] here probably in fidelity to a stereotyped expression.[12]

The partly prosaic,[13] partly poetic passage 1 Maccabees 1:36–40 comments on the establishment of the citadel with its mixed population of Syrian soldiers and renegade Jews. Josephus abandons the imagery of

1 Maccabees. The ominous threat that the presence of the citadel constitutes for the people is communicated instead by an anticipation of the calamities resulting from it: "at their hands the citizens were destined (*synebē*) to suffer many things" (12.252).

Mattathias's bewailing of the situation, which is in the form of direct speech in 1 Maccabees, appears in *Ant.* 12.267; but it is changed in an interesting way. The pointed cry of Mattathias, *hina ti hēmin eti zoē* (1 Macc. 2:13) has become indirect discourse, "and he said it was better for them to die for their country's laws than to live so ingloriously."[14] The verb *zaō*, "live," and the adverb *adoxōs* are immediate loans from 1 Maccabees. Again as in the case of *mega penthos* Josephus chooses a direct rendering of thematic key words. Mattathias's lament is introduced in a precise way by *apōdyreto*[15] ("bewailed") due to Josephus's desire, which we can see operating elsewhere, to classify the specific form of a text. The objects of lament are presented in nonaffective language, e.g., "the plundering of the city," for "the ruin of the holy city" of the source. So far, then, we have observed in the Josephan paraphrase of 1 Maccabees fidelity to formal features of the text, attentiveness to thematic highpoints, and a preference for indirect discourse. Also there is a difference in the modality of his language; it is neutrally descriptive and not emotive.

If Josephus changed the direct discourse of his source in this and other instances,[16] he has not done so for Mattathias's call to rebellion in 12.271: "Whoever is a devotee of our country's customs and the worship of God, let him follow me."[17] Here it could be that Josephus, as Grimm suggests for 1 Maccabees 2:27, alludes to appeals to Roman patriots in time of danger like the one reported by Livy: *Qui rempublicam salvam volunt me sequantur.*[18] At any rate, the cry *ei tis zēlōtēs*[19] has a dramatic effect on the story. It is worth noticing how carefully Josephus utilizes the quotation in his subsequent narrative: "Having said this, Mattathias with his sons set out into the wilderness and many others did the same" (12.271–72).

In 12.276–77, dealing with the issue of fighting on the Sabbath, Josephus again changes the direct discourse of his source to reported speech, properly classifying it as instruction (*edidasken*). Toward the end of the passage Josephus affirms that Mattathias has persuaded his companions. In 1 Maccabees the decision to fight on the Sabbath comes after careful deliberation (1 Macc. 2:40–41). The difference illustrates how Josephus presents the Maccabean leaders in a more distant position vis-à-vis the people.[20] This has repercussions for the form and content of the prayers, as we shall see.

It should not surprise us that the last discourse of Mattathias is quoted rather than reported. An illustrious person is expected to say something worthy of remembrance before he dies.[21] In biblical literature the deathbed speech of Jacob (Gen. 49:1–27), as well as the injunctions of Moses and Joshua to the people of Israel, has served as a model for the development

of the genre of testament, which was popular beginning in the second century B.C.E. One recalls the many versions of the *Testaments of the Twelve
Patriarchs*. This writing, an example of the genre labeled "ethical wills" by
Elias Bickerman, conveys a number of Greek ideas.[22] Josephus, in his shaping of the speech that covers 12.279–84, conforms widely to contemporary
genre conventions, while 1 Maccabees is closer to classical biblical patterns.[23] 1 Maccabees 2:49–71 is well integrated into the narrative, whereas
the Josephan text stands out as a speech in Greek historical literature. Of
the many deviations from the source, the most striking is the omission
of the catalogue of *exempla virtutis* from biblical history.[24] Mattathias in
1 Maccabees starts with a description of the lamentable state of affairs,
which reflects statements earlier in the story. Mattathias in the *Antiquities* opens the address in a genre-specific way: "I am about to go the
destined way."[25] The speech has a fairly consistent form. Explicitly, it is
exhortation *(parakalō/parainō)*, bequest *(paratithemai)*, and implicitly also
consolation *(paramythia)*, channelled through a series of affirmations of
God's faithfulness (12.281).[26] Of these constituents the testament feature is
the strongest.[27] In summation Mattathias gives voice to what is true about
God and human nature.[28] Concordant with the testament feature is the
hopeful tone, the "inner form" of the text according to the terminology of
René Wellek and Austin Warren.[29] The hope centers on "restoration." In
the threefold affirmation of God's faithfulness the proposition "God will
not forget you" is followed by "He will give the laws back to you," and
"He will restore liberty" *(eleutheria)*.[30] The last verb *apokatastēsei* (cf. Acts
1:6), "will restore," is emphasized because of its length[31] and because of its
position in the sentence.[32]

The importance Josephus gives to this speech is revealed in the narrative. The encomium on Judah Maccabee that ends the twelfth book alludes
to the farewell speech by acclaiming Judah "who freed [*eleutherōsas*] his
nation," having suffered for "the liberty of his fellow citizens," and Josephus adds: "mindful of the injunctions of his father" (12.433). Is complete
fulfillment achieved hereby? Or does the statement "God will restore" in
Mattathias's last discourse carry a tinge of eschatological hope? Joseph
Blenkinsopp denies that Josephus ever expressed an eschatological hope of
the restoration of Israel, but he qualifies the statement by saying that after
the fall of Jerusalem, Josephus "deemed it unwise to speak of an eschatological hope."[33] It is striking that Josephus goes beyond his source on this
issue. Mattathias's speech in 1 Maccabees lacks predictions of this kind.
Its statements about the future are bare commissions of the sons as leaders
(vv. 66–68).

Now, in close connection with the address, Mattathias utters the first
prayer of Josephus's account. This is, as we stated above, an addition by
Josephus to his source, which reports only that Mattathias blessed his sons.
The text of the prayer in 12.285 reads: "Having addressed his sons and

implored God to be their ally and to recover [*anasōsai*] for the people its own way of life once more, before long he died." The verb introducing the prayer, *euchomai*, is the most commonly used by Josephus and is the most comprehensive term for prayerful activity.[34] In 1 Maccabees, and in the New Testament, *proseuchomai* prevails over the simple verb. In Mattathias's petition, God is asked to be "their ally" (*symmachos*). This term is often used in military contexts by Greek historians. Dionysius of Halicarnassus uses it in a speech of encouragement addressed to Roman soldiers, saying, "You have for allies [*symmachous*] the gods who have always preserved our city."[35] The most interesting aspect of this prayer is not its terminology, however, but its connections with the farewell address. The fact that the prayer repeats the theme of restoration from the discourse makes the hope expressed therein into something more than a doctrinal statement. The contents of the speech get focused and intensified as its essential message is iterated in prayer form.[36] The ultimate situation of the speaker makes the truth value of his prayer uncontestable, and his utterance becomes a forceful legacy for generations to come, comparable to the intentional impact of *Nunc Dimittis* (Luke 2:29–32). Furthermore, by putting a speech and a prayer on Mattathias's lips, each of which focuses on the destiny of the nation, Josephus enhances the stature of Mattathias beyond the level of 1 Maccabees. The threefold anticipation of God's action lends prophetic features to the figure.[37]

As we look at the few prayers that Josephus has chosen to include in his narrative, we observe that all but one of them are uttered by the leader alone. The intrinsic communal quality of the prayers of the source is also attenuated. The communal prayer of 1 Maccabees 3:50–53 is reduced in *Ant.* 12.300 to a mere exhortation to make supplication (*hiketeuein*). In the prayers of combat, neither Judah nor Jonathan exhorts the soldiers to pray with them. That is the case in 1 Maccabees 4:10 (Judah) and 9:46 (Jonathan). The prayer in 4:30–33 is said by Judah alone, but the use of the term *laos* ("people") in the prayer itself makes it communal. The phrase "before us" in 7:42 does the same. The priests who address a prayer in 1 Maccabees 7:37–38 express a concern of *the people*. This priestly prayer figuring in *Ant.* 12.407 is the only one said by more than one person. As in the exhortation mentioned above, the prayer is presented as a "supplication." The prayer comprises a single accusative with an infinitive construction: "They supplicated God to deliver them from their enemies." In the same way that this prayer is reduced to a bare minimum, so are the two other passages of prayer, both of them introduced by *euxamenos*. The first, in 12.314, is a petition that God be an ally against the mass of enemies.[38] The prayer is part of a carefully rounded off episode ending in a statement about Judah who, by defeating the troops, became an object of fear for the enemy. This statement stresses the figure of Judah more than 1 Maccabees does. The setting of the prayer is similar to the context of the corresponding prayer in 1 Maccabees 4:30–33. At the sight of the massive advance of the enemy (same in both versions) Judah Maccabee fears (implicit in both versions), prays, and having engaged the enemy (same in both), vanquishes them (*nikā toutous*). The last verb, *nikaō*, is not taken from 1 Maccabees, which does not explicitly ascribe victory to Judah. The speech in 3:19 sets a horizon of understanding: "It is not on the size of the army that victory in battle depends, but strength comes from heaven" (NRSV). 2 Maccabees, in a similar way, is circumspect and reverential in talking about victory. However, a petition that God grant victory is included in the second prayer, which is uttered by Jonathan, in *Ant.* 13.13. The providential aspect of victory is thus not absent,[39] but it is comprised in a pattern of correspondence between divine and human action, such as we find on a more general level in the first book of the *Antiquities* (23): "our legislator...having shown that God possesses the very perfection of virtue, thought that human beings should strive to participate in it."

Like the author of 1 Maccabees, Josephus also reports hymns. *Ant.* 12.312 is the first example. After having put Gorgias's army to flight, Judah returned (so also in 1 Maccabees) "rejoicing and praising God for the victories." The corresponding passage in 1 Maccabees 4:24 contains a familiar refrain used in Psalms 117 (118) and 135 (136). The hymn is followed by a concluding phrase indicating, somewhat obliquely, the motivation for the hymn: "And there was a great deliverance in Israel on that day" (1 Macc. 4:25). This statement echoes the victory narratives of ancient times as they appear in 1 and 2 Kings.[40] Thus the author evaluates an event theologically by the use of salvation history. This perspective has obvious political connotations, indicating that the Maccabees and, later, the Hasmoneans, whom the author of 1 Maccabees serves, were national saviors comparable to Israel's earlier kings. Josephus also gives an evaluation from a particular perspective; he thinks of himself as a historian. Strengthening the logic of his source, Josephus concludes: "For this victory contributed not a little to the regaining of their liberty" (12.312). Josephus here instructs his readers as he did by foreshadowing in 12.252: "at their hands the citizens were destined to suffer many things." He wants his audience to envision history as a process; furthermore, he reveals his preoccupation with the question of causation in history.[41]

The two narratives concur stylistically in the double rendering of hymnsinging, probably sharing a liturgical tradition.[42] 1 Maccabees has *hymnoun kai eulogoun* or similar words throughout the book; Josephus uses two equivalents in his three reports of praising: 12.312, 323, and 349. An interesting difference is that in two cases, 12.312 and 12.323, Josephus says, adding to his source, that Judah Maccabee "rejoiced." Similarly, in 12.349, the festival assembly expresses itself in merrymaking, *paidias agontes.*[43] The linking of "joy" to the hymnsinging certainly enhances the atmosphere of the occasion and would assure a Greek audience that real celebration took place.[44] The singing of hymns in *Ant.* 12.349 constitutes the only example of communal singing. The proportions in 1 Maccabees are reversed.

Conclusion

In comparison to 1 Maccabees, the prayers of *Antiquities* 12 and 13 are strongly reduced. In syntactical terms, they all contain one single accusative with an infinitive construction, apart from Mattathias's prayer, which includes two such constructions. The prayers, short and plain as they are, do not contribute much to the story as a whole. Mattathias's prayer does have a distinctive thematic role; but that is only because it is closely related to the preceding speech. The other passages do not add to the story; rather they underscore what is already there. In their relation to the narrative, all prayers are what I call "demonstrational." The prayers of combat demonstrate the forces operating in the story, e.g., victory over an overwhelmingly strong enemy. Similarly, in Mattathias's prayer, the leader's very last words reveal the motivational force behind the uprising, trust in God as *symmachos,* and hope of the restoration of ancestral customs and worship. What the prayers do, then, is that they evidence in a clear and convincing way God's actions in history; this message is enhanced by their close link to the narration of events. This univocal function of the combat prayers gets broadened somewhat if they are seen together with speeches such as the exhortation to combat in 12.290–91. This discourse stresses the importance of "worshipful reverence" (*eusebeia*) for overcoming the enemy. For Josephus, the piety of the Maccabees is part of the plotting of the story.[45] The very fact that they pray and sing hymns is therefore important.

A basic difference between 1 Maccabees and its paraphrase in the *Antiquities* is of a "representational" nature, to use the terminology of Alastair Fowler.[46] Josephus's story is more strictly narrative than 1 Maccabees, since this writing has a distinctive dramatic aspect in addition to its narrative dimension. The narration in 1 Maccabees is interspaced with poetry, speeches, and prayers. The resulting effect is not only enhancement of dramatic tension, but also increased involvement of the reader, particularly because of the communal character of these texts. Josephus, on the other hand, writes a rather straightforward and flowing prose, and he avoids interruption, as Shaye Cohen has stated.[47] As clarified earlier, Josephus prefers indirect discourse and as such prayers emerge parenthetically in the narrative. Most prayers, which are rendered in an infinitive construction, are introduced by the participle *euxamenos*. This participle appears in the context of governing verbs such as *niką* ("defeated"), *synaptei* ("joined battle"), or, in the case of Mattathias, *teleutą* ("died"). Speeches are another matter; they belong intrinsically to the genre of historical narrative. It is essentially through them that Josephus conveys his religious convictions. Furthermore, wishing to present a story of universal impact, Josephus shuns allusive language.[48] Prayer, as literary expression, distinguishes itself precisely by being rich in allusions or unspoken presuppositions such as *mythos,* broadly defined.[49] Josephus writes about fairly recent events,[50] in which *mythos* is not appropriate; a typical topic for *mythos* would be the origins of a people or the destiny of humankind or the why of human behavior.[51] Josephus therefore is cautious with prayer, conscious that, for an audience eager to know the facts of events,[52] persuasion remains with plain words and that the power of exposition derives from simplicity of narrative structure.[53] The different nature of his prayers in *Ant.* 12 and 13 is thus best explained by reference to the historian's concern about norms of literature and by his desire to convince his readers about the truth value of the events through simple narration illuminated by appropriate speeches.

However, another reason, other than literary convention, probably explains more fundamentally why Josephus is cautious with prayer in his version of the story. I would suggest that a difference in the understanding of history has repercussions for the nature of the prayers in the two works. For the author of 1 Maccabees, the paradigmatic nature of the story depends on its relation to the past and therefore is of relevance for those who keep the memory of this past alive. For Josephus, the paradigmatic quality of the events relates to the future and is of universal import. The progressing development of history seems to be more important for him than its momentary events. We noted the address to his audience in *Ant.* 12.312: "For this victory contributed not a little to the regaining of their liberty." By contrast, for the author of 1 Maccabees, the individual events are significant in their echoing the past. The biblically phrased remark in 1 Maccabees 4:25 (quoted above) illustrates this: "And there was a great deliverance in Israel on that day." Prayers can more easily serve a historical perspective that emphasizes the particularity of events than it can a view that stresses history as process; thus Josephus is sparing of prayer in his paraphrase of 1 Maccabees. It is by comments in the narrative and by inserted speeches that Josephus illuminates the nature of history. The prayers, well integrated into the flow of narrative, converge to affirm that, in the development of history, *God is acting.*

The scarcity of prayers in Josephus's version of 1 Maccabees has also to be viewed in relation to the apologetic aim of the *Antiquities.* Interpreters of Josephus have seen the intention of *Antiquities* as being to defend Judaism and the Jewish people and to argue on behalf of their cause.[54] Prayers do not easily serve as tools of argumentation, particularly not in the case of the *Antiquities.* The expected readership of the *Antiquities* was Josephus's own compatriots but also the Greek-speaking Orientals.[55] Per Bilde observes how Josephus's apologetic interests make his paraphrase topical,[56] another literary feature that can be said to work against an extensive use of prayers. Prayers do not deal with topics, but speeches do. Precisely these two considerations, however, make it easier to understand the significance of the prayer of Mattathias, without counterpart in Josephus's source. It continues the theme of the preceding speech, thus being of a topical nature. Furthermore, while Mattathias's prayer in *Ant.* 12.285 might be a vehicle for Josephus's own eschatological hope, as I have suggested above, it can certainly be understood as an apologetic plea: "to recover for the people its own way of life once more."

Notes

1. H. Drüner, *Untersuchungen über Josephus* (Marburg: J. Hamel, 1896), 35–50. See also C. L. W. Grimm, *Das erste Buch der Maccabäer,* in Fritzsche-Grimm, *Kurzgefasstes exegetisches Handbuch zu den Apokryphen des Alten Testaments* (Leipzig: S. Hirzel, 1853), 3:xxviii–xxx.

2. S. J. D. Cohen, *Josephus in Galilee and Rome: His Vita and Development as Historian* (Leiden: E. J. Brill, 1979), 46.

3. By "prayer language" I mean sets of formulaic and poetic expressions and particular thought patterns typical of prayers; cf. A. Fowler, *Kinds of Literature: An Introduction to the Theory of Genres and Modes* (Cambridge, Mass.: Harvard University Press, 1982): "certain lyric kinds have affinities with prayer" (8).

4. See G. W. Neuhaus, *Studien zu den poetischen Stücken im 1.Makkabäerbuch* (Würzburg: Echter Verlag, 1974).

5. A. Enermalm-Ogawa, *Un langage de prière juif en grec: Le témoignage des deux premiers livres des Maccabées* (Stockholm: Almqvist & Wiksell International, 1987), 17 and 23–34.

6. B. Niese, "Kritik der beiden Makkabäerbücher nebst Beiträgen zur Geschichte der makkabäischen Erhebung," *Hermes* 35 (1900), 518–19.

7. *Ant.* 12.1–3 relates Alexander's death and the strife between his successors. Cf. A. Pelletier, *Flavius Josephe adapteur de la Lettre d'Artistée: Une réaction atticisante contre la Koinè* (Paris: Librairie C. Klincksieck, 1962): "Il s'applique, en effet, a insérer la *Paraphrase* sans nuire a l'unité ni a la continuité de son ouvrage tout entier" (251).

8. N. Martola, *Capture and Liberation* (Åbo: Åbo Akademi, 1984), 41, pertinently classifies the poetic passages in the part of 1 Maccabees as description rather than narration: "A description is more picture-oriented than a narrative. When the narrative reaches a description, the reporting of the continuous series of events stops, and the author turns to painting something for the readers in a more graphic way."

9. Neuhaus, *Studien,* 122.

10. H. W. Smyth, *Greek Grammar* (Cambridge, Mass.: Harvard University Press, 1984), par. 3028: "even in prose it is frequent, especially when it secures emphasis on an important idea by placing it at the beginning or end of a sentence." That Josephus pays attention to the locutionary force of his text can be

illustrated by another example: in 1 Maccabees 1:21–24 *hyperēphania* demarcates the episode, in *Ant.* 12.246 and 247 the neutral *hypostrephō* functions the same way.

11. Cohen, *Josephus,* 45.

12. Neuhaus, *Studien,* 79, "geprägte Wendung." Josephus repeats it in 12.285.

13. Martola, *Capture,* 42–43.

14. L. H. Feldman, "Flavius Josephus Revisited: The Man, His Writings and His Significance," *ANRW* II, 21:2, 807 observes that Josephus has emphasized the ideal of martyrdom over 1 Maccabees.

15. The verb is used, e.g., by the tragedians, LSJ; in the LXX the only occurrence is in 3 Maccabees (Hatch-Redpath).

16. Cf. E. J. Bickermann, "Makkabäerbücher (I. und II.)," in PW 14, col. 791, speaking about the style of 1 Maccabees: "Den hebräischen Stil gemäss werden Gedanken und Reden in *oratio recta* mitgeteilt." Illustrative examples: 1 Maccabees 1:11 vs. *Ant.* 12.240b and 1 Maccabees 2:17–18 vs. *Ant.* 12.268. The inserted *phēsin* in 271 does not change the form of discourse, Kühner-Gerth, *Ausführliche Grammatik der Griechischen Sprache* (Hannover and Leipzig: Hansche Buchhandlung, 1904), 2:2, par. 548.3.

17. *Ant.* 12.271 has *ethē,* 1 Maccabees 2:27 has *nomos.* After *ho zēlōn tǭ nomǭ* 1 Maccabees 2:27 has *histōn diathēkēn;* Josephus ignores *diathēkē* as a religious term. A. Jaubert, *La notion d'Alliance dans le judaisme aux abords de l'ère chrétienne* (Paris: Editions du Seuil, 1963), 347 sees precisely in *thrēskeia* ("worship") a Josephan approximate to "covenant."

18. Grimm, *Maccabäer, ad loc.,* referring to Livy XII, 53.

19. Greek *zēlōtēs,* the key term of the call, means devotee in this context. The other occurrences of the noun in the *Antiquities* has "customs," as here, or "practices" as modifiers. The verb *zēloō* is never employed to characterize the activities of the Maccabees, contrasting sharply with 1 Maccabees. The disastrous role of the Zealots in the rebellion of 66–73/74 c.e. is the cause of this omission, O. Betz, "Miracles in the Writings of Flavius Josephus," *Josephus, Judaism, and Christianity* (ed. L. H. Feldman and G. Hata; Detroit: Wayne State University Press, 1987), 219–20.

20. See also *Ant.* 12.332 and compare 1 Maccabees 5:17.

21. E. Stauffer, "Abschiedsreden," *RAC* I, col. 29.

22. E. J. Bickerman, *The Jews in the Greek Age* (Cambridge, Mass.: Harvard University Press, 1988), 204–10.

23. Grimm, *Maccabäer, ad* 1 Maccabees 2:49 refers to Genesis 42:29 and 1 Kings 2:1.

24. It is not that Josephus totally avoids surveys of history. There is one of impressive length in *Wars* 5.379–412, in which Josephus evokes God's deeds in history dissuading his fellows from continuing their fight against the Romans.

25. See *TReu* 1.3: *egō apothnēisko kai poreuomai hodon paterōn mou* (edition de Jonge 1978) and *Ant.* 4.315 (Moses) and, from Graeco-Roman literature, Dio Chrysostom *Disc* 30.9 (Loeb): *tēn teleutēn horōn* (Charidemus); to "depart" is a recurrent motif in this speech.

26. Dio Chrys. *Disc.* 30.26–44 contains *paramythia* in form of a *mythos.* In the passage that immediately follows the discourse (45) Dio himself makes some

remarks about the difficulty of consoling, thereby underscoring this particular feature of the speech.

27. See 12.179, *paratithemai,* and 12.281, *paidas ontas emous emmeinai.*

28. Charidemus in Dio Chrys. 30.14, like Mattathias in *Ant.* 12.282, evokes the fragility of the human being.

29. Wellek and Warren, *Theory of Literature* (San Diego: Harcourt Brace Jovanovich, 1977), 231, suggest as "inner form": "attitude, tone, purpose."

30. For the significance of the term *eleutheria,* see W. Farmer, *Maccabees, Zealots, and Josephus* (New York: Columbia University Press, 1956), 13–14.

31. Pelletier, *Adapteur,* 237; Josephus tends to place compounds with *tithēmi* at the end of a sentence for rhythmical reasons.

32. The verb as the last element of the sentence is stressed, since it is placed as far away as possible from its object, J. Humbert, *Syntaxe,* par. 147.

33. J. Blenkinsopp, "Prophecy and Priesthood in Josephus," *JJS* 25 (1974), 262.

34. A. Schlatter, *Wie sprach Josephus vom Gott?* (Gütersloh: C. Bertelsmann, 1910), 73, and A. Corlu, *Recherches sur les mots relatifs a l'idée de prière, d'Homère aux Tragiques* (Paris: Librairie C. Klincksieck, 1966), 84–118.

35. Dionysius of Halicarnassus, *Ant. Rom. IV* 6.3 (Loeb).

36. O. Plöger, "Reden und Gebete im deuteronomistischen und chronistischen Geschichtswerk," *Festschrift G. Dehn* (Neukirchen-Vluyn: Verlag der Buchhandlung des Erziehungsvereins, 1957), 46–47: "In einer predigtähnlichen Ansprache kann man gewiss bekennen und zu erkennen geben was man glaubt; eindringlicher aber lässt es sich im Gebete sagen, wenn man um die Verwirklichung dessen bittet, was man glaubt und bekennt."

37. Blenkinsopp, *JJS* 25 (1974), 250 suggests that the Maccabean resistance was thought to be prophetically inspired. Mattathias is not called *prophētēs* though, since Josephus reserves that designation for the canonical prophets (p. 240). On this topic, see also Feldman, "Prophets and Prophecy in Josephus," *JTS* 41 (1990), 386–422.

38. Niese reads *ep'autǭ genesthai.* The variant *ep'auton esesthai* is relegated to the apparatus. One expects the accusative case here. Naber emends to *auto* referring immediately to *plēthos (polemiōn),* a reading that seems to commend itself.

39. See Betz in *Josephus,* 212–13.

40. Grimm, *Maccabäer, ad loc.,* struggles with the inexactness of "that day" and explains it as "unbewusstes Verherrlichungsinteresse"; rather, it is a biblicism. See J. A. Goldstein, *1 Maccabees* (Anchor Bible; New York: Doubleday, 1976), *ad loc.*

41. H. W. Attridge, *The Interpretation of Biblical History in the Antiquitates Judaicae of Flavius Josephus* (Missoula, Mont.: Scholars Press, 1976), 43, compares Josephus with Dionysius of Halicarnassus; the quotation from *Ant. Rom.* 1.8.2. illuminates the retrospective of *Ant.* 12.312 and the foreshadowing of 12.252: [wars] "showing from what cause they sprang and ... by what arguments they were brought to an end"; for Josephus's account of causation, see also Attridge, *Interpretation,* 154, note 2.

42. Instances are in Daniel 3:51, etc., and in Sirach 39:35, 47:8 and 51:11.

43. Admittedly the source of *Ant.* 12.349; 1 Maccabees 5:54, has "they went up

with joy and gladness," but the cultic action in this instance consists in offering of burnt offerings, not singing of hymns.

44. Cf. W. Burkert, *Greek Religion* (Cambridge, Mass.: Harvard University Press, 1985), 103: "the hymn must always delight the god afresh at the festival."

45. Cf. the emphasis on the inspiring virtues of the ancient Romans in the work of Dionysius of Halicarnassus, pointed out by Attridge, *Interpretation*, 161. A passage in *Ant. Rom.* VI.6.2 (Loeb) is of particular interest. Postumius assures his soldiers that the gods have promised to grant victory by way of "rewarding us for the piety we have shown [*sebontes*] towards them." Some of Josephus's readers might have understood the *eusebeia* of the Maccabean heroes in the same way. On the role of piety in the Josephan paraphrase of 1 Maccabees, see I. Gafni, "On the use of 1 Maccabees by Josephus Flavius," *Zion* 45 (1980), 86.

46. For the terminology, see Fowler, *Kinds*, 60.

47. Cohen, *Josephus*, 46.

48. D. Daube, "Typology in Josephus," *JJS* 31 (1980), 21–25, illustrates how allusions to the past demand a shared universe of discourse.

49. V. Langholf, *Die Gebete bei Euripides und die zeitliche Folge der Tragödien* (Göttingen: Vandenhoeck & Ruprecht, 1971), 6: "Von den anderen dramatischen Ausdrucksmitteln... unterscheidet sich das Gebet dadurch dass es an unausgesprochenen Voraussetzungen viel reicher ist: diese Voraussetzungen bieten der Mythos, der Kult, der Volksglaube, die persönlichen Einstellungen."

50. See T. Rajak, "Josephus and the 'Archeology' of the Jews," *JJS* 33 (1982), 465; the author distinguishes between the biblical part of the *Antiquities,* undeniably "archeology," and the largely political history in the second half of the work.

51. I have taken "myth" in a fairly broad sense, following Wellek and Warren, *Theory of Literature,* who, referring to E. Cassirer, S. H. Hooke, and others contend: "But in a wider sense myth comes to mean any anonymously composed story telling of origins and destinies: the explanations society offers its young of why the world is and why we do as we do, its pedagogic images of the nature and destiny of man" (191).

52. The historian's patron is presented in *Ant.* 1.8 as *chairōn empeiriais pragmatōn.*

53. Demetrius, *On Style* I, 19 (Loeb) links simplicity with the historical/narrative period.

54. E.g., P. Bilde, *Flavius Josephus between Jerusalem and Rome: His Life, His Works and Their Importance* (Sheffield: Sheffield Academic Press 1988), 98–101, and Attridge, *Interpretation,* 52–54; see also Rajak, *Josephus: The Historian and His Society* (Philadelphia: Fortress Press, 1984), 225; she is concerned with apologetics particularly in the second half of the *Antiquities.*

55. Rajak, *Josephus.*

56. Bilde, *Flavius Josephus,* 98.

· 7 ·

PRAYER RENDERED FOR CAESAR?
1 Clement 59.3–61.3

Barbara E. Bowe

The long prayer text that concludes the letter from Rome to Corinth, commonly known as 1 Clement, offers us a unique glimpse of early Christian prayer. The author of this letter, writing probably near the end of the first century, was surely steeped in Jewish tradition. The prayer text, in particular, weaves together a veritable pastiche of LXX phrases richly colored by the Jewish prayer tradition that was especially formative in the growth of the Roman church. Some even claim that 1 Clement incorporates fragments from the Roman liturgy in use in Clement's day, but this claim finds no certain proof.[1] The entire letter, however, and the prayer text we shall examine, surely reflects, if not actual liturgical texts, at least the style and form of prayer that would have been common among Clement's community, and for that reason it is especially important for our study.

Recently James Jeffers has investigated the social composition of this Roman community.[2] He argues that "the congregation behind 1 Clement was composed largely of imperial freedmen and slaves who formed a "social elite" among the Roman churches."[3] He contends further that this congregation had embraced fully the ideology of imperial Rome and had "found in [its] positive view of Roman institutions the basis for restructuring the congregation as a hierarchy."[4] Elsewhere I have taken a more moderate stance and have suggested, on the contrary, that 1 Clement reflects a continued and important dialectical tension between hierarchical and nonhierarchical patterns of communal organization and self-understanding.[5] These questions concerning the social make-up of Clement's community and how its social composition influenced its overall theology will necessarily inform our analysis of the prayer, but space prevents a thorough discussion of these matters.

This essay will examine instead the meaning and function of the long prayer text that concludes the letter from Rome to Corinth. One section in particular will serve as the primary focus: 1 Clem. 60.2–61.3, a section that contains a series of petitions for the "rulers and governors upon the earth" (60.4). How then should we understand this "prayer rendered for Caesar"?

Clement's Prayer in Context

Comparisons of 1 Clement with the Pauline letter corpus show that expressions of prayer, in the form of benedictions, petitions, and doxologies, were a typical feature in Paul's letters. To be sure, Paul adopted but modified standard epistolary forms from both Jewish and Hellenistic models. Not only did he regularly begin his letters with a prayer of thanksgiving, he often brought his remarks to a close with similar expressions of prayer using the same formulaic liturgical language. Commenting on this Pauline convention, John White has concluded that "the closing statement, at least, in Paul's letter body is expressed customarily as a prayer with eschatological peace as its subject."[6] And Helmut Koester[7] noted long ago that the eschatological emphasis at the end of Paul's letters (e.g., 1 Thess. 4:13–5:11) marked a Pauline innovation that thereafter "became the most distinctive mark of the new genre."[8] These observations will be especially important in considering the prayer text of 1 Clement.

The author of 1 Clement knew and used the Pauline letter tradition. In 47.1 he makes conscious reference to 1 Corinthians and employs several key themes from this letter elsewhere in his own: for example, in his use of the body metaphor in 37.5 and 46.7 and in the hymn to love in 49.1–6. Apart from 1 Corinthians, Clement also shows familiarity with Philippians, for example, in his emphasis throughout on the virtue of tapeinophrosynē, a term so important in Philippians 2. He is familiar also with Romans, again in his use of the body metaphor in 1 Clem. 46.7 and elsewhere. We can assume, therefore, that the author of 1 Clement knew and imitated the Pauline letter form and employed its conventions in a self-conscious way.[9]

As Paul had frequently done, Clement too brings his letter to a close with a prayer. The prayer in 1 Clement, however, is much longer than any of its Pauline or post-Pauline models. This prayer forms part of the letter's elaborate concluding section, which employs in tandem all the typical elements associated with the letter body-closing as outlined, for example, in the studies by John White. These elements White defined as the "disclosure-motivation for writing formulae, responsibility statements, polite requests for a letter, formulaic references to a coming visit, and conditional clauses employed formulaically as a threat."[10] Within the larger closing section of 1 Clem. 58.2–65.2 we find four separate doxologies (58.2, 61.3, 64.1, and 65.2), two blessings (64.1, 65.2), and the long prayer of praise and petition that we will turn to in a moment.

The immediate context of the prayer is a solemn warning to the Corinthians in 59.1 that if they fail to comply with the contents of the letter's exhortation they will risk eternal damnation. This eschatological focus marks the letter throughout but is especially emphasized in the concluding section and prayer. "Safeguarding the number of the elect" (2.4; 58.2; 59.2) is presented as the theological motive and objective for Clement's exhortations.[11] The discord in Corinth, triggered by the deposition of some presbyters, in Clement's view, threatens to jeopardize this "number" and to bring ruin on the church at large. From the perspective of the author, then, the stakes are very high indeed. I don't mean to suggest that Clement's eschatological perspective was as immediate as Paul's, but I do want to argue that his consciousness of the coming end time and the ethical imperative for Christian life in the interim remains strong.[12]

Following the long prayer is a general summary of the letter's contents combining a disclosure formula (62.1 — "We have not written to you, beloved brethren, sufficiently touching the things which befit our worship and are most helpful for a virtuous life...") and an expression of confidence in the addressees (62.3 — "...we knew quite well that we were writing to those who were faithful and distinguished and had studied the oracles of the teaching of God"). These conventions serve to strengthen the letter's entreaty by reminding the Corinthians of the common heritage they share with Christians everywhere and by praising them as faithful "Scripture scholars" able to interpret the many scriptural examples of faithful obedience cited within the letter. Stanley Olson concludes that these "confidence expressions," "whatever the emotion behind the expression, ... function ... to undergird the letter's requests or admonitions by creating a sense of obligation through praise."[13]

Before bringing the letter to its final close, Clement reminds the Corinthians of their solemn responsibility to end the strife and division (*1 Clem.* 63.1). He appeals to the authority of the Spirit (63.2) and the weight of tradition and reiterates the intention of the letter: "...that you may know that our whole care has been and is directed to your speedy attainment of peace" (63.4). The final note sounded is a double liturgical blessing and doxology, the two parts of which encircle an appeal to Corinth to send back the Roman couriers with a favorable report that peace has been restored.

Such an elaborate conclusion places extraordinary weight on the final chapters of this letter. Central to this entire section is the lengthy prayer in 59.3–61.2. Our understanding of the function of this prayer in *1 Clement* has been helped by G. B. Caird's analysis of the function of prayer language in general in the New Testament.[14] He includes prayer in the category of "cohesive language" whose function it is to "establish rapport, to create a sense of mutual trust and common ethos."[15] All forms of worship, especially the more stylized forms, have this group binding function. A call to prayer is frequently an overt invitation to the audience to identify with the speaker [or writer] and with the beliefs that they share in common. This is especially true in the doxologies where the "Amen" response invites the audience to affirm with conviction their common assent. The repeated use of this kind of cohesive language forms a major part of the rhetorical strategy of *1 Clement*. There are eleven separate doxologies scattered through the letter, the final three in the important closing chapters. The prayer that we now turn to is an integral part of this rhetorical strategy.

Form and Structure in *1 Clement* 59.3–61.4

The formal opening of the prayer has been, and remains, a puzzle for interpreters. The text of 59.2 promises that the Roman community:

> ... will pray with eager entreaty and supplication that the Creator of the Universe may guard unhurt the number of his elect that has been numbered in all the world through his beloved Servant Jesus Christ, through whom he called us from darkness to light, from ignorance to the full knowledge of the glory of his name.

The next sentence then begins with the infinitive *elpizein*, "...to hope in your name...." The infinitive *could* be understood to continue the thought of the previous line — "...[God] called us...to hope..." — but the awkward transition from third-person description to second-person address remains puzzling: "...the glory of *his* name" and "...to hope in *your* name."[16] Faced with this anacoluthon, Lightfoot supplied an imperative petition and vocative address: *"Dos hēmin, kyrie,...elpizein...."* (Grant us, Lord, to hope...),[17] but few commentators thereafter have followed his lead.[18] Nor am I convinced that Lightfoot's solution was correct. The suggestion of Grant and Graham seems to me to explain better the integral function of prayer language in *1 Clement*. They maintain that the author unconsciously and almost imperceptibly passes from a reference to the promise of prayer in the future to the actual prayer itself.[19] The catchword — *onoma* — triggers this move. And so, the very nature of the anacoluthon at this point in the letter is significant. It suggests that there is, in the mind of the author, an intimate connection between his description of a future prayer that will call upon God "to safeguard the number of the elect" and the actual words of the prayer that follows. The eschatological consciousness discussed above, therefore, seems to color the entire prayer. The influence of LXX language on almost every phrase of this prayer has been ably demonstrated in the commentaries of Lightfoot and Knopf.[20] Certainly the author uses stock phrases and liturgical formulae, but the structure and composition of the prayer, especially given its length and complexity and the way in which it summarizes the contents of the entire letter, must come from the hand of the author himself.

The general structure throughout the prayer alternates both petitions to God and ascriptions of praise for all the many works and attributes of God.[21] We can easily see this pattern by looking briefly at the alteration of imperative and descriptive forms in the prayer.

59.3a   Praise — "You *alone*"

59.3b   Ascriptions of God's antithetical acts
         "You *alone*"

59.3c   Ascriptions of God's care
         — ending with: Jesus Christ as Servant
                    People as the Elect of God

59.4   Petitions for Salvation
         — ending with: "You *alone*"
                    Jesus Christ as Servant
                    People as Elect of God

60.1a   Ascription of God's work of creation and marvelous virtues

60.1b   Petition for forgiveness

60.2   Petition for forgiveness and cleansing

60.3   Petition for salvation

60.4   Petition for concord, peace, obedience

61.1a   Ascription of God's gifts to rulers

61.1b   Petition for the rulers

61.2a   Ascription of God's gifts to rulers

61.2b   Petition for the rulers

61.3   Final prayer of praise and Doxology
         "You *alone*"
         Jesus Christ as High Priest and Protector

Several key phrases are repeated in the prayer that signal special emphasis. The fourfold repetition of *monos* (in 59.3 [2x]; 59.4; 63.1) underscores the ultimate sovereignty of God above all others. In a similar fashion, the alternate repetitions of the vocative address to God throughout the prayer — *kyrie* and *despota* — leave no doubt about the author's reverence and submission toward the sovereign God.[22] Underlying the whole prayer, and in keeping with the theme of "safeguarding the number of the elect," are repeated references to the elect status of those who join in this prayer: 59.3c, 59.4, and 60.4. We assume, furthermore, that like Paul's letters, this letter, too, would have been read in the Christian liturgical assembly. Given the divisive nature of the Corinthian situation presupposed by Clement, it would have offered a powerful theological reminder of the essential unity all shared in the Elect of God.

Space does not permit a detailed form-critical analysis of the entire prayer, but some general observations concerning the form and style of the prayer will help, I think, to elucidate its function in the letter. The opening section in 59.3 sets the overall tone of the prayer. It is a prayer for knowledge of the Sovereign God. The cumulative effect of the long string of parallel participial phrases in this opening section is to stress the universal power of God over all creation. Antithetical ascriptions reinforce this universal emphasis and demonstrate that *nothing* escapes God's sovereignty. These antitheses conclude with the simple statement: "You alone are the benefactor of spirits and the God of all flesh." God alone, is the *euergetēs*.[23] The opening section then concludes with a resumptive participle followed by another declarative statement: "from [all the nations] you have chosen those who love you through Jesus Christ." Christians were not only chosen, but "taught, sanctified, given honor." These affirmations — about God and about God's elect people — become the basis for the petitions that follow.

The first petition in 59.4 calls upon God to be *Boēthos kai antilēptōr*,[24] helper and defender. These of course are terms familiar from the psalms, for example, in LXX Psalms 17:3; 58:17; 118:114. This general petition is then specified, again with a long list of syntactically parallel imperative phrases: "Save..., have mercy..., raise up..., etc. Two points should be especially noted in this section. First, there is a marked emphasis on the fact that the prayer is meant to speak with the "voice" of all the elect people, shown in the threefold repetition of the pronoun *hēmōn* and the double mention of *laos sou*. Second, the concluding statement in 59.4 shows that God's saving actions on behalf of the Elect are meant to prove to the nations the sovereignty of God. That is, they serve an apologetic function and become the means of conversion for the nations. Therefore, the emphasis thus far in the prayer seems to highlight the unique status of Christians as the elect of God within the world and their mission to be agents of conversion for "the nations."

This same universal emphasis continues in the next section, 60.1, with ascriptions to God of absolute sovereignty over all creation followed by a concluding petition for forgiveness: "Forgive us our lawlessness...." The petitions for forgiveness continue in 60.2: "Do not reckon every sin..., but cleanse us..., and direct our steps to walk in holiness...and to do things good and pleasing before you...." Drawing especially on familiar language from Deuteronomy (Deut. 6:18; 12:28; 13:18; 21:9), the prayer begs God to fashion the community in accord with the divine will. At this point, however, Clement adds the phrase: "...and before our rulers." With this addition, the attention of the prayer turns to the challenge of Christian existence within the Roman world.

Prayer Rendered for Caesar? *1 Clement* 60.2–61.2

This brings us to the main focus of the essay: "prayer rendered for Caesar?" To facilitate the discussion of this section of the prayer, I have reproduced (with some modifications) the stanza divisions of S. Légasse from a recent article that studied the "Jewish antecedents" for the prayer.[25] I'll begin, therefore, with a brief summary of this tradition history. Going back to the time of the Exile, Diaspora Jews saw their fortunes tied to those of secular society. In this context, the prophet Jeremiah (29:4–9) announced the oracle of YHWH in his letter to the Jewish exiles: "...seek the welfare [shalom] of the city to which I have exiled you: pray for it to YHWH, for in its welfare you will have welfare." Baruch 1:10–13 goes even further by advising: "pray for the life of Nebuchadnezzar the king of Babylon, and for the life of Belshazzar his son, that their days on earth may be like the days of heaven. And the Lord will give us strength, and will give light to our eyes and we shall live under the protection of Nebudchadnezzar king of Babylon." During the Persian period, 3 Ezra 6:31 refers to the practice, perhaps originated by Darius himself, of Jews offering in the Temple "libations to the Most High God for the King and his children and prayers offered for his life."[26] In the Greco-Roman period, the Temple prayers for the rulers became the Jewish substitute for the cultic practices of the ruler cult.

Jews, as well as Christians, acknowledged that God gave authority to human beings. In Daniel 2:37, Daniel addressed the king with these words: "You, O King, the king of kings, to whom the God of heaven has given the kingdom, the power, and the might, and the glory." Again, admonishing rulers who misuse their power, Wisdom 6:3 nevertheless acknowledges "for your dominion was given you from the Lord, and your sovereignty from the Most High." Christian texts likewise reflect this belief. John 19:11 affirms that Pilate's power (*exousia*) is "given from above"; Matthew 9:8 refers to God's authority (*exousia*) given to human beings, and all three synoptics record the saying of Jesus to "render to Caesar the things that are Caesar's" (Mark 12:17 = Matt. 22:21, Luke 20:25).

Christian accommodation to civil authority finds expression also in the difficult Pauline text in Romans 13:1–7, which encourages submission to the governing authorities since, as Paul says, their authority comes "from God."[27] Later NT writings encourage submission for more apologetic and utilitarian ends — "to silence the ignorance of the foolish" (1 Pet. 2:13–17). Whereas 1 Peter (2:17) exhorts Christians to "honor the emperor," 1 Timothy 2:1–3 urges "that supplications, prayers, intercessions,

and thanksgivings be made for all, for kings and all who are in high posi-
tions, that we may lead a quiet and peaceable life, godly and respectful in
every way." In a similar fashion, Titus 3:1–2 calls for submissiveness "to
rulers and authorities" and Polycarp *Letter to the Philippians* 12:3 (a text
that postdates *1 Clement*) reminds Christians to "Pray also for the Emperors, and for potentates, and princes." To this he adds the reminder to
pray for those who "persecute and hate you." And in the apologists of the
second century, this theme becomes dominant.[28]

From this brief survey we can conclude that the author of *1 Clement*
found in the Jewish and Christian tradition ample precedent for both the
ascription of God-given power to human agents and the appropriateness,
and even necessity, of prayer offered on their behalf. The motivation for
such prayer was mixed, however, and included a strong element of self-
interest and utilitarian ends. In the text cited, there is little comment or
critique of corrupt rulers and the need to "resist" such evil power. Despite
the threat of persecution, Christians in general (here the Book of Revelation is the striking exception) regarded it as their duty to cooperate with
the state.

Given this tradition, therefore, and especially in view of the situation
addressed by *1 Clement* it should not be surprising to find a prayer for the
rulers that accentuates their ability to effect peace and concord. Let us turn
back to that text now. We can consider the first section of the prayer for
rulers in three stanzas, following Légasse. Stanza A and C both conclude
with mention of the rulers (A — *archōn*; C — *archōn kai hēgoumenoi*)
forming an *inclusio*. All three stanzas continue the petitionary form begun
in 60.1. The vocative of 61.1 as well as the return to ascriptions of praise
in that verse signal a new formal unit. Thus, this section of the prayer can
be divided into Part I and Part II, based on criteria both of form and of
content. The focus of this section is twofold: obedience both to God and to
rulers. Moreover, the "voice" of the one who prays is still the Elect community, even though the prayer is made also on behalf of "all who dwell
on earth."

As Légasse noted, both stanzas A and C contain positive petitions. The
middle stanza, B, offers a counterbalance with a double petition for deliverance (*hrysthēnai hrysai*): deliverance from sin and deliverance "from
those who hate us unjustly" (Ps. 18:17). We are led to draw the conclusion, therefore, that there is an intended connection between the double
objective, namely, God and rulers, and the double demand for deliverance,
namely, from sin and from the enemies of Christians.[29] Obedience to God,
it seems, implies deliverance from sin; likewise, obedience to rulers means
deliverance from "those who hate us unjustly."[30] Deliverance is equated
with the establishment of "concord and peace," *first* among Christians (the
major theme of this letter) and secondly in the world at large. In both cases,
God is the agent of deliverance; God is the one who established peace.

Christians are encouraged to pray for the *pax Romana*[31] for their own interest and protection; in the language of *1 Clement,* that is, "to safeguard the number of the elect." It goes without saying, however, that such a positive view of the existing political reality contains within it a dangerous precedent.

The final section of the prayer, 61.1–3, continues this dual focus on God and the rulers. Here there are four stanzas that again alternate ascription and petition. Each begins with a vocative: in A and C "Master" and in B and D "Lord." The mention of *exousia* at the beginning of 61.1 and the end of 61.2 forms an *inclusio* for the unit before the entire prayer is brought to its conclusion with a final expression of praise and doxology ending with an Amen in 61.3. Multiple repetitions of the verb *didōmi* provide internal coherence for the four stanzas and stress once more the sovereignty of God who is the one who gives *exousia* and directs those to whom it is given.

Far from equating the ruler's sovereignty with that of God, this section of the prayer seems to do just the opposite: namely, to subordinate the rulers who are called merely *huioi tōn anthrōpōn* to "the heavenly Master and King of the ages." God's sovereignty is absolute; God alone is *Basileus.* Although stanza A does stress obedience to the rulers as a way of obeying God, stanzas B and D make clear that the rulers must exercise their authority "without offense." Their authority must be "good and pleasing" before God and must be marked by "peace, gentleness, and piety." For, as with all human creatures, they too are subject to God's mercy . . . and, therefore, by implication also to its opposite: God's righteous judgment. Note, in this respect, the parallel petitions in 60.2 and 61.2:

> 60.2 *Kateuthynon ta diabēmata hēmon*
> 61.2 *Kyrie dieuthynon tēn boulēn autōn*

God directs[32] both the people and their rulers to do "what is good and pleasing" before God.

Clement's prayer concludes with a final ascription of praise to God who alone gives good things to the Elect people through Christ, the "high priest and protector of [their] soul" (61.3).

Meaning and Function of the Prayer

How should we assess this prayer "rendered for Caesar?" To be sure, it continues a tradition originating in Diaspora Judaism and evident in early Christian texts to offer prayer on behalf of the civil authorities. And yet its length and repeated positive assessment of rulers and governors "goes well beyond anything in the New Testament."[33] The *context* of the prayer, however, shapes its content. It forms part of the climactic ending of a long and laborious "entreaty for peace and harmony" (63.2) among Christians in Corinth. In the author's perspective, to the extent that strife and division prevail, in Corinth or anywhere else, the Elect community is in peril. Harmony and peace must be restored before the church destroys itself (*1 Clem.* 46.5–7). Clement's assessment of the severity of the crisis in Corinth can be seen especially in the text of *1 Clem.* 46.7: "Why do we divide and tear asunder the members of Christ, and raise up strife against our own body, and reach such a pitch of madness as to forget that we are members of one another?"

From a literary and rhetorical perspective, this prayer serves to underscore the principal themes presented in the letter. Its theocentric emphasis from beginning to end is unmistakable. As elsewhere in the letter, God is the sovereign Master who creates and orders all things and to whom obedience must be given. Christ is Servant, the model for Christian life, who offers the perfect example of obedience (*1 Clement* 16). Repeated allusions to the LXX remind the readers of the great tradition they share, a tradition that should be the basis of their unity.

The social history underlying this prayer is becoming a bit clearer. The congregation behind *1 Clement* may well reflect a relatively privileged social group composed primarily of imperial freedmen and slaves, as Jeffers has proposed.[34] Given this social make-up a positive view of traditional authority is not surprising, and yet Clement's endorsement of traditional authority is not without critique. *Only* God has absolute power. All others hold their *exousia* under *God's* direction and subject to *God's* will. Only insofar as their actions conform to God's will can those in power continue to rule. This principle, it seems to me, is applied both to civil authority and to church leaders alike.[35]

Nevertheless, this prayer sets a potentially dangerous precedent by its endorsement of the imperial power. Whether we should go so far as to say that Clement "shows himself to be a theological apologist for the *Pax Romana*"[36] who reordered the Christian ecclesial vision solely in accord with Roman hierarchical patterns is, decidedly, a point of debate.

With respect to the question of prayer for civil rulers, however, in the end, we too are left with the enigmatic wisdom of Jesus (Mark 12:21 and parallels):

> Render to Caesar the things that are Caesar's,
> and to God the things that are God's.

Notes

1. J. A. Kleist, S.J. (trans and ed.), *The Epistles of St. Clement of Rome and St. Ignatius of Antioch* (Ancient Christian Writers 1; Westminster, Md.: Newman Press, 1961), 116, n. 166.

2. J. S. Jeffers, "Social Foundations of Early Christianity at Rome: The Congregations Behind 1 Clement and the Shepherd of Hermas," Ph.D. diss., University of California, Irvine, 1988; *idem.* "The Influence of the Roman Family and Social Structures on Early Christianity in Rome," *SBLSP* (1988), 360–84; *idem., Conflict at Rome: Social Order and Hierarchy in Early Christianity* (Minneapolis: Fortress, 1991).

3. "Social Foundations," x.

4. Ibid., 314.

5. B. E. Bowe, *A Church in Crisis: Ecclesiology and Paraenesis in Clement of Rome* (HDR 23; Minneapolis: Fortress, 1988), esp., 120–21.

6. J. L. White, "New Testament Epistolary Literature in the Framework of Ancient Epistolography," *ANRW* II, 25.2 (1984), 1748.

7. H. Koester, "1 Thessalonians — Experiment in Christian Writing," in *Continuity and Discontinuity in Church History: Essays Presented to G. H. Williams* (Leiden: Brill, 1979), esp. 39–40.

8. Koester, "1 Thessalonians," 40.

9. For further analysis of the epistolary features of *1 Clement,* see Bowe, *A Church in Crisis,* 33–58.

10. J. L. White, *The Form and Function of the Body of the Greek Letter: A Study of the Letter-Body in the Non-Literary Papyri and in Paul the Apostle* (SPLDS 2; Missoula, Mont.: Scholars Press, 1972), 42.

11. See on this theme, W. C. van Unnik, "Le Nombre des Elus dans la première épître de Clément," *RHPhR* 42 (1962), 237–46. For a contradictory view see O. Knoch, *Eigenart und Bedeutung der Eschatologie im theologischen Aufriß des ersten Clemensbriefes* (Theophaneia 17; Bonn: Peter Hanstein, 1964), 63, and the unpublished response to this paper by A. Enermalm-Ogawa at the SBL Annual Meeting, New Orleans, November 18, 1990.

12. On this point I disagree strongly with the position of Knoch, *Eigenart und Bedeutung,* passim.

13. S. N. Olson, "Pauline Expressions of Confidence in His Addresses," *CBQ* 47 (1985), 289. For further discussion of the function of these formulae in *1 Clement* see Bowe, *A Church in Crisis,* 50–53.

14. G. B. Caird, *The Language and Imagery of the Bible* (Philadelphia: Westminster, 1980), 32–33.

15. Caird, *The Language and Imagery,* 32.

16. The translation of R. M. Grant and H. H. Graham (*The Apostolic Fathers A New Translation and Commentary,* vol. 2: *First and Second Clement* [New York: Thomas Nelson & Sons, 1965], 93).

17. J. B. Lightfoot, *Apostolic Fathers* (5 vols.; 2d ed.; Macmillan, 1889–90), 2:172.

18. I am grateful to Agneta Enermalm-Ogawa for pointing out the error with regard to this text in the first draft of this essay.

19. Grant and Graham, *The Apostolic Fathers,* 92.

20. Lightfoot, *The Apostolic Fathers,* 2:172–81, and Knopf, *Die apostolischen Väter,* Zwei Clemensbriefe (HNT; Tübingen: Mohr-Siebeck, 1920), 139–48.

21. Ibid., 93–96.

22. Jeffers ("Social Foundations," 133–34) suggests that Clement's predilection for the term *despotēs* for God (twenty-four times in the letter) stems from the fact that he and many of his community were most probably imperial freedmen or slaves "for whom such an allusion had special significance." This appellation for God, used frequently in vocative address in prayers, was also common in the LXX. Hatch-Redpath lists fifty-eight occurrences. See, for example, the prayer of Abraham (LXX Gen. 15:8), the prayer of Joshua (LXX Josh. 5:14), the prayer of Jeremiah (LXX, Letter of Jeremiah 6).

23. Though found in the LXX in both its noun and verb forms, this term is rare in early Christian literature. It appears in the NT only in Luke 22:25 to identify "those in authority," *hoi exousiazontes,*" and, apart from 1 *Clement,* only in Ignatius (*Ign. Rom.* 5.1) and *Diogn.* (8.11; 9.5; 10.6). In 1 *Clement* it is used always and only of God and we might ask whether Clement presents a subtle critique of the client-patron system in Roman society. Jeffers's claim ("Social Foundations," 313) that Clement accepts without question the ideology of the Roman imperial hierarchy warrants further study. On the question of benefaction in early Christianity, see Frederick W. Danker, "The Endangered Benefactor in Luke-Acts," *SBLSP* (1981), 39–48.

24. '*Antilēptōr,* "helper, protector," is another rare term in early Christian literature and occurs only here in 1 *Clement* but is a common address or attribute for God in the LXX psalms (16x). *BAGD* (75) notes its use for a Roman official in BGU 1138.19. Again we could ask whether Clement has chosen this word with care in order to affirm God's sovereignty over against the prevailing Roman patron-client ideology.

25. S. Légasse, "La Prière pour les chefs d'état: Antecédénts judaïques et témoins chrétiens du premier siècle," *NT* 29:3 (1987), 236–53.

26. Ibid., 236–41 presents numerous other examples of this theme: *Ep. Arist.* 45; Josephus, *Ant.* 12.140, 406; 1 Maccabees 7:31; Philo, *Leg. Gaius* 157; 317; 356–57.

27. See the recent exposition of this text by R. H. Stein, "The Argument of Romans 13:1–7," *NT* 31.4 (1989), 325–43.

28. For a summary of the pertinent passages, see Knopf, *Die apostolischen Väter,* 146–47.

29. Légasse, "La Prière," 248.

30. As suggested in an oral response to this essay by Agneta Enermalm-Ogawa, this verse "could, in code language, refer to a particular expression of imperial power, especially as that phrase takes the same position as 'our rulers' in stanzas A and C of Part I."

31. On this theme see especially Klaus Wengst, *Pax Romana and the Peace of Jesus Christ* (London: SCM Press, 1987), 105–18.

32. *Dieuthynon* is a rare word and does not appear in the LXX or NT. Clement uses it earlier (20.8) to describe God's direction of the oceans.

33. Grant and Graham, *The Apostolic Fathers,* 96.

34. Jeffers, "Social Foundations," *passim.*

35. See the discussion in Bowe, *A Church in Crisis,* 144–53.

36. Wengst, *Pax Romana,* 108.

The Prayer in *1 Clement* 59.3–61.3

59.3

...elpizein epi to archēgonon
pasēs ktiseōs onoma sou
anoixas tous ophthalmous tēs kardias hēmon
eis to ginōskein se ton monon
hypsiston en hypsistois hagion en hagiois
anapauomenon; ton tapeinounta hybrin
hyperēphanōn, ton dialyonta logismous
ethnōn, ton poiounta tapeinous eis
hypsos kai tous hypsēlous tapeinounta
ton ploutizonta kai ptōchizonta ton
apokteinonta kai zēn poiounta monon
euergetēn pneumatōn kai theon pasēs
sarkos. Ton epibleponta en tois
abyssois ton epoptēn anthrōpinōn
ergōn ton tōn kindyneuontōn boēthon
ton tōn apēlpismenōn sōtēra, ton
pantos pneumatos ktistēn kai episkopon.
Ton plēthynonta ethnē
epi gēs kai ek pantōn eklexamenon
tous agapōntas se dia
Iēsou Christou tou ēgapēmenou paidos sou,
di hou hēmas epaideusas
hēgiasas etimēsas.

...to hope in your name,
the source of all creation,
You open the eyes of our heart
to know you who alone are the highest
in the highest, [and] who remains holy
among the holy. You humble the pride
of the arrogant, you destroy the reck-
onings of nations, you put the humble
on high, and the proud you humble,
you make rich and poor, you kill and
bestow life, you alone are the benefactor of spirits and the God of all
flesh. You look into the depths and see
human endeavors, You are the helper
of the endangered, the savior of those
without hope, the creator and watcher
over every spirit.
You multiply the nations upon the
earth, and from them all you have
chosen those who love you through
Jesus Christ your beloved Servant,
through whom you have taught us,
sanctified us, given us honor.

59.4

axioumen se despota, boēthon genesthai
kai antilēptora hēmōn.
Tous en thlipsei hēmōn sōson
tous tapeinous eleēson
tous peptōkotas egeiron
tois deomenois epiphanēthi
tous astheneis iasai
tous planōmenous tou laou sou
    epistrepson.
Chortason tous peinōntas
lytrōsai tous desmious hēmōn
exanastēson tous asthenountas
parakaleson tous oligopsychountas
gnōtōsan se apanta ta ethnē, hoti
sy ei ho theos monos kai Iēsous Christos
ho pais sou kai hēmeis laos sou kai
probata tēs nomēs sou.

We beseech you, Master, be our helper
and defender.
Save those in distress among us,
have mercy on the lowly,
raise up the fallen,
show yourself to those in need,
heal the sick,
turn back those of your people who
    have strayed.
Feed the hungry,
ransom our prisoners,
revive the weak,
comfort the fainthearted.
Let all the nations know you, that
You are God alone and that Jesus Christ
is your Servant, and that we are your
people and the sheep of your pasture.

60.1

Sy gar tēn aenaon tou kosmou systasin
dia tōn energoumenōn ephaneropoiēsas.
Sy kyrie, tēn oikoumenēn ektisas
ho pistos en pasais tais geneais, dikaios
en tois krimasin, thaumastos en ischyi
kai megaloprepeia, ho sophos en tō ktizein
kai synetos en tō ta genomena hedrasai
ho agathos en tois horōmenois kai chrēstos
en tois pepoithosin epi se, eleēmōn kai
oiktirmon, aphes hēmin tas anomias hēmōn
kai tas adikias kai ta paraptōmata
kai plēmmeleias.

For through your works you revealed
the eternal fabric of the universe;
You, Lord, created the world.
You are faithful in all generations,
righteous in judgment, marvelous in
might and majesty, wise in creating,
understanding in establishing what is,
good toward what is seen, and kind
to those who trust in you, merciful
and compassionate; Forgive us our
lawlessness and unrighteousness,
and transgressions and faults.

PART I:

A

60.2

Mē logisę pasan hamartian
   doulōn sou kai paidiskōn
alla katharison hēmas
   ton katharismon tēs sēs alētheias
kai kateuthynon ta diabēmata hēmon
   en hosiotēti kardias poreuesthai
kai poiein ta kala kai euaresta
   enōpion sou kai
   enōpion tōn archontōn hēmōn.

Do not reckon every sin
   of your servants and handmaids
but cleanse us
   with the cleansing of your truth
and "direct our steps
   to walk in holiness of heart
and to do the things that are good
   and pleasing before you"
   and before our rulers.

B

60.3

Nai despota epiphanon to prosōpon sou
eph' hēmas eis agatha en eirēnę
   eis to skepasthēnai hēmas
   tę cheiri sou tę krataią
kai hrysthēnai apo pasēs hamartias
   tǫ brachioni sou tǫ hypsēlǫ
kai hrysai hēmas apo tōn
   misountōn hēmas adikōs.

Yes, Master, "make your face shine
on us for our good" in peace
that we might be sheltered
   by your mighty hand
and delivered from all sin
   by your uplifted arm,
and deliver us from those who
   hate us unjustly.

C

60.4

Dos homonoian kai eirēnēn hēmin te kai
   pasin tois katoikousin tēn gēn
kathōs *edōkas* tois patrasin hēmōn
   epikaloumenōn se autōn
   hosiōs en pistei kai alētheia

hypēkoous ginomenous
   tǫ pantokratori kai endoxǫ
   onomati sou
   tois te archousin kai hēgoumenois
   hēmōn epi tēs gēs.

Give concord and peace to us and
   to all who dwell on the earth,
just as you gave to our ancestors
   who called upon you
   with holiness in faith and truth.

[Make us] be obedient
   to your almighty and glorious
   name
   and to our rulers and governors
   upon the earth.

PART II:

A

61.1

Sy despota edōkas tēn exousian
tēs basileias autois
dia tou megaloprepous
kai anekdiēgētou kratous sou
eis to ginōskontas hēmas tēn hypo sou
autois dedomenēn doxan kai timēn
hypotassesthai autois
mēden enantioumenous tǭ thelēmati sou.

You, Master, have given the power
of sovereignty to them
through your excellent
and inexpressible might
that we might know the glory
and honor given to them by you
and be subject to them
in no way resisting your will:

B

hois dos kyrie hygieian eirēnēn
homonoian eustatheian
eis to diepein autous
tēn hypo sou dedomenēn autois
hēgemonian aproskopōs.

to them, give, Lord, health, peace,
concord, stability,
that they may administer
the government which you have
given to them without offense.

C

61.2

Sy gar despota epouranie basileu
tōn aiōnōn
didōs tois huiois tōn anthrōpōn
doxan kai timēn kai exousian
tōn epi tēs gēs hyparchontōn.

For you, heavenly Master, King
of the ages,
give to human agents
glory and honor and power
over the things on earth;

D

Sy kyrie dieuthynon tēn boulēn autōn
kata to kalon kai euareston
enōpion sou
hopōs diepontes en eirēnȩ kai
prautēti eusebōs
tēn hypo sou autois dedomenēn
exousian hileō sou tygchanōsin.

You, Lord, direct their will
according to what is "good and
pleasing" before you,
that they may administer in peace and
gentleness with piety
the power given to them by you
and may find mercy with you.

61.3

ho monos dynatos poiēsai tauta
kai perissotera agatha meth' hēmōn
soi exomologoumetha dia tou
archiereōs kai prostatou
tōn psychōn hēmōn Iēsou Christou,
di' hou soi hē doxa kai hē megalōsynē
kai nyn kai eis genean geneōn kai
eis tous aiōnas tōn aiōnōn.
amēn.

O, You, who alone are able to do these
things, and more abundant good things
for us, we praise you through the
high priest and protector
of our souls — Jesus Christ —
through whom to You be glory and
majesty, both now and for all
generations and forever and ever.
Amen.*

---

*Stanzas for 60.2–61.3 adapted from: S. Légasse, "La Prière pour les chefs d'état:
Antécédents judaïques et témoins chrétiens du premier siècle," *NT* 29:3 (1987), 236–53.

THE LORD'S PRAYER
AND OTHER PRAYER TEXTS
OF THE GRECO-ROMAN ERA:
A BIBLIOGRAPHY

Mark Harding

INTRODUCTION

In February 1990, Mark Kiley, on behalf of the Steering Committee of the Society of Biblical Literature Consultation on New Testament Prayer in Historical Context, invited me to submit a bibliographical "state of research" report to the New Orleans meeting of the consultation. "Our mandate," he wrote, "is to explore prayer texts from Alexander to Constantine in a historical-critical mode." This essay has developed out of that 1990 report on the bibliography. It not only introduces the bibliography, but also expresses what I think is the present state of research in the subject and identifies potentially fruitful avenues of inquiry yet to be fully navigated in the endeavor to come to the fullest possible appreciation of prayer in texts from Alexander to Constantine in their historical context. The bibliography has circulated privately among members of the committee and among interested students and teachers since November 1990. It was produced in partnership with members of the Steering Committee, who submitted items for inclusion. The opportunity to publish it has provided impetus to expand the number of bibliographical items included.

It would be helpful to explain first the criteria by which the bibliography has been compiled. This bibliography does not claim to be exhaustive. Probably no bibliography can claim to be so; time and energy conspire to prevent that illusive possibility. However, I trust that the work does list the significant works in the various fields covered.

The Criteria

1. I have largely excluded material whose primary concern is not prayer. Thus, for instance, I have only rarely included commentaries on New Testament books, general studies of corpora such as the Gospels and Epistles, the New Testament as a whole, the Dead Sea Scrolls, or other works, which might treat prayer as one among many subjects.[1] I have included some works on Jewish, Christian, or Greco-Roman liturgies of the designated period since it is evident that prayer is a constituent feature of these. I have endeavored to provide information respecting relevant chapters, sections, or specific page numbers in those general works that are listed.

2. While the bibliography focuses on texts from Alexander to Constantine, I felt some acknowledgment of studies of prayer in the Hebrew Bible was justified since address to God in that corpus largely determines the shape and content of later Jewish and Christian writings. I have sought to include the major studies in these fields. Generally, articles on specific Psalms of the Hebrew Bible have not been included.

3. No brief was given to me to restrict the time span of the items to be included in the bibliography. As far as I am aware, there is no earlier bibliography of this scope upon which to base one's own. While the majority of entries emanate from this century, I have attempted to account for relevant studies antedating the twentieth century. While a postwar demarcation would certainly focus attention on the most recent scholarly literature and the contemporary direction of scholarship, it is helpful to be able to compare the older scholarly endeavors and consensuses with contemporary ones. It may also be discovered that the conclusions of older scholarship remain valuable. The continuing worth of a work such as Norden's *Agnostos Theos* (Leipzig: Teubner, 1913) is universally recognized.

4. What exactly is a "prayer"? It will be readily noted that many of the entries deal as much with "psalms" and "hymns," as with "prayers." While it may be suggested that "prayer," strictly speaking, has to do with invoking and petitioning God, and "psalms" and "hymns" focus more on confession, acknowledgment, and praise, it is quite clear that much of the material is neither solely one genre or the other. Berger, who discusses "Hymnen" and "Gebete" separately and carefully isolates their respective stylistic and thematic aspects, admits with respect to Greek (i.e., Gentile) hymns:

Since the last section of the Greek hymn in usually a prayer, a close relationship exists between hymns and prayers.[2]

I have therefore inclined to the view that in speaking about prayer we are dealing primarily with addressing God in a liturgical or devotional context. It seems unjustifiable to attempt too neat a distinction between forms of address. I might add that in submissions to me from members of the consultation, I have observed the same reluctance to separate prayers and hymns.

5. As indicated above, my mandate was to produce a bibliography from the standpoint of the historical-critical discipline. Historical-criticism denotes the study and evaluation of texts as documents of particular historical eras, with the concomitant attention to determining (a) the text, (b) the literary form of the text, (c) the historical *Sitz im Leben* of the text, (d) the meaning the text had for the original readers and users of the text, and finally (e) understanding the text in light of its total context and background out of which it has emerged.[3] I have not, therefore, intentionally included studies of prayer from the perspectives of sociological or psycho-

logical analysis or the "new" literary criticism. Nevertheless, there is, of course, every reason for investigating prayer texts from these perspectives. Indeed, in 1990 Mark Kiley suggested to the members of the Consultation that the 1991 annual meeting should focus on the theme "Prayer and Narrative."

6. Finally, the layout of the bibliography derives basically from the agenda proposed by J. H. Charlesworth in recent articles addressing the subject.[4] However, I have added, where appropriate, subcategories in which items germane to a general field of inquiry are listed in advance of studies of the individual texts.

1. Stylistic and Genre Analysis

In the modern discussion as it relates to prayer, the figure of Klaus Berger dominates. His massive 1984 *Hellenistische Gattungen*... (*ANRW* II, 25.2 [1984], 1031–1432, 1831–85) devotes no little space to questions of the style and genre of prayers, hymns, and acclamations.[5] Hamman's 1980 article "La prière chrétienne et la prière païenne, formes et différences" (*ANRW* II, 23.2 [1980], 1190–1247) is a helpful introduction emanating from a scholar who has devoted his scholarly life to the study of prayer in the NT and early Christian literature. Like Berger, though not as extensively, he engages the Greco-Roman prayer tradition.

2. General

I have endeavored to collect in this category works written from the historical-critical point of view that treat the subject of prayer, especially in the Judeo-Christian and Greco-Roman traditions, as a religious phenomenon. A number of works have also been included in this category because they range over more than one religious tradition. By the nature of their general focus, dictionary articles are well represented, e.g., Lesètre in the *Dictionnaire de la Bible,* González in the *Supplément,* and von Severus and Michel in the *Reallexicon für Antike und Christentum.* The English edition of the often cited work of Heiler, *Das Gebet* (Munich: Reinhardt, 1920), the fifth edition of which is now over seventy years old, is lamentably truncated, perhaps representing only half of what Heiler wrote.[6] A work in this area, or at least a supplemented and edited English reissue of Heiler's original, particularly as its strength is its "religionsgeschichtliche" point of view, would be of immense benefit. Much of the appreciation of the depth and range of the Jewish material, however, postdates Heiler.

Two recent works by E. Lodi, his *Enchiridion euchologicum fontium liturgicum* and his *Commentary,* both published in 1979, warrant comment. The former is a massive 2,000-page collection of some 3,500 prayers dating from 500 B.C.E. to the sixteenth century C.E., Christian prayers predominating. Lodi's volume of commentary provides "Notes" on some of these texts. G. H. R. Horsley in his *New Documents Illustrating Early Christianity*, vol. 4 (Macquarie University, N.S.W.: Ancient History Documentary Research Centre, 1987) confesses his frustration in using the commentary volume in particular since only some of the texts receive attention (and then only some features) and the texts are referred to in confusing ways.[7] Furthermore, he complains, Greco-Roman, Jewish, and papyrological materials are scarcely represented. With one possible exception, he writes, the inscriptions and papyri included are all Christian. Horsley's critique highlights the need for anthologies and commentary in the respective and specific areas concerning the subject. Michael Lattke's recent work *Hymnus: Materialien zu einer Geschichte der antiken Hymnologie* (NTOA 19; Freiburg/Göttingen: Universitätsverlag/Vandenhoeck & Ruprecht, 1991) is the most extensive investigation available of the hymnic tradition, not just of early Greece and the Ancient Near East, but of the NT era and beyond. It might be noted that there isn't a modern major English discussion of the prayers of the Bible apart from R. E. Clement's 1985 and 1986 contributions to the field: *In Spirit and Truth: Insights from Biblical Prayers* (Atlanta: John Knox, 1985) and *Prayers of the Bible* (London: SCM, 1986). Based as it is on sound exegesis, the work is designed for a popular readership and is homiletic in style and thrust. Nevertheless, I suspect that there are as yet few books on prayer that attempt to bridge the exegetical and the homiletical gap. In German, one might acknowledge H. Dietzfelbinger's *Zukunft mit der Vaterunser* (Munich: Claudius, 1980) as an attempt to encourage the contemporary preacher to address the issues raised by the Lord's Prayer.

In today's ecumenical environment, there is opportunity for English-language scholars to produce anthologies of prayers and hymns with commentary stressing the common heritage of Jews and Christians. As yet no major work has been produced addressing this need.

3. Hebrew Bible

The interest in the Psalms, both from the form-critical and theological perspective, is totally expected. The frequency with which the name Claus Westermann occurs is a testimony to his immense contribution to the understanding of the Hebrew material. Of special interest, perhaps, is Évode Beaucamp's *Israël en prière*, subtitled *des Psaumes au Nôtre Père* (Paris: Cerf, 1985). This work is one in which we are reminded that Israelite prayer and praise expressed in the Hebrew Bible, especially in the

Psalms, are by no means without their ongoing tradition and vitality down into the era of the New Testament (and, of course, beyond).

P. D. Miller's *Interpreting the Psalms* (Philadelphia: Fortress, 1985) combines the results of earnest scholarly labor with a hermeneutical and homiletic thrust. The churches would derive much benefit from similar books of scholarship that took up the Jewish, New Testament, and Pseudepigraphical prayers and hymns in the interests of encouraging a homiletical end-product based on sound exegesis.

4. Jewish Texts

After the New Testament section, this category is the most extensive in the bibliography. It covers prayer in the liturgical development of early Judaism and the Rabbinic era, as well as the Pseudepigrapha, Qumran, Josephus, Philo, and the Targums. Something of the range of the material is evidenced by the recognition that Jews in the NT era produced works like the "Songs of the Sabbath Sacrifice," the penitential laments of the Apocalypses, the victory songs of the book Judith, liturgical forms still used today such as the Eighteen Benedictions, psalms based on the canonical collection (Apocryphal Psalms), and magic and theurgic texts such as the Prayer of Jacob and those contained in the Jewish Magical Papyri (see category 8, Magic). Clearly the corpus encapsulates a vibrant and energetic tradition, capable of expressing the great themes of the Jewish heritage (Prayer of Manasseh), expressing new and bold conceptions of the world of the divine (Songs of the Sabbath Sacrifice), and adapting itself to marginalized thought-forms (magic).

Research into the origins of Jewish liturgical prayer is clearly high on the agenda of contemporary scholarship. In this it builds upon foundations laid in the last century.[8] More recently the labors of J. J. Petuchowski and J. Heinemann *inter alia* have produced new insights. A number of comparative studies of Jewish and Christian liturgies have been included in this category since they take the Jewish liturgical traditions as their starting point. The debate over the precise nature of the role of the "Benediction of the Minim" in the formation of the Fourth Gospel continues to provoke interest.[9]

Turning to the Pseudepigrapha, it becomes immediately obvious that there is an urgent need of a definitive anthology and commentary on its prayers and hymns. Although we have several excellent studies of prayer in various books of the Apocrypha and Pseudepigrapha,[10] the only book I know devoted to the whole corpus is the 1948 monograph by N. B. Johnson, *Prayer in the Apocrypha and Pseudepigrapha* (Philadelphia: Society of Biblical Literature and Exegesis, 1948). Anyone reading its seventy-seven pages will be struck by its limitations and brevity. Moreover, the study is based on the works included in R. H. Charles's two-volume *Apocrypha and Pseudepigrapha of the Old Testament in English* (Oxford: Clarendon, 1913).[11] It does not discuss, therefore, a large number of works that have been included in Charlesworth's *Old Testament Pseudepigrapha* (Garden City, N.Y.: Doubleday, 1983 and 1985). This lacuna in the field stands in the most urgent need of redress. A definitive work is bound to prove of immense benefit to the understanding of early Judaism, particularly if the research is sensitive to the prayer traditions of the contemporary contiguous communities and to the possibility of mutual enrichment. Moreover, little has been written on the prayers of the Jewish Apocalypses.

The discussion of the relevant material found at Qumran continues apace. Though here again, as is the case with the Pseudepigrapha, there are excellent studies of some individual texts,[12] but no definitive large-scale work devoted to the prayers and hymns as a whole.[13] The bibliographical items on specific texts are listed according to the order found at the head of the section on the corpus.

Given the numerous prayers particularly in the early books of Josephus's *Antiquities,* it is surprising that these have received no detailed attention from scholars. Josephus was a first-century Jew, a man writing to commend the Jewish heritage to a Greco-Roman audience, whose prayer texts have largely been ignored. The only substantial and readily available discussion of this material of which I am aware is the section entitled "Lobpreis und Gebet" in A. Schlatter's *Die Theologie des Judentums nach dem Bericht des Josephus* (Gütersloh: Bertelsmann, 1932), 108–13, and in W. C. van Unnik's "Eine merkwürdige liturgische Aussage bei Josephus (Josephus, *Ant.* 8, 111–13)" in the Michel Festschrift (Göttingen: Vandenhoeck & Ruprecht [1974], 362–69).[14]

Prayer in Philo, another first-century Jewish writer, has also been singularly neglected.[15] C. W. Larson lamented this fact at the beginning of his 1946 article "Prayer of Petition in Philo" (*JBL* 65 [1946], 185–203). J. Laporte's *La doctrine eucharistique chez Philon d'Alexandrie* (Paris: Beauchesne, 1972; ETrans., Lewiston, N.Y.: E. Mellen Press, 1983) it would appear to be the first book devoted to thanksgiving in Philo. More recently, Sharyn Dowd has written on the subject of prayer in Philo (*Perspectives in Religious Studies* 10 [1983], 241–54).

In his article "The Recovery of the Language of Jesus" (*NTS* 3 [1956–57], 305–13 [306]) Matthew Black draws attention to the survival of a number of old Aramaic liturgical hymns in the Palestinian Targum of the Pentateuch. Likewise, J. H. Charlesworth's "Prolegomenon to a New Study of the Jewish Background of the Hymns and Prayers in the New Testament" (*JSJ* 33 [1982], 265–85 [276]) notes a number of prayers in Targums (specifically those of Abraham [Gen. 22:14 in Neofiti and the Fragment Targum], Tamar [Gen. 38:25 in Neofiti, Pseudo-Jonathan, and the Fragment Targum] and Moses [Deut. 32:50 in Pseudo-Jonathan]).

Readers looking for further discussion outside of Le Déaut's very cursory attention in his article "Aspects de l'intercession dans le Judaisme" in *JSJ* 1 (1970), 53–57, may find M. Maher's recent article "The Meturgemanim and Prayer," *JJS* 41 (1990), 226–46 a helpful place to begin.

5. New Testament

The paucity of major works in English listed in the general section is readily apparent. Once again German scholarship is dominant. Deichgräber's *Gotteshymnus and Christushymnus in der frühen Christenheit* (Göttingen: Vandenhoeck & Ruprecht, 1967) is indispensable. Much the same could be said of Hamman's now rather dated *La prière: Le nouveau testament* (Tournai: Desclée, 1959). The nearest to these in English is J. T. Sanders's outline *The New Testament Christological Hymns* (Cambridge: Cambridge University Press, 1971; now out of print).[16] A number of dissertations in this area in English do not appear to have been published as books. These are C. E. Eason's "Traces of Liturgical Worship in the Epistles with Special Reference to Hymns, Prayers and Creeds" (Leeds, 1966), D. J. McFarlane's "The Motif of Thanksgiving in the New Testament" (St. Andrews, 1966), and L. L. Thompson's "The Form and Function of Hymns in the New Testament" (Chicago, 1968). Their titles alone suggest promise. The only other item written by either of these three in the bibliography is Thompson's "Cult and Eschatology in the Apocalypse of John" in *JR* 49 (1969), 330–50. With the publication of Qumran and Nag Hammadi texts and the fresh awareness these have brought to the understanding of the milieu and theology of early Christian thought, there is a need for discussions of New Testament prayer and hymnic texts that reflect these insights.

This may be an appropriate place to focus attention on the understanding of the prayers and hymns of the New Testament as "liturgical." The consensus is that the hymns in Philippians 2:5–11 and Colossians 1:15–20, e.g., are not only pre-Pauline but liturgical. Presumably this means that the early churches, perhaps even in the 40s and certainly in the 50s of the first century were re-casting traditional material about Jesus and, according to Käsemann's reading of the Colossians' hymn, adapting material from a proto-Gnostic source and using it in a liturgical form of "worship." Yet it would appear from the slender information supplied from the NT itself that the early believers met in house groups. In this milieu believers possibly recited or confessed or even sang these highly organized and profoundly christological hymns. This is not such a surprising view, since Paul himself counsels the believers in Corinth when they meet together that each should have "a hymn, a lesson, a revelation, a tongue, or an interpretation" (1 Cor. 14:26; cf. Col. 3:16; Eph. 5:19). Now the question could be asked, What kind of communities and gatherings were these? How different were they from other religious communities in the Greco-Roman world in this respect? Who else met in homes, i.e., in a nonsacral context, as a confraternity and engaged in something we would recognize as a liturgical form, without benefit of sacerdotal functionaries? What are the Jewish parallels? Paul Bradshaw in his *Daily Prayer in the Early Church* (New York: Oxford University Press [1982], 44) notes the liturgical activity of the Therapeutae as recorded in Philo, the liturgical life of the Qumran Essenes, and the hymns and sermons on the occasion of Jewish festal meals providing a precedent for what the Christians did. Has a study been done of these Jewish liturgical contexts and their relationship to early Christian gatherings? Moreover, based on Käsemann's reading of the Colossians' hymn, to what extent do other NT hymns pick up from the contiguous religious outlook concepts by which the believers were enabled to express the Christian gospel in a more culturally attuned way for them and their contemporaries. Perhaps there was a polemic thrust to these hymns also, a point many would concede for the hymns and acclamations of the Apocalypse.

The subsection "Jesus and Prayer" includes entries on the most written-about text of the whole field, viz., the Lord's Prayer. There are some 280 items alone in this field. The interest in the prayers of Jesus, and in his use of *Abba* in particular, shows no sign of abating. In fact, new appreciation of the Jewishness of Jesus has spawned an increasingly voluminous literature on the agreement between Jesus' address to God and Jewish address contemporary with him. This is seen in the challenge to J. Jeremias's understanding of the significance of Jesus' use of *Abba*. Jeremias argued that Jesus' use of *Abba* was without parallel in his era, bearing witness to his profound sense of the uniqueness and intimacy of his filial relationship with God, a relationship that he taught his disciples was theirs to enjoy derivatively. When Jesus addressed God as *Abba,* he was taking up the intimate prattle of Jewish children in their address to their fathers. The challenge to Jeremias can be traced to Haenchen and Conzelmann in the 1960s (in Christian scholarship at least), and more lately to Vermes and Käsemann in the 1970s.[17] More recently, Quere (" 'Naming' God 'Father,' " *CuThM* 12 [1985], 5–14) and Barr ("Abba Isn't Daddy," *JThS* 39 [1988], 28–47) *inter alia* have joined the chorus of dissent.

I note with more than passing interest that confessional Jewish and Christian scholarship finds much common ground and fellowship in the Lord's Prayer. The excellent collection of essays edited by M. Brocke, J. J. Petuchowski, and W. Strolz (the German edition is fuller, the 1978 English version, truncated) under the title *Das Vaterunser: Gemeinsames im Beten von Juden und Christen* (Freiburg: Herder, 1974), manifests a cooperation that ought to be and is being emulated. Nevertheless, the Lord's Prayer, as exegeted from a thoroughgoing eschatological point of view in R. E. Brown's article, "The Pater Noster as an Eschatological Prayer" (*TS* 22

[1961], 175–208), contains much that is surprising, indeed unprecedented in early Jewish literature.

Turning to the Gospels, one is struck by the paucity of material devoted to and focused on prayer in the four Gospels as such. J. Caba's *La oración de petición: estudio exegético sobre los evangelios sinópticos y los escritos joaneos* (Rome: Biblical Institute Press, 1974) is the only major one. While much of the material will be covered in more general works on the New Testament and the Bible, one would have expected the Gospels to have provided more than enough fuel for major study. One question that occurs to me is the reason for the relatively low profile of prayer and hymnic material in Mark compared to, say, Luke. Of interest too is the possible connection of the prayers and hymns of Acts with contemporary synagogal counterparts.[18] Can we determine whether or not the prayers of Acts (esp. chs. 1–12) preserve elements of the pre-70 C.E. synagogal prayer tradition?

Turning to the Epistles, the subjection of Philippians 2:5–11 and Colossians 1:15–20, long regarded as hymnic, to most rigorous scholarly scrutiny shows no sign of abating. Indeed the whole corpus of Epistles has proven to be a remarkably fertile ground for scholarly endeavor into the possible background of the hymns and prayers embedded in these texts. J. H. Charlesworth anticipates an interesting line of research when he informs us that there are fruitful parallels between the hymn in Philippians 2:5–11 and the Odes of Solomon.[19] With the Apocalypse, however, a number of issues intrude that may be unique to it in the NT corpus and that seem to me to be fruitful avenues of research not yet exhausted. I am speaking about three possible influences on the thought-world of the Apocalypse as it can be ascertained through its prayers, hymns, and acclamations, from (a) Qumran, (b) Jewish Apocalypses, and (c) the imperial cult. The bibliography demonstrates that these matters have already been exercising the minds of scholars.[20]

6. Early Christian Texts

It was decided to limit items for inclusion to those that dealt with prayer before Nicaea. The Nicene and post-Nicene Fathers and the literature of monasticism certainly take us beyond the original brief to explore prayer texts from Alexander to Constantine. However, a number of works that address the later state of liturgical life in the church have been included since they draw heavily upon the ante-Nicene heritage.

Whereas the study of early Christian liturgy is a venerable one, the link with contemporary Jewish prayer and developing liturgical practice is a comparatively recent undertaking by Jews and Christians. Moreover, Paul Bradshaw's *Daily Prayer in the Early Church* (New York: Oxford University Press, 1982) states in his Preface that Jewish and Christian liturgical scholars have for the most part worked in isolation.[21] He has followed this work with *The Making of Jewish and Christian Worship* (Notre Dame, Ind.: University of Notre Dame Press, 1991).

7. Greco-Roman Texts

I have included here a number of works that treat prayer and hymnic material emanating from the earlier Greek tradition, as well as subsections on prayers and hymns in a number of specific authors and cult traditions. An extremely helpful and sympathetic introduction to the whole Greco-Roman tradition is K. von Fritz's "Greek Prayers" (*RR* 10 [1945], 5–39). He notes at the outset that Greek prayers have been neglected in many of the works on Greek religion, even by F. Heiler in his *Das Gebet*. That unfortunate trend is continued by W. Burkert, whose *Greek Religion* (Cambridge, Mass.: Harvard University Press, 1985 [German original, 1977]) is the most recent general work I know, and by R. MacMullen, *Paganism in the Roman Empire* (New Haven: Yale University Press, 1981). Nevertheless, there are recent valuable treatments, not least Hamman's "La prière chrétienne et la prière païenne, formes et différences" (*ANRW* II, 23.2 [1980], 1190–1247). One suspects that some popular literature echoes the wholly negative assessment of Greek prayer offered by Jeremias.[22] I would also like to know whether the Greeks and Romans ever prayed outside of the cultic arena. I suspect they didn't.

Although this lies outside of the area, though only just outside, it would be interesting to ascertain the Emperor Julian's understanding of prayer. Assuming that there is available source material, does Julian infuse into his paganizing agenda something of the life-commitment that Jews and Christians understand to be the cult acceptable to God? If so, is there a role for prayer outside of the shrine and outside of the cultic/liturgical context as there was in Judaism and Christianity according to Julian?

8. Magical Texts

Early Jews and Christians demonstrated an interest in magic, an interest they shared with Greco-Roman culture as a whole. The practice of most overt forms of magic was marginalized from both the Jewish and Christian mainstream. However, it surfaces in the former in Merkavah and Kabbalistic mysticism and in the latter in some of the codices of the Nag Hammadi corpus, as well as later Christian papyri. Assimilation of some aspects of magic did occur in orthodox Christianity in the form of amulets, veneration of relics, and multiplication of holy places.

9. Gnostic, Hermetic, Manichaean, and Mandaean Texts

I have little to comment here. It does seem, however, that in the wake of the challenge to the traditional understanding of the relationship of the canonical Gospels to the noncanonical, issued most recently by J. D. Crossan in his study of the Gospel of Peter,[23] that a comparative study of the prayers and hymns in both bodies of literature might be a worthwhile enterprise.

10. Papyri and Inscriptions

Here is a most fruitful area of research. Inscriptions and papyri afford precious glimpses into the religiosity of the Greco-Roman world. In the case of the papyrus letters, we are largely dealing with ordinary people. The many papyrus letters usually include a reference to prayer at least in the form of the formulae *pro men pantōn euchomai para tois theois* (found at the beginning of a letter) and *errōsthai se euchomai* (found at the conclusion). There is an apparent perfunctoriness in the use of these formulae and an expressed connection between prayer and cultic activity. Do the clearly Christian letters continue to use the formulae in perfunctory reference to prayer or cultic activity, and is there is a sense in which the Christian letters bear witness to a change in attitude to God, to prayer and worship? Although such questions take us into material lying beyond the Constantinian terminus ad quem of the bibliography, I suspect that the Christian letters either (a) drop the perfunctory formulae or (b) embellish them with a distinctively Christian formulaic perfunctoriness often stressing the sovereignty of God, and that (c) all drop reference to cultic prostration previously often associated in the letters with prayer.[24] At this level of literary style, with some exceptions, the Christian letters as a body tend to stand apart from the non-Christian ones. Though this study would need to go further to examine the content of the letters, my impression is that it is possible that the evidence of the Christian letters supports the thesis that the Judeo-Christian heritage stressed a life-commitment to God as the true and acceptable cult, and that in the sphere of prayer the contrast between the prevailing Greco-Roman religious attitude and the Judeo-Christian is tellingly played out.[25]

Notes

1. Dictionary articles on prayer and related subjects are legion. Accordingly I have included those recommended to me by members of the Steering Committee and those I myself have found most helpful such as the extensive article with bibliographies by E. von Severus and O. Michel in the *Reallexicon für Antike und*

Christentum (RAC). Also helpful is the article "Gebet" by a number of scholars in the *Theologische Realenzyklopädie* (Berlin/New York: de Gruyter, 1977–), 12:31–65. This six part article also includes generous bibliographical material.

2. "Hellenistische Gattungen im Neuen Testament," *ANRW* II, 25.2 (1984), 1169. It may be observed, for instance, that many of the psalms of the Hebrew Bible combine both complaint and thanksgiving (e.g., Pss. 18; 20; 21; 72; 89; 101; 132; and 144), and the same phenomenon is present in the Qumran Hodayot.

3. I am paraphrasing the suggested procedure of the application of the method as produced by the 1949 Ecumenical Study Conference held at Wadham College, Oxford. See E. Krentz, *The Historical-Critical Method* (Philadelphia: Fortress Press, 1975), 2.

4. I have in mind "Jewish Hymns, Odes, and Prayers (ca. 167 B.C.E.–135 C.E.)," in R. A. Kraft and G. W. E. Nickelsburg (eds.), *Early Judaism and Its Modern Interpreters* (Atlanta: Scholars Press, 1986), 411–36 (see especially 424–25), and "A Prolegomenon to a New Study of the Jewish Background of the Hymns and Prayers in the New Testament," in G. Vermes and J. Neusner (eds.), *Essays in Honor of Yigael Yadin* (Oxford Centre for Postgraduate Studies; Totowa, N.J.: Allanheld Osmun & Co., 1983), 265–85 (see especially 274–77). Charlesworth's studies are especially helpful in attempting to identify the prayers in the literature of the period.

5. Berger's opinions are also accessible in more condensed form in his *Formgeschichte des Neuen Testaments* (Heidelberg: Quelle & Meyer, 1984), 239–47. He also wrote the section on New Testament prayer in *TRE* 12, 47–60.

6. Published as *Prayer: A Study in the History and Psychology of Religion* (trans. and ed. S. McComb; New York: Oxford University Press, 1958). The translator informs the reader that with Heiler's concurrence he excised the portions of the German edition that "did not touch vitally his main argument" (v), adding that he also did not include portions of the work that are "of less interest to an English than to a German reader" (!). Heiler's fourth edition (1921) runs to 558 densely packed pages.

7. See #109, "Liturgical Prayers," 199–200. The first 369 pages of the *Enchiridion* covers texts from our period (Greek/Roman third century C.E. patristic material).

8. I have the work of L. Zunz in mind.

9. On the relationship of the "Benediction of the Minim" and the Fourth Gospel, see J. L. Martyn, *History and Theology in the Fourth Gospel* (rev. and enl. ed.; Nashville: Abingdon, 1979). Cf. W. Horbury, "The Benediction of the Minim and Early Jewish-Christian Controversy," *JThS* 33 (1982), 19–61. However, R. Kimelman, "*Birkat Ha-Minim* and the Lack of Evidence for an Anti-Christian Jewish Prayer in Late Antiquity," in E. P. Sanders, A. I. Baumgarten, and A. Mendelson (eds.), *Jewish and Christian Self-Definition*, 2 (London: SCM, 1981), 226–44, doubts that the "Benediction" exercised the function advocated by Martyn.

10. There have been studies of prayers and hymns in certain books of the Pseudepigrapha. M. Lattke's, *Die Oden Salomos in ihrer Bedeutung für Neues Testament und Gnosis* (OBO 25. 1–3; Göttingen: Vandenhoeck & Ruprecht, 1979–86); J. H. Charlesworth's, *The Odes of Solomon* (Missoula, Mont.: Scholars Press, 1978); D. A. Fiensy's, *Prayers Alleged to be Jewish: An Examination*

of the *"Constitutiones Apostolorum"* (Chico, Calif.: Scholars Press, 1985); and A. Enermalm-Ogawa's, *Un langage de prière juif en grec: le témoignage des deux livres des Maccabees* (Stockholm: Almqvist & Wiksell International, 1987) are among the most extensive of these.

11. See Johnson's "Preface," 1. He also used the Rabbinic material cited by Oesterley in his *The Jewish Background of the Christian Liturgy* (Oxford: Clarendon, 1925). This means that Johnson does not discuss "Joseph and Asenath" and the Jewish Apocalypses, apart from *1 Enoch.*

12. See, e.g., S. Holm-Nielsen, *Hodayot: Psalms from Qumran* (Aarhus: Universitetsforlaget, 1960); C. Newsom, *Songs of the Sabbath Sacrifice* (Atlanta: Scholars Press, 1985); J. A. Sanders, *The Psalms Scroll of Qumrân Cave 11 [11QPs^a]* (Oxford: Clarendon, 1965) and E. Schuller, *Non-Canonical Psalms from Qumran* (Atlanta: Scholars Press, 1986).

13. M. Baillet's "Psaumes, hymnes, cantiques et prières dans les manuscrits de Qumran," in R. de Langhe (ed.), *Le Psautier: ses origines, ses problèmes littéraires, son influence* (Louvain: Institut orientaliste, 1962), 339–405, comes closest to such a study.

14. See my unpublished paper "Prayer Texts in Josephus' *Antiquities*: Function and Form, Theology and Purpose," in *Abstracts AAR/SBL 1991* (Atlanta: Scholars Press, 1991), 9.

15. Symptomatic of the neglect is, e.g., É. Bréhier, *Les idées philosophiques et religieuses de Philon d'Alexandrie* (Paris: Vrin, 1950), who devotes an eleven-line footnote to Philo's understanding of prayer on 229–30. S. Sandmel discusses prayer in Philo in an eight-line paragraph in his *Philo of Alexandria: An Introduction* (New York: Oxford University Press, 1979), 115. A. Mendelson's recent book, *Philo's Jewish Identity* (Brown Judaic Studies 161; Atlanta: Scholars Press, 1988), appears not to treat prayer in Philo at all, referring the reader to discussion of the matter in two footnotes on p. 355 of Winston's book of *Selections.* Somewhat more substantial is H. A. Wolfson, *Philo* (Cambridge, Mass.: Harvard University Press, 1947). In his two volumes, he devotes fifteen pages to prayer (see 2:237–52).

16. Of more recent vintage are L. Sabourin's *Christology: Basic Texts in Focus* (New York: Alba, 1984), and C. Osiek and D. Senior (eds.), *Scripture and Prayer* (Wilmington, Del.: Michael Glazier, 1988). Sabourin does not focus as exclusively on the prayers and hymns as one might have expected, concentrating on the christological titles and treating relevant NT hymns in ch. 7 (101–18); Osiek and Senior provide articles on the Lord's Prayer, Luke's Gospel, the Fourth Gospel, sacrifice and prayer in Judaism, and prayer and mission in the Hodayot.

17. I am indebted to Martina Gnadt of the University of Kasel (Germany) for her research in this aspect of Jesus and *Abba.* She also maintains, correctly, that if it can be shown that Jesus' use of *Abba* is not unique and unprecedented, the question of *Abba* as incontrovertible evidence of an *ipsissimum vox* of Jesus falls to the ground. Moreover, on a wider front, she alleges that the quest of the *ipsissima vox* of Jesus has been undertaken both explicitly and implicitly out of anti-Jewish sentiment since one of the criteria for determining these has been the criterion of dissimilarity, in the case of *Abba,* the dissimilarity of Jesus' recorded words to the Judaism of his day.

18. See, e.g., the prayer of Acts 1:24–25, which begins *Su kyrie kardiognōsta pantōn*. The impression given by NT scholarship is that the term *kardiognōstēs* is a distinctive Christian and liturgical expression since it is found in Acts 15:8, frequently in liturgical contexts in subapostolic literature, and in the Apostolic Constitutions (outside the Jewish collection of prayers). Though the term is not found in the Hebrew Bible, the LXX and the Pseudepigrapha, the concept is widely attested in Jewish literature (see, e.g., 1 Sam 16.7; 1 Kgs 8.39; Jer. 17:10; Sir. 42:18; Josephus *Ant.* 6.263). To delimit the expression to Christian circles, therefore, is unwarranted since the concept of God the Knower of the human heart is a thoroughly Jewish one. I would suggest that the reason for the terminology being found on the lips of Peter (and the 120 disciples) is that it was already common to the liturgical tradition of the synagogue.

19. See his important questions in *The Old Testament Pseudepigrapha and the New Testament* (Cambridge: Cambridge University Press, 1985), 120.

20. For Qumran influence, see D. C. Allison, "4Q403 frag. 1, col. 1, 38–46 and the Revelation to John," *RdQ* 12 (1985–87), 409–14; for the influence of the imperial cult, see D. E. Aune, "The Influence of Roman Imperial Court Ceremonial on the Apocalypse," *BR* 28 (1983), 5–26. It is clear that the writer of the NT Apocalypse shares the view of the Jewish apocalypticists that heavenly worship is determinative for earthly worship.

21. See his Preface, xi. As examples of growing appreciation of the Jewishness of early Christian worship, see, e.g., O. Betz, "Early Christian Cult in the Light of Qumran," *RSB* 2 (1982), 73–85; S. Burns, "The Beginnings of Christian Liturgy in Judaism," *SIDIC* 17 (1984), 11–13; D. Flusser, "Sanktus und Gloria," in *Abraham unser Vater: Festschrift O. Michel* (Leiden: Brill, 1963), 129–52; P. Sigal "Early Christian and Rabbinic Liturgical Affinities," *NTS* 30 (1984), 63–90; D. A. Fiensy, *Prayers Alleged to Be Jewish: An Examination of the "Constitutiones Apostolorum"* (Chico, Calif.: Scholars Press, 1985); and P. F. Bradshaw, *The Making of Jewish and Christian Worship* (Notre Dame, Ind.: University of Notre Dame Press, 1991). However, it is also clear that scholars of earlier generations were concerned to trace the origins of many of the prayer texts of the Christian liturgical tradition to Jewish influence.

22. See *The Prayers of Jesus* (Philadelphia: Fortress, 1967), 66–67. Inspired by Matthew 6:7, he appears to dismiss the whole Greek prayer heritage. He writes, "At no other point does the inner corruption and decay of the Hellenistic world — especially of the Levant — in New Testament times become so apparent as in the sphere of prayer. Measured by biblical standards, Greek prayer was lacking in seriousness and reverence even in the pre-Hellenistic period" (66).

23. *The Cross That Spoke: The Origin of the Passion Narrative* (San Francisco: Harper & Row, 1988).

24. The received formula speaks of an act of homage, i.e., *proskynēma para tǭtois theǭ/theois*. I know of no manifestly Christian letter that speaks about an act of *proskunēma* before God associated with prayer. See further the discussion in B. Couroyer, "*BRK* et les formules égyptiennes de salutation," *RB* 85 (1978), 575–85, and H. Koskenniemi, *Studien zur Idee und Phraseologie des griechischen Briefes bis 400 n. Chr.* (Helsinki/Wiesbaden: Suomalaien Tiedakatamie/Otto Harrassowitz, 1956), 139–45.

25. P. Oxy. 2156 (late fourth/fifth centuries C.E.) anticipates the later sixth/ seventh centuries' trend to ascribe to God the ordering of one's affairs without the expressed or implied act of homage (*proskynēma*) before the deity. P. Oxy. 1844–54 and 1860 (all sixth and seventh century C.E.) show the breaking down of the usual introductory formula. However, see P. Oxy. 1070 (third century C.E.). In this remarkable non-Christian letter the writer details his prayers for his addressees in the first eleven lines.

ABBREVIATIONS

For the most part, abbreviations are taken from S. Schwertner (ed.), *Internationales Abkürzungsverzeichnis für Theologie und Grenzgebiete* (Berlin/New York: de Gruyter, 1976).

ABR	Australian Biblical Review
AfThJ	Africa Theological Journal
AGJU	Arbeiten zur Geschichte des antiken Judentums und Urchristentums
AGSU	Arbeiten zur Geschichte des späteren Judentums und des Urchristentums
AJBA	Australian Journal of Biblical Archaeology
ALGHJ	Arbeiten zur Literatur und Geschichte des hellenistischen Judentums
ALW	Archiv für Liturgiewissenschaft
AmiCl	L'ami du clergé
AnBib	Analecta Biblica
ANRW	W. Haase and H. Temporini (eds.), *Aufstieg und Niedergang der römischen Welt* (Berlin/New York: de Gruyter, 1972–)
Anton	Antonianum
AOAT	Alter Orient und Altes Testament
ArOr	Archiv Orientální
ARW	Archiv für Religionswissenschaft
ASNU	Acta Seminarii Neotestamentici Upsaliensis
AssS	Assemblées du Seigneur
AStE	Annuario di Studi Ebraici
AThANT	Abhandlungen zur Theologie des Alten und Neuen Testaments
AThR	Anglican Theological Review
Aug	Augustinianum
BAGD	W. Bauer, W. F. Arndt, F. W. Gingrich, and F. W. Danker, *Greek English Lexicon of the New Testament* (Chicago: University of Chicago Press, 1979)
BASOR	Bulletin of the American Schools of Oriental Research
BBA	Berliner byzantinische Arbeiten
BEFAR	Bibliothèque des écoles françaises d'Athènes et de Rome
BEThL	Bibliotheca Ephemeridum Theologicarum Lovaniensium
Bib	Biblica

BibOr	Biblica et Orientalia
BibR	Biblia Revuo
BibSac	Bibliotheca Sacra
BiKi	Bibel und Kirche
BiLe	Bibel und Leben
BiLi	Bibel und Liturgie
BiOr	Bibliotheca Orientalis
BiTod	The Bible Today
BiTr	Bible Translator
BJRL	Bulletin of the John Rylands Library
BKP	Beiträge zur klassischen Philologie
BR	Biblical Research
BSOAS	Bulletin of the School of Oriental and African Studies
BTB	Biblical Theology Bulletin
BThZ	Berliner theologische Zeitschrift
BVC	Bible et vie chrétienne
BWANT	Beiträge zur Wissenschaft vom Alten und Neuen Testament
BySl	Byzantinoslavica
BZ	Biblische Zeitschrift
BZAW	Beihefte zur Zeitschrift für die alttestamentliche Wissenschaft
CalThJ	Calvin Theological Journal
CBG	Collationes Brugenses et Gandavenses
CBQ	Catholic Biblical Quarterly
ChrTo	Christianity Today
CivCatt	Civiltà Cattolica
ClB	Classical Bulletin
CleR	Clergy Review
CNT	Coniectanea Neotestamentica
Conc	Concilium
CQ	Classical Quarterly
CQR	Church Quarterly Review
CRINT	Corpus Rerum Iudaicarum ad Novum Testamentum
CrossCur	Cross Currents
CultBib	Cultura Bíblica
CuThM	Currents in Theology and Mission
CV	Communio Viatorum

DB	F. Vigouroux (ed.), *Dictionnaire de la Bible* (Paris: Letouzey et Ané, 1895–1912)
DBM	Deltio Biblikōn Meletōn
DBS	L. Pirot et al. (eds.), *Dictionnaire de la Bible, Suppléments* (Paris: Letouzey et Ané, 1928–)
DR	Downside Review
DTT	Dansk Teologisk Tidsskrift
ED	Euntes Docet
EE	Estudios Ecclesiásticos
EKKNT	Evangelisch-Katholischer Kommentar zum Neuen Testament
EKKNTV	Evangelisch-Katholischer Kommentar zum Neuen Testament Vorarbeiten
EL	Ephemerides Liturgicae
EMH	Early Music History
EspVie	Esprit et vie
EstB	Estudios Bíblicos
ET	Expository Times
EThL	Ephemerides Theologicae Lovanienses
ETR	Études théologiques et religieuses
EvQ	Evangelical Quarterly
EvTh	Evangelische Theologie
EWNT	H. Balz and G. Schneider (eds.), *Exegetische Wörterbuch zum Neuen Testament* (Stuttgart/Berlin/Cologne/Mainz: Kohlhammer, 1980–83)
Exp	Expositor
FRLANT	Forschungen zur Religion und Literatur des Alten und Neuen Testaments
GL	Geist und Leben
Gr	Gregorianum
HDR	Harvard Dissertations in Religion
HervTeolStud	Hervormde Teologiese Studies
HeyJ	Heythrop Journal
HNT	Handbuch zum Neuen Testament
HomPastRev	Homiletic and Pastoral Review
HSCP	Harvard Studies in Classical Philology
HThR	Harvard Theological Review
HTKNT	Herders theologischer Kommentar zum Neuen Testament
HUCA	Hebrew Union College Annual

IDB	G. A. Buttrick et al. (eds.), *Interpreters Dictionary of the Bible* (4 vols.; Nashville: Abingdon, 1962)
IEJ	Israel Exploration Journal
Interp	Interpretation
IRM	International Review of Mission
IsrOrSt	Israel Oriental Studies
JAAR	Journal of the American Academy of Religion
JAC	Jahrbuch für Antike und Christentum
JBL	Journal of Biblical Literature
JCPh. S	Neue Jahrbücher für classische Philologie, Supplement
Jdm	Judaism
JEH	Journal of Ecclesiastical History
JES	Journal of Ecumenical Studies
JEThS	Journal of the Evangelical Theological Society
JJGL	Jahrbuch für jüdische Geschichte und Literatur
JJS	Journal of Jewish Studies
JLW	Jahrbuch für Liturgiewissenschaft
JNES	Journal of Near Eastern Studies
JÖAI	Jahreshefte des österreichen archäologischen Institutes in Wien
JÖB	Jahrbuch der österreichischen Byzantinistik
JQR	Jewish Quarterly Review
JR	Journal of Religion
JRS	Journal of Roman Studies
JSHZ	W. G. Kümmel et al. (eds.), *Jüdische Schriften aus hellenistisch-römischer Zeit* (Gütersloh: Mohn, 1973–)
JSJ	Journal of the Study of Judaism in the Persian, Hellenistic and Roman Period
JSNT	Journal for the Study of the New Testament
JSNTSS	Journal for the Study of the New Testament Supplement Series
JSOT	Journal for the Study of the Old Testament
JSOTSS	Journal for the Study of the Old Testament Supplement Series
JSP	Journal for the Study of the Pseudepigrapha
JSS	Journal of Semitic Studies
JThS	Journal of Theological Studies
KuD	Kerygma und Dogma
LQ	Liturgiegeschichtliche Quellen

LSJ	Liddell-Scott-Jones, *Greek-English Lexicon, with Supplement* (Oxford: Clarendon, 1983)
LTP	Laval théologique et philosophique
LV	Lumen Vitae
MD	Maison-Dieu
MethR	Methodist Review
MGWJ	Monatsschrift für Geschichte und Wissenschaft des Judentums
MH	Museum Helveticum
MM	J. H. Moulton and G. Milligan, *The Vocabulary of the Greek Testament* (reprint; Grand Rapids, Mich.: Eerdmans, 1983)
Mn	Mnemosyne
MQR	Methodist Quarterly Review
MThZ	Münchener Theologische Zeitschrift
NBl	New Blackfriars
NedThT	Nederlands Theologisch Tijdschrift
NGWG. PH	Nachrichten der Gesellschaft der Wissenschaften in Göttingen: Philologisch-historische Klasse.
NRTh	Nouvelle revue théologique
NT	Novum Testamentum
NT. S	Novum Testamentum Supplements
NTAbh	Neutestamentliche Abhandlungen
NTD	Das Neue Testament Deutsche
NTOA	Novum Testamentum et Orbis Antiquus
NTS	New Testament Studies
NTTS	New Testament Tools and Studies
OBO	Orbis Biblicus et Orientalis
OLZ	Orientalische Literaturzeitung
Or	Orientalia
OrChr	Oriens Christianus
OrChrA	Orientalia Christiana analecta
OTP	J. H. Charlesworth (ed.), *The Old Testament Pseudepigrapha* (2 vols.; Garden City, N.Y.: Doubleday, 1983–85)
PEQ	Palestine Exploration Quarterly
PIBA	Proceedings of the Irish Biblical Association

PRE	G. Wissowa et al. (eds.), *Paulys Real-Encyclopädie der classischen Alterthumswissenschaft* (Stuttgart: J. B. Metzlerscher Verlag, 1893–1939; Alfred Druckenmüller Verlag, 1955–80)
PRSt	Perspectives in Religious Studies
PSB	Princeton Seminary Bulletin
PSBA	Proceedings of the Society of Biblical Archaeology
PUCSC	Pubblicazioni della Università Cattolica del Sacro Cuore
RAC	T. Klausner et al. (eds.), *Reallexicon für Antike und Christentum: Sachwörterbuch zur Auseinandersetzung des Urchristentums mit der antiken Welt* (Stuttgart: A. Hiersemann, 1950–)
RAE	Revista Agustiniana de Espiritualidad
RAM	Revue d'ascétique et de mystique
RB	Revue biblique
RCCM	Rivista di Cultura Classica e Medioevale
RdQ	Revue de Qumran
RE	Realencyklopädie für protestantische Theologie und Kirche
REG	Revue des études grecques
REJ	Revue des études juives
RelLife	Religion in Life
RevAfTh	Review of African Theology
RevBib	Revista Bíblica
RevExp	Review and Expositor
RevistEspir	Revista de Espiritualidad
RGG	H. Gunkel and L. Zscharnak (eds.), *Die Religion in Geschichte und Gegenwart* (Tübingen: Mohr, 1927–31²; K. Galling et al. [eds.], 1957–65³)
RHE	Revue d'histoire ecclésiastique
RHPhR	Revue d'histoire et de philosophie religieuses
RHR	Revue d'histoire des religions
RivBib	Rivista Biblica
RLA	E. Ebeling and B. Meißner (eds.), *Reallexicon der Assyriologie* (Berlin, 1928–)
RMP	Rheinisches Museum für Philologie
RR	Review of Religion
RSB	Revista Storica Benedittina
RSPhTh	Revue des sciences philosophiques et théologiques
RSR	Recherches de science religieuse

RThPh	Revue de théologie et de philosophie
RThR	Reformed Theological Review
RTK	Roczniki Teologiczna — Kanoniczne
RVV	Religionsgeschichtliche Versuche und Vorarbeiten
SBL	Society of Biblical Literature
SBLDS	Society of Biblical Literature Dissertation Series
SBLSCS	Society of Biblical Literature Septuagint and Cognate Studies
SBLTT	Society of Biblical Literature Texts and Translations
SBM	Stuttgarter biblische Monographien
SBT	Studies in Biblical Theology
SciEsp	Science et esprit
Sem	Semitica
SEÅ	Svensk Exegetisk Årsbok
SIDIC	Service internationale de documentation judéo-chrétienne
SJLA	Studies in Judaism in Late Antiquity
SJTh	Scottish Journal of Theology
SNTSMS	Studiorum Novi Testamenti Societas Monograph Series
SO	Symbolae Osloenses
SP	Studies in Patrology
SPAW. PH	Sitzungsberichte der preussischen Akademie der Wissenschaften, Philosophisch-historische Klasse
StANT	Studia Antoniana
StDJ	Studies on the Texts of the Desert of Judah
StE	Studia Evangelica
StLi	Studia Liturgica
StNT	Studien zum Neuen Testaments
StTh	Studia Theologica
StUNT	Studien zur Umwelt des Neuen Testaments
SvTK	Svensk Teologisk Kvartalskrift
SVTP	Studia in Veteris Testamenti Pseudepigrapha
SWJTh	Southwestern Journal of Theology
TAPA	Transactions of the American Philological Association
TB	Theologische Bücherei
TBAW	Tübinger Beiträge zur Altertumswissenschaft
TDNT	G. Kittel (ed.), *Theological Dictionary of the New Testament* (trans. G. W. Bromiley; Grand Rapids, Mich.: Eerdmans, 1964–76)

THAT	E. Jenni and C. Westermann (eds.), *Theologisches Handwörterbuch zum Alten Testament* (Munich: Kaiser Verlag, 1971–79)
ThB	Theologische Beiträge
ThBl	Theologische Blätter
ThD	Theology Digest
Theol	Theology
TheolPhil	Theologie und Philosophie
THKNT	Theologischer Handkommentar zum Neuen Testament
ThLZ	Theologische Literaturzeitung
ThQ	Theologische Quartalschrift
ThR	Theologische Rundschau
ThStKr	Theologische Studien und Kritiken
ThTo	Theology Today
ThV	Theologia Viatorum
ThZ	Theologische Zeitschrift
TRE	G. Krause and G. Müller (eds.), *Theologisches Realenzyklopädie* (Berlin: de Gruyter, 1977–)
TrinJ	Trinity Journal
TS	Theological Studies
TThZ	Trierer theologische Zeitschrift
TU	Texte und Untersuchungen zur Geschichte der altchristlichen Literatur
TynB	Tyndale Bulletin
US	Una Sancta
VC	Verbum Caro
VD	Verbum Domini
VF	Verkündigung und Forschung
Vg	Vulgate
VigChr	Vigiliae Christianae
VivPen	Vivre et penser
VoxEv	Vox Evangelica
VT	Vetus Testamentum
VT. S	Vetus Testamentum Supplements
WD	Wort und Dienst
WMANT	Wissenschaftliche Monographien zum Alten und Neuen Testament
WSt	Wiener Studien

WThJ	Westminster Theological Journal
WUNT	Wissenschaftliche Untersuchungen zum Neuen Testament
WZ(L)	Wissenschaftliche Zeitschrift des Karl-Marx-Universität (Leipzig)
ZAW	Zeitschrift für die alttestamentliche Wissenschaft und die Kunde der nachbiblischen Judentums
ZDMG	Zeitschrift der deutschen morgenländischen Gesellschaft
ZKG	Zeitschrift für Kirchengeschichte
ZKTh	Zeitschrift für katholische Theologie
ZNW	Zeitschrift für die neutestamentliche Wissenschaft und die Kunde der älteren Kirche
ZPE	Zeitschrift für Papyrologie und Epigraphik
ZRGG	Zeitschrift für Religions- und Geistesgeschichte
ZThK	Zeitschrift für Theologie und Kirche
ZWTh	Zeitschrift für wissenschaftliche Theologie

1. STYLISTIC AND GENRE ANALYSIS

1   Audet, J.-P.   "Esquisse historique du genre littéraire de la 'Bénédiction' juive et de l' 'Eucharistie' chrétienne," *RB* 65 (1958), 371–99.

2   Audet, J.-P.   "Literary Forms and Contents of a Normal *Eucharistia* in the First Century," *StE* 1 (1959), 643–62.

3   Berger, K.   "Hellenistische Gattungen im Neuen Testament," *ANRW* II, 25.2 (1984), 1149–73, 1359–61, 1371–73.

4   Berger, K.   "Hymnus und Gebet," in *Formgeschichte des Neuen Testaments* (Heidelberg: Quelle & Meyer, 1984), 239–47.

5   Bonsirven, J.   "Genres littéraires dans la littérature juive post-biblique," *Bib* 35 (1954), 328–45.

6   Crüsemann, F.   *Studien zur Formgeschichte von Hymnus und Danklied in Israel* (WMANT 32; Neukirchen-Vluyn: Neukirchener Verlag, 1969).

7   Gerstenberger, E. S.   "Psalms," in J. H. Hayes (ed.), *Old Testament Form Criticism* (San Antonio, Tex.: Trinity University Press, 1974), 179–223.

8   Gunkel, H.   *Einleitung in die Psalmen: Die Gattungen der religiösen Lyrik Israels* (Göttingen: Vandenhoeck & Ruprecht, 1933).

9   Heinen, K.   "Das Nomen *tᵉfilla* als Gattungsbezeichnung," *BZ* N.F. 17 (1973), 103–5.

10   Jewett, R.   "The Form and Function of the Homiletic Benediction," *AThR* 51 (1969), 18–34.

11   Koch, K.   *Was ist Formgeschichte?* (Neukirchen-Vluyn: Neukirchener Verlag, 1989), 195–222.

12   McComiskey, T. E.   "The Hymnic Elements of the Prophecy of Amos: A Study of Form-Critical Methodology," *JEThS* 30 (1987), 139–57.

13   Mullins, T. Y.   "Petition as a Literary Form," *NT* 5 (1962), 46–54.

14   Norden, E.   *Agnostos Theos: Untersuchungen zur Formengeschichte religiöser Rede* (Leipzig: Teubner, 1913).

15   Passioni Dell' Acqua, A.   "Il genere letterario dell'inno e del canto di ringraziamento nell'Antico e nel Nuovo Testamento e negli inni di Qumrân (1QH)," *EL* 90 (1976), 72–80.

16   Peterson, E.   *HEIS THEOS: Epigraphische, formgeschichtliche und religionsgeschichtliche Untersuchungen* (Göttingen: Vandenhoeck & Ruprecht, 1926).

17   Price, C. F.   *What Is a Hymn?* (Springfield, Ohio: Hymn Society of America, 1937).

18   Pridik, K.-H.   "Vergil's 'Georgica': Darstellung und Interpretation
                         des Aufbaus," *ANRW* II, 31.1 (1980), 500–548.
19   Schäfer, P.   "Benediktion, I," *TRE 5*, 560–62.
20   Spanier, A.   "Stilkritisches zum jüdischen Gebet," *MGWJ* 80
                         (1936), 339–50.

2. GENERAL STUDIES

21   Araújo, L. C. (ed.)   *A Oração ao Deus da bíblia* (Petrópolis, Brazil:
                           Editora Vôzes, 1986).

22   Barucq, A.   *L'expression de la louange divine et de la prière
                           dans la Bible et en Egypte* (Bibliothèque d'étude, 33;
                           Cairo: Institut français archéologie orientale, 1962).

23   Benoit, P.   "La prière dans les religions gréco-romaines et dans
                           le christianisme primitif," *Ecumenical Institute for
                           Advanced Theological Studies: Yearbook 1978–79*
                           (Tantur/Jerusalem: Franciscan Printing Press, 1981),
                           19–43.

24   Bickermann, E. J.   "Bénédiction et prière," *RB* 69 (1962), 524–32.
25   Bockmuehl, M.   "Should We Kneel to Pray?," *Crux* 26 (1990), 14–17.
26   Bogaert, P.-M.   "Pour une phénoménologie de l'appropriation de
                           la prière: Le cantique d'Anne dans le 1er Livre
                           de Samuel, dans les Antiquitiés bibliques et dans
                           le Nouveau Testament," in H. Limet and J. Ries
                           (eds.), *L'expérience de la prière dans les grandes re-
                           ligions: actes du colloque de Louvain-la-Neuve et
                           Liège (22–23 novembre 1978)* (Louvain-la-Neuve:
                           Centre d'histoire des religions, 1980), 245–59.

27   Bornkamm, G.   "Lobpreis, Bekenntnis und Opfer," in W. Eltester
                           and F. H. Kettler (eds.), *Apophoreta: Festschrift für
                           E. Haenchen zu seinem siebzigsten Geburtstag am 10
                           Dezember 1964* (BZAW 30; Berlin: A. Töpelmann,
                           1964), 46–63.

28   Clements, R. E.   *In Spirit and Truth: Insights from Biblical Prayers*
                           (Atlanta: John Knox, 1985).

29   Clements, R. E.   *The Prayers of the Bible* (London: SCM Press, 1986).
30   Clowney, E. P.   "A Biblical Theology of Prayer," in D. A. Carson
                           (ed.), *Teach Us to Pray: Prayer in the Bible and the
                           World* (Exeter, U.K.: Paternoster/Baker, 1990), 136–
                           73, 336–38.

31   Filson, F. V.   "Petition and Intercession: The Biblical Doctrine of
                           Prayer (2)," *Interp* 8 (1954), 21–34.

32 Glöcker, R.   *Neutestamentliche Wundergeschichten und das Lob der Wundertaten Gottes in den Psalmen* (Mainz: Matthias-Grünewald, 1983).

33 González, A.   "Prière," *DBS* 8, cols. 555–606.

34 González, A.   *La oración en la Bíblia* (Teología y siglo XX, 9; Madrid: Ediciones Cristiandad, 1968).

35 Greeven, H., and *"euchomai,"* *TDNT* 2, 775–808.
    Herrmann, J.

36 Guth, W. W.   "Prayer in Scripture," *MethR* 90 (1908), 602–10.

37 Hamman, A.   "La prière chrétienne et la prière païenne, formes et différences," *ANRW* II, 23.2 (1980), 1190–1247.

38 Harding, M.   "The Biblical Concept of Praise," in B. G. Webb (ed.), *Church, Worship and the Local Congregation* (Explorations 2; Sydney, N.S.W.: Lancer, 1987), 27–44.

39 Heiler, F.   *Das Gebet: eine religionsgeschichtliche und religionspsychologische Untersuchung* (5th ed.; Munich: E. Reinhardt, 1923). Reprinted 1969.

40 Heiler, F., et al. "Gebet," *RGG*³ 2, 1209–30.

41 Hengel, M.   "Das Christuslied im frühesten Gottesdienst," in W. Baier, S. Horn et al., *Weisheit Gottes — Weisheit der Welt: Festschrift für Kardinal Ratzinger zum 60. Geburtstag* (St. Ottilien: EOS Verlag, 1987), 1, 357–404. Discusses the Jewish Psalm tradition and its contribution to the background to the NT Christological hymns, NT Christ psalms and psalmic fragments, as well as the Christological hymns of the second and third centuries.

42 Heschel, A. J.   "Ce qu'est la prière," in J. Heinemann (ed.), *La prière juive: une anthologie* (trans. J. Dessellier, Les Cahiers de l'Institut Catholique de Lyon 13; Lyon: Profac, 1984), 13–25.

43 Hollenweger, W. J. "Healing through Prayer: Superstition or Forgotten Christian Tradition," *Theol* 92 (1989), 166–74.

44 Horst, F.   "Segen und Segenshandlungen in der Bibel," *EvTh* 7 (1947), 23–37.

45 Jungmann, J. A.   *Christian Prayer through the Centuries* (New York: Paulist, 1978).

46 Kroll, J.   *Die christliche Hymnodik bis zu Klemens von Alexandreia* (2d ed.; Darmstadt: Wissenschaftliche Buchgesellschaft, 1968). A study of NT and early Christian hymns.

47 Lattke, M.   *Hymnus: Materialien zu einer Geschichte der antiken Hymnologie* (NTOA 19; Freiburg/Göttingen: Universitätsverlag/Vandenhoeck & Ruprecht, 1991).

48	Lesètre, H.	"Prière," *DB* 5, cols. 663–75.
49	Limbeck, M.	"Bitt- und Klagegebet aus biblischer Sicht — ein Testfall des Glaubens," in J. Sauer (ed.), *Beten in unserer Zeit* (Freiburg: Herder, 1979), 105–26.
50	Lipinski, E.	*La liturgie pénitentielle dans la Bible* (Paris: Cerf, 1969).
51	Lockyer, H.	*All the Prayers of the Bible* (Grand Rapids, Mich.: Zondervan, 1959).
52	Lodi, E.	*Enchiridion euchologicum fontium liturgicum: Clavis methodologica cum commentariis* (Bologna, 1979).
53	Lodi, E. (ed.)	*Enchiridion euchologicum fontium liturgicum* (Bibliotheca "Ephemerides Liturgicae," Subsidia 15; Rome: Centro Liturgico Vencenziano/Edizioni Liturgiche, 1979).
54	Lohfink, N.	*Lobgesänge der Armen: Studien zum Magnifikat, den Hodajot von Qumran und einigen späten Psalmen: Mit einem Anhang: Hodajot–Bibliographie 1948–89 von Ulrich Dahmen* (Stuttgart: Katholisches Bibelwerk, 1990).
55	McFayden, J. E.	*Prayers of the Bible* (New York: A. C. Armstrong & Sons, 1906).
56	Michel, O.	"Gebet II (Fürbitte)," *RAC* 9, cols. 1–36.
57	Miller, P. D.	"In Praise and Thanksgiving," *ThTo* 45 (1988), 180–88.
58	Navone, J.	"Prayer," *Scripture* 20 (1968), 115–25.
59	Nola, A. M. di	*Anthologie des prières de tous les temps: Préface, choix et notices* (Paris: Seghers, 1958).
60	Ohm, T.	*Die Gebetsgebärden der Völker und des Christentums* (Leiden: Brill, 1948).
61	Otto, G.	"Über das Gebet," in F. Bargheer and J. Röbelen (eds.), *Gebet und Gebetserziehung* (Heidelberg: Quelle & Meyer, 1971), 31–48.
62	Pettazzoni, R.	"Confession of Sins and the Classics," *HThR* 30 (1937), 1–14.
63	Petuchowski, J. J., and Brocke, M. (eds.)	*The Lord's Prayer and Jewish Liturgy* (New York: Seabury Press, 1978). Originally published as *Das Vaterunser: Gemeinsames im Beten von Juden und Christen* (Freiburg i. Breisgau: Herder, 1974), with Brocke, Petuchowski, and W. Strolz as editors. The German edition is more extensive, containing a number of essays not translated in the English version.
64	Piper, O. A.	"Praise of God and Thanksgiving: The Biblical Doctrine of Prayer (1)," *Interp* 8 (1954), 3–20.

65 Quervain, A. de *Das Gebet* (Zürich: Evangelischer Verlag, 1948).

66 Ratschow, C. H. "Gebet, I (Religionsgeschichtlich)," *TRE* 12, 31–34.

67 Ross, J. M. "Amen," *ET* 102 (1991), 166–71.

68 Scheele, P.-W. *Halleluja–Amen: Gebete Israels aus drei Jahrtausenden* (Oecumenismus Spiritualis 1; Paderborn: Verlag Bonifacius-Druckerei, 1974).

69 Schille, G. *Frühchristliche Hymnen* (Berlin: Evangelische Verlagsanstalt, 1965). Discusses NT hymns, Acts of Thomas, Qumran hymns, Odes of Solomon, and hymns in the Apostolic Fathers.

70 Schneider, H. "Die biblische Oden in christlichen Altertum," *Bib* 30 (1949), 28–65, 432–53.

71 Schönweiss, H., et al. "Prayer, etc.," in C. Brown (ed.), *The New International Dictionary of New Testament Theology* (Grand Rapids, Mich.: Zondervan, 1976), 2, 855–86.

72 Severus, E. von "Gebet I," *RAC* 8, cols. 1134–1258.

73 Smith, C. W. F. "Prayer," *IDB* 3, 857–67.

74 Spinks, B. D. *The Sanctus in the Eucharistic Prayer* (Cambridge: University Press, 1991), Part 1. Discussion of the background to the later attested Sanctus in the liturgies of the fourth century and later in the Hebrew Bible, early and Rabbinic era Judaism, and the NT.

75 Stendahl, K. "Prayer and Forgiveness," *SEÅ* 22–23 (1957–58), 75–86.

76 Stuiber, A. "Amen," *JAC* 1 (1953), 153–59.

77 Stuiber, A. "Doxologie," *RAC* 4, cols. 210–26.

78 Sweeney, D. "Intercessory Prayer in Ancient Egypt and the Bible," in S. Israelit-Gross (ed.), *Pharaonic Egypt and Christianity* (Jerusalem: Magnes Press, 1985), 213–30.

79 Towner, W. S. " 'Blessed Be YHWH' and 'Blessed Art Thou, YHWH': The Modulation of a Biblical Formula," *CBQ* 30 (1968), 386–99.

80 Uloth, H. "Geist und Gebet," in K. Heimbucher (ed.), *Das biblische Zeugnis vom Heiligen Geist* (Denkendorf: Gnadauer, 1973), 102–8.

81 Vagaggini, C., and Penco, G. (eds.) *La preghiera nella bibbia e nella tradizione patristica e monastica* (Rome: Edizioni Paoline, 1964).

82 Vouga, F., et al. "Providence et prière: références bibliques," in *Bulletin du Centre Protestant D'Études* 30 (1978), 31–39.

83 Wainwright, G. "Praying for Kings: The Place of Human Rulers in the Divine Plan of Salvation," *Ex Auditu* 2 (1986), 117–27.

84   Weinreich, O.   *Gebet und Wunder* (Darmstadt: Wissenschaftliche Buchgesellschaft, 1968).

85   Willis, G. G.   "Sacrificium Laudis," in B. D. Spinks (ed.), *The Sacrifice of Praise: Studies on the Themes of Thanksgiving and Redemption in the Central Prayers of the Eucharistic and Baptismal Liturgies, in Honour of Arthur Hubert Couratin* (Rome: Edizioni Liturgiche, 1981), 73–87.

3. HEBREW BIBLE

86   Aejmelaeus, A.   *The Traditional Prayer in the Psalms* (New York/Berlin: Walter de Gruyter, 1986).

87   Ahuis, F.   *Der klagende Gerichtsprophet: Studien zur Klage in der Überlieferung von den altestamentlichen Gerichtspropheten* (Stuttgart: Calwer Verlag, 1982).

88   Albertz, R.   "*s'q* schreien," THAT 2 (1976), 568–75.

89   Albertz, R.   "*'tr* beten," THAT 2 (1976), 385–86.

90   Albertz, R.   "Gebet, II (AT)," in TRE 12, 34–42.

91   Anderson, B. W.   *Out of the Depths: The Psalms Speak for Us Today* (Philadelphia: Westminster, 1983).

92   Ap-Thomas, D. R.   "Notes on Some Terms Relating to Prayer," VT 6 (1956), 225–41.

93   Ap-Thomas, D. R.   "Some Notes on the Old Testament Attitude to Prayer," SJTh 9 (1956), 424–29.

94   Auffret, P.   *Hymnes d'Égypte et d'Israël* (OBO 34; Fribourg/Göttingen: Éditions universitaires/Vandenhoeck & Ruprecht, 1981).

95   Balentine, S. E.   "Jeremiah, Prophet of Prayer," RevExp 78 (1981), 331–44.

96   Balentine, S. E.   "Prayer in the Wilderness Traditions: In Pursuit of Divine Justice," *Hebrew Annual Review* 9 (1985), 53–74.

97   Balentine, S. E.   "Prayers for Justice in the Old Testament: Theodicy and Theology," CBQ 51 (1989), 597–616.

98   Balentine, S. E.   "Enthroned on the Praises and Laments of Israel," PSB Supp. 2 (1992), 20–35.

99   Baumgartner, W.   *Die Klagegedichte des Jeremia* (BZAW 32; Gießen: A. Töpelmann, 1917).

100 Beaucamp, E.   *Israël en prière: Des psaumes au Nôtre Père* (Paris: Cerf, 1985).

101 Begrich, J. "Die Vertrauensäußerungen im israelitischen Klagelied des Eizelnen und in seinem Babylonischen Gegenstück," *ZAW* 46 (1928), 221–60.

102 Berg, W. *Die sogennanten Hymnenfragmente im Amosbuch* (Bern/Frankfurt: H. Lang/P. Lang, 1974).

103 Beyerlin, W. *Die Rettung der Bedrängten in den Feindpsalmen der Einzelnen auf institutionelle Zusammenhange untersucht* (FRLANT 99; Göttingen: Vandenhoeck & Ruprecht, 1970).

104 Blank, S. H. "The Confessions of Jeremiah and the Meaning of Prayer," *HUCA* 21 (1948), 331–54.

105 Blank, S. H. "Men against God — The Promethean Element in Biblical Prayer," *JBL* (1953), 1–13 = *Prophetic Thought: Essays and Addresses* (Cincinnati: Hebrew Union College Press, 1977), 91–101.

106 Blank, S. H. "Some Observations Concerning Biblical Prayer," *HUCA* 32 (1961), 75–90 = *Prophetic Thought: Essays and Addresses,* 75–89.

107 Boer, P. A. H. de *De voorbede in het Oude Testament* (Leiden: Brill, 1943).

108 Boyce, R. N. *The Cry to God in the Old Testament* (Atlanta: Scholars Press, 1988).

109 Brueggemann, W. "From Hurt to Joy, From Death to Life," *Interp* 28 (1974), 28–38.

110 Brueggemann, W. "The Formfulness of Grief," *Interp* 31 (1977), 263–75.

111 Brueggemann, W. "Psalms and the Life of Faith: A Suggested Typology of Function," *JSOT* 17 (1980), 3–32.

112 Brueggemann, W. *The Message of the Psalms* (Minneapolis: Augsburg, 1984).

113 Brueggemann, W. "The Costly Cry of Lament," *JSOT* 36 (1986), 57–71.

114 Brueggemann, W. *Israel's Praise: Doxology against Idolatry and Ideology* (Philadelphia: Fortress, 1988).

115 Brueggemann, W. "The Psalms as Prayer," *Reformed Liturgy and Music* 23 (1989), 13–26.

116 Brueggemann, W. *Abiding Astonishment: Psalms, Modernity and the Making of History* (Louisville: Westminster/John Knox, 1991).

117 Buck, F. "Prayer in the Old Testament," in J. Plevnik (ed.), *Word and Spirit: Essays in Honor of David Michael Stanley, S.J. on His 60th Birthday* (Willowdale, Ont.: Regis College Press, 1975), 61–110.

118   Buhl, F.   "Über Dankbarkeit im Alten Testament und die sprachlichen Ausdrücke dafür," in *Abhandlungen zur semitischen Religionskunde zum Sprachwissenschaft: Festschrift Wolf Wilhelm Grafen von Baudissin zum 26. September 1917 überreicht von Freunden und Schülern* (BZAW 33; Gießen: A. Töpelmann, 1918), 71–82.

119   Castellino, G. R.   "I beni richiesti nelle preghiere di Israele," *Communio* 10–11 (1969), 275–97.

120   Cazalles, H.   "Gestes et paroles de prière dans l'Ancien Testament," in C. Andronikof et al. (eds.), *Gestes et paroles dans les diverses familles liturgiques* (Rome: Centro Liturgico Vincenziano, 1978), 87–94.

121   Cimosa, M.   "Il vocabulario della preghiera nella traduzione greca (LXX) dei Salmi," *EL* 105 (1991), 89–119.

122   Crenshaw, J. L.   *Hymnic Affirmations of Divine Justice: The Doxologies of Amos and Related Texts in the Old Testament* (Missoula, Mont.: Scholars Press, 1975).

123   Croft, S. J. L.   *The Identity of the Individual in the Psalms* (JSOTSS 44; Sheffield, U.K.: JSOT Press, 1987).

124   Dalglish, E. E.   *Psalm Fifty-One* (Leiden: Brill, 1962).

125   Deissler, A.   "Der Geist des Vaterunsers im alttestamentlichen Glauben und Beten," in M. Brocke, J. J. Petuchowski, and W. Strolz (eds.), *Das Vaterunser: Gemeinsames im Beten von Juden und Christen* (Freiburg i. Breisgau: Herder, 1974), 131–50.

126   Döller, J.   *Das Gebet im Alten Testament* (Vienna: Buchhandlung "Reichspost" (A. Opitz' Nachfolger), 1914). Repr., Hildesheim: Gerstenberg, 1974.

127   Eaton, J.   "Gifts of Prayer in the Old Testament," *PIBA* 4 (1980), 1–11.

128   Fleming, J.   *Thirty Psalmists: A Study in Personalities of the Psalter as Seen against the Background of Gunkel's Type Study of the Psalter* (New York: G. P. Putnam's Sons, 1938).

129   Fretheim, T. E.   "Prayer in the Old Testament: Creating Space in the World for God," in P. R. Sponheim (ed.), *A Primer on Prayer* (Philadelphia: Fortress, 1988), 51–62.

130   Fuchs, O.   *Die Klage als Gebet: Eine theologische Besinnung am Beispiel des Psalms 22* (Kösel: Verlag Munich, 1982).

131   Gaiser, F. J.   "Individual and Corporate Prayer in the Old Testament," in P. Sponheim (ed.), *A Primer on Prayer* (Philadelphia: Westminster, 1988), 9–22.

132 Gerstenberger, E. S. "Der klagende Mensch," in H. W. Wolff (ed.), *Probleme biblischer Theologie: Festschrift G. von Rad* (Munich: C. Kaiser, 1971), 64–72.

133 Gerstenberger, E. S. *Der bittende Mensch: Bittritual und Klagelied des Einzelnen im Alten Testament* (WMANT 51; Neukirchen-Vluyn: Neukirchener Verlag, 1980).

134 Gerstenberger, E. S. *Psalms, Part 1; With an Introduction to Cultic Poetry* (Grand Rapids, Mich.: Eerdmans, 1988).

135 Goeke, H. "Die Anthropologie der individuelle Klagelieder," *BiLe* 14 (1973), 13–29, 112–37.

136 Goulder, M. D. *The Psalms of Korah: Studies in the Psalter, I* (Sheffield: JSOT Press, 1990).

137 Goulder, M. D. *The Prayers of David Psalms (51–72): Studies in the Psalter, II* (Sheffield: JSOT Press, 1990).

138 Greenberg, M. "On the Refinement of the Conception of Prayer in Hebrew Scriptures," *Association for Jewish Studies Review* 1 (1976), 57–92.

139 Greenberg, M. "Moses' Intercessory Prayer (Exod. 32:11–13, 31–32; Deut. 9:26–29)," in *Ecumenical Institute for Advanced Theological Studies: Yearbook 1977–78* (Tantur/Jerusalem: Franciscan Printing Press, 1980), 21–35.

140 Greenberg, M. "The Patterns of Prayers of Petition in the Bible," *Eretz-Israel* 16 (1982), 47–55 [in Hebrew].

141 Greenberg, M. *Biblical Prose Prayer: As a Window to the Popular Religion of Ancient Israel* (Taubmann Lectures, 6th Series; Berkeley: University of California Press, 1983).

142 Greiff, A. *Das Gebet im Alten Testament* (Münster: Aschendorff, 1915).

143 Grimme, H. "Der Begriff von hebräischem *hôdāh* und *tôdāh*," *ZAW* 58 (1940–41), 234–40.

144 Gunkel, H. *Ausgewählte Psalmen* (Göttingen: Vandenhoeck & Ruprecht, 1911³).

145 Gunkel, H. *Einleitung in die Psalmen: Die Gattungen der religiösen Lyrik Israels* (Gottingen: Vandenhoeck & Ruprecht, 1933).

146 Gunkel, H. *Die Psalmen* (Göttingen: Vandenhoeck & Ruprecht, 1968⁵).

147 Gunneweg, A. H. J. "Konfession oder Interpretation im Jeremiabuch," *ZThK* 67 (1970), 393–404.

148 Haran, M. "Temple and Community in Ancient Israel," in M. V. Fox (ed.), *Temple in Society* (Winona Lake, Ind.: Eisenbrauns, 1988), 17–25.

149 Haspecker, J. "Israel's Gespräch mit Gott," *BiLe* 2 (1961), 81–92.

150 Heinen, K. *Das Gebet im Alten Testament* (Rome: Typis Pontificiae Universitatis Gregorianae, 1971).

151 Heller, J. "Das Gebet im Alten Testament: Begriff Analyse," *CV* 19 (1976), 157–62.

152 Hempel, J. *Gebet und Frömmigkeit in Alten Testament* (Göttingen: Vandenhoeck & Ruprecht, 1922).

153 Hempel, J. "Die israelitischen Anschauungen von Segen und Fluch, im Lichte altorientalischer Parallelen," *ZDMG* N.F. 4 (1925), 20–110.

154 Hertzberg, H. W. "Sind die Propheten Fürbitter?," in E. Würthwein (ed.), *Tradition und Situation Studien zur alttestamentlichen Prophetie: Artur Weiser zum 70 Geburtstag* (Göttingen: Vandenhoeck & Ruprecht, 1963), 63–74.

155 Hesse, F. "Die Fürbitte im Alten Testament" (Dissertation: Erlangen, 1949).

156 Hiebert, T. *God of My Victory: The Ancient Hymn in Habakkuk 3* (Harvard Semitic Museum Monographs 38; Atlanta: Scholars Press, 1986).

157 Holm-Nielsen, S. "Den gammeltestamentlige Salmetradition," *DTT* 18 (1955), 135–48, 193–215.

158 Holm-Nielsen, S. "The Importance of Late Jewish Psalmody for the Understanding of Old Testament Psalmodic Tradition," *StTh* 14 (1960), 1–53.

159 Ittmann, N. *Die Konfession Jeremias: Ihre Bedeutung für die Verkündigung des Propheten* (WMANT 54; Neukirchen-Vluyn: Neukirchener Verlag, 1981).

160 Jacob, E. "Prier avec les psaumes," *Foi et vie* 84 (1985), 58–66.

161 Jahnow, H. *Das hebraische Leichenlied im Rahmen der Völkerdichtung* (BZAW 36; Gießen: A. Töpelmann, 1923).

162 Jeremias, Jörg *Kultprophetie und Gerichtsverkündigung in der späten Königszeit* (WMANT 35; Neukirchen-Vluyn: Neukirchener Verlag, 1970).

163 Keet, C. *The Psalms of Ascent* (London: Mitre Press, 1969).

164 Kegel, M. *Das Gebet im Alten Testament* (Gütersloh: C. Bertelsmann, 1908).

165 Köberle, J. *Die Motive des Glaubens an die Gebetserhörung im Alten Testament* (Erlangen/Leipzig: Deichert'sche Verlagsbuchhandlung Nachfolger [Georg Böhme], 1901).

166 Koenig, J. *Oracles et liturgies de l'exil babylonien* (Études d'histoire et de philosophie religieuses 69; Paris: Presses universitaires de France, 1988).

167 Krecher, J. "Klagelied," *RLA* 6, cols. 1–6.

168 Krinetzki, L. *Israels Gebet im Alten Testament* (Aschaffenburg: Paul Pattloch Verlag, 1965).

169 Ledogar, R. J. "Verbs of Praise in the LXX Translation of the Hebrew Canon," *Bib* 48 (1967), 29–56.

170 Limbeck, M. "Die Klage — eine verschwundene Gebetsgattung," *ThQ* 157 (1957), 3–16.

171 Lipinski, E. "Psaumes," *DBS* 9, cols. 1–125.

172 Macholz, G. C. "Jeremia in der Kontinuität der Prophetie," in H. W. Wolff (ed.), *Probleme biblische Theologie: Festschrift G. von Rad* (Munich: C. Kaiser, 1971), 306–34.

173 Matheus, F. *Singt dem Herrn ein neues Lied: Die Hymnen Deuterojesajas* (Stuttgart: Katholisches Bibelwerk, 1990).

174 Miller, P. D. "Truth and Woe: Interpreting the Biblical Laments," *Interp* 37 (1983), 32–45.

175 Miller, P. D. *Interpreting the Psalms* (Philadelphia: Fortress, 1986).

176 Mowinckel, S. *Zum Israelitischen Neujahr und die Deutung der Thronbesteigungspsalmen* (Oslo: J. Dybward, 1952).

177 Mowinckel, S. *Der achtundsiebzigste Psalm* (Oslo: J. Dybward, 1953).

178 Mowinckel, S. *Psalmenstudien* (Amsterdam: P. Schippers, 1961).

179 Mowinckel, S. *The Psalms in Israel's Worship* (Oxford: Clarendon, 1962).

180 Mowinckel, S. *Zur neueren Psalmenforschung* (Darmstadt: Wissenschaftliche Buchgesellschaft, 1976).

181 Muilenberg, J. "Liturgy on the Triumph of Yahweh," in M. A. Beck et al. (eds.), *Studia Biblica et Semitica Theodoro Christiano Vriezen...dedicata* (Wageningen: H. Veenman & Sons, 1966), 233–51.

182 Müller, A. R. "Stimmungsumschwung im Klagepsalm: Zu Ottmar Fuchs, Die Klage als Gebet," *ALW* 28 (1986), 416–26.

183 Neumann, P. H. (ed.) *Zur neueren Psalmenforschung* (Darmstadt: Wissenschaftliche Buchgesellschaft, 1976).

184 O'Connor, K. *The Confessions of Jeremiah: Their Interpretation and Role in Chapters 1–25* (Atlanta: Scholars Press, 1988).

185   Plöger, O.   "Reden und Gebete im deuteronomistischen und
                          chronistischen Geschichtswerk," in *Mélanges à*
                          G. Dehn à son 75ème anniversaire (Neukirchen-
                          Vluyn: Neukirchener Verlag, 1957), 35–49 = *Aus*
                          der Spätzeit des Alten Testaments (Göttingen:
                          Vandenhoeck & Ruprecht, 1971), 50–66.

186   Pratt, R. L., Jr.   "Royal Prayer and the Chronicler's Program" (Th.D.
                          Dissertation: Harvard University). See abstract in
                          HThR 81 (1988), 453–54.

187   Quell, G.   *Das kultische Problem der Psalmen: Versuch einer*
                          Deutung des religiösen Erlebens in der Psalmendich-
                          tung Israels (BWANT 36; Stuttgart: Kohlhammer,
                          1926).

188   Reventlow, H. Graf *Gebet im Alten Testament* (Stuttgart: Kohlhammer,
                          1986).

189   Rhodes, A. B.   "Israel's Prophets as Intercessors," in A. Merrill (ed.),
                          Scripture in History and Theology: Studies in Honor
                          of J. Coert Rylaarsdam (Pittsburgh: Pickwick Press,
                          1972), 107–28.

190   Richter, W.   "Das Gelübde als theologische Rahmung der Jakobs-
                          überlieferungen," *BZ* N.F. 11 (1967), 21–52.

191   Ridderbos, H. N.   *De "werkers der ongerechtigheid" in de individueele*
                          Psalmen (Kampen: J. H. Kok, 1939).

192   Routenberg, H.   "Biblical Sources Relating to Prayer: Parts I–IV," *Dor*
                          le Dor 4 (1975), 32–36.

193   Sawyer, J. F. A.   "Types of Prayer in the Old Testament: Some Se-
                          mantic Observations on Hitpallel, Hithannen, etc.,"
                          Semitics 7 (1980), 131–43.

194   Scharbert, J.   "Die Fürbitte in der Theologie des Alten Testa-
                          ments," *Theologie und Glaube* 50 (1960), 321–38.

195   Scharbert, J.   "Die Fürbitte im Alten Testament," in R. Beer,
                          A. Leidl, et al. (eds.), *"Diener in Eurer Mitte"*:
                          Festgabe für Dr. Antonius Hofmann, Bischof von
                          Passau zum 75 Geburtstag (Passau: Passavia Uni-
                          versitätsverlag, 1984), 91–109.

196   Schmidt, H.   "Gebet, IIA. Gebet und Gebetsriten in Israel und im
                          nachexilischen Judentum," *RGG²* 2 (1928), 875–79.

197   Schwenn, F.   *Gebet und Opfer* (Heidelberg: C. Winter, 1927).

198   Seybold, K.   *Das Gebet des Kranken im Alten Testament*
                          (BWANT 99, Stuttgart: Kohlhammer, 1973).

199   Seybold, K.   "Reverenz und Gebet: Erwägungen zu der Wendung
                          hilla panîm," *ZAW* 88 (1976), 2–16.

200   Smith, M. S.   *Psalms, the Divine Journey* (New York: Paulist,
                          1987).

201	Smith, M. S.	*The Laments of Jeremiah and Their Contexts: A Literary and Redactional Study of Jeremiah 11–20* (Atlanta: Scholars Press, 1990).
202	Snaith, N.	*The Seven Psalms* (London: Epworth, 1964). A study of the Penitential Psalms.
203	Snijders, L. A.	"Het gebed naar de Tempel toe: Over gebedsrichting in het Oude Testament," *NedTbT* 19 (1964–65), 1–14.
204	Soden, W. von	"Gebet II," *RLA* 3, 160–70.
205	Speiser, E. A.	"The Stem PLL in Hebrew," *JBL* 82 (1963), 301–6.
206	Stähli, H.-P.	"*pll* hitp. beten," *THAT* 2 (1976), 427–32.
207	Stamm, J. J.	"Ein Vierteljahrhundert Psalmenforschung," *ThR* N.F. 23 (1955), 1–68.
208	Stolz, F.	*Psalmen im nachkultischen Raum* (Zürich: Theologische Verlag, 1983).
209	Vawter, B.	"Postexilic Prayer and Hope," *CBQ* 37 (1975), 460–70.
210	Watts, J. M.	*Psalm and Story* (JSOTSS 139; Sheffield: JSOT Press, 1992).
211	Wendel, A.	*Das freie Laiengebet im vorexilischen Israel* (Leipzig: Eduard Pfeiffer, 1931).
212	Westermann, C.	"Gebet, II. Im AT," *RGG*³ 2, 1213–17.
213	Westermann, C.	*Das Loben Gottes in den Psalmen* (Göttingen: Vandenhoeck & Ruprecht, 1953, 1968⁴).
214	Westermann, C.	"Die Begriffe für Fragen und Suchen im AT," *KuD* 6 (1960), 2–30.
215	Westermann, C.	"Zur Sammlung des Psalters," *ThV* 8 (1961–62), 278–84.
216	Westermann, C.	"Die Begriffe für Fragen und Suchen im AT," in *Forschung am AT, II* (TB 55; Munich: C. Kaiser, 1974), 162–90.
217	Westermann, C.	"The Role of Lament in the Theology of the OT," *Interp* 28 (1974), 20–38 = "Die Rolle der Klage in der Theologie des AT," in *Forschung am AT, II* (TB 55; Munich: C. Kaiser, 1974), 250–68.
218	Westermann, C.	*Praise and Lament in the Psalms* (Atlanta: John Knox, 1981).
219	Westermann, C.	*Living Psalms* (Grand Rapids, Mich.: Eerdmans, 1989).
220	Wheeler, S. B.	"Prayer and Temple in the Dedication Speech of Solomon, 1 Kings 8:14–61" (Ph.D. Dissertation: Columbia University, 1977).

221   Widengren, G.   *The Accadian and Hebrew Psalms of Lamentation as Religious Documents* (Uppsala: Almqvist & Wiksell, 1936).

222   Widengren, G.   *Psalm 110 och det sakrale Kungadomet i Israel* (Uppsala: A.-B. Lundequistska Bokhandeln, 1941).

223   Williams, W. G.   "Prayer in the Life of Jeremiah," *RelLife* 15 (1946), 436–45.

224   Willis, J. T.   "The Song of Hannah and Psalm 113," *CBQ* 35 (1973), 139–54.

225   Wilson, G. H.   *The Editing of the Hebrew Psalter* (Chico, Calif: Scholars Press, 1985).

226   Wolff, H. W.   "Der Aufruf zur Volksklage," *ZAW* 76 (1964), 48–65.

4. JEWISH TEXTS

GENERAL

227   Abelson, J.   *The Immanence of God in Rabbinic Literature* (London: Macmillan, 1912), ch. 14.

228   Abrahams, I.   "Some Rabbinic Ideas on Prayer," *JQR* O.S. 20 (1908), 272–93.

229   Albeck, C.   "Die vierte Eulogie des Tischgebets," *MGWJ* N.F. 42 (1943), 430–37.

230   Alexander, P. S.   "Prayer in the Heikhalot Literature," in R. Goetschel (ed.), *Prière, mystique et judaïsme: colloque de Strasbourg 10–12 septembre, 1984* (Paris: Presses universitaires de France, 1987), 43–64.

231   Ben-Chorin, S.   *Betendes Judentum: Die Liturgie der Synagoge* (Tübingen: Mohr, 1980).

232   Blidstien, G. J.   "Limits of Prayer: A Rabbinic Discussion," *Jdm* 15 (1966), 164–70.

233   Bokser, B. M.   *Post-Mishnaic Judaism in Transition: Samuel on Berkhot and the Beginnings of Gemara* (Chico, Calif.: Scholars Press, 1980), 26–30.

234   Bokser, B. M.   "The Wall Separating God and Israel," *JQR* 73 (1983), 349–74.

235   Bousset, W.   *Die Religion des Judentums im späthellenistischen Zeitalter* (ed. H. Greßmann; Tübingen: Mohr, 1926), esp. 364–75.

236   Bradshaw, P. F.   "*Zebah Todah* and the Origins of the Eucharist," *Ecclesia Orans* 8 (1991), 245–60.

237 Bradshaw, P. F. *The Making of Jewish and Christian Worship* (Notre Dame, Ind.: University of Notre Dame Press, 1991).

238 Büchler, A. "The History of the Benediction *Hatob we-hameytyb* in the Grace after Meals," in *Abhandlungen zur Erinnerung an H. P. Chajes* (Vienna: A. Kohut Memorial Foundation, 1933), 137–67 [in Hebrew].

239 Charlesworth, J. H. "A Prolegomenon to a New Study of the Jewish Background of the Hymns and Prayers in the New Testament," in G. Vermes and J. Neusner (eds.), *Essays in Honor of Yigael Yadin* (Oxford: Oxford Centre for Postgraduate Hebrew Studies, 1983), 265–85 = *JJS* 33 (1982), 265–85.

240 Charlesworth, J. H. "Jewish Hymns, Odes, and Prayers," in R. A. Kraft and G. W. E. Nickelsburg (eds.), *Early Judaism and Its Modern Interpreters* (Atlanta: Scholars Press, 1986), 411–36.

241 Charlesworth, J. H. "Jewish Prayers in the Time of Jesus,' *PSB* Supp. 2 (1992), 36–55.

242 Cohn-Sherbok, D. *Jewish Petitionary Prayer: A Theological Exploration* (Lewiston, N.Y.: E. Mellen Press, 1989).

243 Dan, J. "The Emergence of Mystical Prayer," in J. Dan and L. Kaplan (eds.), *Studies in Jewish Mysticism* (Cambridge, Mass.: Association for Jewish Studies, 1982), 85–128. Response to Dan's article by L. Kaplan on 121–28.

244 Daube, D. "A Prayer Pattern in Judaism," *StE* 1 (1959), 539–45.

245 Davidson, I. "Poetic Fragments from the Geniza — A Palestinian Liturgy for the New Year," *JQR* N.S. 8 (1917–18), 425–54.

246 Di Sante, C. *La prière d'Israël: aux sources de la liturgie chrétienne* (trans. Louis Dussaut; Paris: Desclée; Montréal: Éditions Bellarmin, 1986).

247 Elbogen, I. *Der jüdische Gottesdienst in seiner geschichtlichen Entwicklung* (Frankfurt: Kauffmann, 1931³). See, e.g., 92–98 on the Kaddish.

248 Elbogen, I. "Studies in Jewish Liturgy," in J. J. Petuchowski (ed.), *Contributions to the Scientific Study of Jewish Liturgy* (New York: KTAV, 1970), 1–51.

249 Fiedler, P. "Zur Herkunft des gottesdienstlichen Gebrauchs von Psalmen aus dem Frühjudentum," *ALW* 30 (1988), 229–37.

250 Finkelstein, L. "The Development of the Amida," *JQR* 16 (1925–6), 1–43, 127–70.

251   Finkelstein, L.   "The Birkat Ha-mazon," *JQR* 19 (1928–29), 211–62.

252   Finkelstein, L.   "The Origin of the Hallel," *HUCA* 23 (1950–51), 319–28.

253   Finkelstein, L.   "The Origin and Development of the Qedushah," in A. A. Chiel (ed.), *Perspectives on Jews and Judaism: Essays in Honor of Wolfe Kelman* (New York: Rabbinal Assembly, 1978), 61–78.

254   Fleischer, E.   "On the Beginnings of Obligatory Jewish Prayer," *Tarbiz* 59 (1990), 397–441 [in Hebrew]. See also S. C. Reif's critique and Fleischer's rejoinder in *Tarbiz* 60 (1991), 677–82 and 683–88 respectively.

255   Flusser, D.   "Sanktus und Gloria," in O. Betz, M. Hengel, and P. Schmidt (eds.), *Abraham unser Vater: Juden und Christen im Gespräch über die Bibel: Festschrift für Otto Michel* (Leiden: Brill, 1963), 129–52.

256   Flusser, D.   "Psalms, Hymns and Prayers," in M. E. Stone (ed.), *Jewish Writings of the Second Temple Period* (Compendia Rerum Iudicarum ad Novum Testamentum Section Two, II; Assen/Philadelphia: Van Gorcum/Fortress, 1984), 551–77.

257   Freehof, S. B.   "The Structure of the Birchos Hashahar," *HUCA* 23 (1950–51), 329–54.

258   Gaster, M.   "Ein Targum der Amidah," in *MGWJ* 39 (1895), 79–90.

259   Gilbert, M.   "La prière des sages d'Israël," in H. Limet and J. Ries (eds.), *L'expérience de la prière dans les grandes religions: actes du colloque de Louvain-la-Neuve et Liège (22–23 novembre 1978)* (Louvain-la-Neuve: Centre d'histoire des religions, 1980), 227–43.

260   Ginzberg, L.   "Notes sur la Kedoucha et les bénédictions du Chema," *REJ* 98 (1934), 72–80.

261   Goldin, J.   "On Honi the Circle-Maker: A Demanding Prayer," *HThR* 56 (1963), 233–37.

262   Graubard, B.   "The Kaddish Prayer," in J. J. Petuchowski and M. Brocke (eds.), *The Lord's Prayer and Jewish Liturgy* (New York: Seabury Press, 1978), 59–72.

263   Green, A., and Holtz, B. W. (eds.)   *Your Word Is Fire: The Hasidic Masters on Contemplative Prayer* (New York: Paulist Press, 1977).

264   Greenberg, S.   *A Treasury of Thoughts on Jewish Prayer* (Northvale, N.J./London, U.K: Jason Aronson, 1989).

265   Grodner, R.   *The Spirit of Mishnaic Law: Tractate Berachot* (Jerusalem: Gefen, 1989).

266   Gross, S. Y.   *The Amen Response* (Brooklyn, N.Y.: Mosad Bruscha Tova, 5741 [=1980/81]).

267 Hammer, R.   "What Did They Bless?: A Study of Mishnah Tamid 5.1," *JQR* 81 (1991), 305–24.

268 Haran, M.   "Cult and Prayer," in A. Kort and S. Morschauser (eds.), *Biblical and Related Studies Presented to Samuel Iwry* (Winona Lake, Ind.: Eisenbrauns, 1985), 87–92.

269 Heinemann, J.   "The Formula melekh ha-'olam," *JJS* 11 (1960), 177–79.

270 Heinemann, J.   "Prayers of Beth Midrash Origin," *JSS* 5 (1960), 264–80.

271 Heinemann, J.   "Birkat ha-zimmun and Havurah-Meals," *JJS* 13 (1962), 23–29.

272 Heinemann, J.   "Once again Melekh ha-'olam," *JJS* 15 (1964), 149–54.

273 Heinemann, J.   "One Benediction Comprising Seven," *REJ* 125 (1966), 101–11.

274 Heinemann, J.   *Prayer in the Talmud: Forms and Patterns* (ETrans. R. S. Sarason; Berlin/New York: de Gruyter, 1977). Originally published in Hebrew in 1964.

275 Heinemann, J. (ed.) *La prière juive: une anthologie* (trans. J. Dessellier, Les Cahiers de l'Institut Catholique de Lyon 13; Lyon: Profac, 1984).

276 Hengel, M.   "Proseuche und Synagoge," in G. Jeremias and H. W. Kuhn (eds.), *Tradition und Glaube: Festschrift für K. G. Kuhn* (Göttingen: Vandenhoeck & Ruprecht, 1971), 157–84.

277 Hengel, M.   "Proseuche und Synagoge: Jüdische Gemeinde, Gotteshaus und Gottesdienst in der Diaspora und in Palästina," in J. Gutmann (ed.), *The Synagogue: Studies in Origins, Archaeology and Architecture* (New York: KTAV, 1975), 27–54.

278 Hennig, J.   "Mischnatraktat 'Berakot' I–V und das katholisches Gebetsleben," *ZRGG* 18 (1966), 310–25.

279 Hoenig, S. B.   "Historical Inquiries," *JQR* 48 (1957), 123–39, esp. 132–39.

280 Hoffman, L. A. "Gebet III, Judentum," *TRE* 12, 42–47.

281 Hoffman, L. A. "Rabbinic *Berakah* and Jewish Spirituality," *Conc* 26 (1990), 18–30.

282 Holm-Nielsen, S. "The Importance of Late Jewish Psalmody for Understanding Old Testament Psalmodic Tradition," *StTh* 14 (1960), 1–53.

283 Holm-Nielsen, S. "Religiöse Poesie des Spätjudentums," *ANRW* II, 19.1 (1979), 152–86. Discussion inter alia of the hymnic elements in the Apocrypha and Pseudepigrapha, the Hodayot, and the Psalms of Solomon.

284 Holtzmann, O. "Die tägliche Gebetsstundes im Judentum und Urchristentum," ZNW 12 (1911), 90–107.

285 Hruby, H. "Quelques notes sur la Tahanun et la place de la prière individuelle dans la liturgie synagogale," in P. Jacob (ed.), Littera Judaica in Memoriam Edwin Guggenheim (Frankfurt am Main: Europäische Verlagsanhalt, 1963), 78–104.

286 Hruby, H. "L'action de grâces dans la liturgie juive," in H. Cazalles et al. (eds.), Eucharisties d'orient de d'occident, I (Lex orandi 46; Paris: Cerf, 1970), 23–51.

287 Idelsohn, A. Z. Jewish Liturgy and Its Development (New York: H. Holt & Co., 1932), chs. 8, 9, 12, 13.

288 Jacobs, L. Jewish Prayer (London: Jewish Chronicle Publications, 1955).

289 Jacobs, L. Hasidic Prayer (New York: Schocken Books, 1973).

290 Jansen, H. L. Die spätjüdische Psalmendichtung: Ihr Entstehungskreis und Ihr Sitz im Leben (Oslo: Dybwad, 1937).

291 Jansen, H. L. "Psalmody in Late Judaism," in P. Borgen (ed.), The Many and the One: Essays on Religion in the Greco-Roman World: Presented to H. L. Jansen (Trondheim: Tapir, 1985), 17–30.

292 Kitzner, Y. The Art of Jewish Prayer (Northvale, N.J./London, U.K.: Jason Aronson, 1991).

293 Kohler, K. "Über die Ursprünge und Grundformen der synagogalen Liturgie: Eine Studie," MGWJ N.F. 1 (1893), 441–51, 489–97.

294 Krupp, M. "Prayer in the Period of the Tanna'im and the Amora'im by J. Heinemann," Immanuel 2 (1973), 23–27.

295 Lasker, A. A. and D. J. "The Jewish Prayer for Rain in Babylonia," JSJ 15 (1984), 123–44.

296 Lauer, S. "Awinu Malkenu," in M. Brocke, J. J. Petuchowski, and W. Strolz (eds.), Das Vaterunser: Gemeinsames im Beten von Juden und Christen (Freiburg i. Breisgau: Herder, 1974), 120–27.

297 Le Déaut, R. "Aspects de l'intercession dans le Judaisme," JSJ 1 (1970), 53–57.

298 Levertoff, P. P. "Synagogue Worship in the First Century," in W. K. Lowther Clarke (ed.), Liturgy and Worship: A Companion to the Prayer Book of the Anglican Communion (New York: Macmillan, 1932), 60–77.

299 Lévi, I. "Fragments de rituels de prières provenant de la gueniza du Caire," REJ 53 (1907), 231–41.

300 Levinskaya, I. A.   "A Jewish or Gentile Prayer House?: The Meaning of Proseuche," *TynB* 41 (1990), 154–59.

301 Liebreich, L. J.   "Invocation to Prayer at the Beginning of the Yozer Service," *JQR* 39 (1949), 285–90, 407–12.

302 Liebreich, L. J.   "The Pesuke de-Zimra Benedictions," *JQR* 41 (1950–51), 195–206.

303 Liebreich, L. J.   "The Impact of Nehemiah 9:5–37 on the Liturgy of the Synagogue," *HUCA* 32 (1961), 227–37.

304 Liebreich, L. J.   "Aspects of the New Year Liturgy," *HUCA* 34 (1963), 125–76, esp. sections 1 and 6.

305 Maier, J.   "Zur Verwendung der Psalmen in der synagogalen Liturgie (Wochentag und Sabbat," in H. Becker and R. Kaczynski (eds.), *Liturgie und Dichtung: Ein interdisziplinäres Kompendium, 1: Historische Präsentation* (St. Ottilien: EOS, 1983), 55–90.

306 Mann, J.   "Genizah Fragments of the Palestinian Order of Service," *HUCA* 2 (1925), 269–338.

307 Mann, J.   "Changes in the Divine Service of the Synagogue due to Religious Persecution," *HUCA* 4 (1927), 241–310, esp. sections 2 and 3.

308 Manns, F.   *La prière d'Israël à l'heure de Jésus* (Studium Biblicum Franciscanum, Analecta 22; Jerusalem: Franciscan Printing Press, 1986). See esp. section 3.

309 Manson, T. W.   "The Jewish Background," in N. Micklem (ed.), *Christian Worship: Studies in Its History and Meaning* (Oxford: Clarendon, 1936), 35–49.

310 Marmorstein, A.   "The Amidah of the Public Fast Days," *JQR* N.S. 15 (1925), 409–18.

311 Martin, B.   *Prayer in Judaism* (New York: Basic Books, 1968).

312 McKinnon, J. W.   "On the Question of Psalmody in the Ancient Synagogue," *EMH* 6 (1986), 159–91.

313 Moore, G. F.   *Judaism in the First Centuries of the Christian Era* (New York: Schocken, 1971), 2, 212–36.

314 Navè, P.   "Höre Israel — Talmudische und liturgische Traditionen über Dt 6, 4–9; 11, 13–21; Nm 15, 37–41," in M. Brocke, J. J. Petuchowski, and W. Strolz (eds.), *Das Vaterunser: Gemeinsames im Beten von Juden und Christen* (Freiburg i. Breisgau: Herder, 1974), 56–76.

315 Navè, P. (ed.)   *Tu, nuestro padre: oraciones judías para cristianos* (Buenos Aires: Editorial Guadalupe, 1975).

316 Oesterley, W. O. E.   *The Jewish Background of the Christian Liturgy* (Oxford: Clarendon, 1925), see esp. sections 2 and 5.

317 Oesterley, W. O. E., *The Religion and Worship of the Synagogue* (New and Box, G. H. York: Scribners, 1907), ch. 17.

318 Peli, P. H. "From Prophecy to Prayer: On Prayer and the Pray-er in Judaism of Late Antiquity," in *Ecumenical Institute for Advanced Theological Studies: Yearbook 1978–79* (Tantur/Jerusalem: Franciscan Printing Press, 1981), 45–70.

319 Perles, F. *Das Gebet im Judentum* (Frankfurt, 1904).

320 Perles, F. "Prayers, Jewish," in J. Hastings (ed.), *Encyclopædia of Religion and Ethics* (vol. 10; Edinburgh: T. & T. Clark, 1979–81), cols. 191–96.

321 Perrot, C. "La chant hymnique chez les Juifs et les chrétiens au premier siécle," *MD* 161 (1985), 7–31.

322 Peterson, E. "Die geschichtliche Bedeutung der jüdischen Gebetsrichtung," *ThZ* 3 (1947), 1–15 = *Frühkirche, Judentum & Gnosis* (Rome/Freiburg/Vienna: Herder, 1959), 1–14.

323 Peterson, E. "Henoch im jüdischen Gebet und in jüdischer Kunst," in *Frühkirche, Judentum & Gnosis* (Rome/Freiburg/Vienna: Herder, 1959), 36–42.

324 Petuchowski, J. J. "Do This in Remembrance of Me," *JBL* 76 (1957), 293–98.

325 Petuchowski, J. J. "A New Approach to Jewish Liturgy," *Jdm* 15 (1966), 114–20. Review of J. Heinemann, *Prayer in the Talmud: Forms and Patterns* (= *Prayer in the Period of the Tanna'im and Amora'im: Its Nature and Patterns* (Jerusalem: Magnes, 1964) [in Hebrew].

326 Petuchowski, J. J. *Understanding Jewish Prayer* (New York: KTAV, 1972).

327 Petuchowski, J. J. "Einleitende Bemerkungen zum Wesen des jüdischen Gottesdienstes," in M. Brocke, J. J. Petuchowski, and W. Strolz (eds.), *Das Vaterunser: Gemeinsames im Beten von Juden und Christen* (Freiburg i. Breisgau: Herder, 1974), 45–55.

328 Petuchowski, J. J. "Jüdische Gebetstexte," in M. Brocke, J. J. Petuchowski, and W. Strolz (eds.), *Das Vaterunser: Gemeinsames im Beten von Juden und Christen* (Freiburg i. Breisgau: Herder, 1974), 31–44.

329 Petuchowski, J. J. *Beten im Judentum* (Stuttgart: Katholisches Bibelwerk, 1976). Excerpt from *Understanding Jewish Prayer* (see above).

330 Petuchowski, J. J. "The Liturgy of the Synagogue," in J. J. Petuchowski and M. Brocke (eds.), *The Lord's Prayer and Jewish Liturgy* (New York: Seabury Press, 1978), 45–52.

331   Petuchowski, J. J.   "Theology and Poetry in the Liturgy of the Synagogue," in A. Finkel and L. Frizzell (eds.), *Standing before God: Studies on Prayer in Scriptures and in Tradition with Essays in Honor of John M. Oesterreicher* (New York: KTAV, 1981), 223–32.

332   Petuchowski, J. J.   "The Liturgy of the Synagogue: History, Structure, and Contents," in W. S. Green (ed.), *Approaches to Ancient Judaism*, 4 (Brown Judaic Studies 27; Chico, Calif.: Scholars Press, 1983), 1–64.

333   Pines, S.   "From Darkness into Great Light," *Immanuel* 4 (1974), 47–51.

334   Plessner, S.   *Die kostbare Perle oder das Gebet* (Berlin, 1837).

335   Price, C. P.   "Jewish Morning Prayer and Early Christian Anaphoras," *AThR* 43 (1961), 153–68.

336   Rankin, O. S.   "The Extent of the Influence of the Synagogue Service upon Christian Worship," *JJS* 1 (1948–49), 27–32.

337   Reif, S. C.   "Jewish Liturgical Research: Past, Present and Future," *JJS* 34 (1983), 161–70.

338   Reif, S. C.   "Some Liturgical Issues in the Talmudic Sources," *StLi* 15 (1982–83), 188–206.

339   Reif, S. C.   "On the Earliest Developments of Jewish Prayer," *Tarbiz* 60 (1991), 677–82 [in Hebrew].

340   Ricciardi, A.   "El reino de Dios en la oración litúrgica judía," *RevBib* 48 (1986), 239–55.

341   Roth, C.   "Melekh ha-'olam: Zealot Influence in the Liturgy," *JJS* 11 (1960), 173–75.

342   Sarason, R. S.   "On the Use of Method in the Modern Study of Jewish Liturgy," in W. S. Green (ed.), *Approaches to Ancient Judaism: Theory and Practice* (Missoula, Mont.: Scholars Press, 1978), 97–172.

343   Schäfer, P.   "Der synagogale Gottesdienst: Eine Einleitung," in J. Maier and J. Schreiner (eds.), *Literatur und Religion des Frühjudentums* (Würzburg: Echter Verlag, 1973), 391–423.

344   Schechter, A. I.   *Studies in Jewish Liturgy: Based on a Unique Manuscript Entitled Seder Hibbur Berakot* (Philadelphia: Dropsie College for Hebrew and Cognate Learning, 1930).

345   Schirmann, J.   "Hebrew Liturgical Poetry and Christian Hymnology," *JQR* 44 (1953), 123–61.

346   Scholem, G.   *Jewish Gnosticism, Merkavah Mysticism and Talmudic Transition* (New York: KTAV, 1965), sections 4 and 8.

347   Sigal, P.   "Early Christian and Rabbinic Liturgical Affinities," *NTS* 30 (1984), 63–90.

348   Sloyan, G. S.   "Jewish Ritual of the First Century c.e.," *BTB* 15 (1985), 98–103.

349   Sola Pool, D. de   *The Old Jewish-Aramaic Prayer, the Kaddish* (Jerusalem and New York: Sivan Press, 1964[3]). Originally published Leipzig: Robert Haupt, 1909.

350   Spanier, A.   "Zur Formengeschichte des altjüdischen Gebetes," *MGWJ* 78 (1934), 438–47.

351   Spanier, A.   "Dubletten in Gebetstexten," *MGWJ* 83 (1939), 142–49.

352   Spinks, B. D.   "The Jewish Sources for the Sanctus," *HeyJ* 21 (1980), 168–79.

353   Staerk, W.   *Die Mishnatraktat Berakhoth in vokalisiertem Text mit sprachlichen und sachlichen Bemerkungen* (Bonn: A. Marcus and E. Weber, 1910).

354   Staerk, W.   *Altjüdische liturgische Gebete* (Berlin: de Gruyter, 1930).

355   Teichmann, J.   *Unser Gebet* (Zürich: Morascha, 1982).

356   Thackeray,   *The Septuagint and Jewish Worship* (The Schweich
       H. St. John   Lectures; London: Oxford University Press, 1921).

357   Wachs, S. P.   "Eleinu: Rabbinic Theology in Biblical Language," *Conservative Judaism* 42 (1989), 46–49.

358   Weinfeld, M.   "The Heavenly Praise in Unison," in K. Seybold (ed.), *Meqor-Hajjim: Festschrift für Georg Grolin zum 75. Geburtstag* (Graz: Akademische Durck- u. Verlagsanstalt, 1983), 427–37.

359   Weiss, J. G.   "The Kavvanoth of Prayer in Early Hasidism," *JJS* 9 (1958), 163–92.

360   Weiss, J. G.   "On the Formula 'melekh ha-ʿolam' as anti-Gnostic Protest," *JJS* 10 (1959), 169–71.

361   Werner, E.   "The Doxology in Synagogue and Church: A Liturgico-Musical Study," *HUCA* 19 (1945–46), 275–351. Part 1 (276–328) concentrates on early Jewish and Christian liturgies. Discussions of the Qedushah and Kaddish, and early Christian doxologies.

362   Willems, G. F.   "Les psaumes dans la liturgie juive," *Bijtragen* 51 (1990), 397–417.

363   Williams, A. L.   "My Father in Jewish Thought of the First Century," *JThS* O.S. 31 (1929), 42–47.

364   Yahalom, J.   "Piyyut as Poetry," in L. I. Levine (ed.), *The Synagogue in Late Antiquity* (Philadelphia: American Schools of Oriental Research, 1987), 111–26.

365 Zahavy, T.   "A New Approach to Early Jewish Prayer," in
                          B. Bokser (ed.), *History of Judaism — The Next
                          Ten Years* (Brown Judaic Studies 21; Chico, Calif.:
                          Scholars Press, 1980), 45–60.

366 Zahavy, T.   "Kavvanah for Prayer in the Mishnah and the
                          Talmud," in J. Neusner et al. (eds.), *Religion, Lit-
                          erature, and Society* (Lanham, Md.: University Press
                          of America, 1987), 37–48.

367 Zahavy, T.   *The Mishnaic Law of Blessings and Prayers: Trac-
                          tate Berakhot* (Brown Judaic Studies 88; Atlanta:
                          Scholars Press, 1987).

368 Zahavy, T.   "Three Stages in the Development of Early Rab-
                          binic Prayer," in J. Neusner et al. (eds.), *From
                          Ancient Israel to Modern Judaism: Intellect in Quest
                          of Understanding: Essays in Honor of Marvin Fox*
                          (Brown Judaic Studies 159; Atlanta: Scholars Press,
                          1989), 233–65.

369 Zahavy, T.   *Studies in Jewish Prayer* (Lanham, Md.: University
                          Press of America, 1990).

370 Zunz, L.   *Die Ritus des synagogalen Gottesdienstes* (Berlin:
                          Verlag Julius Springer, 1859).

THE EIGHTEEN BENEDICTIONS

371 Aptowitzer, V.   "Bemerkungen zur Liturgie und Geschichte der Li-
                          turgie," *MGWJ* 74 (1930), 104–26, esp. 109–12 on
                          the Benediction of the Minim.

372 Assef, S.   "Mi-seder ha-tefillah b'eres yisra'el," in Y. Baer,
                          Y. Guttermann, and M. Schwabe (eds.), *Sefer Dina-
                          burg* (Jerusalem, 1949), 116–31. Hebrew texts of the
                          Twelve Benedictions.

373 Baer, S.   *Seder 'abodat yisra'el* (Rödelheim, 1868). See 93–95
                          for Hebrew texts of the Twelve Benedictions.

374 Barta, J.   "Das Achtzehngebet — Eine Betrachtung," in M.
                          Brocke, J. J. Petuchowskia, and W. Strolz (eds.), in
                          *Das Vaterunser: Gemeinsames im Beten von Juden
                          und Christen* (Freiburg i. Breisgau: Herder, 1974),
                          77–89.

375 Bickermann, E. J.   "The Civic Prayer for Jerusalem," *HThR* 55 (1962),
                          163–86 = *Studies in Jewish and Christian History, II*
                          (Leiden: Brill, 1980), 290–312 = H. A. Fischel (ed.),
                          Essays in Greco-Roman and Related Talmudic Texts
                          (New York: KTAV, 1977), 266–88.

376 Cohen, N. G. "The Nature of Shimy'on Hapekuli's Act," *Tarbiz* 52 (1982–83), 547–56 [in Hebrew].

377 Finkel, A. "Yavneh's Liturgy and Early Christianity," *JES* 18 (1981), 231–50. Discussion of the Benediction of the Minim.

378 Finkelstein, L. "The Development of the Amidah," *JQR* N.S. 16 (1925–26), 1–43, 127–70. See also J. J. Petuchowski (ed.), *Contributions to the Scientific Study of the Jewish Liturgy* (New York: KTAV, 1970), 91–177. For the Text of the Twelve Benedictions from the Cairo Genizah and elsewhere.

379 Grant, F. C. "Modern Study of the Jewish Liturgy," *ZAW* 65 (1953), 59–77. See also the extensive bibliography on 74–77 (74–76: Eighteen Benedictions; 76: the Jewish Prayer Book; 76–77: the Benediction of the Minim).

380 Horbury, W. "The Benediction of the Minim and Early Jewish-Christian Controversy," *JThS* 33 (1982), 19–61.

381 Jacobs, I. "Kingship and Holiness in the Third Benediction of the Amidah and in the Yozer," *JJS* 41 (1990), 62–74.

382 Kimelman, R. "*Birkat Ha-Minim* and the Lack of Evidence for an Anti-Christian Jewish Prayer in Late Antiquity," in E. P. Sanders, A. I. Baumgarten, and A. Mendelson (eds.), *Jewish and Christian Self-Definition, 2* (London: SCM, 1981), 226–44.

383 Kimelman, R. "The Daily 'Amidah and the Rhetoric of Redemption," *JQR* 79 (1988–89), 165–97.

384 Kohler, K. "The Origin and Composition of the Eighteen Benedictions," *HUCA* 1 (1924), 387–425. See also J. J. Petuchowski (ed.), *Contributions to the Scientific Study of the Jewish Liturgy* (New York: KTAV, 1970), 52–90.

385 Krauss, S. "Imprecation against the Minim in the Synagogue," *JQR* O.S. 9 (1897), 515–17.

386 Kuhn, K. G. *Achtzehngebet und Vaterunser und der Reim* (WUNT 1; Tübingen: Mohr, 1950).

387 Lévy, I. "Les dix-huit Bénédictions et les Psaumes de Salomon," *REJ* 32 (1896), 161–78.

388 Lévy, I. "Fragments de rituels de prières provenant de la gueniza du Caire," *REJ* 53 (1907), 231–41.

389 Liber, M. "Structure and History of the Tefillah," *JQR* N.S. 40 (1950), 331–57.

390 Loeb, I. "Les dix-huit Bénédictions," *REJ* 19 (1889), 17–40.

391	Petuchowski, J. J.	"Der Ketzersegen," in M. Brocke, J. J. Petuchowski, and W. Strolz (eds.), *Das Vaterunser: Gemeinsames im Beten von Juden und Christen* (Freiburg i. Breisgau: Herder, 1974), 90–101.
392	Petuchowski, J. J.	"Das Achtzehngebet," in H. H. Henrix (ed.), *Jüdische Liturgie: Geschichte, Struktur, Wesen* (Freiburg: Herder, 1979), 77–88.
393	Schechter, S.	"Geniza Specimens," *JQR* O.S. 10 (1898), 656–57. Eng. trans. of the Geniza text with the Palestinian recension of the Eighteen Benedictions.
394	Schwaab, E.	*Historische Einführung in das Achtzehngebet* (Beiträge zur Förderung Christlicher Theologie, 17, 5; Gütersloh: C. Bertelsmann, 1913).
395	Sluis, D. J. van der, et al.	*Elke Morgen Nieuw: Het Achttiengebed* (Arnhem: B. Folkersma, 1978).
396	Spanier, A.	"Die erste Benediktion des Achtzehngebets," *MGWJ* 81 (1937), 71–76.
397	Weinfeld, M.	"The Prayers for Knowledge, Repentance and Forgiveness in the 'Eighteen Benedictions' — Qumran Parallels, Biblical Antecedents, and Basic Characteristics," *Tarbiz* 48 (1978–79), 186–200 [in Hebrew].
398	Zolli, I.	"Tefillah," *AStE* 1 (1934), 93–100.

APOCRYPHA AND PSEUDEPIGRAPHA

General

399	Denis, A.-M.	*Introduction aux pseudépigraphes grecs d'Ancien Testament* (SVTP 1; Leiden: Brill, 1970), 60–69 (Psalms of Solomon); 125–27 (Prayer of Joseph); 177–81 (Prayer of Manasseh).
400	Johnson, N. B.	*Prayer in the Apocrypha and Pseudepigrapha: A Study in the Jewish Concept of God* (JBL Monograph Series 2; Philadelphia: Society of Biblical Literature and Exegesis, 1948).
401	Mayer, G.	"Die Funktion der Gebete in den alttestamentliche Apokryphen," in W. Dietrich et al. (eds.), *Theokratia: Festschrift für K. H. Rengstorf* (Jahrbuch des Institutum Judaicum Delitzschianum 2; Leiden: Brill, 1973), 16–25.

402   McNamara, M.   "Prayer and Prayers of the Intertestamental Period," in *Intertestamental Literature* (Old Testament Message 23; Wilmington, Del.: Michael Glazier, 1983), 165–209.

403   Zeitlin, S.   "Prayer in the Apocrypha and Pseudepigrapha," *JQR* 40 (1949–50), 201–3.

Specific Texts

Additions to Daniel

404   Brüll, N.   "Das Gebet der drei Männer im Feuerofen," *JJGL* 8 (1887), 22–27.

405   Christie, E. B.   "The Strophic Arrangement of the Benedicite," *JBL* 47 (1928), 188–93.

406   Frizzell, L.   "The Hymn of Creation in Daniel," in A. Finkel and L. Frizzell (eds.), *Standing before God: Studies on Prayer in Scriptures and in Tradition with Essays in Honor of John M. Oesterreicher* (New York: KTAV, 1981), 41–52.

407   Gilbert, M.   "La prière d'Azarias (Dn 3:26–45 Theodotion)," *NRTh* 96 (1974), 561–82.

408   Kuhl, C.   *Die drei Männer im Feure (Daniel Kapitel 3 und seine Zusatze: Ein Beitrag zur israelitische-jüdischen Literaturgeschichte* (Gießen: A. Töpelmann, 1930).

409   Moore, C. A.   *Daniel, Esther, and Jeremiah: The Additions: A New Translation with Introduction and Commentary* (Anchor Bible 44; Garden City, N.Y.: Doubleday, 1977), 39–76.

Additions to Esther

410   Moore, C. A.   *Daniel, Esther, and Jeremiah: The Additions: A New Translation with Introduction and Commentary* (Anchor Bible 44; Garden City, N.Y.: Doubleday, 1977), 203–7 (Prayer of Mordecai), 208–15 (Prayer of Esther).

Apocryphal Psalms (see also Qumran Apocryphal Psalms)

411   Baars, W.   "Apocryphal Psalms" (Peshitta IV.6; Leiden: Brill, 1972).

412   Noth, M.   "Die fünf syrisch überlieferten apokryphen Psalmen," *ZAW* 48 (1930), 1–23.

413	Skehan, P. W.	"Again the Syriac Apocryphal Psalms," *CBQ* 38 (1976), 143–58.
414	Strelcyn, S.	"Le psaume 151 dans la tradition éthiopienne," *JSS* 23 (1978), 316–29.
415	Strugnell, J.	"Notes on the Text and Transmission of the Apocryphal Psalms 151, 154 (= Syr. II) and 155 (= Syr. III)," *HThR* 59 (1966), 257–81.
416	Woude, A. S. van der	*Die fünf syrischen Psalmen* (JSHZ 4.1; Gütersloh: Mohn, 1974).
417	Wright, W.	"Some Apocryphal Psalms in Syriac," *PSBA* 9 (1887), 257–66.

1 Baruch

| 418 | Moore, C. A. | "Toward the Dating of the Book of Baruch," *CBQ* 36 (1974), 312–20. Comparison of the Baruch prayers and Daniel 9:4–19. |
| 419 | Wambacq, B. N. | "Les prières de Baruch (i 15–ii 19) et de Daniel (ix 5–19)," *Bib* 40 (1959), 463–75. |

2 Baruch

| 420 | Licht, J. | "An Analysis of Baruch's Prayer," *JJS* 33 (1982), 327–31. |

4 Baruch

| 421 | Delling, G. | *Jüdische Lehre und Frömmigkeit in den Paralipomena Jeremiae* (BZAW 100; Berlin: C. Töpelmann, 1967). See esp. section 2, 30–41. |

1 Enoch

| 422 | Ricciardi, A. | "La oración en las Parábolas de Henoc," *RevBib* 47 (1985), 53–73. |

4 Ezra

| 423 | Boyarin, D. | "Penitential Liturgy in 4 Ezra," *JSJ* 3 (1972), 30–34. |
| 424 | Cook, Joan E. | "Ezra's Confession, Appeal to a Merciful God," *JSP* 3 (1988), 89–100. |

Jewish Prayers in the Apostolic Constitutions

425	Bousset, W.	"Eine jüdische Gebetssammlung im siebenten Buch der apostolischen Konstitutionem," repr. in A. F. Verheule (ed.), *Religionsgeschichtliche Studien: Aufsätze zur Religionsgeschichte des Hellenistischen Zeitalters* (NT. S 50; Leiden: Brill, 1979), 231–86. Originally published in 1915.
426	Drews, P. G.	*Untersuchungen über die sog. clementinische Liturgie im VIII Buch der apostolischen Konstitutionem*, 1: *Die clementinische Liturgie in Rom* (Tübingen: Mohr, 1906). See also *Studien zur Geschichte des Gottesdienstes und des gottesdienstlichen Lebens II, III* (Tübingen/Leipzig, 1902–10).
427	Fiensy, D. A.	*Prayers Alleged to Be Jewish* (Brown Judaic Studies 65; Chico, Calif.: Scholars Press, 1985).
428	Fiensy, D. A.	"The Hellenistic Synagogal Prayers: One Hundred Years of Discussion," *JSP* 5 (1989), 17–27.

Joseph and Asenath

429	Berger, K.	"Jüdische-Hellenistische Missionsliteratur und Apokryphe Apostelakten," *Kairos* 17 (1975), 232–48, see esp. 232–40.
430	Burchard, C.	*Untersuchungen zu Joseph und Asenath* (WUNT 8; Tübingen: Mohr [Paul Siebeck], 1965), 106–7.
431	Philonenko, M.	*Joseph et Asénath* (Leiden: Brill, 1968), 156–59.
432	Sänger, D.	*Antikes Judentum und die Mysterien* (WUNT 2.5; Tübingen: Mohr [Paul Siebeck], 1980), 163–65.
433	Smith, E. W.	"Joseph and Asenath and Early Christian Literature: A Contribution to the Corpus Hellenisticum Novi Testamenti" (Ph.D. Dissertation: Claremont Graduate School, Claremont, Calif., 1974), 107–16.

Jubilees

434	Skehan, P. W.	"Jubilees and the Qumran Psalter," *CBQ* 37 (1975), 343–47.
435	Testuz, M.	*Les idées religieuses du livre des Jubilés* (Geneva: E. Droz, 1960). See esp. 189–92 for comparison with the Qumran Hodayot.

Judith

436	Gardner, A. E.	"Judith 16:2–17 (LXX 16:1–17)," *HeyJ* 29 (1988), 413–22.
437	Jansen, H. L.	"La composition du Chant de Judith," *Acta Orientalia* 15 (1937), 63–71.
438	Skehan, P. W.	"The Hand of Judith," *CBQ* 25 (1963), 94–110, see 96–98. Comparison of Judith with 1QM 11 and 13.
439	Zorell, F.	"Canticum Judith, Vg 16, 1–2," *VD* 5 (1925), 329–32.

Maccabees

440	Enermalm-Ogawa, A.	*Un langage de prière juif en grec: le témoignage des deux livres des Maccabees* (Stockholm: Almqvist & Wiksell International, 1987).

Odes of Solomon

441	Abbott, E. A.	*Light on the Gospel from an Ancient Poet* (Diatessarica 9; Cambridge: University Press, 1912).
442	Aune, D. E.	*The Cultic Setting of Realized Eschatology in Early Christianity* (NT. S 28; Leiden: Brill, 1972), ch. 5.
443	Aune, D. E.	"The Odes of Solomon and Early Christianity," *NTS* 28 (1982), 435–60.
444	Bacon, B. W.	"The Odes of Solomon: Christian Elements," *Exp* series 8, vol. 4 (1911), 243–56.
445	Bacon, B. W.	"The Odes of the Lord's Rest, 1: The Problem of Their Origins," *Exp* series 8, vol. 1 (1911), 193–209.
446	Bacon, B. W.	"Songs of the Lord's Beloved," *Exp* series 8, vol. 1 (1911), 319–37.
447	Bauckham, R. J.	"The Parable of the Vine; Rediscovering a Lost Parable of Jesus," *NTS* 33 (1987), 84–101. Discusses inter alia Ode 38:17–19.
448	Bernard, J. H.	*The Odes of Solomon* (Texts and Studies 8.3; Cambridge: University Press, 1912).
449	Blaszcak, G. R.	*A Formcritical Study of Selected Odes of Solomon* (Harvard Semitic Museum Monograph; Atlanta: Scholars Press, 1985).
450	Bultmann, R.	"Ein jüdisch-christliches Psalmbuch aus dem ersten Jahrhundert," *Monatschrift für Pastoraltheologie* 7 (1910), 23–29.
451	Cameron, P.	"The Crux in Ode of Solomon 19:6: A New Solution," *JThS* 42 (1991), 588–96.

452   Carmignac, J.   "Un qumrânien converti au christianisme: L'auteur des Odes de Salomon," in H. Bardtke (ed.), *Qumran-Probleme* (Deutsche Akademie der Wissenschaften zu Berlin 42; Berlin: Akademie-Verlag, 1963), 75–108.

453   Chadwick, H.   "Some Reflections on the Character and Theology of the Odes of Solomon," in P. Granfield and J. A. Jungmann (eds.), *Kyriakon: Festschrift Johannes Quasten* (2 vols.; Münster: Aschendorff, 1970), 1, 266–70.

454   Charlesworth, J. H.   "The Odes of Solomon — Not Gnostic," *CBQ* 31 (1969), 357–69.

455   Charlesworth, J. H.   "Les Odes de Salomon et les manuscrits de la mer morte," *RB* 77 (1970), 522–49.

456   Charlesworth, J. H.   *The Odes of Solomon* (Corrected Reprint, SBLTT; Pseudepigrapha Series 7; Missoula, Mont.: Scholars Press, 1978). Extensive bibliography.

457   Charlesworth, J. H.   "Haplography and Philology: A Study of Ode of Solomon 16:8," *NTS* 25 (1978–79), 221–37.

458   Charlesworth, J. H.   "Qumran, John and the Odes of Solomon," in J. H. Charlesworth (ed.), *John and Qumran* (London: Chapman, 1972), 107–36. Reprinted, New York: Crossroad, 1990.

459   Charlesworth, J. H., and Culpepper, R. A.   "The Odes of Solomon and the Gospel of John," *CBQ* 35 (1973), 298–322.

460   Drijvers, H. J. W.   "Die Oden Salomos und die Polemik mit der Markioniten im Syrischen Christentum," in A. Vööbus (ed.), *Symposium Syriaca 1976* (OrChrA 205; Rome: Pontificum Institutum Orientalium Studiorum, 1978), 39–55.

461   Drijvers, H. J. W.   "Kerygma und Logos in den Oden Salomos dargestellt am Beispiel der 23. Ode," in A. M. Ritter (ed.), *Kerygma und Logos: Festschrift für Carl Andresen* (Göttingen: Vandenhoeck & Ruprecht, 1979), 153–72.

462   Emerton, J. A.   "Some Problems of Text and Language in the Odes of Solomon," *JThS* N.S. 18 (1967), 372–406.

463   Emerton, J. A.   "Notes on Some Passages in the Odes of Solomon," *JThS* N.S. 28 (1977), 507–19.

464   Franzmann, M.   "The Parable of the Vine in Odes of Solomon 38.17–19?: A Response to Richard Bauckham," *NTS* 35 (1989), 604–8.

465   Franzmann, M.   "An Analysis of the Poetical Structure and Form of the Odes of Solomon" (Ph.D. Thesis: University of Queensland, 1990).

466	Franzmann, M.	"The Wheel in Proverbs xx 26 and Odes of Solomon xxiii 11–16," *VT* 41 (1991), 121–23.
467	Grant, R. M.	"The Odes of Solomon and the Church at Antioch," *JBL* 63 (1944), 363–77.
468	Gressmann, H.	"Die Oden Salomos," in E. Hennecke (ed.), *Neutestamentliche Apokryphen* (Zweite Auflage; Tübingen: Mohr, 1924), 437–72.
469	Gunkel, H.	"Die Oden Salomos," *ZNW* 11 (1910), 291–328.
470	Harnack, A. von	*Ein jüdisch-christliches Psalmbuch aus dem ersten Jahrhundert* (TU 35.4; Leipzig: J. C. Hinrichs, 1910).
471	Harris, J. R.	*An Early Christian Psalter* (London: James Nisbet & Co., 1909).
472	Harris, J. R.	*The Odes and Psalms of Solomon: Now First Published from the Syriac Edition* (Cambridge: University Press, 1911).
473	Harris, J. R.	*The Doctrine of Immortality in the Odes of Solomon* (London: Hodder & Stoughton, 1912).
474	Harris, J. R., and Mingana, A.	*The Odes and Psalms of Solomon* (2 vols.; Manchester: University Press; London/New York: Longmans, Green & Co., 1916, 1920).
475	Haussleiter, J.	"Der judenchristliche Charakter der 'Oden Salomos,'" *ThBl* 31 (1910), 265–76.
476	Headlam, A. C.	"The Odes of Solomon," *CQR* 71 (1911), 272–97.
477	Holstijn, H. J. E. W.	*Oden van Salomo: Zangen van Rust in den Heere* (Zutphen: G. J. A. Ruys Uitgevers, 1942).
478	Kittel, G.	"Eine zweite Handschrift der Oden Salomon," *ZNW* 14 (1913), 79–93.
479	Klijn, A. F. J.	"The Influence of Jewish Theology on the Odes of Solomon and the Acts of Thomas," in M. Simon (ed.), *Aspects du judéo-christianisme: Colloque de Strasbourg 23–25 avril 1964* (Paris: Presses universitaires de France, 1965), 167–79.
480	Kruse, H.	"Die 24. Ode Salomos," *OrChr* 74 (1990), 25–43.
481	Labourt, J.	"Les Odes de Salomon," *RB* 8 (1911), 5–21.
482	Labourt, J., and Batiffol, P.	*Les Odes de Salomon: une œuvre chrétienne des environs de L'an 100–120* (Paris: Librairie Victor Lecoffre, 1911).
483	Lattke, M.	*Die Oden Salomos in ihrer Bedeutung für Neues Testament und Gnosis* (OBO 25.1–3; Göttingen: Vandenhoeck & Ruprecht, 1979–86).
484	Marmorstein, A.	"Kranz und Krone in den Oden Salomos," *OLZ* 15 (1912), 306–8.
485	MarYosip, M.	"The Oldest Christian Hymnbook," *Union Seminary Review* 59 (1943), 254–60.

486 Menzies, A.   "The Odes of Solomon," in *Interpreter* 7 (1910), 7–22.

487 Newbold, W. R.   "Bardaisan and the Odes of Solomon," *JBL* 30 (1911), 161–204.

488 Newbold, W. R.   "The Descent of Christ in the Odes of Solomon," *JBL* 31 (1912), 168–209.

489 Philonenko, M.   "Conjecture sur un verset de la onzième Ode de Salomon," *ZNW* 53 (1962), 264.

490 Rudolph, K.   'War der Verfasser der Oden Salomos ein 'Qumran-Christ'?": Ein Beitrag zur Diskussion um die Anfänge der Gnosis," *RdQ* 4 (1964), 523–55.

491 Segelberg, E.   "Evangelium Veritatis: A Confirmation Homily and Its Relation to the Odes of Solomon," *Orientalia Suecana* 8 (1959), 3–42.

492 Spitta, F.   "Zum Verständnis der Oden Salomos," *ZNW* 11 (1910), 259–90.

493 Terzoli, R.   "Le Odi di Salomone," in *Il Tema della Beatitudine nei Patri Siri* (Rome: Morcelliana, 1972).

494 Tondelli, L.   *Le Odi di Salomone: Cantici Christiani degli inizi del II Secolu* (Prefazione del Angelo Mercati; Rome: Francesco Ferrari, 1914).

495 Ungnad, A., and   *Die Oden Salomos: Aus dem Syrischen übersetzt,*
     Staerk, W.   *mit Anmerkungen* (Bonn: A. Marcus & E. Weber's Verlag, 1910).

496 Vööbus, A.   "Neues Licht zur Frage der Originalsprache der Oden Salomos," *Muséon* 75 (1962), 275–90.

497 Winterhalter, P.   *The Odes of Solomon: Original Christianity Revealed* (Llewellyn's Spiritual Perspective Series; St. Paul, Minn.: Llewellyn Publications, 1985).

Orphica

498 Lafargue, M.   "The Jewish Orpheus," in P. J. Achtemeier (ed.), *Society of Biblical Literature Seminar Papers 1978* (Missoula, Mont.: Society of Biblical Literature, 1978), 2, 132–44.

499 Walter, N.   *Der Thoraauslege Aristobulos* (TU 86; Berlin: Akademie-Verlag, 1962), esp. 103–15, 202–61.

Prayer of Jacob

500	Charlesworth, J. H.	"The Portrayal of the Righteous as an Angel," in J. J. Collins and G. W. E. Nickelsburg (eds.), *Ideal Figures in Ancient Judaism: Profiles and Paradigms* (Chico, Calif.: Scholars Press, 1980), 135–51. See 140–42.
501	Goodenough, E. R.	"Charms in Judaism," in *Jewish Symbols in the Greco-Roman Period* (New York: Pantheon Books, 1953–68), 2:161–207.

Prayer of Joseph

502	James, M. R.	*The Lost Apocrypha of the Old Testament* (London: S.P.C.K., 1920), 21–31.
503	Priebatsch, H.	*Die Josephsgeschichte in der Weltliteratur* (Breslau: M. & H. Marcus, 1937), esp. 8–44.
504	Schäfer, P.	"The Rivalry Between Angels and Men in 'The Prayer of Joseph' and Rabbinic Literature," in *Proceedings 6th Congress of Jewish Studies, 1973* (Jerusalem: Magnes, 1977), 3:511–15.
505	Smith, J. Z.	"The Prayer of Joseph," in J. Neusner (ed.), *Religions in Antiquity: Essays in Memory of Erwin Ramsdell Goodenough* (Supplements *Numen* 14; Leiden: Brill, 1968), 253–94.
506	Smith, J. Z.	"Map Is Not Territory," *SJLA* 23 (1978), 24–66. Full bibliography included.
507	Stein, E.	"Zur apokryphen Schrift 'Gebet Josephs,'" *MGWJ* 81 (1937), 280–86.

Prayer of Manasseh

508	Frey, J. B.	"Apocryphes de l'Ancien Testament, 13: La Prière de Manassé," in *DBS* 1, cols. 442–45.
509	Stone, M. E.	"Apocryphal Notes and Readings, 6: The Prayer of Manasses," *IsrOrSt* 1 (1971), 127–28.

Psalms of Solomon

510	Braun, H.	"Von Erbarmen Gottes über den Gerechten: Zur Theologie der Psalmen Salomos," *ZNW* 43 (1950–51), 1–54.
511	Delcor, M.	"Psaumes de Salomon," *DBS* 9, cols. 214–45.
512	Delcor, M.	"Salomon, Salmos de," in J. A. Gutiérrez-Larraya (ed.), *Enciclopedia de la Biblia* (vol. 6; Barcelona: Garriga, 1963), col. 401.

513	Franklyn, P. N.	"The Cultic and Pious Climax of Eschatology in the Psalms of Solomon," *JJS* 18 (1987), 1–17.
514	Gebhardt, O. von	*Die Psalmen Salomos* (Leipzig, 1895).
515	Hann, R. R.	*The Manuscript History of the Psalms of Solomon* (SBLSCS 13; Chico, Calif.: Scholars Press, 1982).
516	Harris, J. R.	*The Odes and Psalms of Solomon: Now First Published from the Syriac Edition* (Cambridge: University Press, 1911).
517	Harris, J. R., and Mingana, A.	*The Odes and Psalms of Solomon* (2 vols.; Manchester: University Press; London: Longmans; New York: Green & Co., 1916, 1920).
518	Holm-Nielsen, S.	"Salomos Salmer," in E. Hammershaimb (ed.), *De Gammeltestamentlige Pseudepigrapher* (vol. 5; Copenhagen: Gad, 1970), 548–95.
519	Jonge, M. de	"The Expectation of the Future in the Psalms of Solomon," *Neotestamentica* 23 (1989), 93–117.
520	Kuhn, K. G.	*Die älteste Textgestalt der Psalmen Salomos insbesondere auf Grund der syrischen Übersetzung der Psalmen Salomos 13–17* (BWANT 4.21; Stuttgart: Kohlhammer, 1937).
521	O'Dell, J.	"The Religious Background of the Psalms of Solomon (Re-evaluated in the Light of the Qumran Texts)," *RdQ* 3 (1961), 241–57.
522	Ryle, H. E., and James, M. R.	*Psalmoi Solomontos: Psalms of the Pharisees Commonly Called the Psalms of Solomon* (Cambridge: University Press, 1891.
523	Schüpphaus, J.	*Die Psalmen Salomos* (ALGHJ 7; Leiden: Brill, 1977).
524	Trafton, J. L.	*The Syriac Version of the Psalms of Solomon: A Critical Evaluation* (SBLSCS 11; Atlanta: Scholars Press, 1985).
525	Trafton, J. L.	"The Psalms of Solomon: New Light from the Syriac Version?," *JBL* 105 (1986), 227–32.
526	Viteau, J.	"Les Psaumes de Salomon," in F. Martin, *Documents pour l'étude de la Bible* (Paris: Letouzey et Ané, 1911).
527	Wright, R. B.	"The Psalms of Solomon, the Pharisees and the Essenes," in R. A. Kraft (ed.), *1972 Proceedings: International Organization for Septuagint and Cognate Studies and the Society of Biblical Literature Pseudepigrapha Seminar* (SBLSCS 2; Missoula, Mont.: Scholars Press, 1972), 136–54.

Pseudo-Philo

528	Delcor, M.	"Remarques sur un hymn essénien de caractère gnostique," *Sem* 11 (1961), 43–54.
529	Delling, G.	"Von Morija zum Sinai," *JSJ* 2 (1971), 1–18. Discusses PsPhilo 32:1–10 (the Hymn of Deborah).
530	Philonenko, M.	"Un paraphrase du cantique d'Anne," *RHPhR* 42 (1962), 157–68.

Sirach

531	Baumgartner, W.	"Die literarischen Gattungen in der Weisheit des Jesus Sirach," *ZAW* 34 (1914), 161–98, see esp. 169–86.
532	Di Lella, A. A.	"Sirach 51:1–12: Poetic Structure and Analysis of Ben Sira's Psalm," *CBQ* 48 (1986), 395–407.
533	Lee, T. R.	*Studies in the Form of Sirach 44–50* (Atlanta: Scholars Press, 1986).
534	Mack, B. L.	*Wisdom and the Hebrew Epic: Ben Sira's Hymn in Praise of the Fathers* (Chicago/London: University of Chicago Press, 1985).
535	Marböck, J.	"Das Gebet um die Rettung Zions Sir 36,1–22 (G. 33,1–13a; 36,16b-22) im Zusammenhang der Geschichtsschau Ben Siras," in J. B. Bauer (ed.), *Memoria Jerusalem: Freundesgabe Franz Sauer zum 70. Geburtstag* (Graz: Akademische Druck- u. Verlagsanstalt, 1977), 93–116.
536	Marmorstein, A.	"Jesus Sirach 51.12ff.," *ZAW* 29 (1909), 287–93.
537	Muraoka, T.	"Sir. 51,13–30: An Erotic Hymn to Wisdom?," *JSJ* 10 (1979), 166–78.
538	Prato, G. L.	*Il problema della teodicea in Ben Sira* (AnBib 65; Rome: Pontifical Biblical Institute, 1975). See 62–115 for the prayer in 39:12–35.
539	Roth, C.	"Ecclesiasticus in the Synagogue Service," *JBL* 71 (1952), 171–78.
540	Siebeneck, R. T.	"May Their Bones Return to Life! Sirach's Praise of the Fathers," *CBQ* 21 (1959), 411–28. A wide-ranging essay discussing the hymnic material in Sirach.
541	Vargha, T.	"De Psalmo hebraico Ecclesiastici c.51," *Anton* 10 (1935), 3–10.

Testament of Moses

542   Collins, A. Yarbro   "Composition and Redaction of the Testament of Moses 10," *HThR* 69 (1976), 179–86.

Tobit

543   Deselaers, P.   *Das Buch Tobit: Studien zu seiner Entstehung, Komposition und Theologie* (Göttingen: Vandenhoeck & Ruprecht, 1982), esp. 76–84, 90–96.

Wisdom of Solomon

544   Marchel, W.   *Abba, Père! La prière du Christ et des chrétiens: Étude exégétique sur les origines et la signification de l'invocation à la divinité comme père, avant et dans le Nouveau Testament* (AnBib 19; Rome: Pontifical Biblical Institute, 1963), 73–81.

545   Winston, D.   *The Wisdom of Solomon* (Anchor Bible; Garden City, N.Y.: Doubleday, 1979), 167–71.

QUMRAN

The following documents, many of fragmentary nature, together with psalms and prayers located in other Qumran works, represent the prayer and hymnic material from Qumran as of December 1992.

Thanksgiving Hymns (Hodayot: 1QH, 1Q35)
Hymn of Praise (3Q6)
Prayer of Joseph (4Q371–372)
Prayer of Nabonidus (4QPrNab)
Patriarchal Blessings (4QPBless)
Psalms of Joshua (4Q378–379)
Qumran Pseudepigraphic Psalms (4QapPs)
 Zion Psalm (4Q380 1)
 Praise of Obadiah (4Q380 2B)
 Creation Psalm (4Q381 1)
 Psalm Based on Psalms 86 and 89 (4Q381 15)
 Psalm of the Man of God (4Q381 24)
 Psalm of Deliverance (4Q381 31A)
 Psalm of Lament 2 (4Q381 31B)
 Penitential Psalm (4Q381 33A)
 Manasseh's Prayer (4Q381 33B)
 Individual Psalm of Lament (4Q381 45)
 A Psalm of the Chosen Ones (4Q381 46)
 A Psalm Based on Psalm 76 (4Q381 48 and 50)

A Discourse on the Land (4Q381 69)
A Psalm of Covenant Lawsuit (4Q381 76–77)
Angelic Liturgy
  4QShirShabb (4Q400–407)
  11QShirShabb
  Masada ShirShabb
Times for Praising God (4Q409)
Blessings (4Q434–439)
Prayer for King Jonathan (4Q448)
Benediction 2 (4Q500)
Lament (4Q501)
Daily Prayers (4Q503)
Psalms (4Q504–506)
Prayers for Feasts (4Q507–509)
Wisdom Canticles (4Q510–11)
Ritual of Purification (4Q512)
Beatitudes (4Q525)
4Q Apocryphal Psalms (4QPs^f)
Blessings (6QBen)
Hymns (pap6Q18)
A Hymn (8Q5)
Benediction 1 (11QBer)
11Q Psalms (11QPs^{a-e}, 11QPsAp^a)
11Q Hymn^{a-b}
Hymnic Fragments
  Holy Messi[ah] Fragment (1Q30)
  Men of the Covenant Fragment (1Q31)
  Liturgical Fragment 1 (1Q34a)
  Day of Atonement Fragment (1Q34b)
  Liturgical Fragment 2 (1Q36)
  Liturgical Fragment 3 (1Q38)
  Liturgical Fragment 4 (1Q39)
  Liturgical Fragment 5 (1Q40)
  Liturgical Fragment (2Q26 ar)
  Hymnic Fragment 1 (4Q498)
  Hymnic Fragment 2 (4Q499)

General

546	Baillet, M.	"Psaumes, hymnes, cantiques et prières dans les manuscrits de Qumran," in R. De Langhe (ed.), *Le Psautier: Ses origines, ses problèmes littéraires, son influence* (Orientalia et biblica lovaniensia 4; Louvain: Publications universitaires, 1962), 389–405.
547	Brooke, G. J.	"Psalms 105 and 106 at Qumran," *RdQ* 14 (1989), 267–92.

548 Carmignac, J.   "Les affinités qumrâniennes de la onzième Ode de Salomon," *RdQ* 3 (1961), 71–102.

549 Carmignac, J.   "Un qumrânien converti au christianisme: L'auteur des Odes de Salomon," in H. Bardtke (ed.), *Qumran-Probleme* (Deutsche Akademie der Wissenschaften zu Berlin 42; Berlin: Akademie-Verlag, 1963), 75–108.

550 Charlesworth, J. H.   "Qumran, John and the Odes of Solomon," in J. H. Charlesworth (ed.), *John and Qumran* (London: Chapman, 1972), 107–36. Reprinted in *John and the Dead Sea Scrolls* (New York: Crossroad, 1990), 107–36.

551 Flusser, D.   "Qumran and Jewish 'apotropaic' Prayers," *IEJ* 16 (1966), 194–205.

552 Haag, H.   "Das liturgische Leben der Qumrangemeinde," *ALW* 10 (1967), 78–109.

553 Klinzing, G.   *Die Umdeutung des Kultus in der Qumrangemeinde und im Neuen Testament* (Göttingen: Vandenhoeck & Ruprecht, 1971). See esp. ch. 4, "Rechter Wandel und Lobpreis als Opfer," 93–106.

554 Kohler, K.   "The Essene Version of the Seven Benedictions as Preserved in the VII Book of the Apostolic Constitutions," *HUCA* 1 (1924), 410–25. Reprinted in J. J. Petuchowski (ed.), *Contributions to the Scientific Study of Jewish Liturgy* (New York: KTAV, 1970), 75–90.

555 Limbeck, M.   "Der Lobpreis Gottes als Sinn des Daseins," *ThQ* 150 (1970), 349–57. Discussion of 1QH 10 and 1QS 10.

556 Maier, J.   "Zu Kult und Liturgie der Qumrangemeinde," *RdQ* 14 (1990), 543–86.

557 Nitzan, B.   "Biblical Influence in Qumran Prayer and Religious Poetry" (Ph.D Dissertation: Tel-Aviv University, 1989) [in Hebrew].

558 Nitzan, B.   "The Obligatory Prayer in Qumran and in Klal Israel," in D. Assaf (ed.), *Proceedings of the 10th World Congress of Jewish Studies, A: The Bible in Its World* (Jerusalem: Magnes Press, 1990), 111–18.

559 Nitzan, B.   *Biblical Influences in Qumran Prayer* (forthcoming).

560 Philonenko, M.   "Culte sacrificiel et 'offrande des lèvres' dans le judaïsme essénien," in R. Goetschel (ed.), *Prière, mystique et judaïsme: colloque de Strasbourg 10–12 septembre, 1984* (Paris: Presses universitaires de France, 1987), 9–19.

561 Ploeg, J. P. M. van der — "L'immortalité de l'homme d'après les textes de la mer Morte (1QS, 1QH)," *VT* 2 (1952), 171–75.

562 Ploeg, J. P. M. van der — "Les manuscrits de la Grotte XI de Qumrân," *RdQ* 12 (1985–87), 3–15, see esp. 5–6 (Psalms); 10–11 (Songs of the Sabbath Sacrifice); 11 (11QBer); 11–12 (11QHymn[a-b]).

563 Schiffman, L. H. — "The Dead Sea Scrolls and the Early History of Jewish Liturgy," in L. I. Levine (ed.), *The Synagogue in Late Antiquity* (Philadelphia: American Schools of Oriental Research, 1987), 33–48.

564 Talmon, S. — "The Order of Prayer in the Sect from the Judean Desert," *Tarbiz* 29 (1959–60), 1–20 [in Hebrew]. Discussion of 1QS 9.26–11.22 and other Qumran hymnic material.

565 Talmon, S. — "The 'Manual of Benedictions' of the Sect of the Judaean Desert," *RdQ* 2 (1959–60), 475–500. Discussion of a number of passages forming part of an alleged "Manual of Benedictions," but now allegedly broken up among the various scrolls, e.g., 1QS 10–11, 1QH 12.

566 Talmon, S. — "The Emergence of Institutionalized Prayer in Israel in the Light of the Qumran Literature," in M. Delcor (ed.), *Qumrân: Sa piété, sa théologie et son milieu* (BEThL 46; Paris and Gembloux: Duculot, 1978), 265–84.

567 Weinfeld, M. — "Traces of Kedushat Yozer and Pesukey de Zimra in the Qumran Literature and Ben Sira," *Tarbiz* 45 (1976), 15–26 [in Hebrew].

568 Weinfeld, M. — "On the Question of Morning Benedictions at Qumran," *Tarbiz* 51 (1981–82), 495–6 [in Hebrew].

569 Weinfeld, M. — "The Morning Prayers (Birkhoth Hashachar) in Qumran and the Conventional Jewish Liturgy," *RdQ* 13 (1988), 481–94. Discusses 1QS 10–11, 11QPs[a] col. xix.

570 Weinfeld, M. — "Prayers and Liturgical Practise in Qumran," in D. Dimant and U. Rappaport (eds.), *The Dead Sea Scrolls: Forty Years of Research* (Leiden/New York/Cologne: Brill, 1992), 241–58.

571 Wilms, F.-E. — "Blutige Opfer oder Opfer der Lippen," *ALW* 25 (1983), 121–36.

Thanksgiving Hymns (Hodayot: 1QH, 1Q35)

572 Arvedson, T. — "De s. k. Tacksagelsepsalmerna från Qumran," *SEÅ* 22–23 (1957–58), 208–18.

573   Bardtke, H.   "Considérations sur les cantiques de Qumran," *RB* 63 (1956), 220–33.

574   Bardtke, H.   "Das Ich des Meisters in den Hodajoth von Qumran," *WZ(L)* 6 (1956–57), 93–104.

575   Bardtke, H.   "Die Loblieder von Qumran," *ThLZ* 81 (1956), col. 149–54, 589–604, 715–24; and *ThLZ* 82 (1957), col. 339–48.

576   Baumgarten, J. M., and Mansoor, M.   "Studies in the New *Hodayot* (Thanksgiving Hymns)," *JBL* 74 (1955), 115–24, 188–95; and *JBL* 75 (1956), 107–13.

577   Becker, J.   *Das Heil Gottes* (StUNT 3; Göttingen: Vandenhoeck & Ruprecht, 1964), section 6 (126–68).

578   Betz, O.   "Die Geburt der Gemeinde durch den Lehrer: Bermerkungen zum Qumranpsalm 1QH III, 1ff," *NTS* 3 (1957), 314–26.

579   Birnbaum, S. A.   "The Date of the Hymns Scroll," *PEQ* 84 (1952), 93–104.

580   Carmignac, J.   "Remarques sur le Texte des Hymnes de Qumrân," *Bib* 39 (1958), 138–55.

581   Carmignac, J.   "Localisation des fragments 15, 18, et 22 des Hymnes," *RdQ* 1 (1958–59), 425–30.

582   Carmignac, J.   "Les eléments historiques des Hymnes de Qumrân," *RdQ* 2 (1959–60), 205–22.

583   Carmignac, J.   "Les citations de l'Ancien Testament, et spécialement des Poèmes du Serviteur, dans les *Hymnes* de Qumrân," *RdQ* 2 (1960), 357–94.

584   Carmignac, J.   "Étude sur les procédés poétiques des Hymnes," *RdQ* 2 (1959–60), 515–32.

585   Chamberlain, J. F.   "Another Qumran Thanksgiving Psalm," *JNES* 14 (1955), 32–41.

586   Chamberlain, J. F.   "Further Elucidations of a Messianic Thanksgiving Psalm from Qumran (1QH 3.6)," *JNES* 14 (1955), 181–82.

587   Charlesworth, J. H.   "The Righteous Teacher and the Historical Jesus: A Study of the Self-Understandings of the Two," in W. P. Weaver (ed.), *Perspectives on Christology* (Nashville: Exodus Press, 1989), 73–94. Discusses 1QH 8.

588   Charlesworth, J. H.   "An Allegorical and Autobiographical Poem by the *Moreh HasSedeq* (1QH 8.4–11),' in M. Fishbane, E. Tov, with W. W. Fields (eds.), *Studies in the Bible, Qumran, and the Ancient Near East Presented to Shemaryahu Talmon* (Winona Lake, Ind.: Eisenbrauns, 1992), 295–307.

589 Delcor, M. *Les Hymnes de Qumran (Hodayot): Texte hébreu, introduction, traduction, commentaire* (Paris: Letouzey et Ané, 1962).

590 Denis, A.-M. "La prière dans les hymnes de Qumrân," in H. Limet and J. Ries (eds.), *L'expérience de la prière dans les grandes religions: actes du colloque de Louvain-la-Neuve et Liège (22–23 novembre 1978)* (Louvain-la-Neuve: Centre d'histoire des religions, 1980), 313–24.

591 Dietzel, A. "Beten im Geist: Eine religionsgeschichtliche Parallele aus den Hodajot zum paulinischen Gebet im Geist," *ThZ* 13 (1957), 12–32.

592 Dimant, D. "Qumran Sectarian Literature," in M. Stone (ed.), *Jewish Writings of the Second Temple Period* (CRINT II; Assen/Philadelphia: Van Gorcum/Fortress, 1984), 522–25.

593 Dombrowski Hopkins, D. "The Qumran Community and I Q Hodayot: A Reassessment," *RdQ* 10 (1981), 323–64.

594 Dupont-Sommer, A. "La mère du Messie et la mère de l'Aspic dans un hymne de Qoumrân," *RHR* 147 (1955), 174–88.

595 Dupont-Sommer, A. *Le Livre des Hymnes découvert près de la mer Morte (1QH)* (Semitica 7; Paris: Librairie d'Amérique et d'Orient Adrien Misonneuve, 1957).

596 Ehlen, A. J. "The Poetic Structure of a Hodayah from Qumran: An Analysis of Grammatical, Semantic, and Auditory Correspondence in 1QH 3:19–36" (Dissertation: Harvard University). Summarized in *HThR* 63 (1970), 516–17.

597 Ehrhardt, A. A. T. "A Penitentiary Psalm from the Dead Sea Scrolls and Its Allies," *StE* 1 (1959), 582–91.

598 Glanzmann, G. S. "The Sectarian Psalms from the Dead Sea," *TS* 13 (1952), 487–524.

599 Greenfield, J. C. "The Root 'GBL' in Mishnaic Hebrew and in the Hymnic Literature from Qumran." *RdQ* 2 (1959–60), 155–62.

600 Holm-Nielsen, S. *Hodayot: Psalms from Qumran* (Acta Theologica Danica 2, Aarhus: Universitetsforlaget, 1960).

601 Holm-Nielsen, S. " 'Ich' in den Hodayot und die Qumrangemeinde," in H. Bardtke (ed.), *Qumran-Probleme* (Berlin: Akademie-Verlag, 1963), 217–29.

602 Holm-Nielsen, S. "Erwägungen zu dem Verhaltnis zwischen den Hodayot und den Psalmen Salomon," in S. Wagner (ed.), *Bibel und Qumran: Festschrift H. Bardtke* (Berlin: Evangelische Haupt-Bibelgesellschaft, 1968), 112–31.

603 Hübner, H.   "Anthropologischer Dualismus in den Hodayoth,"
                          NTS 18 (1972), 268–84.

604 Hyatt, J. P.   "The View of Man in the Qumran 'Hodayot,'" *NTS*
                          2 (1955–56), 276–84.

605 Kittel, B. P.   *The Hymns of Qumran* (SBLDS 50; Chico, Calif.:
                          Scholars Press, 1981).

606 Knibb, M. A.   "The Hymns," in *The Qumran Community* (Cam-
                          bridge: University Press, 1987), 157–82.

607 Kraft, C. F.   "Poetic Structure in the Qumran Thanksgiving
                          Psalms," *BR* 2 (1957), 1–18.

608 Kuhn, H.-W.   *Enderwartung und gegenwärtiges Heil* (StUNT 4;
                          Göttingen: Vandenhoeck & Ruprecht, 1966), 11–
                          112.

609 Laurin, R. B.   "The Question of Immortality in the Qumran 'Ho-
                          dayot,'" *JJS* 3 (1958), 344–55.

610 Licht, J.   "The Doctrine of the Thanksgiving Scroll," *IEJ* 6
                          (1956), 1–13, 89–101.

611 Licht, J.   *The Thanksgiving Scroll* (Jerusalem: Bialik Institute,
                          1957) [in Hebrew].

612 Mansoor, M.   *The Thanksgiving Hymns* (StDJ 3; Grand Rapids,
                          Mich.: Eerdmans, 1961).

613 Morawe, G.   *Aufbau und Abgrenzung der Loblieder von Qumrân:
                          Studien zur gattungsgeschichtlichen Einordnung der
                          Hodajôth* (Theologische Arbeiten 16; Berlin: Evan-
                          gelische Verlagsanstalt, 1960).

614 Morawe, G.   "Vergleich des Aufbaus der Danklieder und hymni-
                          schen Bekenntnislieder von Qumran mit dem Aufbau
                          der Psalmen im Alten Testament und im Spätjuden-
                          tum," *RdQ* 4 (1963–64), 323–56.

615 Mowinckel, S.   "Some Remarks on Hodayoth 39 (V, 5–20)," *JBL* 75
                          (1956), 265–76.

616 Nielsen, E.   "I Q H V, 1.20–27: An Attempt at Filling Out Some
                          Gaps," *VT* 24 (1974), 240–43.

617 Puech, É.   "Un Hymne essénien en partie retrouvé et les Béati-
                          tudes. 1QH V 12–VI 18 (= col XIII–XIV 7) et
                          4QBéat," *RdQ* 13 (1988), 59–88.

618 Puech, É.   "Quelques aspects de la restauration du Rouleau des
                          Hymnes," *JJS* 39 (1988), 38–55.

619 Qimron, E.   "A New Reading in 1QH XV 15 and the Root GYL
                          in the Dead Sea Scrolls," *RdQ* 14 (1989), 127–28.

620 Ringgren, H.   "Die Weltbrand in den Hodajot," in S. Wagner
                          (ed.), *Bibel und Qumran: Festschrift H. Bardtke*
                          (Berlin: Evangelische Haupt-Bibelgesellschaft, 1968),
                          177–82.

621   Robinson, J. M.   "Die Hodajot-Formel in Gebet und Hymnus des Frühchristentums," in W. Eltester and F. H. Kettler (eds.), *Apophoreta: Festschrift für E. Haenchen zu seinem siebzigsten Geburtstag am 10 Dezember 1964* (BZAW 30; Berlin: A. Töpelmann, 1964), 194–235.

622   Rotenberry, P. W.   "A Translation and Study of the Qumran Hodayot" (Ph.D. Dissertation: Vanderbilt University, 1968).

623   Sanders, E. P.   "Chiasmus and the Translation of 1Q Hodayot VII 25–27," *RdQ* 6 (1968), 427–32.

624   Selms, A. van   *Der Rol der Lofprijzingen* (Baarn: Bosch & Kenning, 1957).

625   Silberman, L. H.   "Language and Structure in the Hodayot (1QH 3)," *JBL* 75 (1956), 96–106.

626   Sukenik, E. L.   *The Dead Sea Scrolls of the Hebrew University* (Jerusalem: Magnes Press, 1955).

627   Tanzer, S.J.   "The Sages at Qumran: Wisdom in the Hodayot" (Ph.D. Dissertation: Harvard University, 1986).

628   Thiering, B.   "The Poetic Forms of the Hodayot," *JSS* 8 (1963), 189–209.

629   Thoring, Y.   "Der Vergleich in I Q Hodayot," *RdQ* 11 (1983), 193–217.

630   Wallenstein, M.   *Hymns from the Judean Scrolls* (Manchester: University Press, 1950).

631   Wallenstein, M.   "A Hymn from the Scrolls," *VT* 5 (1955), 277–83.

632   Wallenstein, M.   "A Striking Hymn from the Dead Sea Scrolls," *BJRL* 38 (1955–56), 241–65.

633   Wernberg-Møller, P.   "Contributions of the Hodayot to Biblical Textual Criticism," *Textus* 4 (1964), 133–75.

634   Woude, A. S. van der   *De Dankpsalmen* (Amsterdam: Proost en Brandt, 1957).

Prayer of Joseph (4Q371–372)

635   Schuller, E. M.   "The Psalm of 4Q372 1 within the Context of Second Temple Prayer," *CBQ* 54 (1992), 67–79.

Prayer of Nabonidus (4QPrNab)

636   Cross, F. M.   "Fragments of the Prayer of Nabonidus," *IEJ* 34 (1984), 260–64.

637   Delcor, M.   "Le Testament de Job, la prière de Nabonide et les traditions targoumiques," in S. Wagner (ed.), *Bibel und Qumran: Festschrift H. Bardtke* (Berlin: Evangelische Haupt-Bibelgesellschaft, 1968), 57–74.

638   Grelot, P.   "La prière de Nabonide (4Q or Nab): Nouvel essai
                                   de restauration," *RdQ* 9 (1978), 483–95.

639   Jongeling, B.,   *Aramaic Texts from Qumran with Translations and*
       Labuschagne, C. J.,   *Annotations* (Semitic Studies Series 4; Leiden: Brill,
       and van der Woude,   1976), 121–31.
       A. S. (eds.)

640   Kirschläger, W.   "Exorcismus in Qumran?," *Kairos* 18 (1976), 135–
                                   53.

641   Knibb, M. A.   *The Qumran Community* (Cambridge: University
                                   Press, 1987), 203–6.

642   Meyer, R.   *Das Gebet des Nabonid: Eine in den Qumran —
                                   Handschriften weiterentdeckte Weisheitserzählung*
                                   (Sitzungsberichte der Sächsischen Akademie der Wis-
                                   senschaften zu Leipzig 104/3; Berlin: Akademie-
                                   Verlag, 1962).

643   Milik, J. T.   "Prière de Nabonide et autres écrits d'un cycle de
                                   Daniel: fragments araméens de Qumrân," *RB* 63
                                   (1956), 407–11.

644   Woude, A. S. van der   "Bemerkungen zum Gebet de Nabonid," in M. Del-
                                   cor (ed.), *Qumrân: Sa piété, sa théologie et son milieu*
                                   (BEThL 46; Paris and Gembloux: Duculot, 1978),
                                   121–29.

Patriarchal Blessings (4QPBless)

645   Allegro, J. M.   "Further Messianic References," *JBL* 75 (1956),
                                   174–76.

646   Fitzmyer, J. A.   "A Bibliographical Aid to the Study of the Qumran
                                   Cave IV Texts 158–186," *CBQ* 31 (1969), 59–71.
                                   See appendix, 71, for brief comment on this text and
                                   bibliography.

647   Stegemann, H.   "Weitere Stücke von 4Q Psalm 37, von 4Q Pa-
                                   triarchal Blessings und Hinweis auf eine unedierte
                                   Handschrift aus Höhle 4Q mit Exzerpten aus Deu-
                                   teronomium," *RdQ* 6 (1967), 193–227, esp. 211–17.

648   Yadin, Y.   "Some Notes on Commentaries on Genesis XLIX
                                   and Isaiah, from Qumran Cave 4," *IEJ* 7 (1957),
                                   66–68.

Psalms of Joshua (4Q378–379)

649   Newsom, C. A.   "The 'Psalms of Joshua' from Qumran Cave 4," *JJS*
                                   39 (1988), 56–73.

Pseudepigraphical Psalms 4QapPs (4Q380–381)

| 650 | Schuller, E. M. | *Non-canonical Psalms from Qumran: A Pseudepigraphic Collection* (Atlanta: Scholars Press, 1986). |
| 651 | Schuller, E. M. | "4Q380 and 4Q381: Non-Canonical Psalms from Qumran," in D. Dimant and U. Rappaport (eds.), *The Dead Sea Scrolls: Forty Years of Research* (Leiden/New York/Cologne: Brill, 1992), 90–99. |

Angelic Liturgy (4Q400–407, 11QShirShabb, Masada ShirShabb)

652	Allison, D. C.	"4Q403 frag. 1, col. 1, 38–46 and the Revelation to John," *RdQ* 12 (1985–87), 409–14.
653	Allison, D. C.	"The Silence of Angels: Reflections on the Songs of the Sabbath Sacrifice," *RdQ* 13 (1988), 189–97.
654	Baumgarten, J. M.	"The Qumran Sabbath Shirot and Rabbinic Merkabah Traditions," *RdQ* 13 (1988), 199–213.
655	Carmignac, J.	"Quelques détails de la lecture dans la Règle des chants pour l'holocauste du Sabbat," *RdQ* 7 (1964), 563–66.
656	Carmignac, J.	"Roi, Royauté et Royaume, dans la Liturgie Angélique," *RdQ* 12 (1985–87), 177–86.
657	Newsom, C. A.	*Songs of the Sabbath Sacrifice: A Critical Edition* (Harvard Semitic Studies 27; Atlanta: Scholars Press, 1985).
658	Newsom, C. A.	"Merkabah Exegesis in the Qumran Sabbath Shirot," *JJS* 38 (1987), 11–30.
659	Newsom, C. A., and Yadin, Y.	"The Masada Fragment of the Qumran Songs of the Sabbath," *IEJ* 34 (1984), 77–88.
660	Philonenko, M.	"Prière au soleil at liturgie angélique," in A. Caquot, J. H. Charlesworth, A. Piñero-Saenz et al. (eds.), *La littérature intertestamentaire* (Paris: Presses universitaires de France, 1985), 221–28.
661	Puech, É.	"Notes sur le manuscrit des Cantiques du Sacrifice du Sabbat trouvé à Masada," *RdQ* 12 (1985–87), 573–83.
662	Robinson, J. E.	"The Testament of Adam and the Angelic Liturgy," *RdQ* 12 (1985–87), 105–10.
663	Segert, S.	"Observations on Poetic Structures in the Songs of the Sabbath Sacrifice," *RdQ* 13 (1988), 215–23.
664	Smith, M. S.	"Biblical and Canaanite Notes to the Songs of the Sabbath Sacrifice at Qumran," *RdQ* 12 (1985–87), 585–88.

665   Strugnell, J.   "The Angelic Liturgy at Qumran — *4Q Serek Shirot*
                              'Olat Hashshabbat" (VT. S 7; Leiden: Brill, 1960),
                              318–45.

666   Woude, A. S. van der   "Fragmente einer Rolle der Lieder für das Sab-
                              batopfer aus Höhle XI von Qumran (11QSirSabb),"
                              in W. C. Delsman et al. (eds.), *Von Kanaan bis Ker-*
                              ala: Festschrift für Prof. Mag. Dr. Dr. J. P. M. van
                              der Ploeg zur Vollendung des siebzigsten Lebens-
                              jahres am 4. Juli 1979 (AOAT 211; Kevelaer/
                              Neukirchen-Vluyn: Butzon & Bercker/Neukirchener-
                              Vluyn, 1982), 311–37.

Times for Praising God (4Q409)

667   Qimron, E.   "Times for Praising God: A Fragment of a Scroll from
                             Qumran (4Q409)," *JQR* 80 (1989), 341–47.

Blessings (4Q434–439)

668   Weinfeld, M.   "Grace after Meals in Qumran," *JBL* 111 (1992),
                           427–40.

Prayer for King Jonathan (4Q448)

669   Eshel, E. and H.   "A Scroll from Qumran Which Includes Part of
                           Psalm 154 and a Prayer for King Jonathan and His
                           Kingdom," *Tarbiz* 60 (1991), 295–324 [in Hebrew].

Benedictions (4Q500, 11QBer)

670   Baumgarten, J. M.   "4Q500 and the Ancient Exegesis of the Lord's
                           Vineyard," *JJS* 40 (1989), 1–6.

671   Woude, A. S. van der "Ein neuer Segensspruch aus Qumran (11 Q Ber),"
                           in S. Wagner (ed.), *Bibel und Qumran: Fest-*
                           schrift H. Bardtke (Berlin: Evangelische Haupt-
                           Bibelgesellschaft, 1968), 253–58.

Lament (4Q501)

672   Strugnell, J.   "Notes en marge de Volume V des 'Discoveries in
                           the Judaean Desert of Jordan,' " *RdQ* 7 (1969–71),
                           250–52.

Daily Prayers (4Q503)

673   Baumgarten, J. M.   "4Q503 (Daily Prayers) and the Lunar Calendar," *RdQ* 12 (1985–87), 399–407.

Psalms (4Q504–506)

674   Baillet, M.   "Un recueil liturgique de Qumrân, grotte 4: Les Paroles de Luminaires," *RB* 68 (1961), 195–250.

675   Baillet, M.   "Remarques sur l'édition des Paroles des Luminaires," *RdQ* 7 (1964), 23–42.

676   Chazon, E.   "Is *Divrei ha-me'orot* a Sectarian Prayer?," in D. Dimant and U. Rappaport (eds.), *The Dead Sea Scrolls: Forty Years of Research* (Leiden/New York/Cologne: Brill, 1992), 3–17.

677   Lehmann, M. R.   "A Re-Interpretation of 4Q *Dibrê ham-me'oroth*," *RdQ* 7 (1964), 106–10.

678   Rinaldi, G.   "Une 'Supplice' da Qumrân (4Q Dib Ham)," *BibOr* 14 (1972), 119–31.

Wisdom Canticles (4Q510 and 511)

679   Nitzan, B.   "Hymns from Qumran, 4Q510–4Q511," in D. Dimant and U. Rappaport (eds.), *The Dead Sea Scrolls: Forty Years of Research* (Leiden/New York/Cologne: Brill, 1992), 53–63.

Beatitudes (4Q525)

680   Puech, É.   "4Q525 et les péricopes des Béatitudes en Ben Sira et Matthieu (Planche 1)," *RB* 98 (1991), 80–116.

Apocryphal Psalms from Cave 4 (4QPsf)

681   Starcky, J.   "Psaumes apocryphes de la grotte 4 de Qumrân (4QPs(f) VII–X)," *RB* 73 (1966), 353–71.

Qumran Psalms (Cave 11)

682   Auffret, P.   "Structure littéraire et interprétation du Psaume 151 de la grotte 11 de Qumrân," *RdQ* 9 (1977–78), 163–88.

683   Auffret, P.   "Structure littéraire et interprétation du Psaume 155 de la grotte XI de Qumrân," *RdQ* 9 (1977–78), 323–56.

684 Auffret, P. "Structure littéraire et interprétation du Psaume 154 de la grotte XI de Qumrân," *RdQ* 9 (1977–78), 513–45.

685 Brownlee, W. H. "The 11Q Counterpart to Psalm 151, 1–5," *RdQ* 4 (1963), 379–87.

686 Carmignac, J. "Nouvelles précisions sur le psaume 151," *RdQ* 8 (1975), 593–97.

687 Cross, F. M. "David, Orpheus, and Psalm 151:3–4," *BASOR* 231 (1978), 69–71.

688 Delcor, M. "Cinq psaumes syriaques esséniens," in *Les hymnes de Qumran (Hodayot)* (Paris: Letouzey et Ané, 1962), 299–319.

689 Dupont-Sommer, A. "Le psaume CLI dans 11QPs[a] et la problème de son origine essénienne," *Sem* 14 (1964), 25–62.

690 Dupont-Sommer, A. "Le psaume hébreu extra-canonique (11QPs[a], col. XXVIII)," *Annuaire du Collège de France* 64 (1964), 317–20.

691 Farrell, S. E. "Le rouleau 11QPs[a] et le psautier biblique: Une étude comparative," *LTP* 46 (1990), 353–68.

692 Goshen-Gottstein, M. H. "The Psalms Scroll (11QPs[a]): A Problem of Canon and Text," *Textus* 5 (1966), 22–33.

693 Gurewicz, S. B. "Hebrew Apocryphal Psalms from Qumran," *ABR* 15 (1967), 13–20.

694 Haran, M. "Two Text-Forms of Psalm 151," *JJS* 39 (1988), 171–82.

695 Hurvitz, A. "Observations on the Language of the Third Apocryphal Psalm from Qumran," *RdQ* 5 (1965), 225–32.

696 Lührmann, D. "Ein Weisheitspsalm aus Qumran (11QPs[a] XVIII)," *ZAW* 80 (1968), 87–98.

697 Magne, J. "Recherches sur les psaumes 151, 154 et 155," *RdQ* 8 (1975), 503–7.

698 Magne, J. "Orphisme, pythagorisme, essénisme dans le texte hébreu du psaume?," *RdQ* 8 (1975), 508–47.

699 Magne, J. " 'Seigneur de l'Univers' ou David-Orphée?: Défense de mon interprétation du Psaume 151," *RdQ* 9 (1977–78), 189–96.

700 Moraldi, L. "Dal Rotolo del Salmi (11QPs[a])," in *I Manoscritti di Qumran* (Turin: Unione Tipografico-Editrice Torinese, 1971), 465–94.

701 Philonenko, M. "L'origine essénienne des cinq psaumes syriaques de David," *Sem* 9 (1959), 35–48.

702 Ploeg, J. P. M. van der "Le psaume xci dans une recension de Qumran," *RB* 72 (1965), 210–17.

703 Ploeg, J. P. M. van der | "Fragments d'un manuscrit de psaumes de Qumran (11QPsᵇ)," *RB* 74 (1967), 408–12.

704 Ploeg, J. P. M. van der | "Un petit rouleau de psaumes apocryphes," in G. Jeremias, H. W. Kuhn and H. Stegemann (eds.), *Tradition und Glaube: Festgabe für K. G. Kuhn* (Göttingen: Vandenhoek & Ruprecht, 1971), 128–39.

705 Ploeg, J. P. M. van der | "Fragments d'un psautier de Qumrân," in M. A. Beek et al. (eds.), *Symbolae biblicae et mesopotamicae Francisco Mario Theodoro de Liagre Böhl dedicatae* (Leiden: Brill, 1973), 308–9.

706 Puech, É. | "11QPsApᵃ: Un rituel d'éxorcismes: Essai de reconstruction," *RdQ* 14 (1990), 377–408.

707 Puech, É. | "Les deux derniers psaumes davidiques du rituel d'exorcisme 11QPsApᵃ IV 4–5 14," in D. Dimant and U. Rappaport (eds.), *The Dead Sea Scrolls: Forty Years of Research* (Leiden/New York/Cologne: Brill, 1992), 64–89.

708 Rabinowitz, I. | "The Alleged Orphism of 11QPss 28, 3–12," *ZAW* 76 (1964), 193–200.

709 Sanders, J. A. | *The Psalms Scroll of Qumrân Cave 11 (11QPsᵃ)* (Oxford: Clarendon Press, 1965).

710 Sanders, J. A. | *The Dead Sea Psalms Scroll* (Ithaca, N.Y.: Cornell University Press, 1967).

711 Sanders, J. A. | "The Qumran Psalms Scroll (11QPsᵃ) Reviewed," in M. Black and W. A. Smalley (eds.), *On Language, Culture, and Religion: In Honor of Eugene A. Nida* (The Hague: Mouton, 1974), 76–99.

712 Silberman, L. H. | "Prophets/Angels: LXX and Qumran Psalm 151 and the Epistle to the Hebrews," in A. Finkel and L. Frizzell (eds.), *Standing before God: Studies on Prayer in Scriptures and in Tradition with Essays in Honor of John M. Oesterreicher* (New York: KTAV, 1981), 91–101.

713 Skehan, P. W. | "A Liturgical Complex in 11QPsᵃ," *CBQ* 35 (1973), 195–205.

714 Skehan, P. W. | "Jubilees and the Qumran Psalter," *CBQ* 37 (1975), 343–47.

715 Strugnell, J. | "More Psalms of David," *CBQ* 27 (1965), 207–16.

716 Wacholder, B. Z. | "David's Eschatological Psalter 11QPsalmsᵃ," *HUCA* 59 (1988), 23–72.

717 Yadin, Y. | "Another Fragment (E) of the Psalms Scroll from Qumran Cave 11 (11QPsᵃ)," *Textus* 5 (1966), 1–10.

Hymnic Fragments (from Cave 1)

718   Carmignac, J.   "Le recueil de prières liturgiques de la grotte 1," *RdQ*
                            4 (1963), 271–76.

1QS

719   Becker, J.   *Das Heil Gottes* (StUNT 3; Göttingen: Vandenhoeck
                            & Ruprecht, 1964), section 5.

720   Goedhart, H.   *De Slothymne van het Manual of Discipline* (Rotter-
                            dam: Bronder-Offset, 1965).

721   Loader, J. A.   "The Model of the Priestly Blessing in 1QS," *JSJ* 14
                            (1983), 11–17.

1QSb

722   Leivestad, R.   "Enthalten die Segensprüche 1QSb eine Segnung des
                            Hohenpriesters der messianischen Zeit?," *StTh* 31
                            (1977), 137–45.

War Scroll (1QM, 1Q33)

723   Duhaime, J. L.   "La rédaction de 1QM XIII et l'évolution du dual-
                            isme à Qumrân," *RB* 84 (1977), 210–38.

724   Flusser, D.   "The Magnificat, the Benedictus and the War Scroll,"
                            in *Judaism and the Origins of Christianity* (Jerusa-
                            lem: Magnes Press, 1988), 126–49.

725   North, R.   " 'Kittim' War or 'Sectarian' Liturgy?," *Bib* 39
                            (1958), 84–93.

JOSEPHUS

726   Brüne, B.   *Flavius Josephus und seine Schriften in ihrem Ver-
                            hältnis zum Judentum, zur griechischen-römischen
                            Welt und zum Christentum* (Gütersloh: Bertelsmann,
                            1913). Reprinted, Wiesbaden: Sändig, 1969, 99–103.

727   Grimm, W.   "Der Dank für die empfangene Offenbarung bei
                            Jesus und Josephus: Parallelen zu Mt 11, 25–27," in
                            *Das Institutum Judaicum der Universität Tübingen
                            1971–72* (Tübingen: Mohr, 1972), 69–78. See also
                            BZ 17 (1973), 249–56.

728   Hahn, S.   "Josephus on Prayer in c. Ap. II. 197," in O. Kom-
                            los (ed.), *Études orientales à la mémoire de Paul
                            Hirschler* (Budapest, 1950), 111–15.

729   Langen, J.   "Die theologische Standpunkt des Flavius Josephus," *ThQ* 47 (1865), 3–59, esp. 20–22.

730   Montgomery, J. A.   "The Religion of Flavius Josephus," *JQR* N.S. 11 (1920–21), 277–305, esp. 291–93.

731   Schlatter, A.   *Wie sprach Josephus von Gott?* (Beiträge zur Förderung christlicher Theologie 14; Gütersloh: Bertelsmann, 1910), 73–76. Repr., K. Rengstorf (ed.), Darmstadt: Wissenschaftliche Buchgesellschaft, 1970.

732   Schlatter, A.   "Lobpreis und Gebet," in *Die Theologie des Judentums nach dem Bericht des Josephus* (Gütersloh: C. Bertelsmann, 1932), 108–13.

733   Unnik, W. C. van   "Eine merkwürdige liturgische Aussage bei Josephus (Jos. Ant. 8, 111–13)," in O. Betz, K. Haacker, and M. Hengel (eds.), *Josephus — Studien: Untersuchungen zu Josephus, dem antiken Judentum und dem Neuen Testament, Otto Michel zum 70. Geburtstag gewidmet* (Göttingen: Vandenhoeck & Ruprecht, 1974), 362–69.

PHILO

734   Bréhier, É.   *Les idées philosophiques et religieuses de Philon d'Alexandrie* (Paris: Vrin, 1950), 141, and 229 n.6.

735   Dowd, S. E.   "The Theological Function of Petitionary Prayer in the Thought of Philo," *PRSt* 10 (1983), 241–54.

736   Laporte, J.   *La doctrine eucharistique chez Philon d'Alexandrie* (Paris: Beauchesne, 1972).

737   Laporte, J.   *Eucharistia in Philo* (New York: E. Mellen Press, 1983).

738   Larson, C. W.   "Prayer of Petition in Philo," *JBL* 65 (1946), 185–203.

739   Nikiprowetzky, V.   "Spiritualisation et culte chez Philon d'Alexandrie," *Sem* 17 (1967), 97–116.

740   Sandmel, S.   *Philo's Place in Judaism* (Cincinnati: Hebrew Union College, 1956), 115. Reprinted, New York: KTAV, 1971),

741   Severus, E. von   "Gebet I," *RAC* 8, cols. 1168–69.

742   Wolfson, H. A.   *Philo: Foundations of Religious Philosophy in Judaism, Christianity, and Islam* (Cambridge, Mass.: Harvard University Press, 1947), 2:237–52.

TARGUMS

743   Black, M.   "The Recovery of the Language of Jesus," *NTS* 3 (1956–57), 305–13. See 306 for brief note concerning the survival of liturgical hymns in the Palestinian Pentateuch tradition.

744   Díez Macho, A.   "Le substrat araméen des évangiles: scolies en marge de l'Aramaic Approach de Matthew Black," *Bib* 49 (1968), 388–99. Discussion on 391–92 of the *epiousios* concept in the Lord's Prayer.

745   Díez Macho, A.   "Le targum palestinien," *RSR* 47 (1973), 169–231. See 209, 215, for discussion of the Lord's Prayer and the Targumic traditions. The formula "our Father who art in Heaven" is discussed on 207.

746   Liebreich, L. J.   "The Benedictory Formula in the Targum to the Song of Songs," *HUCA* 18 (1944), 177–97.

747   Maher, M.   "The Meturgemanim and Prayer," *JJS* 41 (1990), 226–46.

748   Martinmort, A. G.   "Essai historiques sur les traductions liturgiques (aussi Juives)," *MD* 86 (1966), 75–105.

749   McNamara, M.   *Targum and Testament: Aramaic Paraphrases of the Hebrew Bible: A Light on the New Testament* (Grand Rapids/Shannon: Eerdmans/Irish University Press, 1972). See 116–17 for discussion of the phrase "your Father in Heaven" in Matt. 6:6, 8. The formula "our Father" is discussed on 115–19. The Prologue of John's Gospel is discussed on 101–6.

750   Patte, D.   "Scripture at the Synagogue: Targums and Liturgy," in *Early Jewish Hermeneutics in Palestine* (SBLDS 22; Missoula, Mont.: Scholars Press, 1975), 49–86.

751   Shinan, A.   " 'Their Prayers and Petitions': The Prayers of the Ancients in the Light of the Pentateuchal Targums," *Sinai* 78 (1975–76), 89–92 [in Hebrew].

752   Shinan, A.   *The Aggadah in the Aramaic Targum to the Pentateuch* (Jerusalem: Magnes Press, 1979), 2:327–35.

5. NEW TESTAMENT

GENERAL

753   Balthasar, H. U. von   "Vom immerwährenden Gebet," in *Internationale Katholische Zeitschrift "Communio"* 4 (1975), 206–17.

754   Behler, G.-M.   "Prier dans l'Esprit et prier sans cesse selon le Nouveau Testament," *MD* 109 (1972), 31–50.

755   Berger, K.   "Gebet, IV (Neues Testament)," in *TRE* 12, 47–60.

756   Bieder, W.   "Gebetswirklichkeit und Gebetsmöglichkeit: Das Beten des Geists und das Beten im Geiste," *ThZ* 4 (1948), 22–40.

757   Bloth, P. C.   "Gebetstheologische Aspekte der Liturgie und das Neuen Testaments," in F. Bargheer and J. Röbelen (eds.), *Gebet und Gebetserziehung* (Heidelberg: Quelle & Meyer, 1971), 48–75.

758   Boyd, R. F.   "Work of the Holy Spirit in Prayer," *Interp* 8 (1954), 35–42.

759   Brun, L.   *Segen und Fluch im Urchristentum* (Oslo: J. Dybwad, 1932).

760   Bruston, C.   "À propos de quelques textes de 'prières cultuelles' du Nouveau Testament," *RHPhR* 10 (1930), 286–88.

761   Buchanan, G. W.   "The Ceremonies of the Early Church," *NTS* 26 (1978–79), 279–97, esp. 287–89.

762   Cahill, M.   "A Structuralist Approach to Prayer in the New Testament," *PIBA* 4 (1980), 12–20.

763   Christ, P.   *Die Lehre vom Gebet nach dem Neuen Testament: eine Beitrag zur Kenntniss und Wurdigung des ursprunglichen Christenthums* (Leiden: Brill, 1886).

764   Cipriani, S.   *La preghiera nel Nuovo Testamento: spunti di esegesi e di spiritualità* (4th ed.; Milan: Edizioni O.R., 1989).

765   Coggan, F. D.   *The Prayers of the New Testament* (London: Hodder & Stoughton, 1968).

766   Cooper, R. M.   "Leitourgos Christou Iesou: Toward a Theology of Christian Prayer," *AThR* 47 (1965), 263–75.

767   Cullmann, O.   *Le culte dans l'église primitive* (Éditions Delachaux & Niestlé: Neuchâtel/Paris, 1945), 11–13, 20–23.

768   Cullmann, O.   *Early Christian Worship* (Philadelphia: Westminster, 1978), 21–25.

769   Cuming, G. J.   "The New Testament Foundation for Common Prayer," *StLi* 10 (1974), 88–105.

770 Deichgräber, R.   *Gotteshymnus und Christushymnus in der frühen Christenheit: Untersuchungen zu Form, Sprache und Stil der frühchristlichen Hymnen* (StUNT 5; Göttingen: Vandenhoeck & Ruprecht, 1967).

771 Delling, G.   Der Gottesdienst im Neuen Testament (Göttingen: Vandenhoeck & Ruprecht, 1952). See esp. "Bekenntnis und Hymnus," 77–88; "Gebet," 99–118. ETrans.: Philadelphia: Fortress, 1962.

772 Dietzel, A.   "Die Gründe der Erhörungsgewißheit nach dem NT" (Dissertation: Johannes Gutenburg Universität, Mainz, 1955).

773 Doohan, H. and L.   *Prayer in the New Testament: Make Your Requests Known to God* (Wilmington, Del.: Michael Glazier, 1992).

774 Eason, C. E.   "Traces of Liturgical Worship in the Epistles with Special Reference to Hymns, Prayers and Creeds" (Dissertation: University of Leeds, 1966).

775 Fisher, R.   *Prayer in the New Testament* (Philadelphia: Westminster, 1964).

776 Friedrich, G.   "Die Fürbitte im Neuen Testament," in *Auf das Wort kommt es an: Gesammelte Aufsätze* (Göttingen: Vandenhoeck & Ruprecht, 1978), 431–56.

777 George, A. R.   *Communion with God in the New Testament* (London: Epworth Press, 1953). See esp. chs. 2, 3, 6, and 8.

778 Glöcker, R.   "Neutestamentliche Wundergeschichten und frühchristliche Gebetsparänese," in L. Scheffczyk (ed.), *Die Mysterien des Lebens Jesu* (Aschaffenburg: Paul Pattlock, 1984), 57–74.

779 Gloer, W. H.   "Homologies and Hymns in the New Testament: Form, Content and Criteria for Identification," *PRSt* 11 (1984), 115–32.

780 Greeven, H.   *Gebet und Eschatologie im Neuen Testament* (Gütersloh: C. Bertelsmann, 1931).

781 Greig, J. C. G.   "Abba and Amen: Their Relevance to Christology," *StE* 5 (1968), 3–13.

782 Hamman, A.   *La prière: Le nouveau testament* (Tournai: Desclée, 1959). *Prayer: The New Testament* (ETrans.; Chicago: Franciscan Herald Press, 1971).

783 Hengel, M.   "Hymn and Christology," in E. A. Livingston (ed.), *Studia Biblica* (JSNTSS 3; Sheffield, U.K.: JSOT Press, 1980), 3:173–97.

784 Hiebert, D. E.   "The Significance of Christian Intercession," *BibSac* 149 (1992), 16–26.

785 Hort, F. J. A., and   *"Eucharistia–eucharistein,"* *JThS* O.S. 3 (1902),
     Murray, J. O. F.   594–98.

786 Hultgren, A. J.   "Expectations of Prayer in the New Testament," in
                             P. Sponheim (ed.), *A Primer on Prayer* (Philadelphia:
                             Westminster, 1988), 23–35.

787 Ignaz, R.   *Das Gebet im Neuen Testament* (Münster: Aschen-
                             dorff, 1924).

788 Jouassard, G.   "L'ancien Testament dans la prière des premiers com-
                             munautés chrétiennes," in M. Jourjon et al. (eds.), *A
                             la rencontre de Dieu mémorial Albert Gelin* (Le Puy:
                             Éditions Xavier Mappus, 1961), 355–62.

789 Käsemann, E.   "Der gottesdienstliche Schrei nach der Freiheit," in
                             W. Eltester and F. H. Kettler (eds.), *Apophoreta:
                             Festschrift für E. Haenchen zu seinem siebzigsten Ge-
                             burtstag am 10 Dezember 1964* (BZAW 30; Berlin:
                             A. Töpelmann, 1964), 142–55.

790 Kerkhoff, R.   *Das unablässige Gebet: Beiträge zur Lehre vom Im-
                             merwährenden Beten im Neuen Testament* (Munich:
                             Karl Zink Verlag, 1954).

791 Klawek, A.   *Das Gebet zu Jesus: Seine Berechtigung und Übung
                             nach den Schriften des Neuen Testaments* (Münster:
                             Aschendorff, 1921).

792 Koenig, J.   *Rediscovering New Testament Prayer: Boldness and
                             Blessing in the Name of Jesus* (San Francisco: Harper
                             & Row, 1992).

793 Kroll, J.   *Die christliche Hymnodik bis zu Klemens von Alex-
                             andreia* (2d ed.; Darmstadt: Wissenschaftliche Buch-
                             gesellschaft, 1968).

794 Langkammer, H.   "Jesus in der Sprache der neutestamentlichen Chris-
                             tuslieder," in H. Frankemölle and K. Kertelge (eds.),
                             Vom Urchristentum zu Jesus für Joachim Gnilka
                             (Freiburg/Basel/Vienna: Herder, 1988), 467–86.

795 Légasse, S.   "La prière pour les chefs d'état: antécédents juda-
                             ïques et témoins chrétiens du premier siècle," *NT* 29
                             (1987), 236–53.

796 Lehmann, O.   "Communal Worship in the New Testament and
                             Contemporary Rabbinic Literature," *StE* 3 (1964),
                             146–49.

797 Martin, R. P.   "Aspects of Worship in the New Testament Church,"
                             VoxEv 2 (1963), 6–32. Background of the NT
                             material in Greek hymns and the Jewish hymns.

798 Martin, R. P.   "Some Reflections on New Testament Hymns," in
                             H. H. Rowdon (ed.), *Christ the Lord: Studies Pre-
                             sented to Donald Guthrie* (Downers Grove, Ill.: IVP,
                             1982), 34–49.

799 Martin, R. P.   "New Testament Hymns: Background and Development," *ET* 94 (1983), 132–36.

800 Marty, J.   "Étude des textes cultuels de prière contenus dans le Nouveau Testament," *RHPhR* 9 (1929), 234–68, 366–76.

801 McCasland, S. V.   "Abba, Father," *JBL* 72 (1953), 79–91.

802 McFarlane, D. J.   "The Motif of Thanksgiving in the New Testament" (Dissertation: St. Andrews University, 1966).

803 Moule, C. F. D.   "A Reconstruction of the Context of *Maranatha*," *NTS* 6 (1959–60), 307–10.

804 Moule, C. F. D.   *Worship in the New Testament* (London: Lutterworth, 1961), sections 4 and 5.

805 Nielen, J. M.   *Gebet und Gottesdienst im Neuen Testament* (Freiburg i. Breisgau: Herder, 1937). ETrans. = *The Earliest Christian Liturgy* (St. Louis: B. Herder, 1941).

806 Nielen, J. M.   "Das Gebet im Neuen Testament," *BiLe* 5 (1964), 1–7.

807 Peterson, D. G.   "Prayer in the General Epistles," in D. A. Carson (ed.), *Teach Us to Pray: Prayer in the Bible and the World* (Exeter, U.K.: Paternoster/Baker, 1990), 102–18, 328–32.

808 Ponthot, J.   "La prière chrétienne dans le Nouveau Testament," in H. Limet and J. Ries (eds.), *L'expérience de la prière dans les grandes religions: actes du colloque de Louvain-la-Neuve et Liège (22–23 novembre 1978)* (Louvain-la-Neuve: Centre d'historie des religions, 1980), 275–81.

809 Quinn, J. D.   "Apostolic Ministry and Prayer," *CBQ* 33 (1971), 479–91.

810 Reicke, B.   "Some Reflections on Worship in the New Testament," in A. J. B. Higgins (ed.), *New Testament Essays: Studies in Memory of Thomas Walter Manson* (Manchester: University Press, 1959), 194–209.

811 Rese, M.   "Formeln und Lieder im Neuen Testament: Einige notwendige Anmerkungen," in *VF* 15 (1970), 75–95.

812 Rohr, I.   *Das Gebet im Neuen Testament* (Münster: Aschendorff, 1924).

813 Sabourin, L.   *Christology: Basic Texts in Focus* (New York: Alba, 1984), ch. 7.

814 Sanders, J. T.   *The New Testament Christological Hymns: Their Historical Religious Background* (SNTSMS 15; Cambridge: University Press, 1971).

815	Schattenmann, J.	*Studien zum neutestamentlichen Prosahymnus* (Munich: Beck, 1965).
816	Schenk, W.	*Der Segen im Neuen Testament* (Berlin: Evangelische Verlagsanstalt, 1967).
817	Schenk, W.	"Reden mit Gott im Neuen Testament," *Die Christuslehre* 25 (1972), 8–16.
818	Schüssler Fiorenza, E.	"Wisdom Mythology and the Christological Hymns of the New Testament," in R. Wilson (ed.), *Aspects of Wisdom in Judaism and Early Christianity* (Notre Dame, Ind.: University of Notre Dame Press, 1975), 17–41.
819	Squillaci, D.	"I cantici del Nuovo Testamento," *Palestra del Clero* 42/15–16 (1963), 805–13.
820	Stanley, D. M.	*Faith and Religious Life: A New Testament Perspective* (New York: Paulist Press, 1971), 31–55.
821	Stolle, V.	"Das Gebet der Gemeinde Jesu Christi nach dem Neuen Testament," *KuD* 37 (1991), 307–31.
822	Thompson, L. L.	"The Form and Function of Hymns in the New Testament: A Study in Cultic History" (Ph.D. Dissertation: University of Chicago, 1968).
823	Versteeg, J.	*Het gebed volgens in het NT* (Amsterdam: Buijten & Schipperheijn, 1976).
824	Wengst, K.	*Christologische Formeln und Lieder des Urchristentums* (2d ed., StNT 7; Gütersloh: Mohn, 1972).

JESUS

825	Barr, J.	" 'Abba, Father' and the Familiarity of Jesus' Speech," *Theol* 91 (1988), 173–79.
826	Baumann, R.	"Abba, lieber Vater: Zum biblischen Gottesbild," *BiKi* 22 (1967), 73–78.
827	Betz, O.	"Jesu Lieblingspsalm: Die Bedeutung von Psalm 103 für das Werk Jesu," *ThB* 15 (1984), 253–69.
828	Bligh, J.	"Christ's Death Cry," *HeyJ* 1 (1960), 142–46.
829	Boman, T.	"Der Gebetskampf Jesu," *NTS* 10 (1964), 261–73.
830	Campenhausen, H. von	"Gebetserhörung in den überlieferten Jesusworten und in der Reflexion des Johannes," *KuD* 23 (1977), 157–71.
831	Crouzel, H.	"Das Gebet Jesu," *Internationale Katholische Zeitschrift "Communio"* 2 (1973), 1–15.

832 Fitzmyer, J. A. "Abba and Jesus' Relation to God," in F. Refoulé (ed.), *À cause de l'Évangile: études sur les Synoptiques et les Actes offertes au P. Jacques Dupont, O.S.B. à l'occasion de son 70ᵉ anniversaire* (Lectio divina 123; Paris: Cerf, 1985), 15–38.

833 Giblet, J. "La prière de Jésus," in H. Limet and J. Ries (eds.), *L'expérience de la prière dans les grandes religions: actes du colloque de Louvain-la-Neuve et Liège (22–23 novembre 1978)* (Louvain-la-Neuve: Centre d'histoire des religions, 1980), 261–73.

834 Gnilka, J. "Jesus und das Gebet," *BiLe* 6 (1965), 79–91.

835 Haden, T. H. "The Prayer-life of Jesus," *MQR* 67 (1918), 689–700.

836 Hahn, F. "Jesu Wort vom bergeversetzenden Glauben," *ZNW* 76 (1985), 149–69.

837 Hamerton-Kelly, R. G. *God the Father: Theology and Patriarchy in the Teaching of Jesus* (Philadelphia: Fortress, 1979), chs. 3 and 4 discuss respectively the teaching of Jesus and the teaching about Jesus.

838 Hamman, A. "La Prière de Jésus," *BVC* 10 (1955), 7–21.

839 Heitmüller, W. *"Im Namen Jesu"* (Göttingen: Vandenhoeck & Ruprecht, 1903).

840 Héring, J. "Simples remarques sur la prière à Gethsémané: Matthieu 26.36–46; Marc 14.32–42; Luc 22.40–46," *RHPhR* 39 (1959), 97–102.

841 Holleran, J. W. "Christ's Prayer and Christian Prayer," *Worship* 48 (1974), 171–82.

842 Jeremias, J. "Das Gebetsleben Jesu," *ZNW* 25 (1926), 123–40.

843 Jeremias, J. *Abba: Studien zur neutestamentlichen Theologie und Zeitgeschichte* (Göttingen: Vandenhoeck & Ruprecht, 1966), section 1.

844 Jeremias, J. "Das tägliche Gebet im Leben Jesu und in der ältesten Kirche," in *Abba: Studien zur neutestamentlichen Theologie und Zeitgeschichte* (Göttingen: Vandenhoeck & Ruprecht, 1966), 67–80.

845 Jeremias, J. *The Prayers of Jesus* (SBT 2, #6; London: SCM, 1967).

846 Lathrop, G. "The Prayers of Jesus and the Great Prayer of the Church," *LQ* 26 (1974), 158–73.

847 Lentzen-Deis, F. "Beten Kraft des Gebetes Jesu," *GL* 48 (1975), 164–78.

848 Léon-Dufour, X. "Le dernier cri de Jésus," *Études* 348 (1978), 666–82.

849 Lescow, T. "Jesus in Gethsemane bei Lukas und in Hebräer-brief," *ZNW* 58 (1967), 215–39.

850 Malatesta, E. "The Prayer of Jesus and His Apostles," *Woodstock Letters* 96 (1966), 312–24.

851 Manson, T. W. *The Sayings of Jesus* (London: SCM, 1949), 165–67.

852 Marchel, W. "Abba, Pater! Oratio Christi et christianorum," *VD* 39 (1961), 240–57.

853 Marchel, W. *Abba, Père: La prière du Christ et des chrétiens: étude exégétique sur les origines et la signification de l'invocation à la divinité comme père, avant et dans le Nouveau Testament* (AnBib 19; Rome: Institut biblique pontifical, 1963, 1971²), Part 2.

854 Mauchline, J. "Jesus Christ as Intercessor," *ET* 64 (1953), 355–60.

855 Reumann, J. H. "Psalm 22 at the Cross," *Interp* 28 (1974), 39–58.

856 Rijk, C. A. "Andere Gebete Jesu," in M. Brocke, J. J. Petu-chowski, and and W. Strolz (eds.), *Das Vaterunser: Gemeinsames im Beten von Juden und Christen* (Freiburg i. Breisgau: Herder, 1974), 196–208.

857 Scaria, K. J. "Jesus' Prayer and Christian Prayer," *Bibelhashyam* 7 (1981), 160–85.

858 Scheifler, J. R. "El Salmo 22 y la Crucifixión del Señor," *EstB* 24 (1965), 5–83.

859 Schlosser, J. "Le règne de Dieu dans les dits de Jésus," *RSR* 53 (1979), 164–76.

860 Schürmann, H. *Praying with Christ* (trans. W. Ducey and A. Simon; New York: Herder and Herder, 1964).

861 Severus, E. von "Cum propheta: Der Christ als Beter alttesta-mentlicher Texte," in H. Becker and R. Kaczynski (eds.), *Liturgie und Dichtung, 2: Ein interdiszi-plinäres Kompendium* (St. Ottilien: EOS Verlag, 1983), 649–60.

862 Soares-Prabhu, G. M. "Speaking to Abba: Prayer as Petition and Thanks-giving in the Teaching of Jesus," in C. Duquoc and C. Floristán (eds.), *Asking and Thanking* (Philadel-phia: Fortress, 1990), 31–43.

863 Spencer, A. B. and W. D. *The Prayer Life of Jesus: Shout of Agony, Revelation of Love, A Commentary* (Lanham, Md.: University Press of America, 1990).

864 Thomson, J. G. *The Praying Christ: A Study of Jesus' Doctrine and Practice of Prayer* (Grand Rapids, Mich.: Eerdmans, 1959).

865 Vansant, N. "Our Lord's Prayer in the Garden," *MethR* 46 (1864), 216–33.

866 Vaz, A. "Lo específico de la oración de Jesús," *RevistEspir* 49 (1990), 121–47.

867 Vermes, G. "Abba: Father!," in *Jesus the Jew: A Historian's Reading of the Gospels* (Philadelphia: Fortress Press, 1973), 210–13.

868 Wilkinson, J. "The Seven Words from the Cross," *SJTh* 17 (1964), 69–82.

869 Zeller, D. "God as Father in the Proclamation and Prayer of Jesus," in A. Finkel and L. Frizzell (eds.), *Standing before God: Studies on Prayer in Scriptures and in Tradition with Essays in Honor of John M. Oesterreicher* (New York: KTAV, 1981), 117–29.

LORD'S PRAYER

870 Aleixandre, D. "En torno a la cuarta petición del Padrenuestro," *EstB* 45 (1987), 325–36.

871 Arichea, D. C. "Translating the Lord's Prayer (Matt. 6:9–13)," *BiTr* 31 (1980), 219–23.

872 Aron, R. "Les origines juives du Pater," *MD* 85 (1966), 36–40.

873 Ashton, J. "Le Nôtre Père," *Christus* 24 (1977), 459–70.

874 Ashton, J. "Our Father," *Way* 18 (1978), 83–91.

875 Ayo, N. *The Lord's Prayer: A Survey Theological and Literary* (Notre Dame, Ind.: University of Notre Dame Press, 1992).

876 Baarda, T. "De korte tekst van het Onze Vader in Lucas 11:2–4: een Marcionitische Coruptie?," *NedThT* 44 (1990), 273–87.

877 Bahr, G. J. "The Use of the Lord's Prayer in the Primitive Church," *JBL* 84 (1965), 153–59.

878 Baker, A. "Lead Us Not into Temptation," *NBl* 52 (1971), 64–69.

879 Baker, A. "What Sort of Bread Did Jesus Want Us to Pray For?," *NBl* 54 (1973), 125–29.

880 Balembo, B. "Et ne nous soumets pas à la tentation," *RevAfTh* 10 (1986), 5–13.

881 Bammel, E. "A New Text of the Lord's Prayer," *ET* 73 (1961–2), 54.

882 Bandstra, A. J. "The Original Form of the Lord's Prayer," *CalThJ* 16 (1981), 15–37.

883 Banning, J. van "Il Padre Nostro nell' Opus Imperfectum in Matthaeum," *Gr* 71 (1990), 293–313.

884 Barr, J. "Abba Isn't Daddy," *JThS* 39 (1988), 28–47.

885 Barth, H.-M. "Das Vaterunser als ökumenisches Gebet," *US* 45 (1990), 99–109, 113.

886   Bauer, J. B.   "Libera nos a malo," *VD* 34 (1956), 12–15.

887   Baumgardt, D.   "Kaddish and Lord's Prayer," *Jewish Bible Quarterly (Dor leDor)* 19 (1991), 164–69.

888   Betz, H. D.   "A Jewish-Christian Cultic *Didache* in Matt. 6:1–18: Reflections and Questions on the Historical Jesus," in *Essays on the Sermon on the Mount* (Philadelphia: Fortress, 1985), 55–70, esp. 62–64.

889   Bindemann, W.   "Das Brot für morgen gib uns heute: Sozialgeschichtliche Erwägungen zu den Wir-Bittendes Vaterunsers," *BThZ* 8 (1991), 199–215.

890   Bischoff, A.   *"Epiousios,"* *ZNW* 7 (1906), 266–71.

891   Black, M.   "The Aramaic of *ton arton hemon ton epiousion* (Matt vi.11=Luke xi.3)," *JThS* 42 (1941), 186–89.

892   Black, M.   "The Doxology to the Pater Noster with a Note on Matthew 6:13b," in P. R. Davies and R. T. White (eds.), *A Tribute to Geza Vermes: Essays on Jewish and Christian Literature and History* (Sheffield, U.K.: JSOT Press, 1990), 327–38.

893   Blenkinsopp, J.   "The Lord's Prayer," *HeyJ* 3 (1962), 51–60.

894   Blenkinsopp, J.   "The Lord's Prayer and the Hill of Olives," *HeyJ* 3 (1962), 169–71.

895   Bonnard, P. E.   "Ne nous induis pas en tentation," *Flambeau* 59 (1980), 380.

896   Bonnard, P. E., Dupont, J., and Refoulé, F.   *Nôtre Père qui est aux cieux, la prière oecuménique* (Cahiers de la truduction oecuménique de la Bible 3; Paris: les Bergers et les Mages, 1968).

897   Botha, F. J.   "Recent Research on the Lord's Prayer," *Neotestamentica* 1 (1967), 42–50.

898   Bourgoin, H.   *"Epiousios* expliqué par la notion de préfixe vide," *Bib* 60 (1979), 91–96.

899   Bouttier, M.   "Le Père manifesté dans les actes et caché à la piété," in F. Refoulé (ed.), *À Cause de l'Évangile: Études sur les Synoptiques et les Actes offertes au P. Jacques Dupont, O.S.B. À l'occasion de son 70ᵉ anniversaire* (Lectio divina 123; Paris: Cerf, 1985), 39–56.

900   Braun, F.-M.   "Le pain dont nous avons besoin: Mt 6, 11; Lc 11, 3," *NRTh* 100 (1978), 559–68.

901   Brooke, G. J.   "The Lord's Prayer Interpreted through John and Paul," *DR* 98 (1980), 298–311.

902   Brown, R. E.   "The Pater Noster as an Eschatological Prayer," in New Testament Essays (New York: Doubleday, 1965), 217–53. See also *TS* 22 (1961), 175–208.

903   Brown, R. E.   "The Meaning of Our Father," *ThD* 10 (1962), 3–10.

904 Brown, R. E. "Review of Carmignac's *Recherches sur la 'Nôtre Père,'*" *CBQ* 32 (1970), 264–66.

905 Bruggen, J. van "Abba, Vader! Tekst en toonhoogte van het Onze Vader," in C. Trimp (ed.), *De Biddende Kerk* (Groningen: De Vuurbaak, 1979), 9–42.

906 Bruggen, J. van "The Lord's Prayer and Textual Criticism," *CalThJ* 17 (1982), 78–87. A reply to Bandstra's article in *CalThJ* 16 (1981).

907 Burkitt, F. C. "As We Have Forgiven," *JThS* 33 (1932), 253–55.

908 Burrows, M. "Thy Kingdom Come," *JBL* 74 (1955), 1–8.

909 Bussche, H. van den "Het Onze Vader," *CBG* 5 (1959), 289–335; 467–95.

910 Bussche, H. van den *Le "Nôtre Père"* (Paris: La Pensée Catholique, 1960). ETrans., London: Sheed & Ward, 1964.

911 Bussche, H. van den "Donne-nous aujourd-hui nôtre pain quotidien," *BVC* 32 (1960), 42–46.

912 Cambe, M., and Lucas, N. "Le 'Nôtre Père' (Matthieu 6, 9–13): Eléments d'analyse structurale," *Foi et vie* 78 (1979), 113–17.

913 Cameron, P. S. "Lead Us Not into Temptation," *ET* 101 (1990), 299–301.

914 Carmignac, J. "Fais que nous n'entrions pas dans la tentation: La portée d'une négation devant une verbe au causatif," *RB* 72 (1965), 218–26.

915 Carmignac, J. *À l'écoute du Nôtre Père* (Paris: Éditions de Paris, 1969).

916 Carmignac, J. *Recherches sur le "Nôtre Père"* (Paris: Letouzay & Ané, 1969).

917 Carmignac, J "Hebrew Translations of the Lord's Prayer: An Historical Survey," in G. A. Tuttle (ed.), *Biblical and Near Eastern Studies: Essays in Honor of William Sanford LaSor* (Grand Rapids, Mich.: Eerdmans, 1978), 18–79.

918 Carmignac, J. "Spiritual Wealth of the Lord's Prayer," in J. J. Petuchowski, and M. Brocke (eds.), *The Lord's Prayer and Jewish Liturgy* (New York: Seabury Press, 1978), 137–46.

919 Carré, A. M. *Le nôtre père: prière du Christ et des chrétiens* (Paris: Cerf, 1971).

920 Celada, B. "El Padre Nuestro: Progresos en la inteligencia de la oración de los cristianos," *CultBib* 22 (1965), 153–59.

921   Charlesworth, J. H.   "The *Beth Essentiae* and the Permissive Hiphil (Aphel)," in H. W. Attridge, J. J. Collins and T. H. Tobin (eds.), *Of Scribes and Scrolls: Studies on the Hebrew Bible, Intertestamental Judaism, and Christian Origins* (College Theology Society Resources in Religion, 5; New York/London: University Press of America, 1990), 67–78. Discusses the temptation clause.

922   Chase, F. H.   *The Lord's Prayer in the Early Church* (Cambridge: University Press, 1891).

923   Collins, R. F.   " 'Thy Will Be Done on Earth as It Is in Heaven' — Matthew 6:10," *BiTod* 1 (1964), 911–17.

924   Cothenet, E.   "La Prière du Seigneur," *EspVie* 80 (1970), 631–34.

925   Cruz Hernández, M.   "El 'Padrenuestro' de Jesús de Nazaret," *Religión y Cultura* 36 (1990), 61–66.

926   Cyster, R. F.   "The Lord's Prayer and the Exodus Tradition," *Theol* 64 (1961), 377–81.

927   Dahms, J. V.   " 'Lead Us Not into Temptation,' " *JEThS* 17 (1974), 223–30.

928   Dalmais, I.-H.   "L'introduction et l'embolisme de l'Oraison dominicale dans la célébration eucharistique," *MD* 85 (1966), 92–100.

929   Dalman, G. H.   *Die Worte Jesu* (Leipzig: J. C. Hinrichs, 1930[2]), Anhang A, "Das Vaterunser," 283–365. ETrans.: Edinburgh: T. & T. Clark, 1909.

930   Davies, W. D., and Allison, D. C.   "Excursus: The Lord's Prayer: Matthew 6.9–13 = Luke 11.2–4," in *Matthew* (ICC; Edinburgh, 1988), 590–617.

931   Debrunner, A.   "Epiousios," *Glotta* 4 (1913), 249–53.

932   Debrunner, A.   " 'Epiousios' und kein Ende," *MH* 9 (1952), 60–62.

933   De Fraine, J.   "Oraison Dominicale," in *DBS* 6, cols. 788–800.

934   Deissler, A.   "Der Geist des Vaterunsers im alttestamentlichen Glauben und Beten," in M. Brocke, J. J. Petuchowski, and and W. Strolz (eds.), *Das Vaterunser: Gemeinsames im Beten von Juden und Christen* (Freiburg i. Breisgau: Herder, 1974), 131–50.

935   Delobel, J.   "The Lord's Prayer in the Textual Tradition: A Critique of Recent Theories and Their View on Marcion's Role," in J. Sevrin (ed.), *The New Testament in Early Christianity: la réception des écrits néotestamentaire dans le christianisme primitif* (Louvain: University Press, 1989), 293–309.

936   Delorme, J.   "La prière du Seigneur: Pour une catéchèse biblique du 'Nôtre Père.' À propos de la nouvelle traduction," *AmiCl* 76 (1966), 225–36.

937 Denis-Boulet, N. M. "La place du Nôtre Père dans la liturgie," *MD* 85 (1966), 69–91.

938 Dewailly, L.-M. " 'Donne-nous nôtre pain': Quel pain?," *RSPhTh* 64 (1980), 561–88.

939 Dewailly, L.-M. "Vilket bröd avses i Fader vår?," *SEÅ* 45 (1980), 77–89.

940 Díaz, J. Alonso "El problema literario del Padre Nuestro," *EstB* 18 (1959), 63–75.

941 Dibelius, M. *Das Vaterunser: Umrisse zu einer Geschichte des Gebets in der alten und mittleren Kirche* (Gießen: Ricker [Töpelmann], 1903).

942 Dibelius, M. "Die dritte Bitte des Vaterunsers," in *Botschaft und Geschichte: Gesammelte Aufsätze* (Tübingen: Mohr, 1953), 1:175–77.

943 Dietzfelbinger, H. *Zukunft mit der Vaterunser: Perspektiven für die achtziger Jahre* (Munich: Claudius, 1980).

944 Dillon, R. J. "On the Christian Obedience of Prayer (Matthew 6:5–13)," *Worship* 59 (1985), 413–26.

945 Dockx, S. "La genèse du 'Nôtre Père' replacé dans le cadre de l'histoire," in *Chronologies néotestamentaires et Vie de l'Église primitive* (Louvain: Éditions Peeters, 1984), 299–308.

946 Dorneich, M. (ed.) *Vaterunser Bibliographie* (Freiburg i. Breisgau: Herder, 1982). Rev. eds., 1987 and 1988.

947 Dornseiff, F. "*Epiousios* im Vaterunser," *Glotta* 35 (1956), 145–49.

948 Du Buit, F. M. "Nôtre Père," *Évangile* 50 (1969), 5–46.

949 Dupont, J. "Jésus et la prière liturgique," *MD* 95 (1968), 16–49.

950 Dupont, J., and Bonnard, P. E. "Le Nôtre Père: notes exégétique," *MD* 85 (1966), 7–35.

951 Duquoc, C. "The Prayer of Jesus," in C. Floristán and C. Duquoc (eds.), *Learning to Pray* (New York: Seabury, 1982), 11–17.

952 Dürig, W. "Die Deutung der Brotbitte des Vaterunsers bei den lateinischen Vätern bis Hieronymus," *Liturgisches Jahrbuch* 18 (1968), 77–86.

953 Edmonds, P. "The Lucan Our Father: A Summary of Luke's Teaching on Prayer?," *ET* 91 (1979–80), 140–43.

954 Elliott, J. K. "Did the Lord's Prayer Originate with John the Baptist?," *ThZ* 29 (1973), 215.

955 Evans, C. F. *The Lord's Prayer* (London: S.P.C.K., 1963).

956 Falcone, S. A.   "The Kind of Bread We Pray for in the Lord's Prayer," in R. F. McNamara (ed.), *Essays in Honor of Joseph P. Brennan* (Rochester, N.Y.: St. Bernard's Seminary, 1977), 36–59.

957 Fiebig, P.   *Das Vaterunser: Ursprung, Sinn und Bedeutung des christlichen Hauptgebetes* (Beiträge zur Förderung christlicher Theologie 30.3; Gütersloh: C. Bertelsmann, 1927).

958 Fischer, B.   "Das Herrengebet als Tauferinnerung," in "Formen privater Tauferinnerung im Abendland," *Liturgisches Jahrbuch* 9 (1959), 157–66 (161–62).

959 Fitzmyer, J. A.   "Abba and Jesus' Relation to God," in F. Refoulé (ed.), *À Cause de l'Évangile: Études sur les Synoptiques et les Actes offertes au P. Jacques Dupont, O.S.B. à l'occasion de son 70ᵉ anniversaire* (Lectio divina 123; Paris: Cerf, 1985), 15–38.

960 Ford, J. M.   "Yom Kippur and the Matthean Form of the Pater Noster," *Worship* 41 (1967), 609–19.

961 Ford, J. M.   "The Forgiveness Clause in the Matthean Form of the Our Father," *ZNW* 59 (1968), 127–31.

962 Foucault, J.-A. de   "Nôtre pain quotidien," *REG* 83 (1970), 56–62.

963 Fresenius, W.   "Beobachtungen und Gedanken zum Gebet des Herrn," *EvTh* 20 (1960), 235–29.

964 Freudenberger, R.   "Zum Text der zweiten Vaterunserbitte," *NTS* 15 (1968–69), 419–32.

965 Fridrichsen, A.   "Helligt vorde dit navn!," *DTT* 8 (1917), 1–16.

966 Fridrichsen, A.   "ARTOS EPIOUSIOS" (SO 2; Oslo: Some & Co., 1924), 31–41 and (SO 9; 1930), 62–68.

967 Froehlich, K.   "The Lord's Prayer in Patristic Literature," *PSB* Supp. 2 (1992), 71–87.

968 Frye, R. M.   "On Praying 'Our Father': The Challenge of Radical Feminist Language for God," *AThR* 73 (1991), 388–402.

969 Furberg, I.   *Das Pater Noster in der Messe* (Lund: Gleerups, 1968).

970 Galot, J.   "La prière au Père," *Telema* 10 (1984), 53–66.

971 Galot, J.   "Per una teologia del Padre," *CivCatt* 135 (1984), 119–31.

972 Galot, J.   "Pour une théologie du Père: Dans le mystère de la Sainte Trinité," *EspVie* 94 (1984), 661–69.

973 Galot, J.   "La preghiera al Padre," *CivCatt* 136 (1985), 222–35.

974 Gatzweiler, K.   "Jesus in Prayer: Texts of the Our Father," *LV* 39 (1984), 148–54.

975 George, A. "Ne nous soumets pas à tentation...Note sur la tra-duction nouvelle du Nôtre Père," *BVC* 71 (1966), 74–79.

976 Gerhardsson, B. "Fader vår i Nya testamentet," *SvTK* 54 (1978), 93–102.

977 Gerhardsson, B. "The Matthaean Version of the Lord's Prayer (Matt 6:9b–13): Some Observations," in W. C. Weinrich (ed.), *The New Testament Age: Essays in Honor of Bo Reicke* (Macon, Ga.: Mercer University Press, 1984), 1:207–20.

978 Gil, L. "Versiones del Pater noster al castellano en el Siglo de Oro," *Filología Neotestamentaria* 1 (1988), 175–91.

979 Ginzel, G. B. (ed.) *Die Bergpredigt: jüdisches und christliches Glau-bensdokument: Eine Synopse* (Heidelberg: Verlag Lambert Schneider, 1985). See 86–95 for Jewish parallels to the Lord's Prayer.

980 Goulder, M. D. "The Composition of the Lord's Prayer," *JThS* N.S. 14 (1963), 32–45. See also *Midrash and Lexi-con in Matthew* (London: S.P.C.K., 1974), 296–301 (amended version of the article).

981 Grelot, P. "La quatrième demande du 'Pater' et son arrière-plan sémitique," *NTS* 25 (1979), 299–314.

982 Grelot, P. "L'arrière-plan araméen du 'Pater,' " *RB* 91 (1984), 531–66 (reconstructed Aramaic version).

983 Grunzweig, F. *Das Vaterunser: Beten in der Schule Jesu* (2. Aufl.; Bad Liebenzell: Verlag der Liebenzeller Mission, 1986).

984 Guardini, R. *The Lord's Prayer* (New York: Pantheon Books, 1958).

985 Hadidian, D. Y. "The Meaning of *epiousios* and the Codices Sergii," *NTS* 5 (1958–59), 75–81.

986 Hadidian, D. Y. "The Lord's Prayer and the Sacraments of Baptism and of the Lord's Supper in the Early Church," *StLi* 15 (1982–83), 132–44.

987 Hamman, A. "La prière du seigneur," in *La prière: 1, Le nouveau testament* (Tournai: Desclée, 1959), 94–134.

988 Hamman, A. "Le Nôtre Père dans la catéchèse des Pères de l'Église," *MD* 85 (1966), 41–68.

989 Harner, P. B. *Understanding the Lord's Prayer* (Philadelphia: For-tress, 1975).

990 Harner, P. B. "Matthew 6:5–15," *Interp* 41 (1987), 173–78.

991 Hauck, F. "*Artos epiousios*," *ZNW* 33 (1934), 199–202.

992 Heinemann, J. "The Background of Jesus' Prayer in the Jewish Liturgical Tradition," in J. J. Petuchowski and M. Brocke (eds.), *The Lord's Prayer and Jewish Liturgy* (New York: Seabury Press, 1978), 81–89.

993 Hemer, C. " 'epiousios,' " *JSNT* 22 (1984), 81–94.

994 Hemmerdinger, B. "Un élément pythagoricien dans le Pater," *ZNW* 63 (1972), 121.

995 Hennig, J. "Our Daily Bread," *TS* 4 (1943), 445–54.

996 Hensler, J. *Das Vaterunser: Text und literarkritische Untersuchungen* (NT Abhandlungen 4/5; Münster i. W: Aschendorff, 1914).

997 Herrmann, J. "Der alttesetamentliche Urgrund des Vaterunsers," in *Festschrift Otto Procksch* (Leipzig: A. Deichert & J. C. Hinrichs, 1934), 71–98.

998 Houk, C. B. "PEIRASMOS: The Lord's Prayer, and the Massah Tradition," *SJTh* 19 (1966), 216–25.

999 Hugh, M. *The Lord's Prayer* (London: SCM, 1951).

1000 Jacob, T. "The Daily Bread in the Teaching of Jesus," *Jeevadhara* 32 (1976), 187–97.

1001 Jacquemin, L. "La portée de la 3me demande du Pater," *EThL* 25 (1949), 61–76.

1002 Jacquemin, L. "La prière du Seigneur," *AssS* 48 (1965), 47–64.

1003 Jaeger, C. "À propos de deux passages du sermon sur la montagne," *RHPhR* 18 (1938), 415–16.

1004 Jaeger, S. *Der Weg zu Gott unserm Vater: Eine Einfuhrung ins Vaterunser als Einleitung in die christliche Lehre* (Halle: Verlag der Buchhandlung des Waisenhauses, 1902).

1005 Jeremias, J. "The Lord's Prayer in Modern Research," *ET* 71 (1960), 141–46.

1006 Jeremias, J. "Fader var i den nyare forskningens ljus," *SEÅ* 27 (1962), 33–54.

1007 Jeremias, J. *Abba: Studien zur neutestamentlichen Theologie und Zeitgeschichte* (Göttingen: Vandenhoeck & Ruprecht, 1966).

1008 Jeremias, J. "Das Vater-Unser im Lichte der neuen Forschung," in *Abba*, 152–71 (see above).

1009 Jeremias, J. *The Lord's Prayer* (ETrans., J. Reumann; Philadelphia: Fortress Press, 1980). See also *The Prayers of Jesus*, ch. 3.

1010 Jeremias, J. "Dio Abba-Patro," *BibR* 18 (1982), 19–30.

1011 John, M. P. "Give Us This Day Our Bread," *BiTr* 31 (1980), 245–47.

1012 Juel, D.   "The Lord's Prayer in the Gospels of Matthew and
                               Luke," *PSB* Supp. 2 (1992), 56–70.

1013 Juel, D., and   "I Believe in God the Father," *Horizons* 20 (1990),
      Keifert, P.   39–60.

1014 Kate, R. ten   " 'Geef ons heden ons 'Dagelijks' brood,' " *NedThT*
                               32 (1978), 125–39.

1015 Killinger, J.   *The God Named Hallowed: The Lord's Prayer for
                               Today* (Nashville: Abingdon Press, 1988).

1016 Kirsch, L.   "Das Vaterunser als Schule des Gebetes (Mt 6, 9–13
                               par Lk 11, 2–4)" (Dissertation: Würzburg, 1982).

1017 Kistemaker, S.   "The Lord's Prayer in the First Century," *JEThS* 21
                               (1978), 323–28.

1018 Klein, G.   "Die ursprüngliche Gestalt des Vaterunsers," *ZNW*
                               7 (1906), 34–50.

1019 Knörzer, W.   "Unser Vater im Himmel: Das Gebet des Herrn als
                               Inbegriff des Evangeliums," *BiKi* 22 (1967), 79–86.

1020 Knörzer, W.   *Vater Unser* (Stuttgart: Verlag Katholisches Bibel-
                               werk, 1969²).

1021 Kratz, R. G.   "Die Gnade des täglichen Brots: Späte Psalmen auf
                               dem Weg zum Vaterunser," *ZThK* 89 (1992), 1–40.

1022 Kruse, H.   " 'Pater Noster' et passio Christi," *VD* 46 (1968),
                               3–29.

1023 Kuhn, K. G.   *Achtzehngebet und Vaterunser und der Reim* (Tü-
                               bingen: Mohr, 1950).

1024 Kuss, O.   "Das Vaterunser," in *Auslegung und Verkündigung*
                               (Regensburg: Pustet, 1967), 2:275–333.

1025 Lachs, S. T.   "On Matthew 6:12," *NT* 17 (1975), 6–8.

1026 Lachs, S. T.   "The Lord's Prayer," in *A Rabbinic Commentary on
                               the New Testament* (Hoboken, N.J.: KTAV, 1987),
                               117–24.

1027 Lampe, G. W. H.   " 'Our Father' in the Fathers," in P. Brooks (ed.),
                               *Christian Spirituality: Essays in Honour of Gordon
                               Rupp* (London: SCM, 1975), 11–31.

1028 Lapide, P.   "Das Vaterunser — ein jüdisches oder ein christliches
                               Gebet?," *Renovatio* 47 (1991), 108–10.

1029 Laymon, C. M.   *The Lord's Prayer in Its Biblical Setting* (Nashville:
                               Abingdon, 1968).

1030 Leaney, A. R. C.   "The Lucan Text of the Lord's Prayer (Lk xi 2–4),"
                               NT 1 (1956), 103–11.

1031 LeVerdiere, E.   "The Lord's Prayer in Literary Context," in C. Osiek
                               and D. Senior (eds.), *Scripture and Prayer* (Philadel-
                               phia: Fortress, 1988), 104–16.

1032 Limbeck, M. *Von Jesus beten lernen: Das Vaterunser auf dem Hintergrund des Alten Testaments* (Stuttgart: Religiöse Bildungsarbeit, 1980).

1033 Lindemann, A. "Die Versuchungsgeschichte Jesu nach der Logienquelle und das Vaterunser," in D.-A. Koch et al. (eds.), *Jesu Rede von Gott und ihre Nachgeschichte im frühen Christentum: Beiträge zur Verkündigung Jesu und zum Kerygma der Kirche: Festschrift für W. Marxsen zum 70. Geburtstag* (Gütersloh: Mohn, 1989), 91–100.

1034 Lingen, W. van *Het Gebed des Heeren* (Leiden: W. T. Werst, 1874).

1035 Lochman, J. M. *The Lord's Prayer* (ETrans., G. W. Bromiley; Grand Rapids, Mich.: Eerdmans, 1990).

1036 Lohfink, G. "Der präexistente Heilsplan: Sinn und Hintergrund der dritten Vaterunserbitte," in H. Merklein (ed.), *Neues Testament und Ethik für Rudolf Schnackenburg* (Freiburg: Herder, 1989), 110–33.

1037 Lohmeyer, E. "Das Vater-Unser als Ganzheit," *ThBl* 17 (1938), 217–27.

1038 Lohmeyer, E. *Das Vaterunser* (3d ed.; Zürich: Zwingli-Verlag, 1952).

1039 Lowe, J. *The Interpretation of the Lord's Prayer* (Evanston, Ill.: Seabury Western Theological Seminary, 1955).

1040 Lüthi, W. *The Lord's Prayer: An Exposition* (Richmond, Va.: John Knox, 1961).

1041 Luz, U. "Das Unservater (6, 9–13)," in *Das Evangelium nach Matthäus* (EKKNT; Neukirchenen-Vluyn: Neukirchener Verlag, 1985), 1:332–53.

1042 Luzi, P. *L'orazione della montagna: il Pater Noster* (Urbino: Edizione S. Chiara, 1961).

1043 Magne, J. "Le Pater — Mt. 6, 9–13," *Bib* 39 (1958), 196–97.

1044 Magne, J. "La variante du Pater . . . Lu 11.2," *LTP* 44 (1988), 369–74.

1045 Manson, T. W. *The Sayings of Jesus* (London: SCM, 1949), 167–71 and 265–66.

1046 Manson, T. W. "God as Father," in *The Teaching of Jesus* (Cambridge: University Press, 1951), 89–115.

1047 Manson, T. W. "The Lord's Prayer?," *BJRL* 38 (1956), 99–113, 436–48.

1048 Marchel, W. *Abba, Père! La prière du Christ et des chrétiens: Étude exégétique sur les origines et la signification de l'invocation à la divinité comme père, avant et dans le Nouveau Testament* (AnBib 19; Rome: Pontifical Biblical Institute, 1963), 191–202.

1049 Maritain, R.   *Notes on the Lord's Prayer* (New York: P. J. Kenedy, 1964).

1050 Martin, H.   *The Lord's Prayer* (London: SCM, 1951).

1051 Matthews, W. R.   *The Lord's Prayer* (London: Hodder & Stoughton, 1958).

1052 Mawhinney, A.   "God as Father: Two Popular Theories Reconsidered," *JEThS* 31 (1988), 181–89.

1053 McCaughey, D.   "Matt. 6.13a: The Sixth Petition in the Lord's Prayer," *ABR* 33 (1985), 31–40.

1054 Mediavilla, R.   "La oración de Jesús en el tercer evangelio," *Mayéutica* 4 (1978), 5–34.

1055 Megivern, J.   "Forgive Us Our Debts," *Scripture* 18 (1966), 33–47.

1056 Menestrina, G.   "Sicut in caelo et in terra (Nota a Matteo 6, 10)," *BiOr* 19 (1977), 5–8.

1057 Metzger, B. M.   "How Many Times Does 'Epiousios' Occur outside the Lord's Prayer?" *ET* 69 (1957), 52–54.

1058 Metzger, B. M.   "The Prayer That Jesus Taught His Disciples," in P. Rogers (ed.), *Sowing the Word: Biblical-Liturgical Essays* (Dublin: Dominican Press, 1983), 125–34.

1059 Miegge, G.   "Le 'Nôtre Père' prière du temps present," *ETR* 35 (1960), 237–53.

1060 Moltmann, J.   "Ich glaube an Gott den Vater: Patriarchalische oder nicht-patriarchalische Rede von Gott," *EvTh* 43 (1983), 397–415.

1061 Moor, J. C. de   "The Reconstruction of the Aramaic Original of the Lord's Prayer," in W. van der Meer and J. C. de Moor (eds.), *The Structural Analysis of Biblical and Canaanite Poetry* (Sheffield, U.K.: JSOT Press, 1988), 397–422.

1062 Moore, E.   "Lead Us Not into Temptation," *ET* 102 (1991), 171–72.

1063 Moule, C. F. D.   "An Unsolved Problem in the Temptation Clause in the Lord's Prayer," *RThR* 33 (1974), 65–76.

1064 Moule, C. F. D.   " '...As we forgive...' — A Note on the Distinction between Deserts and Capacity in the Understanding of Forgiveness," in E. Bammel et al. (eds.), *Donum Gentilicum: Festschrift D. Daube* (Oxford: Clarendon, 1978), 68–77.

1065 Müller, C.   *"Epiousios,"* EWNT 2, 79–81.

1066 Mussner, F.   "Das Vaterunser als Gebet des Juden Jesus," in *Traktät über die Juden* (Munich: Kösel, 1979), 198–208. ETrans., Philadelphia: Fortress, 1984.

1067 Noack, B.   *Om Vadervor* (Copenhagen: Gad, 1969).

1068	Orchard, B.	"The Meaning of *ton epiousion* (Matt. 6.11 = Luke 11.3)," *BTB* 3 (1973), 274–82.
1069	Ott, W.	*Gebet und Heil: Die Bedeutung der Gebetsparänese in der lukanischen Theologie* (Munich: Kösel Verlag, 1965), 112–23.
1070	Philonenko, M.	"La troisième demande du 'Nôtre Père' et l'hymne de Nabuchodonosor," *RHPhR* 72 (1992), 23–31.
1071	Plymale, S. F.	"The Lucan Lord's Prayer: An Act of Recollection," *BiTod* 27 (1989), 176–82.
1072	Popkes, W.	"Die letzte Bitte des Vater-Unser: Formgeschichtliche Beobachtungen zum Gebet Jesu," *ZNW* 81 (1990), 1–20.
1073	Porter, S. E.	"Mt 6:13 and Lk 11:4: 'Lead Us Not into Temptation,'" *ET* 101 (1990), 359–62.
1074	Powell, W.	" 'Lead Us Not into Temptation,' " *ET* 67 (1956), 177–78.
1075	Pytel, J.	"Adveniat regnum tuum: Historia interpretacji prosby," *RTK* 11 (1964), 57–69.
1076	Quere, R.	" 'Naming' God 'Father,' " *CuThM* 12 (1985), 5–14.
1077	Ramaroson, L.	" 'Nôtre part de nourriture' (Mt 6, 11)," *SciEsp* 43 (1991), 87–115.
1078	Rengstorf, K. H.	"Das Vaterunser in seiner Bedeutung für unser Zusammenleben," in W. Blankenburg, H. von Schade, and K. Schmidt-Clausen (eds.), *Kerygma und Melos: Christhard Mahrenholz 70 Jahre* (Berlin: Lutherisches Verlagshaus; Kassel: Bärenreiter-Verlag), 1970, 13–25.
1079	Richardson, R. D.	"The Lord's Prayer as an Early Eucharist," *AThR* 39 (1957), 123–30.
1080	Rimbach, J. A.	"God-Talk or Baby-Talk: More on Abba," *CuThM* 13 (1986), 332–35.
1081	Robinson, J. A. T.	"The Lord's Prayer," in *More New Testament Studies* (London: SCM, 1984), 44–64.
1082	Rommel, K.	*Our Father Who Art in Heaven* (ETrans.; Philadelphia: Fortress, 1981).
1083	Rordorf, W.	" 'Wie auch wir vergeben haben unsern Schuldnern (Matth VI, 12b),' " in F. L. Cross (ed.), *Studia Patristica*, vol. 10, Pt. 1 (Berlin: Akademie-Verlag, 1970), 236–41.
1084	Rordorf, W.	"The Lord's Prayer in the Light of Its Liturgical Use in the Early Church," *StLi* 14 (1980–81), 1–19.
1085	Sabugal, S.	*El Padrenuestro en la interpretación catequética antigua y moderna* (Salamanca: Ediciones Sígueme, 1982).

1086   Sabugal, S.   "La importancia del Padre nuestro," *RAE* 23 (1982),
                         437–86.

1087   Sabugal, S.   "La redacción mateana del Padrenuestro (Mt. 6:9–
                         13)," *EE* 58 (1983), 307–29.

1088   Sabugal, S.   "Didaje 8.2: el 'Padre Nuestro,' " *RevBib* 46 (1984),
                         287–97.

1089   Sabugal, S.   *Abba! — La Oración del Señor* (Madrid: Biblioteca
                         de Autores Cristianos, 1985).

1090   Saphir, A.   *The Lord's Prayer* (London, 1872).

1091   Schelbert, G.   "Sprachgeschichtliches zu 'Abba,' " in P. Cassetti et
                         al. (eds.), *Mélanges Dominique Barthélemy* (Fri-
                         bourg/Göttingen: Éditions universitaires, 1981),
                         395–447.

1092   Schlatter, A.   *Das Unser Vater: Eine Auslegung des Herrengebets*
                         (Berlin: Furche, 1938).

1093   Schlosser, J.   "La règne de Dieu dans les dits de Jésus," *RSR* 53
                         (1979), 164–76.

1094   Schmid, W.   *"Epiousios,"* Glotta 6 (1915), 28–29.

1095   Schnackenburg, R. *Alles kann, wer glaubt: Bergpredigt und Vaterunser
                         in der Absicht Jesu* (2d ed.; Freiburg im Breslau:
                         Herder, 1984).

1096   Schneider, G.   "Das Vaterunser des Matthäus," in F. Refoulé (ed.),
                         *À Cause de l'Évangile: Études sur les Synoptiques
                         et les Actes offertes au P. Jacques Dupont, O.S.B. à
                         l'occasion de son 70ᵉ anniversaire* (Lectio divina 123;
                         Paris: Cerf, 1985), 57–90.

1097   Schneider, G.   "Das Vaterunser," in W. Baier, S. Horn et al., *Weis-
                         heit Gottes — Weisheit der Welt: Festschrift für
                         Kardinal Ratzinger zum 60. Geburtstag* (St. Ottilien:
                         EOS Verlag, 1987), 1:405–17.

1098   Schnurr, K. B.   *Hören und Handeln: Lateinische Auslegungen des
                         Vaterunsers in der Alten Kirche bis zum fünften
                         Jahrhundert* (Freiburger Theologische Studien 132;
                         Freiburg: Herder, 1985).

1099   Schroer, S.   "Konkretionen zum Vaterunser," *US* 45 (1990),
                         110–13.

1100   Schürmann, H.   *Praying with Christ: The 'Our Father' for Today*
                         (ETrans., W. M. Ducey and A. Simon; New York:
                         Herder, 1964).

1101   Schürmann, H.   *Das Gebet des Herrn aus der Verkündigung Jesu*
                         (Freiburg i B.: Herder, 1965³).

1102   Schürmann, H.   *La prière du Seigneur à la lumière de la prédication
                         de Jésus* (trans. by F. Diverres and C. Richard, Et.
                         Théol. 3; Paris: L'Orante, 1965).

1103 Schürmann, H. *Das Gebet des Herrn als Schlussel zum Verstehen Jesu* (4te. verbesserte und erweiterte Aufl.; Freiburg: Herder, 1981).

1104 Schwarz, G. "Matthäus VI. 9–13/Lukas XI. 2–4: Emendation und Rückübersetzung," *NTS* 15 (1969), 233–47.

1105 Scott, E. F. *The Lord's Prayer: Its Character, Purpose, and Interpretation* (New York: Scribner's, 1951).

1106 Seeberg, A. "Vaterunser und Abendmahl," in A. Deissmann and H. Windisch (eds.), *Neutestamentliche Studien Georg Henrici zu seinem 70. Geburtstag* (Leipzig: J. C. Hinrichs, 1914), 108–14.

1107 Shearman, T. G. "Our Daily Bread," *JBL* 53 (1934), 110–17.

1108 Sheed, F. J. *The Lord's Prayer: The Prayer of Jesus* (New York: Seabury Press, 1975).

1109 Sheward, C. G. "The Lord's Prayer: A Study in Sources," *ET* 52 (1940), 119–20.

1110 Sjögren, P.-O. *Jesusbonen* (Stockholm: Diakonistyrelsen, 1967). See also *The Jesus Prayer* (ETrans.; Philadelphia: Fortress, 1975).

1111 Standaert, B. "Crying 'Abba' and Saying 'Our Father': An Intertextual Approach to the Dominical Prayer," in S. Draisma (ed.), *Intertextuality in Biblical Writings: Essays in Honour of Bas van Iersel* (Kampen: J. H. Kok, 1989), 141–58.

1112 Starcky, J. "La quatrième demande du Pater," *HThR* 64 (1971), 401–9.

1113 Steinmetz, F. J. " 'Dein Reich Komme!': Zur zweiten Bitte des Vaterunsers," *GL* 41 (1968), 414–28.

1114 Stendahl, K. "Prayer and Forgiveness," *SEÅ* 22 (1958), 75–86.

1115 Stendhal, K., et al. "The Lord's Prayer," *IRM* 69 (1980), 265–351.

1116 Stendahl, K. "Your Kingdom Come," *CrossCur* 32 (1982), 257–66.

1117 Steuernagel, C. "Die ursprüngliche Zweckbestimmung des Vater- unser," *WZ(L)* 3 (1953–54), 217–20.

1118 Strecker, G. "Vaterunser und Glaube," in F. Hahn and H. Klein (eds.), *Glaube im Neuen Testament* (Neukirchen-Vluyn: Neukichener Verlag, 1982), 11–28.

1119 Strecker, G. "Das Vaterunser: Ein exegetischer Kommentar," in *Die Bergpredigt* (Göttingen: Vandenhoeck & Ruprecht, 1984), 109–32.

1120 Stritzky, M.-B. von *Studien zur Überlieferung und Interpretation des Vaterunsers in der frühchristlichen Literatur* (Münster: Aschendorff, 1989).

1121 Strolz, W. "Moderne Vaterunser-Interpretation," in M. Brocke, J. J. Petuchowski, and and W. Strolz (eds.), *Das Vaterunser: Gemeinsames im Beten von Juden und Christen* (Freiburg i. Breisgau: Herder, 1974), 13–24.

1122 Stubblefield, J. M. "Matthew 6:5–15," *RevExp* 87 (1990), 303–7.

1123 Swetnam, J. "Hallowed Be Thy Name," *Bib* 52 (1971), 556–63.

1124 Sykes, W. H. "And Do Not Bring Us to the Test," *ET* 73 (1964), 189–90.

1125 Taussig, H. "The Lord's Prayer: Foundations and Facets," in *Forum* 4/4 (1988), 25–41.

1126 Theunissen, M. *"ho aitōn lambanei:* Der Gebetsglaube Jesu und die Zeitlichkeit des Christuseins," in B. Caspar (ed.), *Jesus: Ort der Erfahrung Gottes* (Basel/Vienna/Freiburg: Herder, 1976), 13–68.

1127 Thompson, G. H. P. "Thy Will Be Done in Earth, as It Is in Heaven: Matthew 6:11; a Suggested Re-interpretation," *ET* 70 (1959), 379–81.

1128 Tiede, D. L. "The Kingdom Prayer," in P. R. Sponheim (ed.), *A Primer on Prayer* (Philadelphia: Fortress, 1988), 107–20.

1129 Tilborg, S. van "A Form-Criticism of the Lord's Prayer," *NT* 14 (1972), 94–105.

1130 Tillard, J. M. R. "La prière des chrétiens," *LV* 14 (1965), 39–84.

1131 Tittle, E. F. *The Lord's Prayer* (New York/Nashville: Abingdon-Cokesbury, 1942).

1132 Tod, M. N. "Our Daily Bread," *CQR* 158 (1957), 49–51.

1133 Trudinger, P. "The Our Father in Matthew as Apocalyptic Eschatology," *DR* 107 (1989), 49–54.

1134 Venetz, H.-J. *Das Vaterunser: Gebet einer bedrängten Schöpfung* (Fribourg/Brig: Éditions Exodus, 1989).

1135 Verity, G. B. "Lead Us Not into Temptation but...," *ET* 58 (1947), 221–22.

1136 Vogler, W. " 'Gib uns, was wir heute zum Leben brauchen': Zum Auslegung der vierten Bitte des Vaterunsers," in H. Seidel and K.-H. Bieritz (eds.), *Das lebendige Wort* (Berlin: Evangelische Verlagsanstalt, 1982), 52–63.

1137 Vögtle, A. "Das Vaterunser — ein Gebet für Juden und Christen?," in M. Brocke, J. J. Petuchowski, and and W. Strolz (eds.), *Das Vaterunser: Gemeinsames im Beten von Juden und Christen* (Freiburg i. Breisgau: Herder, 1974), 165–95.

1138 Vögtle, A. "Der 'eschatologische' Bezug der Wir-Bitten des Vaterunser," in E. E. Ellis and E. Grässer (eds.), *Jesus und Paulus: Festschrift W. G. Kümmel* (Göttingen: Vandenhoeck & Ruprecht, 1975), 344–62.

1139 Vokes, F. E. "The Lord's Prayer in the First Three Centuries" (Studia Patristica X/TU 107; Berlin: Akademie-Verlag, 1970), 253–60.

1140 Walker, M. B. "Lead Us Not into Temptation," *ET* 73 (1962), 287.

1141 Walker, W. O. "The Lord's Prayer in Matthew and John (Matt 6:9–13; Jn 17)," *NTS* 28 (1982), 237–56.

1142 Walther, G. *Untersuchungen zur Geschichte der griechischen Vaterunser-Exegese* (Leipzig: J. C. Hinrichs, 1914).

1143 Weiser, M. "Das Vaterunser in 'konsequent' — existentialer Interpretation: Zur Predigtmeditation über Matth 6, 5–13 von Herbert Braun," in Å. Andrén et al. (eds.), *Wort und Welt: Festgabe für Erich Hertzsch* (Berlin: Evangelische Verlagsanstalt, 1968), 299–311.

1144 Willis, G. G. "Lead Us Not into Temptation," *DR* 93 (1975), 281–88.

1145 Wimmerer, R. "Noch einmal *epiousios*," *Glotta* 12 (1923), 68–82.

1146 Wolf, C. U. "Daniel and the Lord's Prayer," *Interp* 15 (1961), 398–410.

1147 Wright, R. F. "Our Daily Bread," *CQR* 157 (1956), 340–45.

1148 Wurzinger, A. "Es komme Dein Königreich: Zum Gebetsanliegen nach Lukas," *BiLi* 38 (1964–65), 89–94.

1149 Yamauchi, E. "The 'Daily Bread' Motif in Antiquity," *WThJ* 28 (1966), 145–56.

1150 Young, B. *The Jewish Background to the Lord's Prayer* (Austin, Tex.: Center for Judaic-Christian Studies, 1984).

GOSPELS AND ACTS

Gospels

1151 Barrett, C. K. "The House of Prayer and the Den of Thieves," in E. E. Ellis and E. Grässer (eds.), *Jesus und Paulus: Festschrift für Werner Georg Kümmel zum 70sten Geburtstag* (Göttingen: Vandenhoeck & Ruprecht, 1975), 13–20.

1152 Caba, J. *La oración de petición: estudio exegético sobre los evangelios sinópticos y los escritos joaneos* (Rome: Biblical Institute Press, 1974).

1153 Kee, H. C. "Aretalogy and Gospel," *JBL* 92 (1973), 402–22.

1154 Montefiore, H. W. "God as Father in the Synoptic Gospels," *NTS* 3 (1956–57), 31–46.

1155 Turner, M. M. B.   "Prayer in the Gospels and Acts," in D. A. Carson
                           (ed.), *Teach Us to Pray: Prayer in the Bible and the
                           World* (Exeter, U.K.: Paternoster/Baker, 1990), 58–
                           83, 319–25.

1156 Werner, E.   " 'Hosanna' in the Gospels," *JBL* 65 (1946), 97–122.

Matthew

1157 Brändle, F.   "La oración en San Mateo: Acogida de la voluntad
                           de Dios," *RevistEspir* 49 (1990), 9–25.

1158 Bussby, F.   "A Note on *raka* (Matthew v. 22) and *battalogeō*
                           (Matthew vi. 7) in the Light of Qumran," *ET* 76
                           (1964), 26.

1159 Danielli, G.   " 'Eli, Eli, lema sabactani': Riflessioni sull'origine e
                           il significato della suprema invocazione di Gesù sec-
                           ondo Matteo (Mt 27.46)," in G. Boggio, A. Bonora,
                           and S. Cipriani et al. (eds.), *Gesù e la sua morte*
                           (Brescia: Paideia Editrice, 1984), 29–49.

1160 Dietzfelbinger, C. "Die Frömmigkeitsregeln von Mt 6 1–18 als Zeug-
                           nisse frühchristlicher Geschichte," *ZNW* 75 (1984),
                           184–201.

1161 Dupont, J.   "Pregando, non siate come i pagani (Mt 6, 7–8),"
                           in *Silenzio e parola: Miscellanea in onore del Card.
                           M. Pellegrino* (Turin: Elle Di Ci, 1983), 55–63.

1162 Finkel, A.   "The Prayer of Jesus in Matthew," in A. Finkel and
                           L. Frizzell (eds.), *Standing before God: Studies on
                           Prayer in Scriptures and in Tradition with Essays in
                           Honor of John M. Oesterreicher* (New York: KTAV,
                           1981), 131–69.

1163 Gerhardsson, B.   "Geistiger Opferdienst nach Matth 6, 1–6 16–21,"
                           in H. Baltensweiler (ed.), *Neues Testament und
                           Geschichte: Historisches Geschehen und Deutung
                           im Neuen Testament: Oscar Cullmann zum 70sten
                           Geburtstag* (Zürich/Tübingen: Theologischer Verlag/
                           Mohr, 1972), 69–77.

1164 Gnilka, J.   *Das Matthäusevangelium* (HTKNT; Freiburg: Her-
                           der, 1986), 212–32.

1165 Sievers, J.   " 'Where Two or Three...' and the Rabbinic Con-
                           cept of the *Shekinah* and Matthew 18:20," in A.
                           Finkel and L. Frizzell (eds.), *Standing before God:
                           Studies on Prayer in Scriptures and in Tradition with
                           Essays in Honor of John M. Oesterreicher* (New
                           York: KTAV, 1981), 171–82.

Mark

1166	Biguzzi, G.	"Mc 11, 23–25 e il Pater," *RivBib* 27 (1979), 57–68.
1167	Dowd, S. E.	*Prayer, Power, and the Problem of Suffering: Mark 11:22–25 in the Context of Markan Theology* (SBLDS 105; Atlanta: Scholars Press, 1988).
1168	Grassi, J.	"Abba, Father (Mark 14:36): Another Approach," *JAAR* 50 (1982), 449–58.
1169	Kiley, M.	" 'Lord, Save my Life' (Ps 116:4) as Generative Text for Jesus' Gethsemane Prayer (Mark 14:36a)," *CBQ* 48 (1986), 655–59.
1170	Kio, S. H.	"A Prayer Framework in Mark 11," *BiTr* 37 (1986), 323–28.
1171	Kirschläger, W.	"Jesu Gebetsverhalten als Paradigma zu Mk 1, 35," *Kairos* 20 (1978), 303–10.
1172	Marrion, M.	"Petitionary Prayer in Mark and in the Q Material" (S.T.D. Dissertation: Catholic University of America, 1974).
1173	Oesterreicher, J.	" 'Abba' . . . !' — Jesu Ölberggebet als Zeugnis seiner Menschlichkeit," in M. Brocke, J. J. Petuchowski, and and W. Strolz (eds.), *Das Vaterunser: Gemeinsames im Beten von Juden und Christen* (Freiburg i. Breisgau: Herder, 1974), 209–30.
1174	Schlosser, J.	"Mc 11,25: tradition et rédaction," in F. Refoulé (ed.), *À Cause de l'Évangile: Études sur les Synoptiques et les Actes offertes au P. Jacques Dupont, O.S.B. à l'occasion de son 70ᵉ anniversaire* (Lectio divina 123; Paris: Cerf, 1985), 277–301.
1175	Unnik, W. C. van	" 'Alles ist dir möglich' (Mk 14, 36)," in O. Böcher and K. Haacker (eds.), *Verborum Veritatis: Festschrift für Gustav Stählin* (Wuppertal: Theologischer Verlag Rolf Brockhays, 1970), 27–36.

Luke-Acts

1176	Alsup, J. E.	"Prayer, Consciousness, and the Early Church: A Look at Acts 2:41–47 for Today," *Austin Seminary Bulletin* 101 (1985), 31–37.
1177	Aschermann, H.	"Zum Agoniegebet Jesus, Lk. 22,43–44," *ThV* 5 (1953–4), 143–49.
1178	Aytoun, R. A.	"The Ten Lucan Hymns of the Nativity in Their Original Language," *JThS* O.S. 18 (1916–17), 274–88.
1179	Benko, S.	"The Magnificat: A History of Controversy," *JBL* 86 (1967), 263–75.

1180 Bovon, F. *Luke the Theologian: Thirty-Three Years of Research* (1950–83) (Allison Park, Pa.: Pickwick, 1987), 400–403.

1181 Brown, R. E. *The Birth of the Messiah* (Garden City, N.Y.: Doubleday, 1977), esp. 346–92.

1182 Brown, R. E. "The Presentation of Jesus (Luke 2.22–40)," *Worship* 51 (1977), 2–11.

1183 Catchpole, D. R. "Q, Prayer and the Kingdom: A Rejoinder," *JThS* N.S. 40 (1989), 377–88.

1184 Conn, H. M. "Luke's Theology of Prayer," *ChrTo* (1972), 290–92.

1185 Davies, J. G. "The Ascription of the Magnificat to Mary," *JThS* N.S. 15 (1964), 307–8.

1186 Doohan, L. *Luke: The Perennial Spirituality* (Santa Fe, N.M.: Bear and Co., 1982), 120–22.

1187 Dupont, J. "Le Magnificat comme discours sur Dieu," *NRTh* 102 (1980), 321–43.

1188 Dupont, J. "La prière et son efficacité dans l'évangile de Luc," *RSR* 69 (1981), 45–56.

1189 Farris, S. *The Hymns of Luke's Infancy Narratives: Their Origin, Meaning and Significance* (JSNTSS 9; Sheffield, U.K.: JSOT Press, 1985).

1190 Feldkämper, L. *Der betende Jesus als Heilsmittler nach Lukas* (St. Augustin: Steyler Verlag, 1978).

1191 Feuillet, A. "Le pharisien et le publicain (Luc 18, 9–14): La manifestation de la miséricorde divine en Jésus serviteur souffrant," *EspVie* 91 (1981), 657–65.

1192 Flusser, D. "The Magnificat, the Benedictus and the War Scroll," in *Judaism and the Origins of Christianity* (Jerusalem: Magnes Press, 1988), 126–49.

1193 Forestall, J. T. "The Old Testament Background of the Magnificat," *Marian Studies* 12 (1961), 205–44.

1194 Fuhrman, C. "A Redactional Study of Prayer in the Gospel of Luke" (Dissertation: Southern Baptist Theological Seminary, 1981).

1195 Gertner, M. "Midrashim in the New Testament," *JJS* 7 (1962), 267–92, esp. 273–82 on the Benedictus.

1196 Gnilka, J. "Der Hymnus des Zacharias," *BZ* 6 (1962), 215–38.

1197 Grelot, P. "Le cantique de Siméon (Luc 11, 29–32)," *RB* 93 (1986), 481–509.

1198 Gryglewicz, F. "Die Herkunft der Hymnen des Kindheitsevangelium des Lucas," *NTS* 21 (1974–75), 265–73.

1199 Gunkel, H. "Die Lieder in der Kindheitsgeschichte Jesu bei Lukas," in *Festgabe für A. von Harnack* (Tübingen: Mohr, 1921), 43–60.

1200 Hamp, V. "Der alttestamentliche Hintergrund des Magnificat," *BiKi* 2 (1953), 17–23.

1201 Harnack, A. von *Das Magnificat der Elisabeth (Luc. 1, 46–55) nebst einigen Bemerkungen zu Luc. 1 und 2* (Berlin: Verlag der Königlichen Akademie der Wissenschaften, 1900).

1202 Harris, O. G. "Prayer in Luke-Acts: A Study in the Theology of Luke" (Dissertation: Vanderbilt University: 1966).

1203 Harris, O. G. "Prayer in the Gospel of Luke," *SWJTh* 10 (1967), 59–69.

1204 Jacoby, A. *"Anatolē ex hypsous,"* ZNW 20 (1921), 205–14.

1205 Jones, D. R. "The Background and Character of the Lucan Psalms," *JThS* N.S. 19 (1968), 19–50.

1206 Koontz, J. V. G. "Mary's Magnificat," *BibSac* 116 (1959), 336–49.

1207 Köstlin, H. A. "Das Magnificat Lc 1,46–55, Lobgesang der Maria oder der Elisabeth?," *ZNW* 3 (1902), 142–45.

1208 Ladeuze, P. "De l'origine du Magnificat et son attribution dans le troisième Évangile à Marie ou à Elisabeth," *RHE* 4 (1903), 623–44.

1209 Linden, P. van *The Gospel of Luke and Acts* (Wilmington, Del.: Glazier, 1986), 49–61.

1210 Llamas, R. "La oración desde San Lucas," *RevistEspir* 49 (1990), 27–61.

1211 Loisy, A. "L'origine du Magnificat," *Revue d'histoire et de littérature religieuses* 2 (1897), 424–32.

1212 Martindale, C. C. "Simeon's Canticle," *Worship* 30 (1956), 199–201.

1213 Micalczyk, J. J. "The Experience of Prayer in Luke-Acts," *RR* 34 (1975), 789–801.

1214 Miyoshi, M. "Jesu Darstellung oder Reinigung im Tempel unter Berücksichtigung von 'Nunc Dimittus' Lk. II 22–38," *Annual of the Japanese Biblical Institute* 4 (1978), 85–115.

1215 Miyoshi, M. "Das jüdische Gebet Sema' und die Abfolge der Traditionsstücke in Lk. 10 — 13," *Annual of the Japanese Biblical Institute* 7 (1981), 70–123.

1216 Monloubou, L. *La prière selon saint Luc: recherche d'une structure* (Lectio divina 89; Paris: Cerf, 1976).

1217 Moule, C. F. D. "H. W. Moule on Acts 4.25," *ET* 65 (1953–4), 220–21.

1218 Navone, J. *Themes of St. Luke* (Rome: Gregorian University, 1970), 118–31.

1219 O'Brien, P. T. "Prayer in Luke-Acts," *TynB* 24 (1973), 111–27.

1220 Ott, W. *Gebet und Heil: Die Bedeutung der Gebetsparänese in der lukanischen Theologie* (StANT 12; Munich: Kösel Verlag, 1965).

1221 Plymale, S. F. "Luke's Theology of Prayer," in D. Lull (ed.), Society of Biblical Literature Seminar Papers 1990 (Atlanta: Scholars Press, 1990), 529–51.

1222 Plymale, S. F. *The Prayer Texts of Luke-Acts* (New York: Peter Lang, 1992).

1223 Prete, B. "Le preghiera di Gesù al monte degli Ulivi e sulla croce nel racconto lucano della passione," in G. Boggio, A. Bonora, and S. Cipriani et al. (eds.), *Gesù e la sua morte* (Brescia: Paideia Editrice, 1984), 75–96.

1224 Ramaroson, L. "Ad Structuram Cantici 'Magnificat,'" *VD* 46 (1968), 30–46.

1225 Rimaud, J. "La première liturgie dans le livre des Actes (Actes 4, 23–31; cf. Ps. 2 et 145)," *MD* 51 (1957), 99–115.

1226 Samain, P. "Luc, évangéliste de la prière," *Revue diocésane de Tournai* 2 (1947), 422–26.

1227 Schnackenburg, R. "Das Magnificat, seine Spiritualität und Theologie," *GL* 38 (1965), 342–57. See also *Schriften zum Neuen Testament* (Munich: Kösel Verlag, 1971), 201–19.

1228 Schürmann, H. "Lk. 22, 42a das älteste Zeugnis für Lk. 22, 20?," *MThZ* 111 (1952), 185–88.

1229 Schürmann, H. *Lukasevangelium* (HTKNT 3.1; Freiburg/Basel/Vienna: Herder, 1969), 70–80, 84–94.

1230 Senior, D. "Jesus in Crisis: The Passion Prayers of Luke's Gospel," in C. Osiek and D. Senior (eds.), *Scripture and Prayer* (Philadelphia: Fortress, 1988), 117–30.

1231 Simon, L. "La prière non religieuse chez Luc," *Foi et vie* 74 (1975), 8–22.

1232 Smalley, S. S. "Spirit, Kingdom and Prayer in Luke-Acts," *NT* 15 (1973), 59–71.

1233 Spitta, F. "Das Magnificat, ein Psalm der Maria und nicht der Elisabeth," in *Theologische Abhandlungen: Festgabe zum 17 Mai 1902 für H. J. Holtzmann* (Tübingen: Mohr, 1902), 63–92.

1234 Spitta, F. "Die chronologischen Notizen und die Hymnen in Lc 1 und 2," *ZNW* 7 (1906), 281–317.

1235 Stramare, T. "La presentazione de Gesù al Tempio (Lc. 2, 22–40): Significato esegetico e teologico," *Cahiers de Josephologie* 29 (1981), 37–61.

1236 Tannehill, R. C. "The Magnificat as a Poem," *JBL* 93 (1974), 263–75.

1237 Thornton, T. C. G. "Short Comment: Continuing Steadfast in Prayer," *ET* 83 (1971), 23–24.

1238 Trites, A. A.   "Some Aspects of Prayer in Luke-Acts," in P. J. Achtemeier (ed.), *Society of Biblical Literature 1977 Seminar Papers* (Missoula, Mont.: Scholars Press, 1977), 59–77.

1239 Trites, A. A.   "The Prayer Motif in Luke-Acts," in C. H. Talbert (ed.), *Perspectives on Luke-Acts* (Danville, Va.: Association of Baptist Professors of Religion, 1978), 168–86.

1240 Tuckett, C.   "Q and the Friend at Midnight (Luke 11.5–8/9)," *JThS* N.S. 34 (1983), 407–24.

1241 Vanhoye, A.   "Structure du 'Benedictus,' " *NTS* 12 (1965–66), 382–89.

1242 Vielhauer, P.   "Das Benedictus des Zacharias," *ZThK* 49 (1952), 255–72. See also *Aufsätze zum Neuen Testament* (TB 31; Munich: Kaiser Verlag, 1965), 28–46.

1243 Vogels, W.   "The Magnificat, Marie et Israël," *Église et théologie* 6 (1975), 279–96.

1244 Winter, P.   "Magnificat and Benedictus — Maccabean Psalms?," *BJRL* 37 (1954–55), 328–47.

1245 Zimmermann, H.   "Das Gleichnis vom Richter und der Witwe (Lk 18, 1–8)," R. Schnackenburg (ed.), *Die Kirche des Anfangs* (Leipzig: St. Benno Verlag, 1977), 79–95.

1246 Zorell, F.   "Das Magnificat, ein Kunstwerk hebräischer oder aramäischer Poesie?," *ZKTh* 29 (1905), 754–58.

Fourth Gospel

1247 Betz, O.   *Der Paraklet: Fürsprecher im häretischen Spätjudentum, im Johannesevangelium und in neugefundenen gnostischen Schriften* (AGSU 2; Leiden: Brill, 1963), 185–86.

1248 Boyle, J. L.   "Last Discourse (Jn. 13, 13–16, 33) and Prayer (Jn. 17): Some Observations on Their Unity and Development," *Bib* 56 (1975), 210–22.

1249 Caba, J.   "Jn 7, 37–39 en la teología del IV Evangelio sobre la oración de petición," *Gr* 63 (1982), 647–75.

1250 Cullmann, O.   "La prière dans l'Évangile johannique," in P. Bonnard, G. W. MacRae, and J. Cobb (eds.), *Yearbook of the Ecumenical Institute for Advanced Theological Study 1979–80* (Jerusalem/Tantur: Franciscan Printing Press, 1980), 31–52.

1251 Dowd, S. E.   "Toward a Johannine Theology of Prayer," in M. Parsons and R. Sloan (eds.), *Perspectives on John* (Macon, Ga.: Mercer University Press, forthcoming).

1252 Hamman, A.

"Lignes maîtresses de la prière johannique," *StE* 1 (1959), 309–20.

1253 Luzárraga, J.

"El encuentro con Jesús como fundamento de la oración cristiana en el Evangelio de Juan," *Teología Espiritual* 20 (1976), 275–99.

1254 Luzárraga, J.

Oración y misión en el Evangelio de Juan (Bilbao: Universidad de Deusto, 1978).

1255 Untergassmair, F.

"Die Aktualität der jahanneischen Aussagen über das Bittgebet in unserer Zeit," in H. Merklein and J. Lange (eds.), *Biblische Randbemerkungen: Schülerschrift für Rudolf Schnackenburg zum 60sten Geburtstag* (Würzburg: Echter Verlag, 1974), 169–80.

1256 Valdiporro, B. da

"La preghiera e il nome di Gesù in San Giovanni (14, 13s.; 15, 16; 16, 23s.)," *Studia Patavina* 8 (1961), 177–212.

1257 Vellanickal, M.

"Prayer in the Gospel of John," *Biblebhashyam* 5 (1979), 63–81.

1258 Wilcox, M.

"Prayer of Jesus in John 11:41b-42," *NTS* 24 (1977), 128–32.

The Prologue

1259 Aland, K.

"Eine Untersuchung zu Joh 1:3, 4: Ueber die Bedeutung eines Punktes," *ZNW* 59 (1968), 174–209.

1260 Ashton, J.

"The Transformation of Wisdom: A Study of the Prologue of John's Gospel," *NTS* 32 (1986), 161–86.

1261 Ausejo, S. de

"¿Es un himno a Cristo el prólogo de San Juan?," *EstB* 15 (1956), 223–77, 381–427.

1262 Baldensperger, W. von

Der Prolog des vierten Evangeliums (Leipzig/Tübingen: Mohr, 1898).

1263 Boismard, M.-E.

Le Prologue de Saint Jean (Paris: Cerf, 1953).

1264 Borgen, P.

"Observations on the Targumic Character of the Prologue of John," *NTS* 16 (1970–71), 288–95.

1265 Bultmann, R.

"Der religionsgeschichtliche Hintergrund des Prologs zum Johannes-Evangelium," in H. Schmidt (ed.), *Eucharisterion: Studien zur Religion und Literatur des A. und N-T: Hermann Gunkel zum 60. Geburtstag* (FRLANT 36.2; Göttingen: Vandenhoeck & Ruprecht, 1923), 2:1–26.

1266 Bultmann, R.

"Die Bedeutung der neuerschlossenen mandäischen und manichäischen Quellen für das Verständnis des Johannesevangeliums," *ZNW* 24 (1925), 100–146.

1267 Bultmann, R.

The Gospel of John (ETrans., G. Beasley-Murray; Oxford: Blackwell, 1971), esp. 13–18.

1268 Burney, C. F.   *The Aramaic Origin of the Fourth Gospel* (Oxford: Clarendon Press, 1922), esp. 40–41. Discusses Aramaic hymnic elements of the Prologue.

1269 Cullmann, O.   "The Theological Content of the Prologue to John in Its Present Form," in R. T. Fortna and B. R. Gaventa (eds.), *The Conversation Continues: Studies in Paul and John in Honor of J. Louis Martyn* (Nashville: Abingdon Press, 1990), 295–98.

1270 Demke, C.   "Der sogennante Logos-Hymnus im Johanneischen Prolog," *ZNW* 58 (1967), 45–68.

1271 Dodd, C. H.   "The Prologue to the Fourth Gospel and Christian Worship," in F. L. Cross (ed.), *Studies in the Fourth Gospel* (London: Mowbray, 1957), 9–22.

1272 Dodd, C. H.   *The Interpretation of the Fourth Gospel* (Cambridge: University Press, 1953), 263–85.

1273 Dürr, L.   *Die Wertung des göttlichen Wortes im Alten Testament und im Antiken Orient* (Mitteilungen der vorderasiatisch-aegyptischen Gesellschaft, XLII, 1. Heft; Leipzig: J. C. Hinrichs, 1938). Logos hymns in the ANE and in the Fourth Gospel.

1274 Feuillet, A.   *Le prologue du Quatrième Évangile: étude de théologie johannique* (Paris: Desclée de Brouwer, 1968).

1275 Feuillet, A.   "Prologue du IVe Évangile," in *DBS* 8, cols. 623–88.

1276 Haenchen, E.   "Probleme des johanneischen 'Prologs,'" *ZThK* 60 (1963), 305–34.

1277 Hofius, O.   "Struktur und Gedankengang des Logos-Hymnus in Joh 1, 1–18," *ZNW* 78 (1987), 1–25.

1278 Janssens, Y.   "Une source gnostique du Prologue," in M. de Jonge (ed.), *L'Évangile de Jean* (BEThL 44; Louvain: University Press, 1977), 355–58.

1279 Jeremias, J.   *Der Prolog des Johannesevangeliums* (Stuttgart: Calwer Verlag, 1967).

1280 Käsemann, E.   "The Structure and the Purpose of the Prologue to John's Gospel," in *New Testament Questions of Today* (London: SCM, 1969), 138–67. See also "Aufbau und Anliegen des johanneishen Prologs," in *Libertas Christiana: Festschrift für F. Delekat* (Munich: Kaiser Verlag, 1957), 75–99.

1281 Lamarche, P.   "Le prologue de Jean," *RSR* 52 (1964), 497–537.

1282 Masson, C.   "Le prologue du quatrième évangile," *RThPh* 28 (1940), 297–311.

1283 McNamara, M.   "Logos of the Fourth Gospel and *Memra* of the Palestinian Targum (Ex 12:42)," *ET* 79 (1968), 115–17.

1284	Miller, E. K.	"The Logic of the Logos Hymn: A New View," NTS 29 (1983), 522–61.
1285	Potterie, I. de la	"La structure du Prologue de Jean," NTS 30 (1984), 354–81.
1286	Richter, G.	"Ist en ein strukturbildendes Element im Logoshymnus Joh 1,1ff.?," Bib 51 (1970), 539–44.
1287	Robinson, J. A. T.	"The Relation of the Prologue to the Gospel of John," in More New Testament Studies (London: SCM, 1984), 65–76.
1288	Ruckstuhl, E.	"Kritische Arbeit am Johannesprolog," in W. C. Weinrich (ed.), The New Testament Age: Essays in Honor of Bo Reicke (Macon, Ga.: Mercer University Press, 1984), 2:443–54.
1289	Sabourin, L.	"The MEMRA of God in the Targums," BTB 6 (1976), 79–85.
1290	Sanders, J. T.	The New Testament Christological Hymns (SNTSMS 15; Cambridge: University Press, 1971), 20–25, 29–57.
1291	Schaeder, H. H.	"Der 'Mensch' im Prolog des IV. Evangeliums," in R. Reitzenstein and H. H. Schaeder (eds.), Studien zum antiken Synkretismus aus Iran und Griechenland (Studien der Bibliothek Wartburg, 7; Leipzig: B. C. Teubner, 1926), Part 2, 306–41. Discusses the Mandaean background.
1292	Schnackenburg, R.	"Logos-Hymnus und johanneischer Prolog," BZ N.F. 1 (1957), 69–109.
1293	Yamauchi, E.	"Jewish Gnosticism?: The Prologue of John, Mandaean Parallels, and the Trimorphic Protennoia," in R. van den Broek and M. J. Vermaseren (eds.), Studies in Gnosticism and Hellenistic Religions (Leiden: Brill, 1981), 467–97.

Chapter 17

1294	Agourides, S. C.	"The High-Priestly Prayer of Jesus," StE 4 (1968), 137–43.
1295	Appold, M.	"Christ Alive, Church Alive: Reflections on the Prayer of Jesus in John 17," CuThM 5 (1978), 365–73.
1296	Balagué, M.	"La oración sacerdotal (Juan 17, 1–26)," CultBib 31 (1974), 67–90.
1297	Battaglia, O.	"Preghiera sacerdotale ed innologia ermetica (Giov 17 — CH. 1, 31–32e XIII, 18–20)," RivBib 17 (1969), 209–32.

1298 Becker, J.   "Aufbau, Schichtung und theologiegeschichtliche Stellung des Gebets in Joh 17," *ZNW* 60 (1969), 56–83.

1299 Bonnard, P. E.   "La prière de Jésus pour une église divisée (Jean 17)," in P. Bonnard, G. W. MacRae, and J. Cobb (eds.), *Yearbook of the Ecumenical Institute for Advanced Theological Study 1979–80* (Jerusalem/ Tantur: Franciscan Printing Press, 1980), 15–25.

1300 Bornkamm, G.   "Zur Interpretation des Johannesevangeliums: Eine Auseinandersetzung mit E. Käsemanns Schrift, 'Jesu letzter Wille nach Johannes 17,' " *EvTh* 28 (1968), 8–25.

1301 Boyle, J. L.   "The Last Discourse (Jn 13, 31–16, 33) and Prayer (Jn 17): Some Observations on Their Unity and Development," *Bib* 56 (1975), 210–22.

1302 Cadier, J.   "The Unity of the Church: An Exposition of Jn 17," *Interp* 11 (1957), 166–76.

1303 Carson, D. A.   *The Farewell Discourse and Final Prayer of Jesus: An Exposition of John 14–17* (Grand Rapids, Mich.: Baker, 1980), chs. 9 and 10.

1304 Delorme, J.   "Sacerdoce du Christ et ministère: sémantique et théologie biblique," *RSR* 62 (1974), 199–219.

1305 Evdokimov, P.   "L'Esprit saint et la prière pour l'unité," *VC* 14 (1960), 250–64.

1306 George, A.   "L'heure de Jean XVII," *RB* 61 (1954), 392–97.

1307 Giblet, J.   "Sanctifie les dans la vérité Jn 17, 1–26," *BVC* 19 (1957), 58–73.

1308 Goes, H., and   *Das letzte Gebet Jesu: Eine Auslegung von Jo-*
       Lutz, W.   *hannes 17* (Biblische Studien 22; Neukirchen-Vluyn: Neukirchener Verlag, 1958).

1309 Hanson, A. T.   "Hodayoth xv and John 17: A Comparison of Content and Form," *Hermathena* 118 (1974), 48–58.

1310 Harrison, W. S. "The Prayer of Jesus: John XVII," *MQR* 47 (1898), 387–95.

1311 Käsemann, E.   *The Testament of Jesus according to John 17* (ETrans., G. Krodel; Philadelphia: Fortress, 1968).

1312 Laurentin, A.   "*We 'attah–kai nun*: Formule caractérisque des textes juridiques et liturgiques (à propos de Jn 17, 5)," *Bib* 45 (1964), 168–95, 413–32.

1313 Lloyd-Jones, D. M. *The Basis of Christian Unity: An Exposition of John 17 and Ephesians 4* (Grand Rapids, Mich.: Eerdmans, 1963).

1314 Malatesta, E.   "The Literary Structure of John 17," *Bib* 52 (1971), 190–214.

1315 Maloney, F. "John 17: The Prayer of Jesus' Hour," *CleR* 67 (1982), 79–83.

1316 Minear, P. S. "Evangelism, Ecumenism, and John 17," *ThTo* 35 (1978), 353–60.

1317 Minear, P. S. "John 17:1–11," *Interp* 32 (1978), 175–79.

1318 Morrison, D. C. "Mission and Ethic: An Interpretation of John 17," *Interp* 19 (1965), 259–73.

1319 Newman, B. M. "The Case of the Eclectic and the Neglected Ek of John 17," *BiTr* 29 (1978), 339–41.

1320 Perret, J. "La prière sacerdotale (Jean 17)," *VC* 18 (1964), 119–26.

1321 Poelman, R. "The Sacerdotal Prayer: John XVII," *LV* 20 (1965), 43–66.

1322 Pollard, T. E. " 'That They All May Be One' (John xvii 21) — and the Unity of the Church," *ET* 70 (1958–59), 149–50.

1323 Quinn, J. D. "The Prayer of Jesus to His Father," *Way* 9 (1969), 90–97.

1324 Radermakers, J. "La prière de Jésus, Jn 17," *AssS* 29 (1973), 48–86.

1325 Randall, J. F. "The Theme of Unity in John 17:20–23," *EThL* 41 (1965), 373–94.

1326 Ritt, H. *Das Gebet zum Vater: Zur Interpretation von Joh 17* (Würzburg: Echter Verlag, 1979).

1327 Rosenblatt, M. E. "The Voice of the One Who Prays in John 17," in C. Osiek and D. Senior (eds.), *Scripture and Prayer* (Wilmington, Del.: Glazier, 1988), 131–44.

1328 Sancho Mielgo, G. "La unidad de la Iglesia según Juan 17," *EspVie* 8 (1978), 9–58.

1329 Schnackenburg, R. "Strukturanalyse von Joh 17," *BZ* 17 (1973), 67–78, 196–202.

1330 Segalla, G. "La preghiera di Gesù e le fede dei discepoli in Giov 17," in P.-R. Tragan (ed.), *Fede e sacramenti negli scritti giovannei* (Rome: Edizioni Abbazia S Paolo, 1985), 135–48.

1331 Stachowiak, L. "Modlitwa arcykaplanska (J 17): Refleksje egzegetyczne," *RTK* 21 (1974), 85–94.

1332 Thüsing, W. *Herrlichkeit und Einheit: Eine Auslegung des Hohepriesterlichen Gebetes Jesu (Joh. 17)* (Düsseldorf: Patmos, 1962).

1333 Thüsing, W. "Die Bitten des johanneischen Jesus in dem Gebet Joh 17 und die Intention Jesu von Nazaret," in R. Schnackenburg et al. (eds.), *Die Kirche des Anfangs: Festschrift H. Schürmann* (Freiburg/Basel/Vienna: Herder, 1978), 307–37.

1334 Ukpong, J. S.   "Jesus' Prayer for His Followers: (Jn 17) in Mission Perspective," *AfThJ* 18 (1989), 49–60.

PAUL

1335 Bieder, W.   "Gebetswirklichkeit und Gebetsmöglichkeit bei Paulus: Das Beten des Geistes und das Beten in Geiste," *ThZ* 4 (1948), 22–40.

1336 Boobyer, G. H.   *"Thanksgiving" and the "Glory of God" in Paul* (Borna-Leipzig: R. Noske, 1929).

1337 Cerfaux, L.   "Hymnes au Christ des lettres de Saint Paul," *Revue diocésaine de Tournai* (1947), 2:3–11.

1338 Champion, L. G.   *Benedictions and Doxologies in the Epistles of Paul* (Oxford: Kemp Hall, 1934).

1339 Cullmann, O.   "La prière dans les Épîtres de St. Paul," *DBM* N.S. 1 (1979), 85–101 [in Greek].

1340 Cullmann, O.   "La prière selon les Épîtres pauliniennes," *ThZ* 35 (1979), 90–101 = *Ecumenical Institute for Advanced Theological Studies: Yearbook 1977–78* (Tantur/ Jerusalem: Franciscan Printing Press, 1980), 67–82.

1341 Dietzel, A.   "Beten im Geist: Eine religionsgeschichtliche Parallele aus den Hodajot zum paulinischen Gebet im Geist," *ThZ* 13 (1957), 12–32.

1342 Fowl, S. E.   *The Story of Christ in the Ethics of Paul: An Analysis of the Function of the Hymnic Material in the Pauline Corpus* (Sheffield: JSOT Press, 1990).

1343 Harder, G.   *Paulus und das Gebet* (Gütersloh: C. Bertelsmann, 1936).

1344 Jeremias, J.   "Zur Gedankenführung in den paulinischen Briefen," in *Abba*, 269–76. See also J. N. Sevenster and W. C. van Unnik (eds.), *Studia Paulina in honorem Johannes de Zwaan, septuagenarii* (Haarlem: Bohm, 1953), 146–54.

1345 Juncker, A.   *Das Gebet bei Paulus* (Berlin, 1905).

1346 Marcheselli Casale, C.   *La preghiera in s. Paolo* (Napoli: Pontificia Facoltà teologica, M. D'Auria, 1975).

1347 Monloubou, L.   *Saint Paul et la prière: prière et évangélisation* (Lectio divina 110; Paris: Cerf, 1982).

1348 Obeng, E. A.   "The Spirit Intercession Motif in Paul," *ET* 95 (1984), 360–64.

1349 O'Brien, P. T.   "Thanksgiving and the Gospel in Paul," *NTS* 21 (1974/5), 144–55.

1350 O'Brien, P. T.   *Introductory Thanksgivings in the Letters of Paul* (NT. S 49; Leiden: Brill, 1977).

1351 Orphal, E.   *Das Paulusgebet* (Gotha, 1933).

1352 Osiek, C.   "Paul's Prayer: Relationship with Christ?," in C. Osiek and D. Senior (eds.), *Scripture and Prayer: A Celebration for Carroll Stuhlmueller* (Wilmington, Del.: Glazier, 1988), 145–57.

1353 Peterson, D. G.   "Prayer in Paul's Writings," in D. A. Carson (ed.), *Teach Us to Pray: Prayer in the Bible and the World* (Exeter, U.K.: Paternoster/Baker, 1990), 84–101, 325–28.

1354 Provera, M.   "Preghiera e vita nelle lettere paoline," in E. Testa, M. Ignazio, and M. Piccirillo (eds.), *Studia hiersolymitana in onore del p. Bellarmino Bagatti, 2, Studi eseagetici* (Jerusalem: Franciscan Printing Press, 1976), 169–79.

1355 Romaniuk, K.   "Spiritus clamans (Gal 4, 6; Rom 8, 15)," *VD* 40 (1962), 190–98.

1356 Schneider, C.   "Paulus und das Gebet," *Angelos* 4 (1932), 11–28.

1357 Schubert, P.   *Form and Function of the Pauline Thanksgivings* (Berlin: A. Töpelmann, 1939).

1358 Stanley, D. M.   *Boasting in the Lord: The Phenomenon of Prayer in Saint Paul* (New York: Paulist, 1973).

1359 Stendahl, K.   "Paul at Prayer," *Interp* 34 (1980), 240–49.

1360 Swain, L.   "Prayer and Apostolate in Paul," *CleR* 51 (1966), 458–65.

1361 White, J. L.   "Introductory Formulae in the Body of the Pauline Letter," *JBL* 90 (1971), 91–97.

1362 Wiles, G. P.   "The Function of Intercessory Prayer in Paul's Apostolic Ministry with Special Reference to the First Epistle to the Thessalonians" (Dissertation: Yale University, 1965).

1363 Wiles, G. P.   *Paul's Intercessory Prayers: The Significance of the Intercessory Prayer Passages in the Letters of St. Paul* (SNTSMS 24; Cambridge: University Press, 1974).

1364 Wobbe, J.   *Der Charis-Gedanke bei Paulus: Ein Beitrag zur neutestamentlicher Theologie* (Münster: Aschendorff, 1932).

1365 Wright, N. T.   "Adam in Pauline Christology," in K. H. Richards (ed.), *Society of Biblical Literature 1983 Seminar Papers* (Chico, Calif.: Scholars Press, 1983), 359–89, see 373–84 (Phil. 2:5–11); 384–87 (Col. 1:15).

1366 Zimmer, F.   *Das Gebet nach den Paulinischen Schriften* (Königsberg: Hartung, 1887).

EPISTLES AND APOCALYPSE

Romans

1367	Armogathe, J. R.	"Gemitibus inenarrabilibus: Note sur Rom 8,26," in V. Saxer (ed.), *Ecclesia orans: mélanges patristiques offerts au Père Adalbert G. Hamman OFM à l'occasion de ses quarante ans d'enseignement* (Rome: Institute Patristicum "Augustinium," 1980), 19–22.
1368	Barth, M.	"Theologie — ein Gebet (Röm 11:33–36)," *ThZ* 41 (1985), 330–48.
1369	Bornkamm, G.	"The Praise of God: Romans 11:33–36," in *Early Christian Experience* (London: SCM, 1969), 105–11.
1370	Boyd, R. F.	"The Work of the Holy Spirit in Prayer," *Interp* 8 (1954), 35–42.
1371	Dupont, J.	*Gnosis: La connaissance religieuse dans les épîtres de Saint Paul* (Louvain/Paris: Nauwelaerts/Gabalda, 1949), 91–93, 329–47. Discussion of 11:33–36.
1372	Jeremias, J.	"Einige vorwiegend sprachliche Beobachtungen zu Röm 11:25–36," in L. Lorenzi (ed.), *Die Israelfrage nach Römer 9–11* (Rome: Abtei von St. Paul, 1977), 203–5.
1373	Kamlah, E.	"Traditionsgeschichtliche Untersuchungen zur Schlußdoxologie des Römerbriefes" (Dissertation: Tübingen, 1955).
1374	Keck, L. E.	"Christology, Soteriology and the Praise of God (Romans 15:7–13)," in R. T. Fortna and B. R. Gaventa (eds.), *The Conversation Continues: Studies in Paul and John in Honor of J. Louis Martyn* (Nashville: Abingdon Press, 1990), 85–97.
1375	MacRae, G.	"Romans 8:26–27" *Interpretation* 34 (1980) 288–92. Rept. in *Studies in the New Testament and Gnosticism* (Wilmington, Del.: Glazier, 1987), 65–71.
1376	Obeng, E. A.	"The Origins of the Spirit Intercession Motif in Romans 8:26," *NTS* 32 (1986), 621–32.
1377	Obeng, E. A.	"The Reconciliation of Rom. 8.26f. to New Testament Writings and Themes," *SJTh* 39 (1986), 165–74.
1378	O'Brien, P. T.	"Romans 8:26, 27: A Revolutionary Approach to Prayer?," *RThR* 46 (1987), 65–73.
1379	Zeller, D.	*Juden und Heiden in der Mission des Paulus: Studien zum Römerbrief* (Stuttgart: Katholisches Bibelwerk, 1973), 267–69.

Corinthians

1380 Betz, H. D.   "Eine Christus-Aretalogie bei Paulus (2 Kor 12, 7–10)," *ZThK* 66 (1969), 288–305.

1381 Unnik, W. C. van   "Reisepläne und Amen-Sagen, Zusammenhang und Gedankenfolge in 2 Korinther 1:15–24," in J. N. Sevenster and W. C. van Unnik (eds.), *Studia Paulina in Honorem J. de Zwaan* (Haarlem: Bohm, 1953), 215–34.

Ephesians

1382 Barkhuizen, J. H.   "The Strophic Structure of the Eulogy of Ephesians 1:3–14," *HervTeolStud* 46 (1990), 390–413.

1383 Barth, M.   "Hymns and Traditional Material," in *Ephesians 1–3* (Anchor Bible; Garden City, N.Y.: Doubleday, 1974), 6–10.

1384 Cambier, J.   "La Bénédiction d'Eph 1, 3–14," *ZNW* 54 (1963), 58–104.

1385 Cerfaux, L.   "À genoux en présence de Dieu (la prière d'Éph III, 14–19)," in *Recueil Lucien Cerfaux*, 3: *Études d'exégèse et d'histoire religieuse de Monsigneur Cerfaux* (Gembloux: Éditions J. Duculot, 1962), 309–22.

1386 Coutts, J.   "Ephesians I. 3–14 and I Peter I. 3–12," *NTS* 3 (1956–57), 115–27.

1387 Dahl, N. A.   "Adresse und Proömium des Epheserbriefes," *ThZ* 7 (1951), 241–64.

1388 Grelot, P.   "La structure d'Éphésiens 1, 3–14," *RB* 96 (1989), 193–209.

1389 Innitzer, T.   "Der 'Hymnus' im Epheserbrief (1, 3–14)," *ZKTh* 28 (1904), 612–21.

1390 Kendrick, W. G.   "Prayer in Colossians and Ephesians" (Dissertation: Baylor University, 1976).

1391 Lohmeyer, E.   "Das Prooemium des Epheserbriefes," *ThBl* 5 (1926), 120–25.

1392 Lyonnet, S.   "La bénédiction de Éph. I, 3–14 et son arrière-plan judaïque," in *À la rencontre de Dieu, Mémorial A. Gelin* (Paris: Xavier Mappus, 1961), 341–52.

1393 Maurer, C.   "Der Hymnus von Epheser 1 als Schlüssel zum ganzen Briefe," *EvTh* 11 (1951–52), 151–72.

1394 O'Brien, P. T.   "Ephesians 1: An Unusual Introduction to a New Testament Letter," *NTS* 25 (1978–79), 504–16.

1395 Sanders, J. T.   "Hymnic Elements in Ephesians 1–3," *ZNW* 56 (1965), 214–32.

| 1396 | Trinidad, J. T. | "The Mystery Hidden in God, A Study of Eph. 1, 3–14," *Bib* 31 (1950), 1–26. |
| 1397 | Wilhelmi, G. | "Der Versöhner-Hymnus in Eph 2,14ff.," *ZNW* 78 (1987), 145–52. |

Philippians

1398	Arvedson, T.	"Phil. 2, 6 und Mt. 10. 39," *StTh* 5 (1951), 49–51.
1399	Badham, F. P.	"Phil. II. 6 *"Harpagmos,"* *ET* 19 (1908), 331.
1400	Bakken, N. K.	"The New Humanity: Christ and the Modern Age: A Study Centering on the Christ-Hymn: Philippians 2:6–11," *Interp* 22 (1968), 71–82.
1401	Bandstra, A. J.	" 'Adam' and 'the Servant' in Phil. 2:5ff.," *CalThJ* 1 (1966), 213–16.
1402	Barclay, W.	"Great Themes of the New Testament — 1. Philippians ii. 1–11," *ET* 70 (1958), 4–7, 40–44.
1403	Barnikol, E.	*Der marcionitische Ursprung des Mythos-Satzes Phil. 2. 6–7* (Kiel: W. G. Kuhlau, 1932).
1404	Bartsch, H. W.	*Die konkrete Wahrheit und die Lüge der Spekulation: Untersuchung über den vorpaulinischen Christushymnus und seine gnostische Mythisierung* (Frankfurt: Lang, 1974).
1405	Binder, H.	"Erwägungen zu Phil 2, 6–7b," *ZNW* 78 (1987), 230–43.
1406	Bornhaüser, K. B.	*Jesus Imperator Mundi (Phil. 3, 17–21 und 2, 5–11)* (Gütersloh: C. Bertelsmann, 1938).
1407	Bornkamm, G.	"Zum Verständnis der Christus-Hymnus Phil. 2, 6–11," in *Studien zu Antike und Urchristentum: Gesammelte Aufsätze, II* (Beiträge zur Evangelischen Theologie 28; Munich: Kaiser Verlag, 1959), 177–87. See also *Early Christian Experience,* 112–20.
1408	Bouyer, L.	*"Harpagmos,"* *RSR* 39 (1951–52), 281–88.
1409	Brown, S.	"The Christ-Event according to Philippians 2:6–11," *HomPastRev* 73 (1973), 31–32, 55–59.
1410	Carmignac, J.	"L'importance de la place d'une négation OUCH HARPAGMON ĒGĒSATO (Philippiens II.6)," *NTS* 18 (1971–72), 131–66.
1411	Cerfaux, L.	"L'hymne au Christ-Serviteur de Dieu (Phil 2, 6–11 = Is 52, 13–53, 12)," in *Receuil Lucien Cerfaux, 2: Études d'exégèse et d'histoire religieuse* (BEThL 6–7; Gembloux: Duculot, 1954), 425–37.
1412	Contri, A.	"Il 'Magnificat' alla luce dell'inno christologico di Filippesi 2, 6–11," *Marianum* 40 (1978), 164–68.
1413	Coppens, J.	"Phil. 2, 7 et Is. 53, 12," *EThL* 41 (1965), 147–50.

1414   Coppens, J.   "Une nouvelle structuration de l'hymne christolo-gique de l'épître aux Philippiens," *EThL* 43 (1967), 197–202.

1415   Dupont, J.   "Jésus-Christ dans son abaissement et son exaltation d'après Phil., II, 6–11," *RSR* 37 (1950), 500–514.

1416   Eckman, B.   "A Quantitative Metrical Analysis of the Philippians Hymn," *NTS* 26 (1979–80), 258–66.

1417   Ernesti, H. F.   "Phil. II. 6–11 aus einer Anspielung auf Gen. II.–III. erläutert," *ThStKr* 21 (1848), 858–924 and 24 (1851), 596–630.

1418   Feinberg, P. D.   "The Kenosis and Christology: An Exegetical-Theological Analysis of Phil. 2:6–11," *TrinJ* 1 (1980), 21–46.

1419   Feuillet, A.   "L'homme-Dieu considéré dans sa condition terrestre (Phil. II. 5 seq. et parall.)," *RB* 51 (1942), 58–79.

1420   Feuillet, A.   "L'hymne christologique de l'épître aux Philippiens (2. 6–11)," *RB* 72 (1965), 352–80, 481–507.

1421   Feuillet, A.   *Christologie paulinienne et tradition biblique* (Paris: Desclée, 1973), 83–161.

1422   Flanagan, N.   "A Note on Philippians iii. 20, 21," *CBQ* 18 (1956), 8–9.

1423   Furness, J. M.   " '*harpagmon...heauton ekenōse,*" *ET* 69 (1957–58), 93–94.

1424   Furness, J. M.   "The Authorship of Phil 2, 6–11," *ET* 70 (1958–59), 240–43.

1425   Furness, J. M.   "Behind the Philippians Hymn (II.6–11)," *ET* 79 (1967–68), 178–82.

1426   Gamber, K.   "Der Christushymnus im Philipperbrief in Liturgie-geschichtlicher Sicht," *Bib* 51 (1970), 369–76.

1427   Gander, G.   "L'hymne de la passion: Exégèse de Philippiens i. 27–ii. 18" (Dissertation: Geneva, 1939).

1428   Georgi, D.   "Der vorpaulinische Hymnus Phil. 2. 6–11," in E. Dinkler (ed.), *Zeit und Geschichte: Dankesgabe an R. Bultmann zum 80. Geburtstag* (Tübingen: Mohr, 1964), 263–93.

1429   Gewiess, J.   "Zum altkirchlichen Verständnis der Kenosis-stelle (Phil 2. 5–11)," *ThQ* 128 (1948), 463–87.

1430   Gifford, E. H.   *The Incarnation: A Study of Philippians ii. 5–11* (ed. H. Wace; London: Longmans, 1911).

1431   Glasson, T. F.   "Two Notes on the Philippians Hymn (ii. 6–11)," *NTS* 21 (1974–75), 133–39.

1432   Grelot, P.   "Deux expressions difficiles de Philippiens 2, 6–7," *Bib* 53 (1972), 495–507.

1433	Grelot, P.	"La valeur de *ouk...alla...* dans Philippiens 2, 6–7," *Bib* 54 (1973), 25–42.
1434	Grelot, P.	"Deux notes critiques sur Philippiens 2, 6–11," *Bib* 54 (1973), 169–86.
1435	Griffiths, D. R.	"*harpagmos* and *heauton ekenōsen,*" *ET* 69 (1958), 237–39.
1436	Guignebert, C.	"Quelques remarques d'exégèse sur Phil. 2. 6–11," *RHPhR* 3 (1923), 522–32.
1437	Harvey, J.	"A New Look at the Christ Hymn of Philippians 2:6–11," *ET* 76 (1964–65), 337–39.
1438	Hofius, O.	*Der Christushymnus Philipper 2, 6–11* (WUNT 17; Tübingen: Mohr, 1976).
1439	Hooker, M. D.	"Philippians 2, 6–11," in E. E. Ellis and E. Grässer (eds.), *Jesus und Paulus: Festschrift für W. G. Kümmel* (Göttingen: Vandenhoeck & Ruprecht, 1975), 151–64.
1440	Hoover, R. W.	"The *Harpagmos* Enigma: A Philological Solution," *HThR* 64 (1971), 95–119.
1441	Howard, G.	"Phil. 2:6–11 and the Human Christ," *CBQ* 40 (1978), 368–87.
1442	Hudson, D. F.	"A Further Note on Philippians ii:6–11," *ET* 77 (1965–66), 29.
1443	Hunzinger, C.-H.	"Zur Struktur der Christus-Hymnen in Phil 2 und 1 Petr 3," in E. Lohse (ed.), *Der Ruf Jesu und die Antwort der Gemeinde: Exegetische Untersuchungen Joachim Jeremias zum 70sten Geburtstag* (Göttingen: Vandenhoeck & Ruprecht, 1970), 142–56.
1444	Hurst, L. D.	"Re-enter the Pre-existent Christ in Philippians 2. 5–11?," *NTS* 32 (1986), 449–57.
1445	Hurtado, L.	"Jesus as Lordly Example in Phil. 2:5–11," in J. C. Hurd and G. P. Richardson (eds.), *From Jesus to Paul: Studies in Honour of Francis Wright Beare* (Waterloo, Ont.: Wilfred Laurier University Press, 1984), 113–26.
1446	Jeremias, J.	"Zur Gedankenführung in den paulinischen Briefen," in J. N. Sevenster and W. C. van Unnik (eds.), *Studia Paulina in Honorem Johannes de Zwaan* (Haarlem: Bohm, 1953), 146–54.
1447	Jeremias, J.	"Zu Phil. ii. 7: *heauton ekenōsen,*" *NT* 6 (1963), 182–88.
1448	Jervell, J.	*Imago Dei: Gen. i, 26f im Spätjudentum in der Gnosis und in den Paulinischen Briefen* (FRLANT 63; Göttingen: Vandenhoeck & Ruprecht, 1960).

1449   Jewett, R.   "The Epistolary Thanksgiving and the Integrity of
                             Philippians," *NT* 12 (1970), 40–53.

1450   Käsemann, E.   "Kritische Analyse von Phil 2, 5–11," *ZThK* 47
                             (1950), 313–60. See also "A Critical Analysis of
                             Philippians 2:5–11," in *God and Christ: Existence
                             and Province* (New York: Harper and Row, 1968),
                             45–88.

1451   Kattenbusch, F.   "*Harpagmos? Hapragmon!* Phil. 2, 6: Ein Beitrag
                             zur paulinischen Christologie," *ThStKr* 104 (1932),
                             373–420.

1452   Krinetzki, L.   "Der Einfluß von Js 52, 13–53, 12 par auf Phil 2,
                             6–11," *ThQ* 139 (1959), 157–93, 292–336.

1453   Kruse, H.   " 'At the Name of Jesus All Beings Should Bend Their
                             Knees (Phil. 2:10),' " *Katorikku Kenkyu* 59 (1991),
                             39–56 [in Japanese].

1454   Larsson, E.   *Christus als Vorbild* (ASNU 23; Uppsala: Almqvist
                             & Wiksell, 1962), 230–75.

1455   Ligier, L.   "L'hymne christologique de Phil. 2, 6–11: La liturgie
                             eucharistique et la bénédiction synagogal 'Nishmat
                             Kol hay,' " in *Studia Paulina Congressus 1961, II*
                             (AnBib 18; Rome: Pontifical Biblical Institute, 1963),
                             65–74.

1456   Lohmeyer, E.   *Kyrios Jesus: Eine Untersuchung zur Phil. 2, 5–11*
                             (Heidelberg: C. Winter, 1928). Repr., Darmstadt:
                             Wissenschaftliche Buchgesellschaft, 1961.

1457   Loofs, F.   "Das altkirchliche Zeugnis gegen die herrschende
                             Auffassung der Kenosisstelle (Phil. 2. 5 bis 11),"
                             ThStKr 100 (1927–8), 1–102.

1458   Losie, L. A.   "A Note on the Interpretation of Phil. 2, 5," *ET* 90
                             (1978), 52–54.

1459   Magne, J.   "L'exaltation de Sabaôth dans *Hypostase des Ar-
                             chontes* 143, 1–31 et l'exaltation de Jésus dans
                             Philippiens 2, 6–11 ou la naissance de Jésus Christ,"
                             in *Cahiers du Cercle Ernest-Renan* 21 (1973), 1–56.

1460   Manns, F.   "Un hymne judéo-chrétien: Philippiens 2, 6–11," *ED*
                             29 (1976), 259–90.

1461   Marcheselli   "La celebrazione di Gesù Cristo Signore in Fil 2, 6–
       Casale, C.   11: Riflessioni letterario-storico-esegetiche sull' inno
                             cristologico," *Ephemerides Carmeliticae* 29 (1978),
                             2–42.

1462   Marshall, I. H.   "The Christ-Hymn in Philippians 2:5–11," *TynB* 19
                             (1968), 104–27.

1463   Martin, R. P.   *An Early Christian Confession: Philippians II. 5–11
                             in Recent Interpretation* (London: Tyndale, 1960).

1464   Martin, R. P.   "Carmen Christo," *VoxEv* 3 (1964), 51–57.

1465 Martin, R. P.   "The Form-Analysis of Philippians ii, 5–11," in *StE* 2 (1964), 611–20.

1466 Martin, R. P.   *Carmen Christi: Philippians ii, 5–11 in Recent Interpretation and in the Setting of Early Christian Worship* (SNTSMS 3; Cambridge: University Press, 1967). Rev. ed., Grand Rapids, Mich.: Eerdmans, 1983.

1467 Michel, O.   "Zur Exegese von Phil 2,5–11," in *Theologie als Glaubenswagnis: Festschrift für K. Heim* (Hamburg: Furche, 1954), 79–95.

1468 Minear, P. S.   "Singing and Suffering in Philippi," in R. T. Fortna and B. R. Gaventa (eds.), *The Conversation Continues: Studies in Paul and John in Honor of J. Louis Martyn* (Nashville: Abingdon Press, 1990), 202–19.

1469 Moule, C. F. D.   "Further Reflections on Philippians 2:5–11," in W. W. Gasque and R. P. Martin (eds.), *Apostolic History and the Gospel: Essays Presented to F. F. Bruce* (Exeter: Paternoster, 1970), 264–76.

1470 Müller, U. B.   "Der Christushymnus Phil 2,6–11," *ZNW* 79 (1988), 17–44.

1471 Murphy-O'Connor, J.   "Christological Anthropology in Phil 2:6–11," *RB* 83 (1974), 25–50.

1472 Nagata, T.   "Philippians 2:5–11: A Case Study in the Contextual Shaping of Early Christology" (Ph.D. Dissertation: Princeton Theological Seminary, 1981).

1473 Neufeld, V. H.   *The Earliest Christian Confessions* (NTTS 5; Leiden: Brill, 1963).

1474 O'Brien, P. T.   "Divine Provision for Our Needs: Assurances from Philippians 4," *RThR* 50 (1991), 21–29.

1475 O'Brien, P. T.   *Commentary on Philippians* (New International Greek Testament Commentary; Grand Rapids, Mich.: Eerdmans, 1991), 186–271.

1476 Pintard, J.   "Christologie paulinienne: Observations sur l'hymne christologique de l'Épître aux Philippiens et sur l'ensemble de la christologie paulinienne," *EspVie* 83 (1973), 328–33.

1477 Reule, G.   "The Christology of Philippians 2:5–11," *Springfielder* 35 (1971), 81–85.

1478 Riesenfeld, H.   "Unpoetische Hymnen im Neuen Testament? Zu Phil 2, 1–11," in J. Kiilunen, V. Riekkinen und H. Räisänen (eds.), *Glaube und Gerechtigkeit: In Memoriam Rafael Gyllenberg* (Helsinki: Suomen Eksegeettisen Seura, 1983), 155–68.

1479 Rissi, M.   "Der Christushymnus in Phil 2, 6–11," *ANRW* II, 25.4 (1987), 3314–26.

1480 Robinson, D. W. B.   *"harpagmos:* The Deliverance Jesus Refused?," *ET* 80 (1968–69), 253–54.

1481 Ross, J.   "HARPAGMOS (Phil. ii. 6)," *JThS* O.S. 10 (1909), 573–74.

1482 Sanders, J. A.   "Dissenting Deities and Philippians 2, 1–11," *JBL* 88 (1969), 278–90.

1483 Schumacher, H.   *Christus in seiner Präexistenz und Kenose nach Phil. 2, 5–8: I, Exegetisch-kritische Untersuchung* (Rome: Verlag des päpstlichen Bibelinstituts, 1914). Ibid., *II, Historische Untersuchung* (Rome: Verlag des päpstlichen Bibelinstituts, 1921).

1484 Schweizer, E.   *Erniedrigung und Erhöhung bei Jesus und seinen Nachfolgern* (AThANT 28; Zürich: Zwingli-Verlag, 1962), esp. 51–55, 112–16.

1485 Söding, T.   "Erniedrigung und Erhöhung: Erwägungen zum Verhältnis von Christologie und Mythos am Beispiel des Philipperhymnus (Phil 2,6–11)," *TheolPhil* 67 (1992), 1–28.

1486 Stagg, F.   "The Mind of Jesus Christ: Philippians 1:27–2:18," *RevExp* 77 (1980), 337–47.

1487 Stanley, D. M.   "The Theme of the Servant of Yahweh in Primitive Christian Soteriology and Its Transcription by St. Paul," *CBQ* 16 (1954), 385–425, esp. 420–25.

1488 Strecker, G.   "Redaktion und Tradition im Christushymnus: Phil. 2. 6–11," *ZNW* 55 (1964), 63–78.

1489 Strecker, G.   "Freiheit und Agape: Exegese und Predigt über Phil 2, 5–11," in H. D. Betz and L. Schottrof (eds.), *Neues Testament und christliche Existenz: Festschrift für Herbert Braun* (Tübingen: Mohr, 1973), 523–38.

1490 Strimple, R. B.   "Philippians 2:5–11 in Recent Studies: Some Exegetical Conclusions," *WThJ* 41 (1979), 247–68.

1491 Talbert, C. H.   "The Problem of Pre-existence in Phil. 2:6–11," *JBL* 86 (1967), 141–53.

1492 Thekkekara, M.   "A Neglected Idiom in an Overstudied Passage (Phil 2:6–8)," *Louvain Studies* 17 (1992), 306–14.

1493 Thomas, J.   "L'hymne de l'Épître aux Philippiens," *Christus* 22 (1975), 334–45.

1494 Thomas, T. A.   "The Kenosis Question," *EvQ* 42 (1970), 142–51.

1495 Trudinger, P.   "A Down-to-Earth Ascension?: A Note on Philippians 2:6–9," *Faith and Freedom* 44 (1991), 126–29.

1496 Vokes, F. E.   *"harpagmos* in Phil. 2:5–11," *StE* 2 (1964), 670–75.

1497 Wallace, D. H.   "A Note on morphé," *ThZ* 22 (1966), 19–25.

1498 Wanamaker, C. A.   "Philippians 2. 6–11: Son of God or Adamic Christology?," *NTS* 33 (1987), 179–93.

1499	Warren, W.	"On *heauton ekenōsen*," *JThS* O.S. 12 (1911), 461–63.
1500	Wong, T. Y. C.	"The Problem of Pre-Existence in Philippians 2, 6–11," *EThL* 62 (1986), 267–82.
1501	Wong, T. Y. C.	"Christ's Mind, Paul's Mind," *Louvain Studies* 17 (1992), 293–305.
1502	Wright, N. T.	"*harpagmos* and the Meaning of Philippians 2:5–11," *JThS* N.S. 37 (1986), 321–52.

Colossians

1503	Aletti, J. N.	*Colossiens 1, 15–20: genre et exégèse du texte fonction de la thématique sapientielle* (AnBib 91; Rome: Pontifical Biblical Institute, 1981).
1504	Bammel, E.	"Versuche zu Col 1, 15–20," *ZNW* 52 (1961), 88–95.
1505	Beasley-Murray, P.	"Colossians 1:15–20: An Early Christian Hymn Celebrating the Lordship of Christ," in D. A. Hagner and M. J. Harris (eds.), *Pauline Studies* (Grand Rapids, Mich.: Eerdmans, 1980), 169–83.
1506	Benoit, P.	"L'hymne christologique de Col 1, 15–20: jugement critique sur l'état des recherches," in J. Neusner (ed.), *Christianity, Judaism and Other Greco-Roman Cults: Studies for Morton Smith at Sixty. Part One, New Testament* (SJLA 12; Leiden: Brill, 1975), 226–63.
1507	Burger, C.	*Schöpfung und Versöhnung: Studien zum liturgischen Gut im Kolosser und Epheserbrief* (WMANT 46; Neukirchen-Vluyn: Neukirchener Verlag, 1975).
1508	Eckart, K.-G.	"Exegetische Beobachtungen zu Kol 1, 9–20," *ThV* 7 (1960), 87–106.
1509	Eckart, K.-G.	"Ursprüngliche Tauf- und Ordinationsliturgie," *ThV* 8 (1962), 23–37.
1510	Feuillet, A.	*Christologie paulinienne et tradition biblique* (Paris: Desclée, 1973), 48–81.
1511	Gabuthuler, H. J.	*Jesus Christus: Haupt der Kirche — Haupt der Welt: Der Christushymnus Colosser 1, 15–20 in der theologischer Forschung der letzten 130 Jahre* (AThANT 45; Zürich: Zwingli-Verlag, 1965).
1512	Glasson, T. F.	"Colossians I 18, 15 and Sirach XXIV," *NT* 11 (1969), 154–56.
1513	Hegermann, H.	*Die Vorstellung vom Schöpfungsmittler im hellenistischen Judentum und Urchristentum* (TU 82; Berlin: Akademie-Verlag, 1961).

1514   Hiebert, D. E.   "Epaphras, Man of Prayer," *BibSac* 136 (1979), 54–64.

1515   Jervell, J.   *Imago Dei: Gen. i, 26f im Spätjudentum in der Gnosis und in den Paulinischen Briefen* (FRLANT 63; Göttingen: Vandenhoeck & Ruprecht, 1960).

1516   Käsemann, E.   "A Primitive Baptismal Liturgy," in *Essays on New Testament Themes* (Philadelphia: Fortress Press, 1982), 149–68. See also E. Wolf (ed.), *Festschrift Rudolph Bultmann zum 65. Geburtstag überreicht* (Stuttgart: Kohlhammer, 1949), 133–48.

1517   Kehl, N.   *Der Christushymnus im Kolosserbrief: Eine motivgeschichtliche Untersuchung zu Kol. 1, 12–20* (SBM 1; Stuttgart: Katholisches Bibelwerk, 1955, 1967).

1518   Kendrick, W. G.   "Prayer in Colossians and Ephesians" (Dissertation: Baylor University, 1976).

1519   Lyonnet, S.   "L'hymne christologique de l'Épître aux Colossiens et la fête juive du Nouvel An," *RSR* 48 (1960), 92–100.

1520   Marcheselli   "Der christologische Hymnus: Kol 1, 15–20 im Di-
        Casale, C.   enste der Versöhnung und des Friedens," *Teresianum* 40 (1989), 3–21.

1521   Martin, R. P.   "An Early Christian Hymn (Col. 1:15–20)," *EvQ* 36 (1964), 195–205.

1522   Masson, C.   "L'hymne christologique de l'épître aux Colossiens I,15–30 (sic)," *RThPh* N.S. 36 (1948), 138–42.

1523   Maurer, C.   "Die Begründung der Herrschaft Christi über die Mächte nach Kolosser 1, 15–20," *WD* N.F. 4 (1955), 75–93.

1524   McCown, W.   "The Hymnic Structure of Colossians 1:15–20," *EvQ* 51 (1979), 156–62.

1525   Mullens, T. Y.   "The Thanksgivings of Philemon and Colossians," *NTS* 30 (1984), 288–93.

1526   O'Brien, P. T.   "Col. 1:20 and the Reconciliation of All Things," *RThR* 33 (1974), 45–53.

1527   O'Neill, J. C.   "The Source of the Christology in Colossians," *NTS* 26 (1979–80), 87–100.

1528   Robinson, J. M.   "A Formal Analysis of Colossians 1:15–20," *JBL* 76 (1957), 270–87.

1529   Schnackenburg, R.   "Die Aufnahme des Christushymnus durch den Verfasser des Kolosserbriefes" (EKKNTV 1; Neukirchen/Zürich: Neukirchener/Benziger, 1969), 33–50.

1530	Schweizer, E.	"Kolosser 1, 15–20" (EKKNTV 1; Neukirchen/ Zürich: Neukirchener/Benziger, 1969), 7–31 = Beiträge zur Theologie des Neuen Testaments: Neutestamentliche Aufsätze (1955–70) (Zürich: Zwingli, 1970), 113–45.
1531	Teste, E.	"Gesù Pacificatore universale: Inno liturgico della Chiesa Madre (Col 1, 15–20 + Ef 2, 14–16)," (Franciscan) Liber Annuus 19 (1969), 5–64.
1532	Tripp, D.	"The 'Colossian Hymn': Seeking a Version to Praise With," One in Christ 26 (1990), 231–37.
1533	Vawter, B.	"The Colossians Hymn and the Principle of Redaction," CBQ 33 (1971), 62–81.
1534	Wink, W.	"The Hymn of the Cosmic Christ," in R. T. Fortna and B. R. Gaventa (eds.), The Conversation Continues: Studies in Paul and John in Honor of J. Louis Martyn (Nashville: Abingdon Press, 1990), 235–45.
1535	Wright, N. T.	"Poetry and Theology in Colossians 1. 15–20," NTS 36 (1990), 444–68.

1 and 2 Thessalonians

1536	Aus, R. D.	"The Liturgical Background of the Necessity and Propriety of Giving Thanks according to 2 Thess 1:3," JBL 92 (1973), 432–38.
1537	Friedrich, G.	"Ein Tauflied hellenistischer Judenchristen, 1. Thess 1,9f.," ThZ 21 (1965), 502–16.

1 Timothy

1538	Dibelius, M., and Conzelmann, H.	The Pastoral Epistles (ETrans.; Philadelphia: Fortress, 1972), 61–63, for concise comparison of 1 Tim 3:16 with contemporary literature.
1539	Gundry, R. H.	"The Form, Meaning and Background of the Hymn Quoted in 1 Timothy 3:16," in W. W. Gasque and R. P. Martin (eds.), Apostolic History and the Gospel: Festschrift F. F. Bruce (Exeter, U.K.: Paternoster, 1970), 203–22.
1540	Klöpper, A.	"Zur Christologie der Pastoralbriefe (1 Tim 3, 16)," ZWTh 45 (1902), 347–61.
1541	Manns, F.	"L'hymne judéo-chrétien de 1 Tim 3, 16," ED 32 (1979), 323–39.
1542	Metzger, W.	Der Christushymnus 1. Timotheus 3, 16: Fragment einer Homologie der paulinischen Gemeinden (Stuttgart: Calwer Verlag, 1979).

1543 Oke, G. C.   "A Doxology Not to God but to Christ," *ET* 67 (1956), 367–68.

1544 Schweizer, E.   "Two New Testament Creeds Compared, I Corinthians 15.3–5 and I Timothy 3.16," in W. Klassen (ed.), *Current Issues in New Testament Interpretation: Studies in Honor of Otto A. Piper* (New York: Harper, 1962), 166–77, 291–93. See also *Neotestamentica: Deutsche und Englisch Aufsätze 1951–1963* (Zürich: Zwingli-Verlag, 1963), 122–35.

1545 Stenger, W.   "Der Christushymnus in 1 Tm 3, 16. Aufbau — Christologie — Sitz im Leben," *TThZ* 78 (1969), 33–48.

1546 Stenger, W.   *Der Christushymnus 1 Tim 3,16: Eine strukturanalytische Untersuchung* (Regensburger Studien zur Theologie 6; Frankfurt: Peter Lang, 1977).

1547 Windisch, H.   "Zur Theologie der Pastoralbriefe," *ZNW* 34 (1935), 213–38, esp. 222–30.

Hebrews

1548 Attridge, H. W.   " 'Heard Because of His Reverence" (Heb 5:7)," *JBL* 98 (1979), 90–93.

1549 Colless, B. E.   "The Letter to the Hebrews and the Song of the Pearl," *Abr-Nahrain* 25 (1987), 40–55.

1550 Grässer, E.   "Hebräer 1, 1–4: Ein exegetischer Versuch," in R. Pesch (ed.), EKKNTV 3 (Neukirchen: Neukirchener Verlag, 1971), 55–91. Repr. in *Text und Situation: Gesammelte Aufsätze zum Neuen Testament* (Gütersloh: Mohn, 1973), 182–230.

1551 Hernández, V. M.   "La vida sacerdotal de los cristianos según la carta a los Hebreos," *RevBib* 52 (1990), 145–52.

1552 Jeremias, J.   "Hebr 5 7-10," *ZNW* 44 (1952–53), 107–11.

1553 Kelly, D. F.   "Prayer and Union with Christ," *Scottish Bulletin of Evangelical Theology* 8 (1990), 109–27.

1554 Loader, W. R. G.   *Sohn und Hoherpriester: Eine traditionsgeschichtliche Untersuchung zur Christologie des Hebräerbriefes* (WMANT 53; Neukirchen-Vluyn: Neukirchener Verlag, 1981), 68–80.

1555 Robinson, D. W. B.   "The Literary Structure of Hebrews 1:1–4," *AJBA* 2 (1972), 178–86.

1556 Vanhoye, A.   *Situation du Christ: épître aux Hébreux 1–2* (Lectio divina 58; Paris: Cerf, 1969), 11–14.

James

1557	Bottini, G. C.	*La preghiera di Elia in Giacomo 5, 17–18: Studia della traduzione biblica e giudaica* (Jerusalem: Francisan Printing Press, 1981).
1558	Hamman, A.	"Prière et culte dans la lettre de Saint Jacques," *EThL* 34 (1958), 35–47.
1559	Mayer, B.	"Jak 5:13 — ein Plädoyer für das Bittgebet in der Kirche," in R. Hübner (ed.), *Der Dienst für den Menschen in Theologie und Verkündigung* (Regensburg: Pustet Verlag, 1981), 165–78.
1560	Omanson, R. L.	"The Certainty of Judgment and the Power of Prayer: James 5," *RevExp* 83 (1986), 427–38.
1561	Vouga, F.	"Jacques 5, 13–18," *ETR* 53 (1978), 103–9.
1562	Warrington, K.	"Some Observations on James 5:13–18," *EPTA Bulletin* 8 (1989), 160–77.
1563	Wells, C. R.	"The Theology of Prayer in James," *Criswell Theological Review* 1 (1986), 85–112.

1 Peter

1564	Boismard, M.-E.	*Quatre hymnes baptismales dans la première épître de Pierre* (Lectio divina 30, Paris: Cerf, 1961).
1565	Bultmann, R.	"Bekenntnis- und Liedfragmente im ersten Petrusbrief," *CNT* 11 (1947), 1–14.
1566	Clarke, W. K. L.	"The First Epistle of St. Peter and the Odes of Solomon," *JThS* O.S. 15 (1914), 47–52.

Johannine Letters

1567	Bauernfeind, O.	"Die Fürbitte angesichts der 'Sünde zum Tode,' " in *Von der Antike zum Christentum: Untersuchungen als Festgabe für Victor Schultze zum 80. Geburtstag am 13. Dezember 1931, dargebracht von Greifswalder Kollegen* (Stettin: Fischer & Schmidt, 1931), (43) 45–54.
1568	Manueliguens, M.	"Sin, Prayer, Life in 1 Jn. 5:16," in E. Testa, M. Ignazio, and M. Piccirillo (eds.), *Studia hierosolymitana in onore del p. Bellarmino Bagatti, 2, Studi eseagetici* (Jerusalem: Franciscan Printing Press, 1976), 64–82.

Apocalypse of John

1569 Aune, D. E. "The Influence of Roman Imperial Court Ceremonial on the Apocalypse of John," *BR* 28 (1983), 5–26, esp. 14–20.

1570 Bauckham, R. J. "The Worship of Jesus in Apocalyptic Christianity," *NTS* 27 (1981), 322–41.

1571 Cabaniss, A. "A Note on the Liturgy of the Apocalypse," *Interp* 7 (1953), 78–80.

1572 Carnegie, D. R. "Worthy Is the Lamb: The Hymns in Revelation," in H. H. Rowdon (ed.), *Christ The Lord: Studies in Christology Presented to D. Guthrie* (Downers Grove, Ill.: IVP, 1982), 243–56.

1573 Comblin, J. *Le Christ dans l'Apocalypse* (Bibliothèque de Théologie, série 3, vol. 6; Tournai: Desclée, 1965). See esp. discussion of the Apocalypse and the imperial cult on 99–106.

1574 Cothenet, E. "Earthly and Heavenly Liturgy according to the Book of Revelation," in *Roles in the Liturgical Assembly* (ETrans. M. J. O'Connell; New York: Pueblo Publishing Co., 1981), 115–35.

1575 Delling, G. "Zum gottesdienstlichen Stil der Johannesapokalypse," *NT* 3 (1959), 107–37.

1576 Hahn, F. "Liturgische Elemente in den Rahmenstücken der Johannesoffenbarung," in W. D. Hauschild, C. Nicolaisen, and D. Wendebourg (eds.), *Kirchengemeinschaft — Anspruch und Wirklichkeit: Festschrift für Georg Kretschmar zum 60. Geburtstag* (Stuttgart: Calwer Verlag, 1986), 43–57. Brief analysis of the hymnic material, as well as the doxologies and acclamations of the Apocalypse.

1577 Harris, M. A. "The Literary Function of Hymns in the Apocalypse of John" (Ph.D. Dissertation: Southern Baptist Theological Seminary, 1989).

1578 Horst, J. *Proskynesis* (Gütersloh: Bertelsmann, 1932), 269–91.

1579 Jörns, K.-P. *Das hymnische Evangelium: Untersuchungen zu Aufbau, Funktion und Herkunft der hymnischen Stücke in der Johannesoffenbarung* (StNT 5; Gütersloh: Mohn, 1971), esp. 17–22, 161–66.

1580 Mowry, L. "Revelation 4–5 and Early Christian Liturgical Usage," *JBL* 71 (1952), 75–84.

1581 Ng, Esther Yue L. "Prayer in Revelation," in D. A. Carson (ed.), *Teach Us to Pray: Prayer in the Bible and the World* (Exeter, U.K.: Paternoster/Baker, 1990), 119–35, 332–35.

1582 O'Rourke, J. J. "The Hymns of the Apocalypse," *CBQ* 30 (1968), 399–409.

1583 Piper, O. A. "The Apocalypse of John and the Liturgy of the Ancient Church," *Church History* 20 (1951), 10–22.

1584 Prigent, P. *Apocalypse et liturgie* (Cahiers théologiques 52; Neuchâtel: Éditions Delachaux et Niestlé, 1964).

1585 Sattler, W. "Das Buch mit der sieben Siegeln, I: Das Gebet der Märtyrer," *ZNW* 20 (1921), 231–40.

1586 Shepherd, M. H. *The Paschal Liturgy and the Apocalypse* (Ecumenical Studies in Worship 6; London: Lutterworth, 1960).

1587 Thompson, L. L. "Cult and Eschatology in the Apocalypse of John," *JR* 49 (1969), 330–50.

6. EARLY CHRISTIAN TEXTS (TO C. 325 C.E.)

1588 Atchley, E. G. Cuthbert F. *On the Epiclesis of the Eucharistic Liturgy and in the Consecration of the Font* (London: Oxford University Press, 1935), esp. section B §1–11 (pps. 3–50).

1589 Bardy, G. *La vie spirituelle d'après les pères des trois premiers siècles* (2 vols.; Tournai: Desclée, 1968), 1:24–33 (Didache), 95–97 (Apostolic Constitutions), 113–22 (Clement of Rome); 2:22–25, 41–49 (Clement of Alexandria), 113–26 (Origen), 167–70 (Tertullian).

1590 Barnes, W. E. *Early Christians at Prayer* (London: Methuen, 1925).

1591 Baumstark, A. "Abendgebet," *RAC* 1, cols. 9–12.

1592 Baumstark, A. "Trishagion und Qeduscha," *JLW* 3 (1923), 18–32.

1593 Baumstark, A. *Comparative Liturgy* (ETrans.; Westminster, Md.: Newman Press, 1958), chs. 4 and 5.

1594 Baumstark, A. *Vom geschichtlichen Werden der Liturgie* (Darmstadt: Wissenschaftliche Buchgesellschaft, 1971).

1595 Baus, K. "Das Gebet der Märtyrer," *TThZ* 62 (1953), 19–32.

1596 Beckwith, R. T. "The Daily and Weekly Worship of the Primitive Church in Relation to Its Jewish Antecedents, Part 1," *EvQ* 56 (1984), 65–80.

1597 Beeck, F. J. van "The Worship of Christians in Pliny's Letter," *StLi* 18 (1988), 121–31.

1598 Békés, G. *De continua oratione Clem. Alexandrini doctrina* (Rome, 1942).

1599 Berselli, C., and Gharib, G. (ed.) *Sing the Joys of Mary: Hymns from the First Millennium of the Eastern and Western Churches* (Wilton, Conn.: Morehouse-Barlow, 1983).

1600 Betz, O. "Early Christian Cult in the Light of Qumran," *RSB* 2 (1982), 73–85.

1601 Biehl, L. *Das liturgische Gebet für Kaiser und Reich* (Paderborn: Schöningh, 1937).

1602 Bondi, R. C. *To Pray and to Love: Conversations on Prayer with the Early Church* (Philadelphia: Fortress, 1991).

1603 Bouyer, L. *The Theology and Spirituality of the Eucharistic Prayer* (ETrans. C. U. Quinn; Notre Dame, Ind.: University of Notre Dame Press, 1968), 119–35.

1604 Bradshaw, P. F. *Daily Prayer in the Early Church: A Study of the Origin and Development of the Divine Office* (New York: Oxford University Press, 1982).

1605 Bradshaw, P. F. "The Search for the Origins of Christian Liturgy: Some Methodological Reflections," *StLi* 17 (1987), 26–34.

1606 Burney, C. F. *Aramaic Origin of the Fourth Gospel* (Oxford: Clarendon, 1922), 161–63. Discussion of the prayers in Ignatius.

1607 Burns, S. "The Beginnings of Christian Liturgy in Judaism," *SIDIC* 17 (1984), 11–13.

1608 Cabrol, F. "La doxologie dans la prière chrétienne des premiers siècles," *RSR* 18 (1928), 9–30.

1609 Cabrol, F. *La prière des premiers chrétiens* (La vie chrétienne 8; Paris: Grasset, 1929). ETrans.: New York: Benziger Brothers, 1930.

1610 Capelle, B. "Le texte du Gloria in excelsis," *RHE* 44 (1949), 437–57.

1611 Cerfaux, L. "La prière dans le christianisme primitif," *Recueil Lucien Cerfaux, III (Suppl.)* (Gembloux: J. Duculot, 1962), 253–62.

1612 Chadwick, H. "Prayer at Midnight," in J. Fontaine and C. Kannengiesser (eds.), *Epektasis: offerts au cardinal Jean Daniélou* (Paris: Éditions Beauchesne, 1972), 47–49.

1613 Chadwick, O. "The Origins of Prime," *JThS* O.S. 49 (1948), 178–82.

1614 Church, F. Forrester, and Mulray, T. J. (eds.) *The Macmillan Book of Earliest Christian Hymns* (London: Collier Macmillan, 1988).

1615 Clerici, L. *Einsammlung der Zerstreuten: Liturgiegeschichtliche Untersuchung zur Vor- und Nachgeschichte der Fürbitte für die Kirche in Didache 9, 4 und 10, 5* (Münster: Aschendorff, 1966).

1616 Connolly, R. H. "The Eucharistic Prayer of Hippolytus," *JThS* O.S. 39 (1938), 350–69.

1617 Couratin, A. H.   "The Thanksgiving: An Essay," in B. D. Spinks (ed.), *The Sacrifice of Praise: Studies on the Themes of Thanksgiving and Redemption in the Central Prayers of the Eucharistic and Baptismal Liturgies, in Honour of Arthur Hubert Couratin* (Rome: Edizioni Liturgiche, 1981), 20–61, esp. 20–36.

1618 Crouzel, H.   "Les doxologies finales des homélies d'Origène selon le texte grec et les versions latines," in V. Saxer (ed.), *Ecclesia orans: mélanges patristiques offerts au Père Adalbert G. Hamman OFM à l'occasion de ses quarante ans d'enseignement* (Rome: Institute Patristicum "Augustinium," 1980), 95–107.

1619 Cuming, G. J.   "Egyptian Elements in the Jerusalem Liturgy," *JThS* 25 (1974), 117–24. Eucharistic prayer.

1620 Cunningham, A.   *Prayer: Personal and Liturgical* (Message of the Fathers of the Church 6; Wilmington, Del.: Glazier, 1985).

1621 Cyprian, St.   *L'oraison dominicale: Text, Translation, Introduction and Notes by Michel Reveillaud* (Paris: Presses universitaires de France, 1964).

1622 Daneels, G., and Maertens, T.   *La prière eucharistique, formes anciennes et conception nouvelle du canon de la messe* (Paris: Éditions du Centurion, 1967).

1623 Deiss, L.   *Hymnes et prières des premiers siècles: Textes choisis et traduits* (Paris: Fleurus, 1963).

1624 Deiss, L.   *Early Sources of the Liturgy* (London: G. Chapman, 1967), ch. 2.

1625 Dibelius, M.   "Die Mahl-Gebete der Didache," *ZNW* 37 (1938), 32–41.

1626 Dinesen, P.   "Die Epiklese im Rahmen altchristlicher Liturgien," *StTh* 16 (1962), 42–107.

1627 Dix, G.   "The Origins of the Epiclesis," *Theol* 28 (1934), 125–37, 187–202.

1628 Dix, G.   *The Shape of the Liturgy* (London: A. & C. Black, 1964), 126–31, ch. 7.

1629 Dix, G.   *The Apostolic Tradition of St. Hippolytus* (London: S.P.C.K., 1968²; reissued Alban Press/Morehouse, 1992), 29, 39, 57–58, 61–68. See also bibliography at the conclusion of the Preface to the second edition.

1630 Dölger, F.-J.   *Sol Salutis: Gebet und Gesang im christlichen Altertum* (Münster: Aschendorff, 1920, 1925²).

1631 Dölger, F.-J.   "Lumen Christi: Untersuchungen zum abendlichen Licht-Segen im Antike und Christentum," in *Antike und Christentum, Kultur- und religionsgeschichtliche Studien 5* (Münster: Aschendorff, 1936), 1–43.

1632 Dölger, F.-J. "Das Niedersitzen nach dem Gebet: Eine Auseinandersetzung zwischen Christentum und Heidentum im häuslich und liturgischen Gebetsbrauch: Ein Kommentar zu Tertullianus de Oratione 16," in Antike und Christentum, Kultur- und religionsgeschichtliche Studien 5 (Münster: Aschendorff, 1936), 116–37.

1633 Duchesne, L. Origines du culte chrétien: étude sur la liturgie avant Charlemagne (Paris: Thorin, 1920), esp. 47–57.

1634 Evans, E. Tertullian's Tract on Prayer (London: S.P.C.K., 1953).

1635 Ferguson, E. "Spiritual Sacrifice in Early Christianity and Its Environment," ANRW II, 23.2 (1980), 1164, 1168–69, 1172–78, 1181–86, 1188.

1636 Ferguson, J. "Hymns in the Early Church," Bulletin of the Hymn Society of Great Britain and Ireland 12 (1989), 114–23.

1637 Fischer, B. "Le Christ dans les Psaumes: la devotion aux Psaumes dans l'Église des Martyrs," MD 27 (1951), 86–109.

1638 Fischer, B. "The Common Prayer of Congregation and Family in the Ancient Church," StLi 10 (1974), 106–24. See also "La prière ecclésiale et familiale dans le christianisme ancien," MD 116 (1973), 41–58.

1639 Froger, J. Les origines de prime (Rome: Edizioni Liturgiche, 1946).

1640 Gamber, K. Sacrificium Laudis: Zur Geschichte des frühchristlichen Eucharistiegebets (Regensburg: Pustet, 1973).

1641 Gelineau, J. "Les psaumes à l'époque patristique," MD 135 (1978), 99–116.

1642 Gero, S. "The So-called Ointment Prayer in the Coptic Version of the Didache: A Re-evaluation," HThR 70 (1977), 67–84.

1643 Gessel, W. Die Theologie des Gebetes nach "De Oratione" von Origenes (Munich/Paderborn/Vienna: Schöningh, 1975).

1644 Giraudo, C. La struttura lettereria della preghiera eucaristica (AnBib 92; Rome: Pontifical Biblical Institute, 1981).

1645 Glaue, P. "Amen nach seiner Bedeutung und Verwendung in der alten Kirche," ZKG 44 (1925), 184–98.

1646 Goltz, E. A. Freiherr von der Das Gebet in der ältesten Christenheit (Leipzig: J. C. Hinrichs, 1901). See esp. ch. 3 (123–240) "Das Gebet der Christen im apostolischen und nachapostolischen Zeitalter."

1647 Goltz, E. A. Freiherr von der — *Tischgebete und Abendmahlsgebete in der altchristliche und in der griechische Kirche* (Leipzig: J. C. Hinrichs, 1905).

1648 Grossi, V. — "Il contesto battesimale dell'oratio dominica nei commenti di Tertulliano, Cipriano, Agostino," in V. Saxer (ed.), *Ecclesia orans: mélanges patristiques offerts au Père Adalbert G. Hamman OFM à l'occasion de ses quarante ans d'enseignement* (Rome: Institute Patristicum "Augustinium," 1980), 205–20.

1649 Guillaumont, A. — "Le problème de la prière continuelle dans le monarchisme ancien," in H. Limet and J. Ries (eds.), *L'expérience de la prière dans les grandes religions: actes du colloque de Louvain-la-Neuve et Liège (22–23 novembre 1978)* (Louvain-la-Neuve: Centre d'histoire des religions, 1980), 285–94.

1650 Hadidian, D. Y. — "The Background and Origin of the Christian Hours of Prayers," *TS* 25 (1964), 59–69.

1651 Hamman, A. — "Genèse et signification de la prière aux origines chrétiennes," in *Studia Patristica* 2 (TU 64; Berlin: Akademie-Verlag, 1957), 468–84.

1652 Hamman, A. — *Prières eucharistiques des premiers siècles* (Paris: Desclée, 1957).

1653 Hamman, A. — *La prière: les trois premiers siècles* (Paris, 1963).

1654 Hamman, A. — "Du symbole de la foi à l'anaphore eucharistique," in P. Granfield and J. A. Jungmann (eds.), *Kyriakon: Festschrift Johannes Quasten* (2 vols.; Münster: Aschendorff, 1970), 835–43.

1655 Hamman, A. — *Vie quotidienne des premiers chrétiens* (Paris: Hachette, 1971), 197–218.

1656 Hamman, A. — *Abrégé de la prière chrétienne* (Paris: Desclée, 1987).

1657 Hamman, A. — *Das Gebet in der Alten Kirche* (Bern/New York: P. Lang, 1989).

1658 Hamman, A. (ed.) — *Prières des premiers chrétiens* (Paris: A. Fayard, 1952).

1659 Hamman, A. (ed.) — *Early Christian Prayers* (ETrans., W. Mitchell; Chicago: Regnery, 1961).

1660 Hanson, R. P. C. — "The Liberty of the Bishop to Improvise Prayer in the Eucharist," *VigChr* 15 (1961), 173–76.

1661 Hatzinikolaou, N. S. (ed.) — *Voices in the Wilderness: An Anthology of Patristic Prayers* (Brookline, Mass.: Holy Cross Orthodox Press, 1988).

1662 Hausherr, I. — "Comment priaient les Pères," *RAM* 32 (1956), 33–58, 282–96.

1663 Holtzmann, O.   "Die täglichen Gebetsstunden im Judentum und Urchristentum," *ZNW* 12 (1911), 90–107.

1664 Houssiau, A.   "Les moments de la prière eucharistique," in H. Limet and J. Ries (eds.), *L'expérience de la prière dans les grandes religions: actes du colloque de Louvain-la-Neuve et Liège (22–23 novembre 1978)* (Louvain-la-Neuve: Centre d'histoire des religions, 1980), 325–34.

1665 Instinsky, H. U.   *Die alte Kirche und das Heil des Staates* (Munich: Kösel, 1963), esp. 41–60, 61–65.

1666 Jasper, R. C. D., and Cuming, G. J. (eds.)   *Prayers of the Eucharist: Early and Reformed* (New York: Pueblo Publishing House, 1987), Part 1, esp. chs. 1–5. Originally published London: Collins, 1975.

1667 Jay, E. J.   *Origen's Treatise on Prayer* (London: S.P.C.K., 1954).

1668 Jouassard, G.   "L'Ancien Testament dans la prière des premières communautés chrétiennes," in M. Jourjon et al. (eds.), *À la rencontre de Dieu, Mémorial A. Gelin* (Le Puy: Éditions Xavier Mappus, 1961), 355–62.

1669 Jungmann, J. A.   "Altkristliche Gebetsordnungen im Lichte des Regelbuches von 'En Fescha,'" *ZKTh* 75 (1953), 215–19.

1670 Jungmann, J. A.   *The Early Liturgy to the Time of Gregory the Great* (Notre Dame, Ind.: University of Notre Dame Press, 1959), 97–108.

1671 Jungmann, J. A.   *Der Gottesdienst der Kirche* (Innsbruck/Vienna/Munich: Tyrolia Verlag, 1962), esp. 11–27.

1672 Jungmann, J. A.   *The Place of Christ in Liturgical Prayer* (New York: Alba House, 1965), esp. chs. 1, 2, 9, and 10.

1673 Kehl, A.   "Beiträge zum Verständnis einiger gnostischer und frühchristlicher Psalmen und Hymnen," *JAC* 15 (1972), 92–119.

1674 Kilmartin, E. J.   "The Eucharistic Prayer: Content and Function of Some Early Eucharistic Prayers," in R. Clifford and G. W. MacRae (eds.), *Word in the World* (Cambridge, Mass.: Weston College Press, 1973), 117–34.

1675 Kilmartin, E. J.   "Sacrificium Laudis: Content and Function of Early Eucharistic Prayers," *TS* 35 (1974), 268–87.

1676 Kraemar, C. J.   "Pliny and the Early Church Service," *ClB* 39 (1934), 293–300.

1677 Kroll, J.   "Hymnen," in E. Hennecke (ed.), *Neutestamentliche Apokryphen* (Tübingen: Mohr, 1924²), 596–601.

1678 Kroll, J.   "Die Hymnendichtung des frühen Christentums," *Antike* 2 (1926), 258–81.

1679 Kurfess, A. "Plinius und der urchristliche Gottesdienst," ZNW 35 (1936), 295–98.

1680 Lamb, J. A. The Psalms in Christian Worship (London: Faith Press, 1962). See esp. chs. 1–3: (1) The Psalms in Hebrew Worship, (2) the Psalms in the New Testament, (3) the Psalms in the Early Church.

1681 Lebreton, J. "La prière dans l'église primitive," RSR 14 (1924), 5–32, 97–133.

1682 Ledogar, R. J. Acknowledgement: Praise-Verbs in the Early Greek Anaphora (Rome: Herder, 1968).

1683 Légasse, S. "La prière pour les chefs d'état: antécédents judaïques et témoins chrétiens du premier siècle," NT 29 (1987), 236–53. Discusses in particular the Pastoral Epistles and sub-apostolic literature.

1684 Leipoldt, J. Der Gottesdienst der ältesten Kirche: jüdisch? griechisch? christlich? (Leipzig: Dorffling & Franke, 1937).

1685 Leloir, L. "La prière des Pères du désert d'après les Paterika arméniens," in H. Limet and J. Ries (eds.), L'expérience de la prière dans les grandes religions: actes du colloque de Louvain-la-Neuve et Liège (22–23 novembre 1978) (Louvain-la-Neuve: Centre d'histoire des religions, 1980), 295–311.

1686 Lietzmann, H. Messe und Herrenmahl: Eine Studie zur Geschichte der Liturgie (Berlin: de Gruyter, 1955), ch. 9. ETrans. = Mass and Lord's Supper (Leiden: Brill, 1979).

1687 MacDonald, A. B. Christian Worship in the Primitive Church (Edinburgh: T. & T. Clark, 1934), chs. 8, 9, 13.

1688 Malachi, Z. "Christian and Jewish Liturgical Poetry: Mutual Influences in the First Four Centuries," Aug 28 (1988), 237–48.

1689 Manns, F. "L'origine judéo-chrétienne de la prière "Unde et memores" du Canon Romain," EL 101 (1987), 60–67.

1690 Marcovich, M. "The Naassene Psalm in Hippolytus (Haer. 5.10.2)," in B. Layton (ed.), The Rediscovery of Gnosticism: Proceedings of the International Conference on Gnosticism at Yale, New Haven, Connecticut, March 28–31, 1978: vol. 2, Sethian Gnosticism (Leiden: Brill, 1981), 770–78. Also in M. Marcovich, Studies in Graeco-Roman Religions and Gnosticism (Leiden: Brill, 1988), 80–88.

1691 Martin, R. P. Worship in the Early Church (Grand Rapids, Mich.: Eerdmans, 1974). See esp. chs. 2–4.

1692 Marty, J. "Étude des textes cultuels de prière conservés par les "Pères apostoliques," *RHPhR* 10 (1930), 90–98.

1693 Mateos, J. "The Origins of the Divine Office," *Worship* 41 (1967), 477–85.

1694 May, G. "Der Christushymnus des Clemens von Alexandrien," in H. Becker and R. Kaczynski (eds.), *Liturgie und Dichtung: Ein interdisziplinäres Kompendium,* 1: *Historische Präsentation* (St. Ottilien: EOS, 1983), 257–73.

1695 McKay, K. J. "Door Magic and the Epiphany Hymn," *ClQ* 17 (1967), 184–94.

1696 McKinnon, J. W. "The Fourth-Century Origin of the Gradual," *EMH* 7 (1987), 91–106.

1697 Mearns, J. *Early Latin Hymnaries: An Index of Hymns in Hymnaries before 1100* (Cambridge: University Press, 1913).

1698 Meijer, J. A. "Tertullianus over het gebed," in C. Trimp (ed.), *De biddende kerk: Ein bundel studies over het gebed aangeboden bij gelegenheid van het 125-jarig bestaan van de Theologische Hogeschool de Kampen* (Groningen: De Vuurbaak, 1979), 139–80.

1699 Michel, K. *Gebet und Bild in frühchristlicher Zeit: Studien über Christlicher Denkmäler,* 1 (Leipzig: Dieterich, 1902).

1700 Michel, O., and Klauser, T. "Gebet II (Fürbitte)," *RAC* 9, 1–36.

1701 Mitsakis, K. "The Hymnography of the Greek Church in the Early Christian Centuries," *JÖB* 20 (1971), 31–49.

1702 Mitsakis, K. *Byzantine Hymnography,* vol. 1, *From the New Testament to the Iconoclastic Controversy* (Thessaloniki: Patriarchal Institute for Patristic Studies, 1971).

1703 Mohlberg, C. "Carmen Christi quasi Deo," *Revista di Archeologie cristiana* 14 (1937), 105–6.

1704 Mohrmann, C. *Études sur le latin des chrétiens* (vol. 3; Rome: Edizioni di storia e letterature, 1958). Vol. 3 examines the evolution of Christian Latin prayers.

1705 Moule, C. F. D. "A Note on *Didache* ix.4," *JThS* N.S. 6 (1955), 240–43.

1706 Nemeshegyi, P. *La paternité de Dieu chez Origène* (Bibliothèque de théologie, ser. 4, vol. 2; Tournai: Desclée, 1960).

1707 Neunheuser, B. "Les gestes de la prière à genoux de la génuflection dans les Églises de rite romain," in C. Andronikof et al. (eds.), *Gestes et paroles dans les diverses familles liturgiques* (Rome: Centro Liturgico Vincenziano, 1978), 153–65.

1708 Origen   *La prière: pourquoi prier, que demander, comment prier sans cesse, prière et action* (Introduction et orientation par A.-G. Hamman; Paris: Desclée de Brouwer, 1977).

1709 Origen   "Prayer," in *An Exhortation to Martyrdom, Prayer, First Principles: Book IV, Prologue to the Commentary on the Song of Songs, Homily XXVII on Numbers* (trans. and intro. by R. A. Greer; New York: Paulist Press, 1979).

1710 Pepin, J.   "Prière et providence au 2e siècle (Justin, Dial 1,4)," in F. Bossier et al. (eds.), *Images of Man in Ancient and Medieval Thought: Studia Gerardo Verbeke ab amicis et collegis dicata* (Louvain: Louvain University Press, 1976), 111–25.

1711 Perler, O.   "Das Gebet in der Frühkirche," *Anima* 14 (1959), 13–22.

1712 Perrot, C.   "Worship in the Primitive Church," *Conc* 162 (1983), 3–9.

1713 Peterson, E. "Das Kreuz und das Gebet nach Osten," in *Frühkirche, Judentum und Gnosis* (Rome/Freiburg/Vienna: Herder, 1959), 15–35.

1714 Phillips, L. E. "Daily Prayer in the *Apostolic Traditions* of Hippolytus," *JThS* N.S. 40 (1989), 389–400.

1715 Porter, H. B., Jr. *The Ordination Prayers of the Ancient Western Churches* (London: S.P.C.K., 1967), esp. ch. 1 on the prayers of the Apostolic Tradition of Hippolytus.

1716 Quecke, H.   *Untersuchungen zum koptische Stundengebet* (Louvain: Université catholique de Louvain: Institut orientaliste, 1970).

1717 Ratcliff, E. C. "The Sanctus and the Pattern of the Early Anaphora," *JEH* 1 (1950), 29–36, 125–34. See also A. H. Couratin and D. Tripp (eds.), *E. C. Ratcliff: Liturgical Studies* (London: S.P.C.K., 1976), 18–40.

1718 Reitschel, G. "Kirchenlied, I: der alten Kirche (bis ca. 600)," in *RE* 10 (1970³), 399–409.

1719 Richardson, C. C. "The So-called Epiclesis in Hippolytus," *HThR* 40 (1947), 101–8.

1720 Richardson, C. C. "A Note on the Epicleses in Hippolytus and the Testamentum Domini," *Recherches de théologie ancienne et médiévale* 15 (1948), 357–59.

1721 Rordorf, W.   "Les gestes accompagnant la prière d'après Tertullien, *de Oratione* 11–30, et Origine, *Peri euchēs* 31–32," in C. Andronikof et al. (eds.), *Gestes et paroles dans les diverses familles liturgiques* (Rome: Centro Liturgico Vincenziano, 1978), 191–203.

1722   Rose, A.   "L'usage et la signification de l'Alleluia en Orient et en Occident," in C. Andronikof et al. (eds.), *Gestes et paroles dans les diverses familles liturgiques* (Rome: Centro Liturgico Vincenziano, 1978), 205–33.

1723   Rousseau, O.   "La plus ancienne liste de cantiques liturgiques tirés de l'Écriture," *RSR* 35 (1948), 120–29.

1724   Schermann, T.   *Griechische Zauberpapyri und das Gemeinde- und Dankgebet im 1. Klemensbrief* (TU 34, 2b; Leipzig: J. C. Hinrichs, 1909).

1725   Schoedel, W. R.   *Ignatius of Antioch: A Commentary on the Letters of Ignatius of Antioch* (Philadelphia: Fortress, 1985), 87–94.

1726   Segelberg, E.   "The Benedictio Olei in the Apostolic Tradition of Hippolytus," *OrChr* 48 (1964), 268–81.

1727   Segelberg, E.   "The Ordination Prayers in Hippolytus," in E. A. Livingstone (ed.), *Studia Patristica,* vol. 13.2 (Berlin: Akademie-Verlag, 1975), 397–408.

1728   Simpson, R.   *The Interpretation of Prayer in the Early Church* (Philadelphia: Westminster, 1965).

1729   Smith, M. A.   "The Anaphora of the *Apostolic Tradition* Reconsidered," *Studia Patristica* 10 (1970), 426–30.

1730   Spinks, B. D.   "The Jewish Sources for the Sanctus," *HeyJ* 21 (1980), 168–79.

1731   Srawley, J. H.   *The Early History of the Liturgy* (Cambridge: University Press, 1947), see ch. 2 inter alia.

1732   Stadlhuber, J.   "Das Stundengebet des Laien im christlichen Altertum," *ZKTh* 71 (1949), 129–83.

1733   Stander, H. F.   "The Starhymn in the Epistle of Ignatius to the Ephesians (19:2–3)," *VigChr* 43 (1989), 209–14.

1734   Stanley, D. M.   "Carmenque Christo quasi deo dicere," *CBQ* 20 (1958), 173–91.

1735   Talley, T. J.   "The Eucharistic Prayer of the Ancient Church according to Recent Research: Results and Reflections," *StLi* 11 (1976), 138–58.

1736   Tarby, A.   *La prière eucharistique de l'Église de Jerusalem* (Paris: Beauchesne, 1972).

1737   Tertullian   *La preghiera* (Torino: Edizioni Paoline, 1984).

1738   Thierry, J. J. (ed.)   *Christ in Early Christian Greek Poetry: An Anthology* (Leiden: Brill, 1972). Hymns from Ignatius, Sibylline Oracles, the gnostic corpus, Clement of Alexandria, Hippolytus inter alia.

1739   Tripp, D.   "The Prayer of St. Polycarp and the Development of Anaphoral Prayer," *EL* 104 (1990), 97–132.

1740   Vagaggini, C., and   *La preghiera nella bibbia e nella tradizione patristica*
      Penco, G. (eds.)   *e monastica* (Rome: Edizioni Paoline, 1964).

1741   Verheul, A.   "La prière eucharistique dans la Didachè," *Questions liturgiques* 60 (1979), 197–207.

1742   Vischer, L.   "Das Gebet in der alten Kirche," *EvTh* 17 (1957), 531–46.

1743   Vogel, C.   "Anaphores eucharistiques préconstantiniennes: Formes non traditionnelles," in V. Saxer (ed.), *Ecclesia orans: mélanges patristiques offerts au Père Adalbert G. Hamman OFM à l'occasion de ses quarante ans d'enseignement* (Rome: Institute Patristicum "Augustinium," 1980), 401–10.

1744   Volz, C. A.   "Prayer in the Early Church," in P. Sponheim (ed.), *A Primer on Prayer* (Philadelphia: Westminster, 1988), 36–47.

1745   Vööbus, A.   *Liturgical Traditions in the Didache* (Papers of the Estonian Theological Society in Exile, 16; Stockholm: Etse, 1968).

1746   Walker, J. H.   "Terce, Sext and None: An Apostolic Custom?," *SP* 5 (1962), 206–12.

1747   Walpole, A. S. (ed.)   *Early Latin Hymns with Introduction and Notes* (Cambridge: University Press, 1922), 16–114.

1748   Warren, F. C.   *The Liturgy and Ritual of the Ante-Nicene Church* (London: S.P.C.K., 1897), esp. section 3 (early Christian texts), section 4 (early Jewish texts).

1749   Wetter, G. P.   *Altchristliche Liturgien, 1, Das christliche Mysterium: Studie zur Geschichte des Abendmahles* (FRLANT, N.F. Heft 13; Göttingen: Vandenhoeck & Ruprecht, 1921), discusses early eucharistic prayer, and prayers in the Acts of Thomas.

1750   Willis, G. G.   *Essays on Early Roman Liturgy* (London: S.P.C.K., 1964), esp. I, ch. 1 "The Prayer of the Faithful' (pp. 3–10).

7. GRECO-ROMAN TEXTS

GENERAL

1751   Adami, F.   "De poetis scaenicis Graecis hymnorum sacrorum imitatoribus," *JCPh. S* 26 (1901), 213–62.

1752 Appel, G.   *De Romanorum precationibus* (New York: Arno Press, 1975). Originally published RVV 7.2; Gießen: Töpelmann, 1909.

1753 Ausfeld, C.   "De Graecorum precationibus quaestiones," *JCPh*. *S* 28 (1903), 502–47.

1754 Bergmann, J.   "Die Rachegebete von Rheneia," *Philologus* N.F. 70 (1911), 503–10. Discussion of possible first-century C.E. texts.

1755 Bremond, A.   "Un texte de Proclus sur la prière et de l'union divine," *RSR* 19 (1929), 448–62.

1756 Burkert, W.   *Greek Religion* (Cambridge, Mass.: Harvard University Press, 1985). See "Prayer," 2.3, 73–75 (notes on 375–76). "Dancing and Hymns," = 2.7, 102–3 (notes on 388).

1757 Cameron, A.   "Sappho's Prayer to Aphrodite," *HThR* 32 (1934), 1–17.

1758 Clay, D.   "Socrates' Prayer to Pan," in G. Bowersock, W. Burkert, and M. Putnam (eds.), *Arktouros: Hellenic Studies Presented to Bernard M. W. Knox on the Occasion of His 65th Birthday* (Berlin: de Gruyter, 1979), 345–53.

1759 Corlu, A.   *Recherches sur les mots relatifs à l'idée de prière, d'Homère aux tragiques* (Études et commentaires 64; Paris: C. Klincksieck, 1966).

1760 Creaghan, J. S.   "Content and Form of the Prayer of Sophocles' (Dissertation: Fordham University, 1939).

1761 Des Places, É.   "Hymnes grecs au seuil de l'ère chrétienne," *Bib* 38 (1957), 113–29.

1762 Des Places, É.   "La preghiera nella poesia classica della grecia antica," *CivCatt* 110 (1959), 274–82, 502–11.

1763 Des Places, É.   "La prière cultuelle dans la Grèce ancienne," *RSR* 33 (1959), 343–59.

1764 Des Places, É.   "La prière des philosophes grecs," *Gr* 41 (1960), 253–72.

1765 Des Places, É.   "Deux études sur la prière en Grèce," *REG* 81 (1968), 167–71.

1766 Des Places, É.   *La religion grecque: dieux, cultes, rites, et sentiment religieux dans la Grèce antique* (Paris: Éditions A. et J. Picard, 1969), 123–25.

1767 Ehrenberg, V.   "Athenischer Hymnus auf Demetrios Poliorketes," *Antike* 7 (1931), 279–97.

1768 Esser, H.-P.   "Untersuchungen zu Gebet und Gottesverehrung der Neoplatoniker" (Dissertation: Cologne, 1967).

1769 Festugière, A.-J.   "ANTH HŌN: La formule 'en échange de quoi' dans la prière grecque hellénistique," *RSPhTh* 60 (1976), 389–418.

1770 Fowler, W. W.   *The Religious Experience of the Roman People* (New York: Macmillan, 1911). See esp. 181–91 on prayer and sacrifice.

1771 Freyburger, G.   "La supplication d'action de grâces dans la religion romaine archaïque," *Latomus* 36 (1977), 283–315.

1772 Freyburger, G.   "La supplication d'action de grâces sous le Haut-Empire," *ANRW* II, 16.2 (1978), 1418–39.

1773 Fritz, K. von   "Greek Prayers," *RR* 10 (1945), 5–39.

1774 Guittard, C.   "L'expression du verbe de la prière dans le 'carmen' latin archaïque," in P. Bloch (ed.), *Recherches sur les religions de l'antiquité classique* (Geneva: Droz, 1980), 395–403.

1775 Halkin, L. E.   *La supplication d'Action de grâces chez les Romains* (Paris: Les Belles Lettres, 1953).

1776 Hickson, F. V.   *Voces precationum: The Language of Prayer in the History of Livy and the Aeneid of Vergil* (Dissertation: University of North Carolina, Chapel Hill, 1986).

1777 Keil, J.   "Zur Geschichte der Hymnoden in der Provinz Asia," *JÖAI* 11 (1908), 101–10.

1778 Kern, O.   "Der Kultus," in *Die Religion der Griechen*, 1: *Von den Anfängen bis Hesiod* (Berlin: Weidmannsche Buchhandlung, 1926), 150–56.

1779 Keyssner, K.   *Gottesvorstellung und Lebensauffassung in der griechischen Hymnus* (Stuttgart: W. Kohlhammer, 1932).

1780 Kleinknecht, H.   *Die Gebetsparodie in der Antike* (Hildesheim: Georg Olms, 1967).

1781 Körte, A.   "Der Demeter-Hymnos des Philikos," *Hermes* 66 (1931), 442–54.

1782 Kytzler, B., and Fischer, C. (eds.)   *Carmina Priapea: Gedichte an den Gartengott* (Zürich/Munich: Artemis, 1978).

1783 Langhof, V.   *Die Gebete bei Euripides und die zeitliche Folge Tragödien* (Göttingen: Vandenhoeck & Ruprecht, 1971).

1784 Leeuw, G. van der   "Do ut des," *ARW* 20 (1921), 241–53.

1785 Maas, P.   *Epidaurische Hymnen* (Halle: M. Niemeyer, 1933).

1786 Nilsson, M. P.   "Lied und Gebet," in *Geschichte der Griechische Religion, I: bis zur griechischen Weltherrschaft* (Munich: C. H. Beck'sche Verlagsbuchhandlung, 1941), 146–49.

1787 Perrett, J. "Aux origines de l'hymnodie latine — l'apport de la civilisation romaine," *MD* 173 (1988), 41–60.

1788 Pradel, F. *Griechische und süditalienische Gebete* (RVV 3.3; Gießen: A. Töpelmann, 1907).

1789 Ratkowitsch, K. "Ein Hymnus in Ciceros erster Catalinaria," *WSt* N.F. 15 (94) (1981), 157–67.

1790 Saffrey, H. D. "The Piety and Prayers of Ordinary Men and Women in Late Antiquity," in A. H. Armstrong (ed.), *Classical Mediterranean Spirituality: Egyptian, Greek, Roman* (New York: Crossroad, 1986), 195–213. See 202–4 for the prayers of "ordinary people." Discussion centered on epigraphic texts found in Book VI of the Palatine Anthology.

1791 Savino, E. *Preghiera e rito nella Grecia antica* (1st ed., Oscar Uomini e religioni; Milan: A. Mondalori, 1986).

1792 Schermann, T. "*Eucharistia* und *eucharistein* in ihrem Bedeutungswandel bis 200 n. Chr.," in *Philologus: Zeitschrift für das klassische Altertum* 69 (1910), 375–410.

1793 Schmidt, H. *Veteres philosophi quomodo iudicaverint de precibus* (RVV 4.1; Gießen: A. Töpelmann, 1906).

1794 Schmidt, L. *Die Ethik der alten Griechen* (Berlin: Hertz, 1882), 2:31–40.

1795 Schwenn, F. *Gebet und Opfer* (Heidelberg: C. Winter, 1927).

1796 Simon, M. "Prière du philosophe et prière chrétienne," in H. Limet and J. Ries (eds.), *L'expérience de la prière dans les grandes religions: actes du colloque de Louvain-la-Neuve et Liège (22–23 novembre 1978)* (Louvain-la-Neuve: Centre d'histoire des religions, 1980), 205–24.

1797 Tschiedel, H.-J. "Ein Pfingstwunder im Apollonhymnus (Hymn, Hom. Ap. 156–64) und Apg. 2, 1–13," *ZRGG* 27 (1975), 22–39.

1798 Vellay, C. "Étude sur les hymnes de Synésius de Cyrène" (Dissertation: Paris, 1904).

1799 Versnel, H. S. "A Parody on Hymns in Martial and Some Trinitarian Problems," *Mn* 4, 27 (1974), 365–455.

1800 Versnel, H. S. *Faith, Hope, and Worship: Aspects of Religious Mentality in the Ancient World* (Leiden: Brill, 1981).

1801 Wagenwoort, H. "Orare: Precari," in T. P. van Baaren (ed.), *Verbum: Essays on Some Aspects of the Religious Function of Words Dedicated to H. W. Obbink* (Utrecht: Kemink, 1964), 101–11 [in Latin].

1802 West, M. L. "Cynaethus' Hymn to Apollo," *CQ* 25 (1975), 161–70.

1803 Wissowa, G.   *Religion und Kultus der Römer* (Munich: Beck, 1902), 333–34.

1804 Wünsch, R.   "Hymnos," *PRE* 9.1, cols. 140–83.

1805 Ziegler, K.   "De precationum apud Graecos formis quaestiones selectae" (Dissertation: Breslau, 1905).

HYMN OF CLEANTHES

1806 Festugière, A.-J.   " 'L'hymne à Zeus' de Cléanthe," in *La Révélation d'Hermès Trismégiste II* (Paris: Lecoffre, 1944–54), 310–25, 607.

1807 Lauer, S.   "Der Zeushymnus des Kleanthes," in M. Brocke, J. J. Petuchowski, and and W. Strolz (eds.), *Das Vaterunser: Gemeinsames im Beten von Juden und Christen* (Freiburg i. Breisgau: Herder, 1974), 156–62.

1808 Meijer, P. A.   "*Geras* in the Hymn of Cleanthes to Zeus," *RMP* 129 (1986), 31–35.

1809 Neustadt, E.   "Der Zeushymnus des Kleanthes," *Hermes* 66 (1931), 387–401.

1810 Slings, S. R.   "*Themis* in Hymnos des Kleanthes," *RMP* 125 (1982), 188–89.

1811 Zuntz, G.   "Zum Hymnus des Kleanthes," *RMP* 94 (1951), 337–41.

1812 Zuntz, G.   "Zum Kleanthes-Hymnus," *HSCP* 63 (1958), 289–308.

ISIS ARETALOGIES

1813 Engelmann, H.   *Die delische Sarapisaretalogie* (BKP 15; Meisenheim: A Hain, 1964). *The Delian Aretalogy of Sarapis* (ETrans.; Leiden: Brill, 1975).

1814 Festugière, A.-J.   "À propos des arétalogies d'Isis," *HThR* 42 (1949), 209–34.

1815 Festugière, A.-J.   "L'arétalogie isiaque de la "Korè Kosmou," in *Mélanges Ch. Picard* (Paris, 1949), 376–81.

1816 Harder, R.   *Karpokrates von Chalkis und die Memphitische Isispropaganda* (Berlin: de Gruyter, 1944).

1817 Horsley, G. H. R.   "A Personalised Aretalogy of Isis," in *New Documents Illustrating Early Christianity: A Review of the Greek Inscriptions and Papyri Published in 1976* (Macquarie University, N.S.W.: The Ancient History Documentary Research Centre, 1981), 10–21.

1818 Junker, H.   *Der große Pylon des Tempels der Isis zu Philae* (Vienna, 1958).

1819 Lexa, F.   "L'hymne grec de Kyme sur la déesse Isis," *ArOr* 2 (1930), 138–52.

1820 Malaise, M.   "La piété personnelle dans la religion isiaque," in H. Limet and J. Ries (eds.), *L'expérience de la prière dans les grandes religions: actes du colloque de Louvain-la-Neuve et Liège (22–23 novembre 1978)* (Louvain-la-Neuve: Centre d'histoire des religions, 1980), 83–117.

1821 Nock, A. D.   "Review of R. Harder, *Karpokrates von Chalkis und die Memphitische Isis-propaganda*," *Gnomon* 21 (1949), 221–28.

1822 Peek, W.   *Der Isishymnos von Andreos und verwandte Texte* (Berlin: Weidmanns, 1930).

1823 Roussel, P.   "Un nouvel hymne grec à Isis," *REG* 42 (1929), 137–68.

1824 Vanderlip, V. F.   *The Four Greek Hymns of Isidorus and the Cult of Isis* (Toronto: A. M. Hakkert, 1972).

1825 Zabkar, L. V.   *Hymns to Isis in Her Temple at Philae* (Hanover, N.H.: Brandeis University Press, 1988).

ORPHICA

1826 Abel, E.   *Orphica: Accedunt Procli Hymni, Hymni Magici, Hymnus in Isim, aliaque eiusmodi carmina* (Leipzig/Prague: Freytag & Tempsky, 1885).

1827 Athanassakis, A. N.   *The Orphic Hymns* (Text, Translation and Notes, SBL Texts and Translations 12, Graeco-Roman Religion Series 4; Missoula, Mont.: Scholars Press, 1977).

1828 Diehls, H.   "Ein orphischer Demeterhymnus," in *Festschrift Th. Gomperz* (Vienna, 1902), 1–15.

1829 Dieterich, A.   "De hymnis Orphicus Capitula V" (Habilitationschrift, Marburg, 1891). See also *Kleine Schriften* (Leipzig: Teubner, 1911).

1830 Kern, O.   *Die Herkunft des orphischen Hymnenbuchs* (Berlin, 1910).

1831	Kern, O.	"Das Demeterheiligtum von Pergamon und die orphischen Hymnen," *Hermes* 46 (1911), 431–46.
1832	Kern, O.	*Orphicorum fragmenta* (Berlin, 1922).
1833	Keydell, R.	"Orphische Dichtung, 1) Hymnen," *PRE* 18.2, cols. 1321–33.
1834	Linforth, I. M.	*The Arts of Orpheus* (Berkeley and Los Angeles: University of California Press, 1941).
1835	Maass, E.	*Orpheus: Untersuchungen der griechischen, römischen, altchristlichen Jenseitsdichtung* (Munich: Beck, 1895).
1836	Plassmann, J. O.	*Orpheus altgriechische Mysterien: aus dem Urtext übersetzt und erläutert* (Frankfurt/Main, 1982).
1837	Quandt, W.	*Orphei Hymni* (Dublin/Zürich: Weidmann, 1973). Contains an extensive bibliography.
1838	Reitzenstein, R.	"Ein orphisches Fragment," in R. Reitzenstein and H. H. Schäder (eds.), *Studien zum antiken Synkretismus aus Iran und Griechenland* (Studien der Bibliothek Wartburg, 7; Leipzig: B. C. Teubner, 1926), Part 1, ch. 3, 69–103.
1839	Weinreich, O.	"Hymnologica," *ARW* 17 (1914), 524–31. Discusses Aelius Aristeides and the Orphica.
1840	West, M. L.	*The Orphic Hymns* (Oxford: Clarendon Press, 1984).

MITHRAS CULT

1841	Cumont, F.	*Textes et monuments figurés relatifs aux mystères de Mithra* (Bruxelles, 1898–99).
1842	Cumont, F.	*Les mystères de Mithra* (Paris, 1902[2]). ETrans.: Chicago: Open Court Publishing Company, 1903. For discussion of the Mithraic mysteries, see 150–74.
1843	Dieterich, A.	*Eine Mithrasliturgie* (ed. R. Wünsch; Leipzig, 1903[1], 1910[2]; edited by O. Weinreich, 1923[3]). Repr., Darmstadt: Wissenschaftliche Buchgesellschaft, 1966.
1844	Meyer, M. W.	*The "Mithras Liturgy"* (Texts and Translations 10, Graeco-Roman Religion Series 2; Missoula, Mont.: Scholars Press, 1976).
1845	Preisendanz, K. (ed.)	*Papyri Graecae Magicae: Die griechischen Zauberpapyri* (2 vols., Leipzig/Berlin, 1931). 2d rev. ed. by A. Henrichs; Stuttgart: Teubner, 1974. See vol. 1, 88–101 for Mithras liturgy.
1846	Turcan, R.	"Note sur la liturgie mithriaque," *RHR* 194 (1978), 147–57.

HYMNS OF ARISTEIDES

1847 Amann, J.   *Die Zeusrede des Ailios Aristeides* (TBAW 12; Stuttgart: Kohlhammer, 1931). See esp. ch. 1, "Die Topik der Götterreden nach der rhetorischen Schultheorie und bei Aristeides," 1–14.

1848 Gigli, D.   "Teoria e prassi metrica negli inni a Sarapide e Dioniso di Elio Aristide," *Prometheus* 1 (1975), 237–65.

1849 Heitsch, E. (ed.)   *Dichterfragmente der römischen Kaiserzeit gesammelt und herausgegeben,* Band I.2 (Göttingen: Vandenhoeck & Ruprecht, 1963–4), 1:165, #XVII (text).

1850 Herzog, R.   "Ein Asklepios-Hymnus des Aristeides v. Smyrna" (SPAW. PH 23; Berlin, 1934), 753–70.

1851 Höfler, A.   *Der Sarapishymnus des Ailios Aristeides* (TBAW 27; Stuttgart: W. Kohlhammer, 1935).

1852 Jöhrens, G.   "Der Athenahymnus des Ailios Aristeides: Mit einem Anhang zum Höhenkult der Athena und Testimonien zur allegorischen Deutung der Athena" (Dissertation: Berlin, 1980).

1853 Lenz, F. W.   "Der Dionysoshymnus des Aristeides," *RCCM* 3 (1961), 153–66.

1854 Lenz, F. W.   "Der Athenahymnos des Aristeides," *RCCM* 5 (1963), 329–47.

1855 Mesk, J.   "Zu den Prosa- und Vershymnen des Aelius Aristides," in *Raccolta di scritti in onore di Felice Ramorino* (PUCSC 4,7; Mailand, 1927), 660–72.

1856 Uerschels, W.   *Der Dionysoshymnos des Ailios Aristeides* (Bonn: Rheinische Friedrich-Wilhelms-Universität, 1962).

1857 Voll, W.   "Der Dionysos-Hymnus des Ailios Aristeides" (Dissertation: Tübingen, 1948).

1858 Wahl, W.   "Der Herakleshymnos des Ailios Aristeides" (Dissertation: Tübingen, 1946).

1859 Weinreich, O.   "Hymnologica," *ARW* 17 (1914), 524–31. Discusses Aelius Aristeides and the Orphica.

HYMNS OF CALLIMACHUS

1860 Bornmann, F.   *Callimachi Hymnus in Dianam: Introduzione, testo critico, commento* (Florence: La nuova Italia, 1968.

1861 Bulloch, A. W.   *Callimachus: The Fifth Hymn* (Cambridge: University Press, 1985).

1862 Cahen, E.   *Les hymnes de Callimaque: Commentaire explicatif et critique* (BEFAR 124; Paris, 1930).

1863 Chlebowski, A.   *De Callimachi in Iovem hymno, Progr* (Königsberg: E. J. Dalkowski, 1879).

1864 Erbse, H.   "Zum Apollonhymnus des Kallimachos," *Hermes* 83 (1955), 411–28.

1865 Küchler, K. C. G. *De vestigiis nonnullis Veteris Testamenti quae in Hymnis Callimachi deprehenduntur* (Neostadii ad Orilam, 1788). Comparison of the material of the Hebrew Bible with Hellenism as represented by Callimachus.

1866 Ludwich, A.   *Homerischer Hymnenbau nebst seinen Nachahmungen bei Kallimachos, Theokrit, Vergil, Nonnus und anderen* (Leipzig: S. Hirzel, 1908).

1867 Mair, A. W.   *Callimachus: Hymns and Epigrams* (London: Heinemann, 1955[5]).

1868 McLennan, G. R. *Callimachus: Hymn to Zeus: Introduction and Commentary* (Rome: Edizioni dell'Ateneo & Bizzari, 1977).

1869 Pfeiffer, R. (ed.) *Callimachus:* vol. 2, *Hymni et epigrammata* (Oxford: Clarendon Press, 1953).

1870 Williams, F.   *Callimachus: Hymn to Apollo, A Commentary* (Oxford: Clarendon Press, 1978).

IMPERIAL CULT

1871 Beurlier, E.   *Le culte rendu aux empereurs romains* (Paris: Thorin, 1890). See esp. 55–76 for honors rendered to the emperors after their death, and 271–81 for Christians and prayer in the context of the Imperial Cult.

1872 Cerfaux, L.   "Le titre *Kyrios* et la dignité royale de Jésus," *RSPhTh* 12 (1923), 125–53. See also *Recueil Lucien Cerfaux*, 1 (Gembloux: Éditions J. Duculot, 1954), 35–63.

1873 Cerfaux, L., and Tondriau, J. *Un concurrent du christianisme: Le culte des souverains dans la civilisation gréco-romaine* (Bibliothèque de théologie, sér. 3, vol. 5; Paris: Desclée, 1957). Prayer mentioned specifically on 202 (the cult of the Theoi Soteres) and 224 (the Jews and imperial claims, as evidenced in Daniel). See also 394 for brief discussion of Rev. 13 and the worship offered to the Beast.

1874 Comblin, J.   *Le Christ dans l'Apocalypse* (Bibliothèque de Théo-
                           logie, série 3, vol. 6; Tournai: Desclée, 1965). See
                           discussion of the Apocalypse of John and the liturgy
                           of the imperial cult on 99–106.

1875 Fears, J. R.   "The Cult of Jupiter and Roman Imperial Ideology,"
                           ANRW II, 17.1 (1980), 7–141. Discussion of prayer
                           and of Zeus as Father.

1876 Kühn, W.   *Plinius der Jüngere: Panegyrikus: Lobrede auf den
                           Kaiser Trajan* (Darmstadt: Wissenschaftliche Buch-
                           gesellschaft, 1985).

1877 Prigent, P.   "Au temps de l'Apocalypse, II: le culte impérial au
                           1er siècle en Asie Mineure," *RHPhR* 55 (1975), 215–
                           35, esp. 221–23.

1878 Thaede, K.   "Die Poesie und der Kaiserkult," in W. den Boer (ed.),
                           Le culte des souverains dans l'empire romain (Entre-
                           tiens sur l'antiquité classique 19; Geneva: Fondation
                           Hardt, 1973), 273–303.

8. MAGICAL TEXTS

1879 Aune, D. E.   "Magic in Early Christianity," *ANRW* II, 23.2
                          (1980), 1507–57, esp. 1551–55.

1880 Basset, R.   *Enseignements de Jésus-Christ à ses disciples et
                          prières magiques* (Les Apocryphes étopiennes, 7;
                          Paris 1893–1900).

1881 Betz, H. D. (ed.)   *The Greek Magical Papyri in Translation. Including
                          the Demotic Spells:* vol. 1, *Texts* (Chicago/London:
                          University of Chicago Press, 1986). Most of the texts
                          are dated fourth century C.E. or earlier.

1882 Blau, L.   *Das altjüdische Zauberwesen* (Berlin: L. Lamm,
                          1914²), see esp. section 4, chapter 4 (96–117).

1883 Deissmann, A.   "An Epigraphic Memorial of the Septuagint," in
                          Bible Studies (Edinburgh: T. & T. Clark, 1901),
                          272–300. Discussion of a second-/third-century C.E.
                          incantation (Adrumetum Tablet) with a brief com-
                          parison of the language of Prayer of Manasseh and
                          2 Macc. 1:24ff. on 297–300.

1884 Dieterich, A.   *Abraxas: Studien zur Religionsgeschichte des Spät-
                          eren Altertums* (Leipzig, 1891), see esp. section 2.

1885 Festugière, A.-J.   "La valeur religieuse des papyrus magiques," in
                          L'idéal religieux des grecs et de l'Évangile (Paris:
                          Gabalda, 1932), 281–328.

1886 Goldin, J.   "The Magic of Magic and Superstition," in E. Schüssler Fiorenza (ed.), *Aspects of Religious Propaganda in Judaism and Early Christianity* (Notre Dame, Ind.: University of Notre Dame Press, 1976), 115–47, esp. 132–38.

1887 Leipoldt, J.   "Gebet und Zauber in Urchristentum: Von der Mysterien zur Kirche," in *Gesammelte Aufsätze* (Leipzig: Koehler-Amelang, 1961), 104–15.

1888 Lewy, H.   *Chaldaean Oracles and Theurgy: Mysticism, Magic and Platonism in the Later Roman Empire* (Cairo: L'Institut français d'archéologie orientale, 1956, 1979²), esp. ch. 1.

1889 Luck, G.   "Theurgy and Forms of Worship in Neoplatonism," in J. Neusner, E. S. Frerichs, and P. V. McC. Flesher (eds.), *Religion, Science and Magic* (New York/Oxford: Oxford University Press, 1989), 185–225, esp. 192–99.

1890 Luck, G. (ed.)   *Arcana Mundi: Magic and the Occult in the Greek and Roman Worlds: A Collection of Ancient Texts* (Baltimore: Johns Hopkins University Press, 1985), see esp. section 1, 3–60 (Introduction) and 61–140 (magical texts with commentary).

1891 Nilsson, M. P.   "Die Religion in der griechischen Zauberpapyri," in *Opuscula Selecta* (Skrifter Utgivna av Svenska Institutet i Athen 8, 2.3; Lund: Gleerup, 1960), 3:129–66.

1892 Nock, A. D.   "Greek Magical Papyri," *Journal of Egyptian Archaeology* 15 (1929), 219–35. See also *Essays on Religion and the Ancient World* (Cambridge, Mass.: Harvard University Press, 1972), 1:176–94.

1893 Pfister, F.   "Ekstasis," *RAC* 4, col. 968, "Gebet und Zauberspruch."

1894 Preisendanz, K. (ed.)   *Papyri Graecae Magicae: Die griechischen Zauberpapyri* (2 vols.; Leipzig/Berlin, 1931). 2d rev. ed. edited by A. Henrichs; Stuttgart: Teubner, 1973.

1895 Reitzenstein, R.   "Zwei hellenistische Hymnen," *ARW* 8 (1905), 167–90.

1896 Riesenfeld, H.   "Remarques sur les hymnes magiques," *Eranos* 44 (1946), 153–60.

1897 Schäfer, P.   "Jewish Magic Literature in Late Antiquity and Early Middle Ages," *JJS* 41 (1990), 75–91, esp. "Incantation Prayers" on 76–79.

1898 Schermann, T.   *Griechische Zauberpapyri und das Gemeinde- und Dankgebet im 1. Klemensbriefe* (TU 34, 2b; Leipzig: J. C. Hinrichs, 1909).

1899   Sudhaus, S.   "Lautes und leises Gebet," *ARW* 9 (1906), 185–200.

1900   Wessely, C. (ed.)   *Griechische Zauberpapyrus von Paris und London* (Denkschriften der kaiserlichen Akademie der Wissenschaften in Wien, philosophisch-historisch Classe 36; Vienna: Kaiserliche Akademie der Wissenschaften, 1888).

9. GNOSTIC, HERMETIC, MANICHAEAN, AND MANDAEAN TEXTS

GNOSTIC TEXTS

1901   Adam, A.   *Die Psalmen des Thomas und das Perlenlied als Zeugnisse vorchristlicher Gnosis* (Berlin: C. Töpelmann, 1959).

1902   Bevan, A. A.   *The Hymn of the Soul Contained in the Syriac Acts of Thomas* (Cambridge: University Press, 1897).

1903   Bevan, E. R.   *Hellenism and Christianity* (London: Allen & Unwin, 1921). Hymn of the Pearl discussed on 87–108.

1904   Beyer, A. A.   "Das syrische Perlenlied: Ein Erlösungsmythos als Märchengedicht," *ZDMG* 140 (1990), 234–59.

1905   Broadribb, D.   "La Kanto pri la Perlo," *BibR* 4 (1968), 23–37.

1906   Burch, V.   "A Commentary on the Syriac Hymn of the Soul," *JThS* O.S. 19 (1918), 145–61.

1907   Claude, P. (ed.)   *Les Trois Stèles de Seth* (Bibliothèque Copte de Nag Hammadi 8; Québec: Les presses de l'Université Laval, 1983).

1908   Dewey, A. J.   "The Hymn in the Acts of John: Dance as Hermeneutic," *Semeia* 38 (1986), 67–80.

1909   Dirkse, P. A., and Brashler, J. (ed.)   "The Prayer of Thanksgiving," in D. M. Parrott (ed.), *Nag Hammadi Studies* 11 (Leiden: Brill, 1979), 375–87.

1910   Funk, W.-P.   "Die zweite Apokalypse des Jakobus aus Nag Hammadi Codex V" (TU 119; Berlin: Akademie-Verlag, 1976), 179–91, 211–20. Discussion of Gnostic and Manichean prayers.

1911   Gressmann, H.   "Das Gebet des Kyriakos," *ZNW* 20 (1921), 23–35.

1912   Helmbold, A. K.   "Redeemer Hymns — Gnostic and Christian," in R. N. Longenecker and M. C. Tenney (eds.), *New Dimensions in New Testament Study* (Grand Rapids, Mich.: Zondervan, 1974), 71–78.

1913 Hoffman, G.   "Zwei Hymnen der Thomasakten," *ZNW* 4 (1903), 273–309. Discusses parallels to the Hymn of the Pearl.

1914 Janssens, Y.   *La Prôtennoia Trimorphe* (Bibliothèque Copte de Nag Hammadi 4; Louvain: Peeters, 1978).

1915 Kasser, R., et al. (eds.)   *Tractatus Tripartitus* (vol. 2 [pars 2, pars 3]; Berne: Francke, 1975), 243–85. The Prayer of Paul the Apostle.

1916 Kehl, A.   "Beiträge zum Verständnis einiger gnostischer und frühchristlicher Psalmen und Hymnen," *JAC* 15 (1972), 92–119.

1917 Klijn, A. F. J.   "The Influence of Jewish Theology on the Odes of Solomon and the Acts of Thomas," in *Aspects du judéo-christianisme: Colloque de Strasbourg, 23–25 avril 1964* (Paris: Presses universitaires de France, 1965), 165–77.

1918 Köbert, R.   "Das Perlenlied," *Or* N.S. 38 (1969), 447–56.

1919 Kragerud, A.   *Die Hymnen der Pistis Sophia* (Oslo: Universitetsforlaget, 1967).

1920 Krause, M., and Girgis, V.   "Die drei Stelen des Seth," in F. Altheim (ed.), *Christentum am Roten Meer* (vol. 2; Berlin/New York: de Gruyter, 1971–73), 180–99.

1921 Macke, K.   "Syrische Lieder gnostischen Ursprungs," *ThQ* 56 (1874), 5–70. Hymns in the Acts of Thomas.

1922 Macke, K.   *Hymnen aus dem Zweiströmland* (Mainz: Franz Kirchheim, 1882), 246–56. Hymns in the Acts of Thomas.

1923 MacRae, G. W.   "Prayer and Knowledge of Self in Gnosticism," *Ecumenical Institute for Advanced Theological Studies: Yearbook 1978/79* (Tantur/Jerusalem: Franciscan Printing Press, 1981), 97–114. See also *Studies in the New Testament and Gnosticism* (Wilmington, Del.: Glazier, 1987), 218–36.

1924 Magne, J.   "Le chant de la perle à la lumière des écrits de Nag Hammadi," *Cahiers du Cercle Ernest-Renan* 100 (1977), 25–36.

1925 Marcovich, M.   "The Wedding Hymn of Acta Thomae," in *Studies in Graeco-Roman Religions and Gnosticism* (Leiden: Brill, 1988), 156–73.

1926 Mead, G. R. S.   *The Hymn of Jesus* (London: J. M. Watkins, 1963). Text, translation, and notes on the prayer found in the Acts of John.

1927 Ménard, J. E.   "Le Chant de la Perle," *RSR* 42 (1968), 289–325.

1928 Merkelbach, R.   "Der Seelenhymnus der Thomasakten und die Weihe Julians," in *Roman und Mysterium in der Antike* (Beilage 1; Munich/Berlin, 1962), 299–325.

1929 Merrill, E. W.   "The Odes of Solomon and the Acts of Thomas: A Comparative Study," *JEThS* 17 (1974), 231–34.

1930 Michel, O.   "Zur Frage des Seelenliedes," *ZNW* 25 (1926), 312–13.

1931 Miller, R. H.   "Liturgical Materials in the Acts of John," *TU* 116 (1975), 375–81.

1932 Mueller, D.   "Prayer of Paul the Apostle," in H. W. Attridge (ed.), *Nag Hammadi Codex 1* (Leiden: Brill, 1985), 1:5–11. See also 2:1–5.

1933 Nöldeke, T.   "Lied von der Seele," *ZDMG* 25 (1871), 676–79.

1934 Painchaud, L. (ed.)   *Le Deuxième Traité du Grand Seth (NH VII,2)* (Québec: Presses de l'université Laval, 1982).

1935 Poirier, P.-H.   *L'Hymne de la perle des Actes de Thomas: Introduction, texte, traduction, commentaire* (Homo Religiosus 8; Louvain-la-Neuve: Centre d'histore des religions, 1981).

1936 Preuschen, E.   *Zwei gnostische Hymnen* (Gießen: J. Ricker [Töpelmann], 1904).

1937 Quispel, G.   "Das Lied von der Perle," *Eranos-Jahrbuch* 34 (1965), 9–32.

1938 Quispel, G.   "Makarius und das Lied von der Perle," in U. Bianchi (ed.), *Le origini dello gnosticismo: Colloquio di Messina, 13–18 aprile 1966* (Studies in the History of Religions 12; Leiden: Brill, 1967), 625–44.

1939 Reitzenstein, R.   "Ein Gegenstück zu dem Seelenhymnus der Thomasakten," *ZNW* 21 (1922), 35–37.

1940 Robinson, J. M.   "The Three Steles of Seth and the Gnostics of Plotinus," in *Proceedings of the International Colloquium on Gnosticism, Stockholm August 20–25, 1973* (Stockholm: Almqvist & Wiksell, 1977), 133–42.

1941 Robinson, J. M., and Wisse, F.   "The Three Steles of Seth (VII, 5): Introduction and Translation," in J. M. Robinson (ed.), *The Nag Hammadi Library in English* (San Francisco: Harper & Row, 1977), 362–67.

1942 Sanders, J. T.   *The New Testament Christological Hymns: Their Historical Religious Background* (SNTSMS 15; Cambridge: University Press, 1971), 121–32.

1943 Schenke, G.   *Die dreigestaltige Protennoia (Nag-Hammadi-Codex XIII)* (Berlin: Akademie-Verlag, 1984).

1944	Schoedel, W. R.	"The Hymn of the Pearl," in R. M. Grant (ed.), *Gnosticism: A Source Book of Heretical Writings from the Early Christian Period* (New York: Harper, 1961), 116–22.
1945	Segelberg, E.	"Evangelium Veritatis: A Confirmation Homily and Its Relation to the Odes of Solomon," *Orientalia Suecana* 8 (1959), 3–42.
1946	Segelberg, E.	"Prayer among the Gnostics," in M. Krause (ed.), *Gnosis and Gnosticism* (Nag Hammadi Studies 8; Leiden: Brill, 1977), 55–69.
1947	Sevrin, J.-M.	"La prière gnostique: L'expérience de la prière dans les grandes religions," in H. Limet and J. Ries (eds.), *Actes du colloque de Louvain-la-Neuve et Liège (22–23 novembre 1978)* (Louvain-la-Neuve: Centre d'histore des religions, 1980), 367–74.
1948	Tardieu, M.	"Les Trois Steles de Seth," *RSPhTh* 57 (1973), 545–75.
1949	Unnik, W. C. van	*Evangelien aus dem Nilsand* (Frankfurt a. M: H. Scheffler, 1960). Discusses inter alia the question of a pre-Christian tradition of Gnostic redeemer hymns.
1950	Widengren, G.	"Die Hymnen der Pistis Sophia und die gnostische Schriftauslegung," in G. Widengren et al. (eds.), *Liber amicorum: Studies for C. J. Bleecker* (Leiden: Brill, 1969), 269–81.
1951	Wohlbergs, T.	*Griechische religiöse Gedichte der ersten nachchristlichen Jahrhundert, 1: Psalmen und Hymnen der Gnosis und des frühen Christentums* (BKP 40; Meisenheim: A. Hain, 1971).
1952	Yamauchi, E.	"The Apocalypse of Adam, Mithraism and Pre-Christian Gnosticism," in J. Duchesne-Guillemin (ed.), *Études mithriaques, textes et mémoires* (Teheran/Liège: Bibliothèque Pahlavi, 1978), 4:537–63.
1953	Yamauchi, E.	"Jewish Gnosticism?: The Prologue of John, Mandaean Parallels, and the Trimorphic Protennoia," in R. Van Den Broek and M. J. Vermaseren (eds.), *Studies in Gnosticism and Hellenistic Religions: Festschrift Gilles Quispel* (Leiden: Brill, 1981), 467–97.

CORPUS HERMETICUM

| 1954 | Festugière, A.-J. | "le style de la 'Korè Kosmou,'" *VivPen* 2 (1942), 15–57. |

1955 Festugière, A.-J.   *Traités I–XII* (Corpus Hermeticum 1, texte établi par A. D. Nock et traduit par A.-J. Festugière; Paris: Les Belles Letteres, 1945).

1956 Grese, W. C.   *Corpus Hermeticum XIII and Early Christian Literature* (Leiden: Brill, 1979).

1957 Kroll, J.   *Die Lehren des Hermes Trismegistus* (Münster: Aschendorff, 1914). See esp. 308–10, 328–38.

1958 Mahé, J.-P.   *Hermès en Haute-Égypte: Les textes hermétiques de Nag Hammadi et leurs parallèles grecs et latins,* tome 1 (Bibliothèque Copte de Nag Hammadi 3; Louvain: Peeters, 1978). On the prayers of Tractate XIII, see 146–55.

1959 Philonenko, M.   "Une utilisation du Shema dans le Poimandres," *RHPhR* 59 (1979), 369–72.

1960 Scott, W.   *Corpus Hermeticum* (Oxford: Clarendon, 1925), 2:372–418. Discussion of and notes to Tractate XIII.

1961 Whitehouse, D. J. M.   "The Hymns of the Corpus Hermeticum: Forms with a Diverse Functional History" (Th.D. Dissertation: Harvard University, 1985).

1962 Zuntz, G.   "On the Hymns in Corpus Hermeticum XIII," *Hermes* 83 (1955), 68–92. See also *Opuscula selecta: Classica, Hellenistica, Christiana* (Manchester: University Press, 1972), 150–77.

MANICHAEAN TEXTS

1963 Allberry, C. R. C. (ed.)   *Manichaean Manuscripts in the Chester Beatty Collection,* vol. 2: *A Manichaean Psalm-Book, part 2: With a Contribution by Hugo Ibscher* (Stuttgart: W. Kohlhammer, 1938).

1964 Bang, W.   "Manichäische Hymnen," *Muséon* 38 (1925), 1–55.

1965 Boyce, M.   *The Manichaean Hymn-Cycles in Parthian* (London/ New York/Toronto: G. Cumberlege/Oxford University Press, 1954).

1966 Brunner, C. J.   "Liturgical Chant and Hymnody Among the Manichaeans of Central Asia," *ZMDG* 130 (1980), 342–68.

1967 Henning, W. B. H.   "Ein manichäischer kosmogonischer Hymnus," *NGWG. PH* (1932), 214–28.

1968 Henning, W. B. H.   *Ein manichäisches Bet- und Beichtbuch* (Abhandlund der Preussischen Akademie der Wissenschaft 1936, nr. 10; Berlin: de Gruyter, 1937).

1969	Kasser, R.	"Le cheminement de l'âme, second chant de Thôm le Manichéen," *RThPh* 122 (1990), 505–15.
1970	Kasser, R.	"Le sixième et le septième chants de Thôm le Manichéen," *RHPhR* 70 (1990), 421–32.
1971	Nagel, P.	"Die Psalmoi Sarakoton des manichäischen Psalmbuches," *OLZ* 62 (1967), 123–30.
1972	Oerter, W.-B.	"Die Thomaspsalmen des Manichäischen Psalters als genuiner Bestandteil der manichäischen Literatur," *BySl* 41 (1980), 44–49.
1973	Ries, J.	"La prière de Bêma dans l'Église de Mani," in H. Limet and J. Ries (eds.), *L'expérience de la prière dans les grandes religions: actes du colloque de Louvain-la-Neuve et Liège (22–23 novembre 1978)* (Louvain-la-Neuve: Centre d'histoire des religions, 1980), 375–90.
1974	Säve-Söderbergh, T.	*Studies in the Coptic Manichaean Psalm-Book: Prosody and Mandaean Parallels* (Arbeten Utgivna med Understöd av Vilhelm Ekmans Universitetsfond, Uppsala, 55; Uppsala: Almqvist & Wiksell Boktrykeri AB, 1949).
1975	Schaeder, H. H.	"Zur manichäischen Urmenschlehre," in R. Reitzenstein and H. H. Schäder (eds.), *Studien zum antiken Synkretismus aus Iran und Griechenland* (Studien der Bibliothek Wartburg, 7; Leipzig: B. C. Teubner, 1926), Part 2, 240–305. See esp. 263–70 for discussion of a hymn of Mani.
1976	Scheftelowitz, I.	"Die manichäische Zarathustra-Hymne M 7," *OrChr* 3.1 (1927), 261–83.
1977	Tsui Chi, M.	"The Lower (Second?) Sectian [sic] of the Manichaean Hymns," *BSOAS* 11 (1943–46), 175–219.

MANDAEAN TEXTS

1978	Baumstark, A.	"Der Mandäerpsalm Ginza R. V 2," *OrChr* 35 (1938), 157–74.
1979	Drower, G. S.	*The Canonical Prayerbook of the Mandaeans: Translated with Notes* (Leiden: Brill, 1959).
1980	Lidzbarski, M.	*Ginza: Der Schatz oder das große Buch der Mandäer* (Göttingen/Leipzig: Vandenhoeck & Ruprecht/J. C. Hinrichs, 1925).
1981	McCullough, W. S.	*Jewish and Mandaean Incantation Bowls in the Royal Ontario Museum* (Toronto: University Press, 1967).

1982 Yamauchi, E.   *Mandaic Incantation Texts* (New Haven, Conn.: American Oriental Society, 1967).

10. PAPYRI AND INSCRIPTIONS

1983 Daniel, R. W.   "Christian Hymn: P. Vindob. G 40195 and P.Ryl. Copt. 33," *ZPE* 42 (1981), 71–77.

1984 Del Grande, C. (ed.) *Liturgiae preces hymni Christianorum e papyris collecti* (Napoli: Loffredo, 1934).

1985 Emmett, A. M.   "A Fourth Century Hymn to the Virgin Mary?," in G. H. R. Horsley, *New Documents Illustrating Early Christianity: A Review of the Greek Inscriptions and Papyri Published in 1977* (Macquarie University, N.S.W.: Ancient History Documentary Research Centre, 1982), 141–46.

1986 Farid, F.   *"Euchomai ... para tois theos:* Evaluation of a Religious Practice," in *Atti del XVII Congresso Internazionale di Papirologia, Napoli, 19–26 maggio 1983* (s.n.), 3:1017.

1987 Gronewald, M.   "Ein liturgischer Papyrus: Gebet und Ode 8, P. Mich. Inv. 6427," *ZPE* 14 (1974), 193–200.

1988 Hagedorn, D.   "Zu den christlichen Hymnen in P. Amhurst I 9 (a)," *ZPE* 52 (1983), 275–78.

1989 Horsley, G. H. R.   "Bilingual Curse Tablet," in G. H. R. Horsley (ed.), *New Documents Illustrating Early Christianity,* 2 (Macquarie University, N.S.W.: Ancient History Documentary Research Centre, 1982), 46. Late imperial inscription.

1990 Horsley, G. H. R.   "The Lord's Prayer in a Necropolis," in G. H. R. Horsley (ed.), *New Documents Illustrating Early Christianity,* 3 (Macquarie University, N.S.W.: Ancient History Documentary Research Centre, 1983), 103–5. Discussion of an undated papyrus with a list of thirteen mostly magical texts among which the Lord's Prayer is found, and includes the texts of two recently published papyri.

1991 Knopf, R.   "Eine Thonscherbe mit dem Texte des Vaterunsers," *ZNW* 2 (1901), 228–33.

1992 Koenen, L.   "Ein christlicher Prosahymnus des 4. Jahrhunderts (O. Zucker 36)," in E. Boswinkel et al. (eds.), *Antidoron Martino David oblatum: Miscellenea Papyrologica* (Leiden: Brill, 1968), 31–52.

1993 Koenen, L., and Kramer, J.   "Ein Hymnus auf den Allgott," *ZPE* 4 (1969), 19–21.

1994 Lebek, W. D.   "Ein Hymnus auf Antinoos," *ZPE* 12 (1973), 101–37.

1995 Roncaglia, M.   "La vie liturgique en Égypte du 1er au 111e siècle (notes et hypothèses)," *Al-Machrig* 63 (1969), 81–134.

1996 Schmidt, C., and Schubart, W. (eds.)   *Altkristliche Texte* (Berliner Klassiker Texte 6; Berlin: Wiedmann, 1910), 110–17. A third-century C.E. collection of Christian prayers.

1997 Smith, Morton   "A Note on Some Jewish Assimilationists: The Angels (P. Berlin 5025b, P. Louvre 2391)," *Journal of the Ancient Near Eastern Society* 16–17 (1984–85), 207–12. Invocation of angels. These papyri are dated c. 400 and c. 300 C.E. respectively.

1998 Thieme, G.   "Inschriftliches zur Geschichte des Gebets," *ZNW* 7 (1906), 264–66.

1999 Treu, K.   "Liturgische Traditionen in Ägypten (zu P. Oxy. 2782)," in P. Nagel (ed.), *Studia Coptica* (BBA 45; Berlin: Akademie-Verlag, 1974), 43–66.

INDEX TO THE BIBLIOGRAPHY

Versnel, H. S., 1799, 1800
Versteeg, J., 823
Vielhauer, P., 1242
Vischer, L., 1742
Viteau, J., 526
Vogel, C., 1743
Vogels, W., 1243
Vogler, W., 1136
Vögtle, A., 1137, 1138
Vokes, F. E., 1139, 1496
Voll, W., 1857
Volz, C. A., 1744
Vööbus, A., 496, 1745
Vouga, F., 82, 1561

Wacholder, B. Z., 716
Wachs, S. P., 357
Wagenwoort, H., 1801
Wahl, W., 1858
Wainwright, G., 83
Walker, J. H., 1746
Walker, M. B., 1140
Walker, W. O., 1141
Wallace, D. H., 1497
Wallenstein, M., 630, 631, 632
Walpole, A. S., 1747
Walter, N., 499
Walther, G., 1142
Wambacq, B. N., 419
Wanamaker, C. A., 1498
Warren, F. C., 1748
Warren, W., 1499
Warrington, K., 1562
Watts, J. M., 210
Weinfeld, M., 358, 397, 567, 568, 569, 570, 668
Weinreich, O., 84, 1839, 1859
Weiser, M., 1143
Weiss, J. G., 359, 360
Wells, C. R., 1563
Wendel, A., 211
Wengst, K., 824
Wernberg-Møller, P., 633
Werner, E., 361, 1156
Wessely, C., 1900
West, M. L., 1802, 1840

Westermann, C., 212, 213, 214, 215, 216, 217, 218, 219
Wetter, G. P., 1749
Wheeler, S. B., 220
White, J. L., 1361
Whitehouse, D. J. M., 1961
Widengren, G., 221, 222, 1950
Wilcox, M., 1258
Wiles, G. P., 1362, 1363
Wilhelmi, G., 1397
Wilkinson, J., 868
Willems, G. F., 362
Williams, A. L., 363
Williams, F., 1870
Williams, W. G., 223
Willis, G. G., 85, 1144, 1750
Willis, J. T., 224
Wilms, F.-E., 571
Wilson, G. H., 225
Wimmerer, R., 1145
Windisch, H., 1547
Wink, W., 1534
Winston, D., 545
Winter, P., 1244
Winterhalter, P., 497
Wisse, F., 1941
Wissowa, G., 1803
Wobbe, J., 1364
Wohlbergs, T., 1951
Wolf, C. U., 1146
Wolff, H. W., 226
Wolfson, H. A., 742
Wong, T. Y. C., 1500, 1501
Woude, A. S. van der, 416, 634, 639, 644, 666, 671
Wright, N. T., 1365, 1502, 1535
Wright, R. B., 527
Wright, R. F., 1147
Wright, W., 417
Wünsch, R., 1804
Wurzinger, A., 1148

Yadin, Y., 648, 659, 717
Yahalom, J., 364
Yamauchi, E., 1149, 1293, 1952, 1953, 1982
Young, B., 1150

INDEX OF SCRIPTURAL REFERENCES

HEBREW BIBLE / OLD TESTAMENT

NEW TESTAMENT

INDEX OF ANCIENT LITERATURE

EARLY CHRISTIAN LITERATURE

INDEX OF HEBREW/ARAMAIC, GREEK, AND LATIN TERMS

HEBREW

abba abba hab lan mitra, 9
adonay elohenu, 10
al abinu šebbaššhamayim, 6
elohim, 10
'ap, 41

biqqēš pānîm, 45
berakah, 57
bēth qôdēš, 9

hakkōl šellô, 70
hištahǎweh, 70

wĕhôn 'āḏām yāqār hārûṣ, 69

zîw, 42

hillâ pānîm, 45
hāmûḏ, 71
hĕmôr, 71

yāqār, 69

lm' ṣlm 'npyk kdn' 'lyk šn' wšht, 43

mar'eh, 40

nātān pānîm 'el, 45, 52

pānîm, 41

ṣᵃlēm 'anpôhî, 42

ribbôn ha'ôlāmîm, 68
ribbônô šel 'ôlām, 57

sîm pānîm, 52

šānâ pānîm, 43

tô'ar, 40
tᵃhaddēhû bᵃśimhâ 'et-pānêkā, 45

GREEK

adoxos, 75
agathos, 40, 42, 69
aggelos, 49, 68
agnoein, 59
agōnia, 43
hairesis, 55, 65
aischynesthai, 42

aiōn, 57
akroatēs, 60
alloiousthai, 42, 43
amoibē, 71
anaballein, 74
anasōzein, 77
anaphainein, 43, 47
anechein, 60
anthrōpos, 68
antilēptor, 90, 96
hapas, 71
apodidonai, 69
apodyresthai, 75
apothnēskein, 82
apokathistenai, 76
apostellein, 68
apostrephein, 44
aprosdeēs, 63, 64, 71
haptesthai, 70
arkos, 42
archesthai, 65
archē, 68
archōn, 92
astrapē, 47
asyngkritos, 71
aphistēnai, 63
aphoran, 59

basileus, 93
boēthos, 90
boulē, 93

genesis, 60
gē, 41
ginesthai, 18
glykys, 58
gony, 70
gynē, 42

deesthai, 45
despotēs, 30, 57, 59, 61, 68, 89, 96
dēmiourg(ein), 57, 58, 60, 64, 68
diabēma, 93
diathēkē, 82
didaskein, 75
didonai, 45, 93
dieuthunai, 93, 96
dikaios(yne), 55, 69

286

INDEX OF MODERN AUTHORS

INDEX OF SUBJECTS AND NAMES

All indexes, except the Index to the Bibliography,
were prepared by Mark Kiley.